TOP NOTCH 1

Teacher's Edition
and Lesson Planner

Joan Saslow ■ Allen Ascher

with Julie C. Rouse

PEARSON
Longman

Includes
Teacher's Resource Disk
with printable activities

Top Notch
English for Today's World   1
Teacher's Edition and Lesson Planner

Pearson Education, 10 Bank Street, White Plains, NY 10606

Editorial director: Pamela Fishman
Senior development editor: Trish Lattanzio
Vice president, director of design and production: Rhea Banker
Director of electronic production: Aliza Greenblatt
Managing editor: Mike Kemper
Art director: Ann France
Digital Layout Specialist: Warren Fischbach
Senior manufacturing buyer: Dave Dickey
Photo research: Aerin Csigay
Text composition: The Mazer Corp.
Text font: 11/12 Palatino
Cover photograph: "From Above," by Rhea Banker. Copyright © 2005 Rhea Banker.

ISBN: 0-13-110417-9

Photo credits: All original photography by Michal Heron; Page 4 (top left) Michael S. Yamashita/ Corbis, (top right) Peter Turnley/Corbis, (middle left) Jose Luis Pelaez, Inc./Corbis, (middle right) Ariel Skelley/Corbis; p. 5 (J. Groban) Robert Mora/Getty Images, (M. Streep) Mitchell Gerber/Corbis, (Y. Ming) AP/Wide World Photos; p. 8 Benjamin Rondel/Corbis; p. 9 (left) Tom Wagner/Corbis SABA, (right) Gary Brasch/Corbis; p. 22 (top) Dinodia Picture Agency, (bottom) Bassouls Sophie/Corbis Sygma; p. 23 (top) Salsatap.com, (bottom) Elizabeth Hansen, Adams/Hansen Photography; p. 28 (grandparents) Lindy Powers/Index Stock Imagery, (uncle, aunt, cousins) Getty Images, (parents) Ryan McVay/Getty Images, (mother-in-law) Ron Chapple/Getty Images, (father-in-law) James Darell/Getty Images, (sister-in-law ,brother, nephew, niece) Royalty Free/Corbis, (sister) Cleve Bryant/PhotoEdit, (brother-in-law) Bill Cannon/Getty Images; p. 29 Rachel Epstein/PhotoEdit; p. 31 (middle) Lisette Le Bon/SuperStock, (bottom) Getty Images; p. 32 (chef) Gary Conner/Index Stock Imagery, (Sydney) David R. Frazier Photolibrary, Inc., (Bankok) Steve Vidler/estock Photography LLC; p. 33 (doctors) Jeff Isaac Greenberg/Photo Researchers, Inc., (girls with flowers) Myrleen Ferguson Cate/PhotoEdit, (shoe store) Jeff Greenberg/PhotoEdit; p. 36 (top) B. Kraft/Corbis, (bottom) Yang Liu/Corbis; p. 39 (tree) Alan Kearney/Getty Images, (Anne Douglas) Kevin Winter/Getty Images, (Kirk Douglas) Chris Pizzello, (Diana Dill) Scott Gries/Getty Images, (Diandra Douglas) Ralph Dominguez/Globe Photos, Inc., (Michael Douglas) Chris Pizzello, (Catherine Zeta-Jones) Sean Gallup/Getty Images, (Cameron Douglas) Scott Gries/Getty Images, (Dylan Douglas) Dave Parker/Globe Photos, Inc., (Carys Douglas) Chris Pizzello/WireImage.com; pp. 40, 46 (Communicator) Seiko Instruments USA, Inc., (woman) Image Source/SuperStock; p. 42 (laptop) Michael Newman/PhotEdit; p. 43 (TV) Ryan McVay/Getty Images, (laptop) Apple Computer, Inc., (PDA) Ryan McVay/Getty Images, (printer) Epson America, Inc., (cell phone) Nokia, (CD burner) Iomega Corporation; p. 44 (microwave) Anthony Meshkinyar/Getty Images, (coffee maker) Andy Crawford/ Dorling Kindersley Media Library, (hair dryer) Slver Burdett Ginn, (fax) EyeWire Collection/Getty Images, (photocopier) Getty Images; p. 47 (alarm) Zhenjiang Sanwei Plastic & Electrical Appliances Co.,Ltd., (pen) photo courtesy of Sharper Image; p. 52 (Thai shrimp) Live Streeter/Patrick Mcleavy/Dorling Kindersley Media Library, (Mexican soup) Brian Hagiwara/PictureArts Corporation, (Tomato salad) Image Source/Picturequest, (chicken) Tom Vano/PictureQuest, (Brazilian steak) (Fried fish) David Murray and Jules Selmes/Dorling Kindersley Media Library, (Ice cream) (apple pie) (German chocolate cake) Francisco Cruz/SuperStock; p. 55 EyeWire Collection/Getty Images; p. 56 John A. Rizzo/Getty Images; p. 60 (Veggies) C Squared Studios/Getty Images; p. 69, (track) Tom Carter/PhotoEdit, (pool) Pat Lanza/Bruce Coleman Inc., (golf) David Cannon/Dorling Kindersley Media Library, (tennis) R.W. Jones/Corbis; pp. 69, 74 (park) Rudi Von Briel/PhotoEdit, (gym) David Sacks/Getty Images, (athletic field) Sergio Piumatti; p. 72 Martell/Boston Herald/Corbis Sygma p. 76 (men's boxers, bathrobe) Comstock Royalty Free Division, pp. 76, 79 (windbreaker) Gerald Lopez/Dorling Kindersley Media Library, (handbag) Steve Gorton/Dorling Kindersley Media Library, (belt) Richard Megna, Fundamental Photographs, (running shoes) Siede Preis/Getty Images; p. 84 (top) Henry Herholdt/Getty Images, (middle) Wolfgang Kaehler Photography, (bottom) Fridmar Damm/eStock Photography LLC.; p. 88 (Rome) Louis A. Goldman/Photo Researchers, Inc., (Venice) Karen McCunnall/eStock Photography LLC, (Disney) Ron Dahlquist/SuperStock, (Magic Kingdom) Len Kaufman, (Africa) Gregory G. Dimijam MD/Photo Researchers, Inc.; p. 90 PhotoLibrary.com and Mark E. Gibson/Corbis; p. 92 Larry Williams/Corbis; p. 93 (zoo) Lawrence Migdale/Pix, (baseball game) SuperStock, (movie) Andre Jenny/ ImageState, (museum) Bob Krist/eStock Photography LLC.; p. 94 (Bhutan) Pete Oxford/Robert Harding World Imagery, (Rio) Stephanie Maze/Woodfin Camp & Associates, (students) Royalty Free/Corbis, (Sea Mountain) Rob Lewine/Corbis; p. 100 Gary Conner/Index Stock Imagery; p. 101 (station) Jeffrey Blackman/Index Stock Imagery, (train) Steve Vidler/eStock Photography LLC; p. 102 (Puebla) Chris Sharp/D. Donne Bryant Stock Photography; p. 104 Hans Georg Roth/Corbis; p. 106 Andres Morya Hinojosa/Morya Photography; p. 108 (train) Jim Winkley/Corbis, (ship) Ron Chapple/Getty Images; p. 114 (background) David Young-Wolff/PhotoEdit; p. 115 (digital camera) Epson America, Inc., (camcorder) Sony Electronics Inc., (DVD player) George B. Diebold/Corbis & Tom Carter/PhotoEdit, (MP3) William Whitehurst/Corbis, (scanner) Churchill & Klehr/Pearson Education/PH College; p. 121 Getty Images; Cover photograph: "From Above," by Rhea Banker. Copyright © 2005 Rhea Banker.

Illustration credits: M. Teresa Aguilar, pp. 100, 103; Kenneth Batelman, pp. 21, 55, 80, 83, 88, 89, 102, 109, 110, 117 (middle); Pierre Berthiaume, pp. 106, 110; Rich Burlew, pp. 39, 64; John Ceballos, pp. 15, 27, 51, 63, 75, 87, 99, 111, 123; Lane DuPont, p. 82 (bottom); Scott Fray, pp. 3, 61; Steve Gardner, p. 112; (bottom); Marty Harris, p. 91 (middle); Brian Hughes, pp. 20, 22, 43, 45, 82 (top) 115; Andy Meyer, pp. 10, 14, 38, 46, 107, 108 (top); Sandy Nichols, pp. 26, 49, 58, 65, 66, 69, 70, 94, 104, 108 110, 119; Dusan Petricic, pp. 19, 57, 68, 96, 120; Rodico Prato, p. 16; Robert Saunders, pp. 31, 34, 90, 91 (top); Phil Scheuer, pp. 48, 116, 117 (top).

Printed in the United States of America
2 3 4 5 6 7 8 9 10–QWD–10 09 08 07 06 05

Contents

Pictorial Section .... **Tiv**
    Unit walk-through .... **Tiv**
    Other *Top Notch* Components .... **Tx**
    The *Top Notch* Teacher's Resource Disk .... **Txii**

A concise methodology for the *Top Notch* course .... **Txiv**

The Lesson Planner

          Welcome to *Top Notch*! **T2**

UNIT 1   **Getting Acquainted** **T4**

UNIT 2   **Going out** **T16**

UNIT 3   **Talking about Families** **T28**

UNIT 4   **Coping with Technology** **T40**

UNIT 5   **Eating in, Eating out** **T52**

UNIT 6   **Staying in Shape** **T64**

UNIT 7   **Finding Something to Wear** **T76**

UNIT 8   **Getting Away** **T88**

UNIT 9   **Taking Transportation** **T100**

UNIT 10 **Shopping Smart** **T112**

REFERENCE SECTION

Alphabetical word list **124**

Social language list **126**

Pronunciation table **128**

Non-count nouns **128**

Irregular verbs **128**

GRAMMAR BOOSTER **G1**

Lyrics for *Top Notch Pop* songs .... **last page**

Workbook Answer Key **AK1**

Teacher's Resource Disk .... **Inside back cover**

Top Notch unit walk-through

UNIT 5

Eating in, Eating out

UNIT GOALS

1 Discuss what to eat
2 Make food choices
3 Order and pay for a meal
4 Discuss food and health

UNIT GOALS. Clearly state the communicative goal of this unit.

A **TOPIC PREVIEW.** Read the menu. Which foods do you like? Which foods do you dislike?

TOPIC PREVIEW. Comprehensible "+1" input previews the content of the unit, accesses prior knowledge and provides a reference for student study.

LANGUAGE SUPPORT. Illustrations ensure comprehensibility of +1 language.

World Café

Chef and Owner: Ronald Gebert

"The Best Food in the World!" Max Reed, *Journal News*, April 22

Appetizers
Thai grilled shrimp
Mexican black bean soup

Entrées
Brazilian steak
Fried fish Chinese style
Roast chicken

Salads
Mixed green salad
Tomato salad

Desserts
Ice cream
Apple pie
German ch...

Beverages
Coffee • Tea • Soft drinks • Fru...
Bottled water

B Look at the menu again. Check ☑ the information you...

- ☑ **1.** food choices
- ☐ **2.** beverage choices
- ☐ **3.** prices
- ☐ **4.** the name of the restaurant owner
- ☐ **5.** the names of the waiters and waitresses
- ☐ **6.** the name of the chef
- ☐ **7.** a restaurant review

52 UNIT 5

C 🎧 **SOUND BITES.** Read along silently as you listen to a natural conversation.

WAITER: Are you ready to order? Or do you need some more time?
CUSTOMER: I'm ready. I think I'll start with the black bean soup. Then I'll have the roast chicken. That comes with salad, doesn't it?
WAITER: Yes, it does. And there's also a choice of vegetables. Tonight we have carrots or grilled tomatoes.
CUSTOMER: The carrots, please.
WAITER: Certainly. Anything to drink?
CUSTOMER: I'll have bottled water, no ice.

D Read the conversation carefully again. Then write <u>true</u> or <u>false</u>.

____ **1.** The customer orders carrots.
____ **2.** The customer doesn't order soup.
____ **3.** The chicken comes with salad.
____ **4.** The chicken comes with a vegetable.

SOUND BITES. Previews the language of the unit and provides exposure to +1 natural language for observation.

WHAT ABOUT YOU?

Look at the menu from the World Café again. Write the items that <u>you</u> would like to order.

| appetizer: |
| salad: |
| entrée / main course: |
| dessert: |
| beverage: |

WHAT ABOUT YOU? Confirms students' understanding and readies them for the unit.

PAIR WORK. Compare your choices. Are they the same or different?

COMMUNICATION GOAL. Each lesson clearly announces its communication goal, ensuring that students will know what they will be able to do at the end of that day's lesson.

CONVERSATION MODEL. Transferable conversation models make target social language, grammar, and vocabulary memorable. Photos support meaning and provide a stimulus for additional oral work.

VOCABULARY. Clear defining illustrations take the guesswork out of the meaning of new words and provide a permanent reference for student study.

LISTENING COMPREHENSION. Frequent listening comprehension activities teach critical listening skills and reinforce vocabulary.

---

1 Discuss What to Eat

🎧 CONVERSATION MODEL Read and listen.

A: What is there to eat?
B: Not much. Cheese, bread, . . . eggs.
A: Is that all? I'm in the mood for seafood.
B: Sorry. You're out of luck. Let's go out!
A: Good idea!

🎧 Rhythm and intonation practice

A GRAMMAR. Count and non-count nouns / there is and there are

Count and non-count nouns

Count nouns name things you can count. They are singular or plural.

singular count noun	plural count noun
an apple	
an egg	ten eggs

Non-count nouns name things you can not count. They are not singular or plural. Don't use a, an, or a number with non-count nouns.

rice   NOT a rice   NOT rices

count nouns
an appetizer   an onion
an apple   an orange
a cookie   a sandwich
an egg   a vegetable

There is and there are

Use there is with non-count nouns and singular count nouns.
Use there are with plural count nouns.

There's milk and an apple in the fridge.
There are oranges, too. But there aren't any vegetables.

Use there is with something, anything, or nothing.

Is there anything to eat? No, there isn't anything.

non-count nouns
bread   juice   rice
candy   lettuce   salt
cheese   meat   seafood
chocolate   milk   soup
coffee   pasta   sugar
fruit

GRAMMAR BOOSTER
PAGES G7–G9
For more . . .

Complete each sentence or question with a form of there is or there are.

1. _Is there_ anything in the fridge?
2. _____ any cookies?
3. I hope _____ no chocolate in this cake. I'm allergic.
4. _____ anything to eat in this house? I'm hungry.
5. _____ eggs in the fridge. We could make an omelette.
6. I don't think _____ any vegetables on the menu.
7. _____ too much sugar in this coffee.
8. _____ enough lettuce to make a salad?

UNIT 5

C 🎧 VOCABULARY BUILDING. Categories of food. Add another food you know to each list. Then listen and practice.

fruit
① apples ② bananas ③ grapes ④ oranges

mangoes

vegetables
⑤ carrots ⑥ peppers ⑦ broccoli ⑧ onions

meat
⑨ chicken ⑩ lamb ⑪ sausage ⑫ beef

seafood
⑬ fish ⑭ clams ⑮ shrimp ⑯ crab ⑰ squid

grains
⑱ pasta ⑲ rice ⑳ noodles ㉑ bread

dairy products
㉒ butter ㉓ cheese ㉔ milk ㉕ yogurt

oils
㉖ corn oil ㉗ olive oil ㉘ coconut oil

sweets
㉙ candy ㉚ pie ㉛ cake ㉜ cookies

D 🎧 LISTENING COMPREHENSION. Listen to the conversations. Then listen again. Classify the foods in each conversation.

1. _dairy products_
2. _____
3. _____
4. _____
5. _____
6. _____

CONVERSATION PAIR WORK

Discuss what to eat. Use foods you like and eat.
Use the guide, or create a new conversation.

A: What is there to eat?
B: _____.
A: Is that all? I'm in the mood for _____.
B: . . .

Continue the conversation in your own way.

CONTROLLED PRACTICE

55

GRAMMAR. Grammar presented with clear explanations and examples, integrating form, meaning, and use. Use of color text ensures that students focus on the target grammar.

GRAMMAR BOOSTER. For those who want more, a Grammar Booster in the back of the Student's Book expands the presentation with additional explanations, examples, grammar points, timely reviews, as well as additional practice.

CONTROLLED COMMUNICATION PRACTICE. Students personalize the Conversation Model, using the new vocabulary and grammar and confirming their progress on a daily basis.

Make Food Choices

COMMUNICATION GOAL. Keeps students aware that they'll achieve something of value to use in their lives outside the classroom.

🎧 CONVERSATION MODEL Read and listen.

A: I'll have the pasta for my main course, please. What does that come with?
B: It comes with soup or a salad.
A: What kind of soup is there?
B: There's tomato soup or chicken soup.
A: I think I'll have the salad.
B: Certainly. And to drink?
A: Water, please.

🎧 Rhythm and intonation practice

CONVERSATION MODEL. Conversation models motivate students because of their practical application.

RHYTHM AND INTONATION PRACTICE. Provides targeted practice of rhythm and intonation to ensure comprehensibility of student speech.

A GRAMMAR. A / an / the

a / an
It comes with a salad and an appetizer.

the
Use the to name something a second time.
A: It comes with a salad.
B: OK. I'll have the salad.

Also use the to talk about something specific.
A: Would you like an appetizer? [not specific]
B: Yes. The fried clams sound delicious. [specific: they're on the menu]

GRAMMAR BOOSTER
PAGES G9–G10
For more …

B 🎧 PRONUNCIATION. The. Compare the pronunciation of the before consonant and vowel sounds. Read and listen. Then repeat.

/ə/ (before consonant sounds)
the chicken
the soup
the juice
the hot appetizer
the fried eggs

/i/ (before vowel sounds)
the orange juice
the onion soup
the apple juice
the appetizer
the eggs

PRONUNCIATION. A comprehensive pronunciation syllabus promotes accurate and comprehensible pronunciation.

CONTEXTUALIZED PRACTICE. Increases memorability and mastery of new language.

C Write a, an, or the.

HUSBAND: What do you feel like eating tonight?
WIFE: Well, _____ seafood special sounds delicious. I think I'll order that. What about you?
HUSBAND: I'm not sure. I'm really in the mood for _____ spicy dish.
WIFE: Well, what about _____ Thai chicken? Thai food is usually spicy.
HUSBAND: Sounds good.

HUSBAND: Excuse me! We're ready to order.
WAITER: Certainly. Would you like to start with _____ appetizer or soup? Our soup of the day is tortilla soup—that's _____ Mexican specialty.
HUSBAND: Is _____ tortilla soup spicy?
WAITER: Not very. But we can give you hot pepper sauce to put into it if you'd like.
HUSBAND: OK. I'll have _____ tortilla soup—with the hot sauce on the side.
WIFE: I'll have the same thing, please.
WAITER: And for your main course? We have _____ nice seafood special on _____ menu tonight.
WIFE: Good. I'll have _____ seafood special.

HUSBAND: Hmm. I love Thai food. I'll have _____ Thai chicken.
WAITER: You won't need hot sauce with that, sir!

CONVERSATION PAIR WORK

Make food choices from the menu with a partner. Use the guide, or create a new conversation.

A: I'll have the _____ for my main course, please. What does that come with?
B: _____.
A: What kind of _____ there?
B: _____.
A: I think I'll have the _____.
B: _____. And to drink?
A: _____, please.

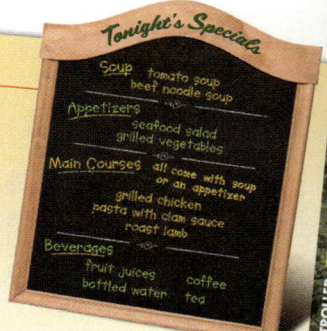

Tonight's Specials

Soup   tomato soup
        beef noodle soup

Appetizers   seafood salad
              grilled vegetables

Main Courses   all come with soup
                or an appetizer
                grilled chicken
                pasta with clam sauce
                roast lamb

Beverages   fruit juices   coffee
             bottled water   tea

COMMUNICATION GOAL. Underscores practical application of the lesson.

VOCABULARY. Vocabulary is also treated at phrase level or as collocation, furnishing students with ready-to-use social language "chunks."

FREE COMMUNICATION PRACTICE. Offering students an opportunity to integrate language taught from previous lessons, *Top Notch* Interactions are rehearsals for real-life communication.

AUTHENTICITY. Life-like documents recycle known language and prepare students to cope with authentic documents in English.

LESSON

3

Order and Pay for a Meal

4 🎧 **VOCABULARY.** What to say to a waiter or waitress. Listen and practice.

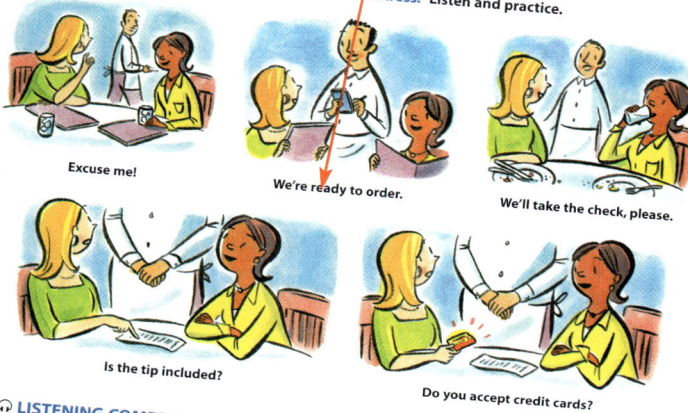

Excuse me!

We're ready to order.

We'll take the check, please.

Is the tip included?

Do you accept credit cards?

B 🎧 **LISTENING COMPREHENSION.** Listen to the conversations in a restaurant. Then listen again and predict the next thing the customer will say to the waiter or waitress.

1. ☐ Is the tip included in the check?
2. ☐ Is the tip included?
3. ☐ Excuse me!
4. ☐ Is the tip included?
5. ☐ I'll have the seafood soup, please.

☐ We'll take the check, please.
☐ We're ready to order.
☐ No, thanks. We'll take the check, please.
☐ Do you accept credit cards?
☐ Excuse me!

C **PAIR WORK.** Imagine you're in a restaurant. Practice asking and answering the questions. Write the answers. Then reverse roles and do it again.

Your questions

1. What do you feel like eating for an appetizer?
2. What do you want for a main course?
3. What would you like for a beverage?
4. How about a dessert? What are you in the mood for?

Your partner's answers

_____
_____
_____
_____

58   UNIT 5

TOP NOTCH
INTERACTION • *Let's Eat!*

ROLE PLAY. Form groups of diners and servers at tables. Practice discussing the menu and ordering and paying for food.

LAND AND SEA

All Entrées include
Bread • Pasta or Salad • Vegetable
Coffee or Tea

APPETIZERS
Fried clams • Mini vegetable pies (2) • Shrimp salad

SOUP
French onion • Beef vegetable • Spicy fish

ENTRÉES
Steak • Chicken and rice • Mixed grilled seafood

Children's menu available

DESSERTS
Chocolate cake • Carrot cake

NEED HELP? Here's language you already know:

Discuss food
What do you feel like eating?
I'm in the mood for ___.
There's ___ on the menu.
The ___ sound(s) delicious!
What about ___?

Serve food
Are you ready to order?
Do you need more time?
That comes with ___.
Would you like ___?
Anything to drink?
And to drink?
And for your main course / dessert / beverage?

Order food
Excuse me!
I'm / We're ready.
I'd like to start with ___.
I think I'll have ___.
And then I'll have ___.
Does that come with ___?
What kind of ___ is there?

Pay for food
I'll / We'll take the check, please.
Is the tip included?
Do you accept credit cards?

59

FREE PRACTICE

LISTENING COMPREHENSION. Listening tasks go beyond auditory discrimination to include critical thinking skills, such as prediction.

EXTENSIVE PAIR WORK ACTIVITIES. Ensure a student-centered approach.

NEED HELP? Provides reminders to students of the language they have previously learned—in this unit and earlier units—that can be used in the *Top Notch* Interaction. Guarantees that students will not forget the language they know.

Discuss Food and Health

A 🎧 **VOCABULARY. Food and health. Listen and practice.**

healthy (or healthful) good for your body
Take care of your body! Choose foods that are healthy.

fatty containing a lot of fat or oil
Some fatty foods are meat, fried foods, and cheese.

a portion the amount of a food that you eat at one time
Eat at least five portions of fruit and vegetables every day.

a meal breakfast, lunch, or dinner
Many people eat three meals a day.

a snack food you eat between meals
Raw vegetables are a healthy low-calorie snack, but
many people prefer high-fat snacks like potato chips and nuts.

in moderation not too much
Eat sweets in moderation. Small portions are better.

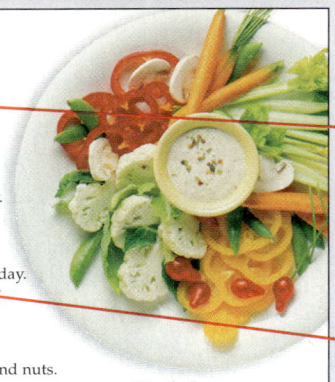

"Veggies"

B **READING WARM-UP. Is eating healthy food important to you?**

C 🎧 **READING. Read the tips from the nutrition website. Which tip do you think is the most important?**

Healthy Eating Tips

search

| Home | Healthy Eating | Kid-Friendly Snacks | Food Shopping Tips | Eat Out, Eat Smart |

Here are some tips for healthy eating at home, work, and elsewhere.

Try some of these ideas.

- Start your day off right! Eat breakfast.
- Take a piece of fruit to munch on during your commute. It tastes great, is filling, and provides energy.
- Use "lite" dairy products, which are low-fat and better for your health.

- If you like to eat meat, trim all visible fat.
- Fried foods? Snacks? Desserts? Sweets? They taste great but are not great for you. They are high in calories and can be high in fat, salt, and sugar.
- Pack your own snacks of raw veggies. Buy healthy snacks like pretzels.
- Cut down on portion size so you don't eat too much unhealthy food.
- Eat everything in moderation.

Home
About
FAQ's
Links
Contact

E-Mail This Page ✉   Print This Page 🖨   Next Page ➡

SOURCE: http://www.nlm.nih.gov/medlineplus/

60 UNIT 5

D **UNDERSTANDING MEANING FROM CONTEXT. Use each sentence to help you understand the meaning of each underlined word or phrase.**

1. Take a piece of fruit to <u>munch on</u> during your commute.
   ☐ eat   ☐ buy
2. If you like to eat meat, <u>trim</u> all visible fat.
   ☐ eat   ☐ cut off
3. Use "<u>lite</u>" dairy products which are low-fat and better for your health.
   ☐ fatty   ☐ not fatty
4. <u>Cut down on portion size</u> so you don't eat too much unhealthy food.
   ☐ Eat larger portions   ☐ Eat smaller portions

TOP NOTCH INTERACTION • What's Good?

STEP 1. PAIR WORK. Together write a check mark ✔ next to the foods you think are healthy. Write an ✗ next to the foods you think are not healthy. Do you agree or disagree?

rice

french fries

peppers and garlic

ice cream

nuts and chips

chicken

salad

pasta with sauce

STEP 2. On the notepad, classify the foods from the pictures.

spicy:	peppers and garlic
fatty:	
salty:	
sweet:	

STEP 3. DISCUSSION. What kind of food do you like? Do you eat healthy foods? What do you eat in moderation? Discuss with your classmates.

COMMUNICATION GOAL. *Top Notch* has a fully-developed discussion syllabus. Students progress beyond functional language and express their ideas successfully in high-frequency discussion topics.

VOCABULARY. Dictionary-style definitions and examples ensure understanding of new vocabulary that can't be taught through simple illustrations. Provide students with a model for explaining meaning.

READING. Warm-Up questions build expectation and get students talking. Authentic readings from identified sources prepare students to comprehend real reading materials in English.

UNDERSTANDING MEANING FROM CONTEXT. Students learn the essential skill of guessing meaning through context.

ADEQUATE PREPARATION. Concrete "steps"—such as notepadding activities, surveys, and critical thinking activities—prepare students for successful and productive free communication.

FREE PRACTICE

T 5
CHECKPOINT

LISTENING COMPREHENSION. Listen critically to the conversations. Are they in a restaurant or at home? Check ☑ the boxes.

	Restaurant	Home
1.	☐	☐
2.	☐	☐
3.	☐	☐
4.	☐	☐

Classify foods. Complete the chart with some foods in each category.

Fruit	Vegetables	Meat	Dairy products	Seafood	Grains

Write four questions you can ask a waiter or a waitress.

1. _____ ?
2. _____ ?
3. _____ ?
4. _____

Complete with a form of there is or there are.

1. _____ too much pepper in the soup.
2. I hope _____ not too much sugar in the cake. Sugar isn't good for you.
3. I'm looking for a good restaurant. _____ any restaurants near you?
4. _____ any low-fat desserts on the menu?
5. _____ an inexpensive restaurant nearby?
6. You should eat some fruit. _____ some oranges on the kitchen table.
7. _____ enough cheese in the fridge for two sandwiches?
8. I'm in the mood for soup. What kind of soup _____ on the menu?

♪ **TOP NOTCH SONG**
"The World Café"
Lyrics on last book page.

TOP NOTCH PROJECT
• In groups, choose traditional dishes to describe to a visitor to this country.
• Practice describing the dishes and their ingredients, and how they taste.

TOP NOTCH WEBSITE
For Unit 5 online activities, visit the *Top Notch* Companion Website at www.longman.com/topnotch.

WRITING. On a separate piece of paper, write information about food in this country for the readers of a travel newsletter.

UNIT 5

UNIT WRAP-UP
• **Vocabulary.** Look at the pictures. Then close your book and write the names of all the foods you remember.
• **Grammar.** Write statements with <u>there is</u>/<u>there are</u> for the foods.
• **Social language.** Create conversations for the people.
• **Writing.** Write a story about the family.

LATER

✓ **Now I can...**
☐ discuss what to eat.
☐ make food choices.
☐ order and pay for a meal.
☐ discuss food and health.

63

Other *Top Notch* Components

TOP NOTCH 1

Workbook

Joan Saslow ■ Allen Ascher

with Barbara R. Denman

WORKBOOK

An illustrated workbook contains exercises that provide additional practice and reinforcement of language concepts and skills from the *Top Notch* Student's Book and its Grammar Booster.

COMPLETE ASSESSMENT PACKAGE WITH EXAM*VIEW*® SOFTWARE

Ten easy-to-administer and easy-to-score unit achievement tests assess listening, vocabulary, grammar, social language, reading, and writing. Two review tests — one mid-book and one end-of-book — provide additional cumulative assessment. Two speaking tests assess progress in speaking.

In addition to the photocopiable achievement tests, Exam*View*® software enables teachers to customize tests that best meet their own needs.

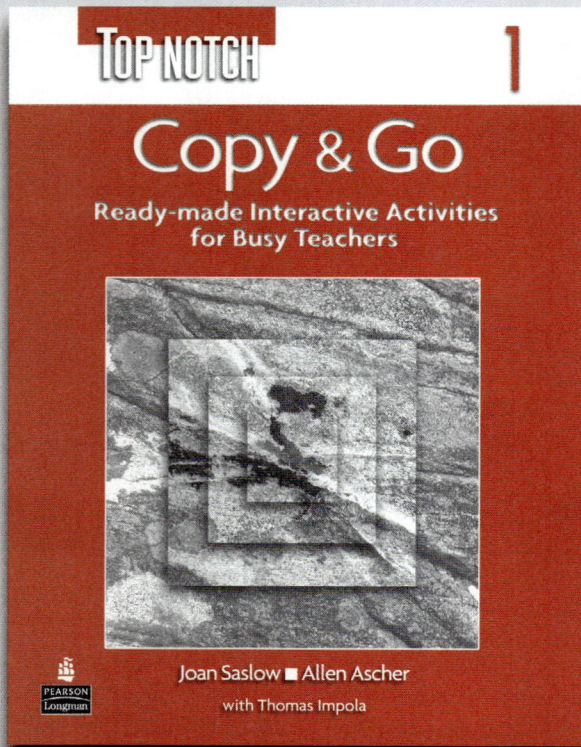

TOP NOTCH 1

Copy & Go

Ready-made Interactive Activities for Busy Teachers

Joan Saslow ■ Allen Ascher

with Thomas Impola

TOP NOTCH

Full-Course Placement Tests

TOP NOTCH 1

Complete Assessment Package

with ExamView® Software

Joan Saslow ■ Allen Ascher

with Angela M. Castro

COPY & GO: READY-MADE INTERACTIVE ACTIVITIES FOR BUSY TEACHERS

Motivating games, puzzles, and other practice activities in convenient photocopiable form support Student's Book content and provide a welcome change of pace.

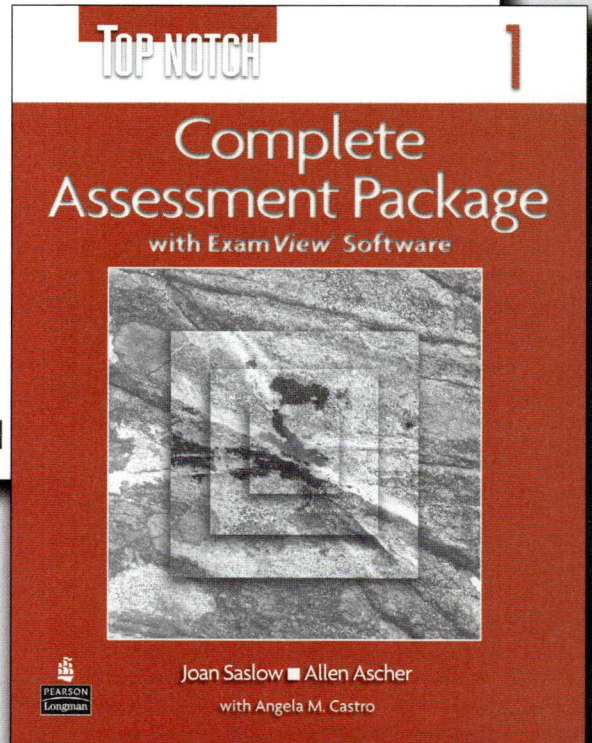

COMPANION WEBSITE

A companion website at www.longman.com/topnotch provides numerous additional resources for students and teachers. This no-cost, high-benefit feature includes opportunities for further practice of language and content from the *Top Notch* Student's Book.

CLASS AUDIO PROGRAM

The audio program contains listening comprehension activities, rhythm and intonation practice, and targeted pronunciation activities that focus on accurate and comprehensible pronunciation.

To prepare students to communicate with a variety of speakers, regional and non-native accents are included. Each class audio program also includes five *Top Notch Pop* songs in standard and karaoke form.

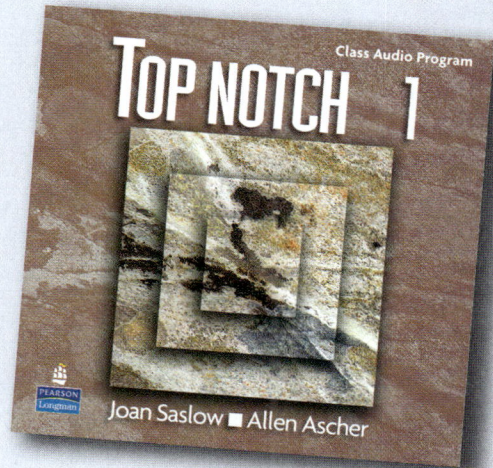

TOP NOTCH TV

A hilarious TV-style situation comedy reintroduces language from each unit. Also includes authentic unrehearsed interviews and *Top Notch Pop* karaoke. Comes with Activity Worksheets and Teaching Notes.

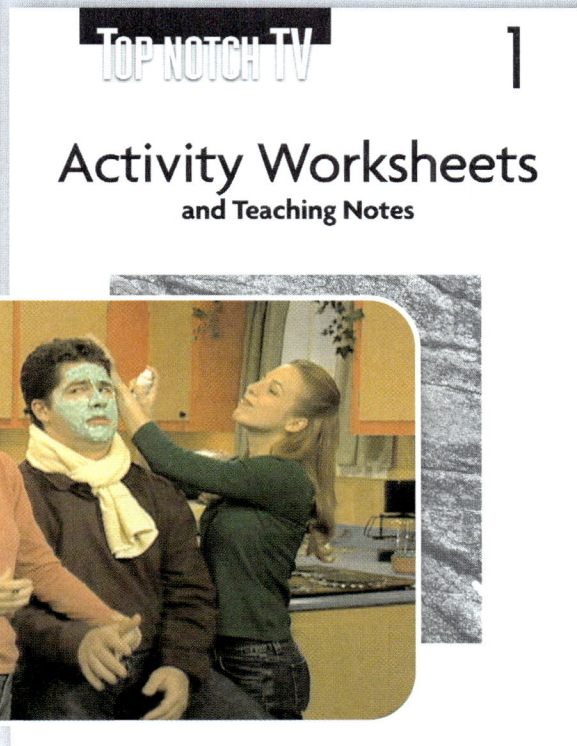

The *Top Notch* Teacher's Resource Disk

A complete menu of free printable activities to personalize YOUR *Top Notch* classroom.

Categories of Food

shrimp

Top Notch 1, Unit 5, page 55

Copyright © 2006 by Pearson Education, Inc. Permission granted to reproduce for classroom use.

Conversation Pair Work, page 57
Practice with a partner. Use your own words.

A: I'll have the _____ for my main course, please. What does that come with?
B:
A: What kind of _____ there?
B:
A: I think I'll have the _____.
B:
A: _____, please.

➤ **Vocabulary cards:** for games and other reinforcement activities

➤ **Pair work cards:** for an alternative approach to Conversation Pair Work

➤ **Grammar self-checks:** for reinforcement or for an inductive presentation

➤ **Cumulative vocabulary activities:** for additional vocabulary-building strategies

➤ **Learning strategies:** for conversation, listening, reading, and vocabulary building

➤ **Graphic organizers:** for reading and listening support

NAME: _____

DATE: _____

Grammar Self-check
(Unit 5, page 54)

GRAMMAR. Count and non-count nouns
Look at these nouns. Some are count nouns and some are non-count nouns.

Count nouns		Non-count nouns	
an appetizer	an onion	bread	
an apple	an orange	candy	juice	rice
a cookie	a sandwich	cheese	lettuce	salt
an egg	a vegetable	chocolate	meat	seafood
		coffee	milk	soup
		fruit	pasta	sugar

FIGURE IT OUT . . .
Count or non-count? Complete the grammar rules.
_____ nouns name things you can count. They can be singular or plural.
_____ nouns name things you cannot count. They do not have a plural form.
Don't use a, or an with _____ nouns.

GRAMMAR. There is and there are
at these sentences with there is and there are.
's milk and an apple in the fridge.
are oranges too. But there aren't any vegetables.
are anything to eat? No, there isn't anything.

E IT OUT . . .
or there are? Complete the grammar rules.
_____ with non-count nouns and singular nouns.
_____ with plural count nouns.
_____ with the pronouns something, anything, or nothing.

Pearson Education. Permission granted to reproduce for classroom use.

Unit 5

NAME: _____

DATE: _____

Cumulative Vocabulary Activity
(Unit 5)

Categorization: foods

Write examples of foods for each description below.

Foods that are spicy	Foods that you can eat raw	Foods that usually come in a container	Fo us co

Top Notch 1
Copyright © 2006 by Pearson Education. Permission granted to reproduce for classroom use.

NAME: _____

DATE: _____

Learning Strategy
(Unit 5, page 60, Reading)

READING STRATEGY: reading for general idea
When reading for the general idea of an article, skim the article for the most important information. Don't spend time on every word.

For example, in the article "Healthy Eating Tips," only these pieces of information are important.

- Start your day -- ------. Eat breakfast.
- Take a piece of fruit -- ------ -- during your commute. -- -------, -------, -- -------, -- -------, ------.
- Use "lite" dairy products, ------ --- low-fat and better for your health.
- --- ---- ------- meat, trim all ------- fat.
- Fried foods? Snacks? Desserts? Sweets? ------ ------ --- ---- --- ---, ---- --- high in calories and -- ---- high in fat, salt, and sugar.
- Pack ---- ---- ------- raw veggies. Buy healthy snacks ---- -------.
- Cut down on portion size -- ------- -- -------, ------- -------.
- Eat -------- in moderation.

PRACTICE
Restate each tip in your own words.
1. *In the morning, eat breakfast*
2. _____
3. _____
4. _____
5. _____
6. _____
7. _____
8. _____

Top Notch 1
Copyright ©2006 by Pearson Education. Permission granted to reproduce for classroom use.

NAME: _____

(U

	b
fruit	
vegetables	
meat	
seafood	
grains	
dairy products	
sweets	

- ➤ **Pronunciation supplements:** for additional pronunciation topics and practice
- ➤ **Writing process worksheets:** for pre-writing and peer-editing activities
- ➤ **Extra reading comprehension activities:** for both traditional comprehension and critical thinking
- ➤ **Pronunciation activities:** for additional reinforcement of pronunciation
- ➤ *Top Notch Pop* song activity sheets: for reinforcement of target language

---

Page 1 of 2

NAME: _____   DATE: _____

Top Notch Pop Song Activities
(Unit 5, "The World Café")

A. Listen to the song "The World Café." Complete the lyrics with the names of the foods. Listen again to check your work.

The World Café

Is there something that you want?
Is there anything you need?
Have you made up your mind
what you want to eat?
Place your order now,
or do you need more time?
Why not start with some juice—
lemon, orange, or lime?
Some like it hot, some like it sweet,
some like it really spicy.
You may not like everything you eat,
but I think we're doing nicely.

[CHORUS]
I can understand every word you say.
Tonight we're speaking English at The World Café.

I'll take the main course now.
I think I'll have the ___

NAME: _____   DATE: _____

Pronunciation Activity
(Unit 5, page 56)

PRONUNCIATION OF THE

Practice with a partner. Read the following words out loud. Use the correct pronunciation of the.

the Thai grilled shrimp   the orange cake

the olive oil   the coconut oil

the vegetable soup   the Australian dishes

the apple pie   the yogurt

NAME: _____   DATE: _____

Extra Reading Comprehension Activities
(Unit 5, page 60)

COMPREHENSION QUESTIONS
A. Look at the reading on page 60 and complete the sentences.
1. In the morning, it's important to eat ___
   a. fruit   b. breakfast   c. a piece of fruit
2. A delicious food that you can eat on your way to work or school is ___
   ___ mute   c. piece of fruit
   ___ nd better than high-fat ones.
   ___ foods   c. veggies
   ___ n course   c. fat
   ___ n sugar.
   ___ eets   c. Snacks
   ___ w vegetables.
   ___ essert   c. meat
   ___ dessert   c. pretzels
   ___ rtions

___ hat high-fat foods can sometimes be low in fat?

Unit 5

Permission granted to reproduce for classroom use

NAME: _____   DATE: _____

Pronunciation Supplement
(Unit 5)

PRONUNCIATION OF t AND d

The t and d between vowels or before an l are pronounced with a rapid movement of the tongue. This sound is called a flap /t/.
For example:
water   butter   ready   order
Fried egg?
That includes coconut oil?

The t and d at the beginning of a syllable or after any other ___ except t, are pronounced ___ respectively. For exam ___
attendant   customer
What kind of soup?
That comes with bread?

Exercise 1
A. Read and practice.

B. Read and practice.
pasta
candy
appetizer
salty
And to drink?
In the mood for a salad?
What kind of salad?

Page 1 of 2

NAME: _____   DATE: _____

Writing Process Worksheet
(Accompanies Unit 5, page 62, E)

ASSIGNMENT: Write information about food in this country for the readers of a travel newsletter.

1. PREWRITING
In small groups, brainstorm ideas about food in this country. Fill in the menu below with your ideas. You may use a dictionary.

LAND AND SEA

All entrées include
Bread ♦ Pasta or salad ♦ Vegetable
Coffee or Tea

APPETIZERS
_____

SOUP
_____

ENTRÉES
_____

DESSERTS
_____

2. WRITING
On a separate piece of paper, write a first draft of your menu.

Unit 5

Top Notch 1
Copyright ©2006 by Pearson Education. Permission granted to reproduce for classroom use.

NAME: _____   DATE: _____

___ Building)

___ rsation Model on page 54 of the S ___

___ gs.
___ afood.
___ out!

dinner	snacks

granted to reproduce for classroom use

Top Notch: A concise methodology

The *Top Notch* approach

The following paragraphs describe the major features of the *Top Notch* approach.

Explicit presentation of language. So that students may use their textbook both to learn from in class and as a study tool, *Top Notch* provides explicit presentation of language. The heavily illustrated Student's Book depicts or defines all vocabulary taught for productive use; it provides clear grammar charts with explanations of form, meaning, and use; and it features numerous practical model conversations.

English for today's world. More than two out of every three speakers of English in today's world are non-native speakers. This fact has profound implications for English language instruction. Learners today are more likely than ever to use English to communicate with other non-native speakers in travel, business, study, and work. For that reason, in addition to presenting the traditional cultural-linguistic features of English and preparing students to communicate with native speakers of English, *Top Notch* deliberately helps students build cultural literacy. Numerous activities in the text prepare students to communicate with people from different cultures in formal and informal situations.

Focus on the needs of the false beginner. *Top Notch 1* is designed for adult and young adult false beginners. False beginners typically have a moderate receptive vocabulary and are able to understand some spoken and written English, so long as it doesn't go much beyond the fundamentals in topics, vocabulary, social language, or grammatical structure. False beginners are often reluctant or unable to communicate orally or in writing. They lack confidence and are frustrated by the disparity between the number of years they may have studied English and their ability.

False beginners typically understand more language than they produce. For that reason, *Top Notch 1* has differing and realistic expectations for receptive and productive tasks.

Daily confirmation of progress. Adult students are often highly motivated and anxious for results, and are unwilling to continue if they don't see progress. Moreover, they are often hesitant to reveal their lack of ability and are embarrassed to speak incorrectly. Materials and lessons need to provide observable results and safe opportunities for controlled and free practice. Students should leave each class session with clear knowledge of what they have achieved. Each daily lesson in *Top Notch* has a clearly identified communicative goal and culminates in an activity to confirm students' progress.

Memorable conversation models. *Top Notch* uses a selection of topics and short practical language models that represent the language adult students want and need to learn—for professional, social, and travel situations. Systematic guided practice helps to make these essential models memorable and transferable to students' own lives.

Top Notch has a practical social language syllabus that provides adult students with essential language for their real needs. In addition to classic level 1 topics, vocabulary, and grammar, *Top Notch 1* includes highly practical, communicative language, such as how to ask whether a tip is included in a bill, how to complain when the air-conditioning in a hotel room doesn't work, how to bargain for a lower price, and so on.

Deliberate movement from controlled to free practice. If language is to be acquired, remembered, and accessible to students when they need it, ample practice is required. Because the language learner often lacks the opportunity to use English outside of the classroom, *Top Notch* offers opportunities for increasingly free and rigorous practice within the class.

Learner-supportive instruction. The following features provide support to students learning from *Top Notch*.

Comprehensible directions. The *Top Notch* Student's Book contains simple directions that students can readily understand and follow. Models and examples take any confusion out of what is expected.

Conversation pair work guides. Conversation pair work is supported with clear in-book speaking guides so students can practice with or without teacher observation.

Notepadding. Free-discussion activities are often preceded by notepad preparation so students have a clear and concrete stimulus to get them started and keep them going.

Need Help? A unique *Need Help?* feature reminds students of language they have previously learned that can be used in free discussions and role plays.

Authentic, sourced reading texts. To lend interest, seriousness, and authentic practice, the *Top Notch* Student's Book contains a variety of texts from authentic sources. Careful attention has been given to comprehensibility of these texts so that students are not frustrated. Source lines in the Student's Book show students that they have the ability to cope with real-world material.

Real language. Carefully exposing students to authentic, natural English, both receptively and productively, is a necessary component of building understanding and expression. All conversation models in *Top Notch* feature the language people really use, not "textbook English" written merely to exemplify grammar.

Usage information backed by the Longman Corpus Network. CN Informed by the Longman Corpus Network—Longman's unique computerized language database of over 328 million words of spoken and written English as well as learner errors—*Top Notch* provides concise and useful information about frequency, collocations, and typical native-speaker usage. Corpus Notes can be found at a glance on the Student's Book pages bound into this Teacher's Edition. In addition, teachers are alerted to frequent learner errors so they can target their attention to troublesome vocabulary and structures.

Top Notch Pop **songs.** Five songs especially composed and recorded for *Top Notch* provide focused language reinforcement as well as essential stress, intonation, and pronunciation practice, making language memorable and fun.

Teacher's Resource Disk. Because teachers have differing ideas of what constitutes the best pedagogy, the Teacher's Resource Disk bound in the inside back cover of this book provides printable, ready-made classroom activities to extend or adapt each section of a *Top Notch* unit.

The following worksheets and cards can be printed from the Teacher's Resource Disk:

Extra reading comprehension activities. Each unit's reading selection appears on a worksheet with in-depth traditional comprehension and critical thinking questions.

Writing process worksheets. Brainstorming and peer-editing activities help students become better writers by offering them an opportunity to take initiative in generating ideas for writing and in correcting for accuracy and clarity.

Learning strategies. These activities teach and practice learning strategies students can apply over and over again, such as vocabulary building, predicting, scanning, and clarification.

Grammar self-checks. Inductive grammar charts provide an alternative grammar presentation as well as cognitive activities to promote students' grammar awareness.

Pronunciation activities and supplements. Pair work activities provide extra practice of each unit's pronunciation point. Pronunciation supplements

focus on additional pronunciation points that can be illustrated and practiced in the unit's conversation models.

Vocabulary cards and cumulative vocabulary activities. *Top Notch* vocabulary is further reinforced in two effective ways. Two-sided vocabulary flash cards come with teacher's notes that provide ideas for games, alternative presentations, substitution in pair work activities, and other ways to ensure vocabulary mastery. Cumulative vocabulary activities reinforce vocabulary meaning throughout the course through critical thinking and application of practical learning strategies.

Pair work cards. These cards reproduce each unit's guided conversation models. Partner A's part is on one card and Partner B's part is on another, with slots for controlled manipulation of vocabulary and social language. These cards get students "out of the book" and communicating.

Graphic organizers. Charts and visual representations enhance and extend activities in the *Top Notch* unit through classification and brainstorming activities.

Top Notch Pop **song activities.** Using the lyrics to each of the *Top Notch Pop* songs, these activities provide practice of the target grammar and vocabulary embedded in the song.

A Teacher's Edition as a management tool. In the Lesson Planner beginning on page T2 of this Teacher's Edition, there are links to all components of *Top Notch 1*. Icons indicate places where extra and optional activities are available on the Teacher's Resource Disk, where *Top Notch* Workbook activities can be assigned, where an Achievement Test or a Speaking Test is available from the Complete Assessment Package, and when to use the *Top Notch TV* video. In addition, icons provide references to activities in *Copy & Go*. While the *Top Notch* Student's Book is a complete course without the need for additional components, those who have chosen to use one or more of the components will see them integrated at a glance in the Lesson Planner.

A Student's Take-Home Audio CD. Located in the back of each *Top Notch* Student's Book, the Student's Take-Home Audio CD provides an opportunity for students to listen and practice at their own convenience—on their commute, in the privacy of their homes—any time they have an opportunity. The CD provides rhythm and intonation practice of the Conversation Models as well as the *Top Notch Pop* songs. Encourage students to listen to the CD on their own time to increase their confidence; make the language in the models memorable; improve their rhythm, stress, and intonation; and learn the songs.

A "Pronunciator." To remove any doubts about pronunciation of proper names in English, the *Top Notch* Companion Website includes a section in which proper names in *Top Notch* that are not heard on the Class Audio Program can be found transcribed in the International Phonetic Alphabet [IPA]. The transcription shows the way a native speaker of English is most likely to pronounce a word. When non-English names or places are included, the pronunciation given is that used in English, which may differ from the one used in the other language. For example, /mɛksɪkoʊ/ NOT /mɛhiko/. To find the Pronunciator, go to the *Top Notch* Companion Website and click on "Pronunciator" in Teacher Resources.

Methodology for the *Top Notch* course

The following paragraphs describe suggestions for managing a *Top Notch* classroom.

The goal of *Top Notch* is to prepare students to understand spoken and written English and to express themselves confidently, accurately, and fluently. Much practice is necessary to reach that goal. Because the typical student has limited opportunity to observe English and to practice it, *Top Notch* seeks to replicate as much as possible the authentic "voice" of English so that students can become successful in understanding, and to provide enough practice for students to truly acquire language.

Communicative teaching methodologies, especially at the lower levels of language instruction, often stop short of enabling students to bridge the gap between controlled and free practice. The student of today wants to be able to go beyond info-gaps and pair work activities to use English in real discussions about ideas with real people.

The following general methodology is recommended for *Top Notch*. Specific suggestions for teaching every exercise of the Student's Book are given in the Lesson Planner beginning on page T2. Note that the extent to which you use these recommendations is up to you. All suggestions may not be appropriate for all groups, and you should tailor the lesson to reflect your own background, personal approach, training, and the specific needs of your students.

Pair work and collaborative activities. On every page of *Top Notch*, opportunities for pair work, group work, and collaborative activities enable students to take a more active and creative role in learning and allow the maximum number of students to participate. These activities encourage students to use their own language resources, making the lesson more personalized and meaningful. They also ensure that students initiate as well as respond in English. Furthermore, in working together, students get to know each other faster and become more independent, relying less on the teacher for guidance and ultimately taking more responsibility for their own learning. We recommend the following approaches for pair and group work activities:

A student-centered approach. Some students, particularly those accustomed to teacher-centered lessons, may not immediately see the benefits of working in pairs or groups. The first time you do pair and group work, point out to students that working together allows them more time to practice English and allows you to listen to more students individually.

Cooperative learning. Encourage students to help and learn from each other. Whenever possible, try to elicit answers from other students before answering a question yourself. If a student asks a question that was previously asked by another student, direct the question to the student who first asked the question. In restating in their own words information they have recently obtained, students internalize the language, increasing the likelihood that it will be retained.

Flexible seating arrangement. To ensure that students interact with a variety of partners, have students sit in a different location for each class. When dividing the class into pairs or groups, try to match students of different abilities. One method of forming groups is to have students count off according to the number of groups needed. (The 1s work together, the 2s work together, and so on.)

Teacher monitoring. During pair and group work activities, circulate around the room, keeping students on task and offering help as needed. When dividing the class into pairs, avoid playing a partner role yourself, as this will limit your ability to monitor and offer assistance to the class. If faced with an odd number of students, create a group of three students, with a third role added as a helper to encourage eye contact and to correct mistakes.

Building student confidence. Before asking students to speak in front of the class, build students' confidence by having them rehearse language in pairs, small groups, or chorally as a class. Students can also collaborate with a partner or group on writing exercises, either by completing the activity together or by comparing their answers.

Time management. To keep students on task, set time limits for each activity. End activities before most of the class is finished to avoid dead time. For students who finish early, prepare additional activities, either your own or ones from any of the *Top Notch* supplements. One idea, for example, would be to have students who have finished their Conversation Pair Work (see page Txxii) write the conversation that they created.

Correction. Most students of languages, particularly adult learners, like feedback and expect to be corrected when they make a mistake. However, recent research indicates that correcting errors in students' speech and writing is less effective in promoting correct language use than is commonly believed. Studies have shown that it is repeated exposure to correct usage, rather than constant correction, that results in the internalization of new language. In addition, excessive correction in a communicative course can embarrass and discourage students, making them reluctant to attempt the experimentation and practice essential to language acquisition. We recommend the following approaches for providing effective positive feedback and striking a balance between the need for correction and maintaining feelings of success:

Accuracy. For activities where accuracy is the focus, such as in the Conversation Pair Work, correct mistakes shortly after they occur. Immediate correction is important for controlled activities where students need guidance in using new language.

Fluency. For freer and more challenging activities where fluency is the focus, such as in the *Top Notch* Interactions, refrain from stopping the flow of student discussion with corrections. In these activities, accuracy is less important than the ability to communicate ideas and improvise with known language. Developing these improvisation skills is critical if students are to convert the English they have learned in the classroom into the English they need in their own lives. Interrupting students with corrections discourages this experimentation. Instead, take notes on common student mistakes and then review those errors as a class at the end of the activity.

Self-correction. Students are often able to correct their own mistakes. First, allow the student to finish the thought, then show by sound or gesture that there has been a mistake. Try to indicate where the mistake was and give the student an opportunity to self-correct. Some techniques for eliciting self-correction include counting off each word of the phrase on your fingers and pausing at the mistake, repeating the student sentence or pausing at the mistake, and prompting the student with a missing word. For example: S: *He has two child.* T: *He has two . . . ?* S: *He has two children.* A less intrusive method is to correct the student's mistake by reformulating what the student said without stopping the flow of conversation. For example: S: *He have a car.* T: *Oh, he has a car?* S: *Yes, he has a car.* Note that these techniques often prompt the student to self-correct.

Selectivity. Don't discourage or overwhelm students by correcting every mistake. Focus corrections on the skills that are being taught in that particular lesson or mistakes that prevent comprehension.

Support. Above all, avoid making students feel pressured. Give students enough time to think. Be careful not to stigmatize or embarrass students. Be aware that students may be sensitive to criticism in front of their peers and may prefer more private feedback. There is nothing more effective in promoting student practice than their belief that you are "on their side." To that end, it is suggested that you show approval for student experimentation, even if the language is inaccurate. Experimentation is an essential step in language mastery.

Checking answers. For exercises or homework requiring a written response, have students check their answers with a partner. This encourages students to correct their own mistakes and also helps students avoid the possible embarrassment of giving incorrect answers in front of the entire class. When the class has finished comparing answers, review the correct answers as a class, either by eliciting the answers from individual students or by having volunteers write their answers on the board. In classes with time constraints, write answers on the board and have the class self-correct.

Repetition. Repetition of the Conversation Models and the Vocabulary (see pages Txx and Txxi) helps students acquire comprehensible and accurate pronunciation, stress, and intonation. Repetition also helps to make language memorable, an important goal. On the Student's Take-Home Audio CD and in the Class Audio Program, a pause following the speaker's utterance facilitates repetition and permits students to imitate the pronunciation and intonation of the native speaker on the audio. Teacher's notes provide specific suggestions for how to focus students' attention on rhythm, stress, and intonation for each Conversation Model. Here are some general options for using repetition to facilitate learning:

Open or closed books. For activities requiring students to listen and repeat, we recommend having students first listen while looking at the written form in their textbooks. This allows students to link the written form in the book to the sound they hear. In the next step, when students are asked to listen and repeat, have them listen and repeat with their books closed. This serves to reduce distractions and allows students to focus exclusively on listening and repeating rather than reading. It also reduces the confusing effect of English spelling on pronunciation.

Practice drills. Introduce short, fast-paced repetition drills to offer the class more pronunciation practice, reinforce word structures, and provide a fresh change of pace. Practice drills will also help students see how much they can personalize the language they are learning. Start by modeling a sentence from the Conversation Model and having the class repeat after you. For example: T: *I'm going to go running this weekend.* Class: *I'm going to go running this weekend.* Then prompt students to change the sentence. For example: T: *go swimming.* Students: *I'm going to go swimming this weekend.* Continue in this manner several times. Point to individual students and have them repeat. Modeling the new language before and after each student response helps students build auditory memory while providing them with a correct model for repetition.

Pace. Keeping the pace of repetition drills lively gives the greatest number of students a chance to speak and maximizes exposure to the language. If a student cannot respond or makes a mistake, move on quickly to another student and then return to the student who made the mistake. Maintaining the pace gives weaker students the time that they need to internalize and ultimately acquire new language.

Realia—bringing the outside in. Research has demonstrated that language is easier to comprehend and retain if presented in conjunction with sensory input such as pictures, sounds, props, and authentic documents. In addition, bringing real material into the classroom serves to motivate students and helps them understand the relevance of their language study to their own lives.

Projects in most units direct students to collect authentic documents; do Internet or library research; or bring in books, magazines, or other printed material. These materials provide real-world content for students to communicate about in English, whether or not the original material is in English. If English materials are available, they build awareness of authentic English in the world outside the classroom.

The Topic Preview on the first page of the unit and many of the readings come from authentic sources or are near-authentic documents created by integrating two or more authentic documents. Teaching notes in the Lesson Planner include suggestions for maximizing the value of this material.

Elicitation. Asking questions keeps the class active and involved and helps you to identify what students understand and what they do not. An effective method for eliciting language from the class is to first provide a model that students understand and then have them create language using that model. For instance, before eliciting a list of occupations from the class, provide examples by writing on the board several occupations that students have learned. Some additional elicitation techniques to consider include the following:

Warm-up. Direct questions to the entire class before eliciting answers from individual students. This technique reduces the pressure on individual students to produce a response before they are ready and provides the class with a model of a correct response.

One-word answers. It is not always necessary for students to answer in full sentences. Often a one-word answer is sufficient to demonstrate understanding of the question and to respond appropriately. Using one-word answers is particularly valuable for beginning students because it allows them to communicate even if they have acquired only a little productive English. Moreover, it allows students to speak "real" language from the start, as one-word responses are often more authentic in informal contexts than full-sentence responses.

Teaching multi-level classes. To accommodate diverse levels within the same classroom, we recommend the following approaches:

Modeling. Use more advanced students to model activities. Advanced students, with their quicker comprehension time, are more likely to respond quickly and correctly. Modeling will allow weaker students, who need longer exposure time to new language, to use the stronger students' responses as a model and respond successfully.

Grouping. In pair and group work activities, vary the approach to grouping students to keep the activities fresh. Partnering more advanced students with weaker students encourages the class to help and learn from each other. Partnering students with similar ability levels also has advantages, as this allows pairs to speak at their own pace and level of production.

Methodology for a *Top Notch* Unit

A *Top Notch* unit is made up of six two-page lessons:

▶ ***Preview:*** Introduction

▶ ***Lesson 1:*** Controlled practice

▶ ***Lesson 2:*** Controlled practice

▶ ***Lesson 3:*** Free practice

▶ ***Lesson 4:*** Free practice

▶ ***Checkpoint:*** Review

The icon 💿 in this section indicates that extension activities can be printed from the Teacher's Resource Disk in the back of this Teacher's Edition.

▶ *Preview*

It is suggested that you open your *Top Notch* textbook to any unit in order to see each section described below.

The purpose of the Preview is to provide an introduction to the topic and the social language of the unit. It's important to understand that the Preview includes language at "+1" level. The reason for this is to expose students to the authentic language they will encounter in the world outside the classroom and to familiarize them with language they will be dealing with in the unit. Great care has been taken to ensure that +1 language is comprehensible. Embedded illustrations and contextual photographs were especially created to aid comprehension and motivate students.

When teaching *Top Notch* to a group for the first time, make students aware that they will not be expected to "learn" or "use" all the language in the Preview. The reason for including it is to give students a motivating glimpse of real language at a comprehensible level, to build their expectations of the topic and language that follows in the unit, to access some prior knowledge, and to build the strategy of determining meaning from context. Exercises and discussion questions in this Preview are written at the productive level of the student.

TOPIC PREVIEW. Begin each unit by asking a few questions about the content of the advertisement, menu, website, etc. that is featured in the Topic Preview. The purpose of Exercise A is to focus attention on the realia that follows. If necessary, model some answers to the questions in Exercise A yourself. Be sure to answer using language your students already know.

One of the purposes of including a piece of realia with +1 language is to teach students to find meaning in texts that contain some unknown language. Encourage students to use the illustrations and context to determine the meaning of unfamiliar words and phrases—an important learning strategy for understanding material above one's productive level. Help students build their ability to use illustrations and context by asking

questions that prompt students to do so. For example, if students don't know the word *accommodations* on the first page of Unit 8, ask *What's the picture to the right of the word?* (a bed) and *On a cruise, you have food, drinks, and entertainment. What more do you need?* (a room, a place to sleep)

Additional exercises on the left-hand page of the Preview get students to start talking about the unit topic. These discussion activities are designed so that students can use language they already know or that is readily available on the page. When grouping isn't specified, students can discuss in pairs or small groups. After students have discussed, review by asking a few students to share their responses with the whole class.

SOUND BITES. The Sound Bites on the right-hand page of the Preview are not a conversation for student practice, but rather for student observation. These examples of natural conversation will promote comprehension of authentic language and will begin to familiarize students with language they will learn later. An attempt has been made to include highly natural idiomatic language, language ordinarily not included in textbooks. Because the language is very appealing, many students will pick it up and make it their own. But that should not be your expectation or requirement.

Before students read and listen to the conversation, ask questions about the photo(s), if possible. For variety and to provide listening practice, you may sometimes want to have students listen with books closed. After students listen to the conversation, ask questions to check comprehension. Use the questions that are provided in each unit or your own questions. (Additional questions are included in the Lesson Plans in this book.) If students have listened with books closed, ask the comprehension questions, allow students to listen again, and then repeat the questions. Comprehension questions can be asked in open class, written on the board for students to answer with a partner, or read out loud for students to write answers to. If appropriate, ask additional questions that relate the content of the conversation to students' own lives.

...w language in the Sound Bites is highlighted
...se(s) that follow. The meaning of almost all
...ge can be determined from the context of
...sation, but where doubts might occur, notes
...son Plans offer suggestions for conveying
... Have students underline in the conversation
..., phrase, or sentence that is asked about in the
... Encourage students to reread the lines before
...er the underlined portion of the conversation.
...n also ask questions about the context that lead
...ts to figure out the meaning of the new language.

...T ABOUT YOU? Each two-page Preview culminates
...hat about you? activities that prompt students to
...te content from the Preview to their own lives,
...ferences, and opinions. Have students complete the
...hat about you? exercise independently. Then talk
...bout their responses. If a Pair Work or other speaking
...ctivity follows, your own responses can serve as a
...model. If the Pair Work activity asks partners to
compare, ask a couple of students about their responses
before pairs discuss. An option for this section is to
have students use the third person to tell the class
something about their classmate.

UNIT GOALS. Finally, note that each Preview lists in a
box four communicative goals for the unit. These are
the goals for the four lessons that follow.

▶ Lessons 1 and 2

Lessons 1 and 2 offer new language and controlled
practice. Each lesson is titled with its communication
goal, such as "Order food in a restaurant," so students
see what they will learn to do in the lesson.

CONVERSATION MODEL. To build awareness and facilitate
comprehension, begin by asking questions about the
photo, if possible. Many questions are provided in
the Lesson Plans, but it's not necessary to stop there.
When you ask questions however, be mindful of what
students are capable of answering. Don't elicit language
or information that students would not know prior to
reading the conversation. Another option is for students
to say as much as they can about the photo to a partner.
Note that to preview the target grammar of the lesson,
one or more examples of that grammar are embedded in
the Conversation Model.

Play the recording of the Conversation Model or read
it aloud yourself while students read and listen with
books open. Then check students' understanding of the
conversation by asking comprehension questions. The
questions provided in the Lesson Plans help students
focus on the essential information in the conversation
and determine the meaning of any new language from

context. The questions also prepare students to
understand any grammar presentation that follows.

An alternative presentation technique, especially in
stronger groups, is to have students listen to the
conversation with books closed first. When electing this
option, have students look at the picture first to build
awareness of the social situation of the conversation.

RHYTHM AND INTONATION PRACTICE. Following the
Conversation Model is a direction line for "Rhythm
and intonation practice." This second recording of the
model directs students to listen and repeat in the pauses.
The pause following each line of the model is an
opportunity for students to listen and focus on imitating
the pronunciation, intonation, rhythm, and stress of the
native speaker in the model. The Lesson Plans suggest
specific rhythm, stress, and intonation points to pay
attention to.

Some instructors like to have students look at the text as
they repeat. Many prefer to have students do the
rhythm and intonation practice with books closed, to
avoid the interference of English spelling. We encourage
experimentation to see which is more effective. With
books closed, students listen and repeat after each line.
Encourage students to imitate the rhythm, stress, and
intonation of the conversation as closely as possible.
Correct where necessary, helping students to pronounce
the language clearly. Encourage students to continue
practicing the rhythm and intonation using the
Student's Take-Home Audio CD included in the back
of their textbook.

Stress patterns. To help teachers focus on the stress
patterns of the Conversation Models, the stress patterns
have been transcribed with a "Morse code-like" feature
in the Lesson Plans.

GRAMMAR. Each new grammar structure is previewed
in the Conversation Model so students read, hear, and
understand the structure in context before they are
required to manipulate it. Have students read the
information in the Grammar box independently. Then
ask them to look again at the Conversation Model and
find and underline any examples of the new structure.

In the Grammar box, the new structure is presented
through examples and clear, concise, easy-to-understand
rules. The Lesson Plans offer specific suggestions for
presenting the grammar from the box and for
reinforcing the grammar taught in each unit. Students
internalize grammatical structures when they have the
opportunity to use them in a meaningful and relevant
context. Suggestions prompt students to begin using the
new structure in the context of their own lives to express
opinions, preferences, and other ideas.

You can also use an inductive approach by printing out the Grammar Self-Checks (see below) or by writing the example sentences from the grammar chart on the board for discussion.

THE GRAMMAR BOOSTER. Following most Grammar boxes is an icon referring students to the Grammar Booster. In some cases, the grammar is expanded and presented more fully. In others, additional and related grammar points are included. Teachers and programs differ in their interest in grammar, so the Grammar Booster should be considered an option for teachers who want to go beyond what is normally included in a textbook for this level. In some cases, you may wish to direct stronger students who can do more to the Grammar Booster while not using it for the whole class. In addition to the presentations, the Grammar Booster contains confirming exercises.

Even if you elect not to use the Grammar Booster, students will still appreciate having additional material for permanent reference in their textbook.

Controlled exercises follow each grammar presentation in the Student's Book. The exercises provide written and/or oral practice with the structure(s) just taught and offer additional examples of its use in context. If necessary, model how to do the first item in each task. Have students complete the exercises independently, in pairs, or in small groups. Review answers in open class, or have students check answers with a partner. The Teacher's Edition contains all answers printed right on the Student's Book page facing the Lesson Plan.

Grammar Self-Checks. * If you prefer an inductive presentation of the grammar point, print out a Grammar Self-Check from the Teacher's Resource Disk. The Grammar Self-Checks are an inductive presentation and awareness activity for use in class. Grammar Self-Checks are also designed to check how well students understand the grammar, and can be used as a follow-up activity after the grammar charts have been presented.

VOCABULARY. Vocabulary is explicitly presented through pictures or definitions. The vocabulary presentations in the Student's Book serve to convey meaning of each new vocabulary item and to provide reference for self-study, especially valuable as students prepare for tests. Vocabulary in *Top Notch* is presented at word, phrase, and sentence level—including expressions, idioms, and collocations.

Students will use the vocabulary presented to manipulate the Conversation Pair Work at the end of the lesson. Begin by focusing students' attention on the illustrations or definitions. An option is to have students cover the words with a sheet of paper and look only at the pictures. Pairs can see which words and phrases they already know. Printable Vocabulary Cards are also available for this purpose on the Teacher's Resource Disk in the back of the Teacher's Edition (see below).

Play the audio program. If you don't have the audio program, read the words aloud as a model. Students listen and repeat. Note that singular count nouns are preceded by the indefinite article a/an. Students should use the article when they repeat. Depending on your students' language background, the concept of count and non-count nouns may provide a great challenge. Using the indefinite article to contrast singular count nouns with non-count nouns will help students to begin internalizing this difficult concept.

If necessary, clarify the meaning of any words or phrases students have difficulty understanding. Convey the meaning physically—through gestures, mime, or reference to people or objects in the room—or give examples or a simple definition. Specific ideas on how to do this are provided in the Lesson Plans.

When possible, personalize the vocabulary. Use the vocabulary to talk about or ask questions about content familiar to your students—for example, *What is across the street, down the street, and around the corner from your school?* (Unit 2, page T20) In open class, or with pairs and small groups, have students talk about their likes/dislikes, preferences, plans, relationships, belongings, habits, etc., in relation to the vocabulary.

Vocabulary cards. For further practice with the vocabulary, print out the Vocabulary Cards from the Teacher's Resource Disk. These cards can be used for presentations and a variety of games and activities. An icon alerts you that cards are available.

Cumulative vocabulary activities. At the end of each unit, there is an icon for the Cumulative Vocabulary Activities. These activities are designed to provide both cumulative and cognitive practice of vocabulary learned in *Top Notch*. You can print out these Cumulative Vocabulary Activities from the Teacher's Resource Disk after completing the relevant Student Book units.

Learning strategies for vocabulary building. To enable students to learn strategies that can help them learn English more effectively, print out a Learning Strategies worksheets from the Teacher's Resource Disk. These worksheets include practical strategies students can apply throughout the course. For vocabulary learning, vocabulary building strategies such as word associations, classification, and marking stress are included.

---

*Throughout the Lesson Plans, each time you see this icon there is a printable extension activity from the Teacher's Resource Disk.

PRONUNCIATION. In addition to the rhythm and intonation practice, each unit provides practice with a specific pronunciation point. Play the audio program or read the examples to the class. Students first read and listen, then listen again and repeat. After students repeat, they can practice reading the examples to a partner. Pronunciation activities are generally related to each unit's content. Use the unit's content to provide additional examples. The Lesson Plans identify words or sentences within the unit—for example, in a Grammar box or another exercise—that students can practice reading to a partner with the correct intonation, pronunciation, or stress. An option is to have students exaggerate correct intonation, pronunciation, or stress when they practice. Remind students to also practice the pronunciation skill when they do the Conversation Pair Work activity at the end of the lesson.

Pronunciation activities and supplements. 🌐 Extra interactive pronunciation activities provide more practice of the unit pronunciation point. In addition, each unit has a supplemental pronunciation activity that extends students' understanding of English pronunciation through further presentation and practice. You can print out both of these extra activities from the Teacher's Resource Disk whenever you see the icon.

LISTENING COMPREHENSION. Lessons 1 and 2 often contain exercises labeled Listening Comprehension. These short exercises serve to practice comprehension and recollection of the vocabulary or the grammar. Some exercises provide practice in simple auditory discrimination, but in most cases listening tasks require very careful listening for sense and critical thinking. The unit's major presentation of Listening Comprehension is included in Lessons 3 and 4 and is more fully described there (see below).

Learning strategies for listening comprehension. 🌐 To help students to learn listening strategies, such as listening for general ideas or making inferences, print out a Learning Strategies worksheet from the Teacher's Resource Disk.

CONVERSATION PAIR WORK. The Conversation Pair Work activity at the end of each lesson is the culminating activity. In this activity, students demonstrate progress and mastery of the lesson's communication goal. Each activity is facilitated by a "guide"—a version of the Conversation Model with blank slots for students to personalize as they like, using names, different vocabulary, or other appropriate social language they have learned. Illustrations and other cues are often provided to help students think of how to change the Conversation Model. This controlled practice is an essential first step, and it must be mastered before

students can be successful at applying the models to free conversation or discussion.

The most important way to maximize the value of this practice is to encourage experimentation, showing approval when students use a variety of possible slot fillers. <u>Be sure students don't think the point of the practice is to test their memory of the original Conversation Model.</u> It is exactly the opposite. As they practice, students should insert new language in the slots. The slots have been carefully chosen to offer a number of possibilities, based on what the students have learned. They should be largely foolproof.

Some slots have been included specifically because students have already learned a number of ways to express a particular thought. For instance, following "Thank you," a slot is provided because students can respond in a number of previously learned ways, such as "You're welcome," "No problem!" and "Sure!" Each slot has been tested to be sure students have enough language "in their pockets" to provide one or more responses. Having different pairs of students perform their Conversation Pair Work in front of the class reminds all students of how much social language they have learned.

Begin by reading the instructions out loud. Then model the conversation with a more advanced student to demonstrate that students should change the Conversation Model by filling in new language from the lesson or from other sources. If helpful, point out the language available on the two-page lesson for students to use. The Lesson Plans provide examples of conversations using language your students can produce. However, the conversation each pair of students creates will vary.

Students practice the Conversation Pair Work activity with a partner. The importance of this activity cannot be overstated, for it is in producing their own language in this controlled activity that students take their first steps toward truly free language. Encourage students to find a new partner for each Conversation Pair Work activity. As students practice, circulate and offer help as needed. Remind students to make eye contact during conversations, to encourage natural pronunciation and tone. An option is to have students practice the conversation a few times with different partners. Also, you can ask a couple of pairs to role-play their conversation for the class or have pairs role-play their conversations for each other.

Pair work cards. 🌐 If you wish to get your students "out of the book" for conversation practice, print out Pair Work Cards from the Teacher's Resource Disk. These cards provide the Conversation Model guide split into two with Partner A's part on one card and Partner B's part on the other. Teaching suggestions are provided on the Teacher's Resource Disk. For example, one activity suggests students work in threes, with Partner C flashing Vocabulary Cards as cues for Partners A and B.

Learning strategies for speaking. 🌀 If you want students to learn the speaking strategies of clarification and keeping a conversation going, print out a Learning Strategies worksheet from the Teacher's Resource Disk.

▶ *Lessons 3 and 4*

Lessons 3 and 4 begin with a communication goal, such as "Discuss food and health," and culminate in a *Top Notch* Interaction in which students achieve that communication goal.

Lessons 3 and 4 open with either a reading or a listening. These exercises provide key input that leads students to free communication. Vocabulary is usually included and ranges from one-word items to phrases to collocations and idioms. Vocabulary meaning is clearly conveyed through illustrations, definitions, and/or contextual sentences. The vocabulary is usually used in the reading or listening and then practiced in the exercises and activities that follow.

READING WARM-UP. This exercise consists of a question or a series of questions that prompt students to start thinking about the topic of the reading. Before students read, they relate the content of the reading to their own lives. This process generates interest and aids understanding.

READING. All readings are based on authentic sources. When appropriate, the sources are identified. To avoid frustrating students at this level, we have had to simplify some of the language from the original sources, but we have taken great care to maintain the authentic character of the material. Students should be encouraged to understand the reading without looking up every new word in the dictionary. Reading in a foreign language always presents the challenge of *some* unknown language. Students need to learn that they can comprehend main ideas, can get specific information and infer information even without knowing every word. Comprehension activities always follow the reading, sometimes in the form of straight factual questions or true/false activities or clozes that demonstrate understanding of information or of vocabulary from context.

Note that all readings are recorded in the Class Audio Program. Listening to them gives excellent ear training for the rhythm, stress, and intonation of extended (as opposed to conversational) speech. It also helps students learn collocations—words that "go together" as phrases. It is recommended that students be given an opportunity to read and listen to each reading. You may choose to play the recording after students have already read the text or while they are reading. In some cases, you may choose to play the recording as a listening activity with closed books.

Read the Reading Warm-up question(s) out loud. Model the activity by answering the questions yourself. Students can answer the questions with a partner or in small groups. To review, ask a few students to share their responses with the class. Specific suggestions can be found in the Lesson Plans.

Before students read, have them look at any photos or illustrations. If appropriate, ask questions about these visuals. Give students a few minutes to look at the selection independently. Encourage them to look at the title and any headings to help give them an idea of what the reading is about. The instructions before most readings also ask a question to help focus students' attention as they read. Ask students to try to answer the question as they read. Then, if you choose, play the audio program and have students read along.

The readings contain language that students have not yet learned but that they should be able to comprehend through context and similarity to language they know. However, it is not necessary for students to know what every word means in order to understand the selection. Encourage students to guess at the meaning of new words as much as possible, or to comprehend as much as they can without understanding every word. After students read, ask questions or use activities that lead them to figure out the meaning of new language and that help them to identify the essential information from the reading. Such questions and activities are provided in the Lesson Plans.

Many of the exercises that follow the reading also prompt students to use context to figure out the meaning of new language or to identify the most important information from the reading. Read the directions for each exercise out loud, or ask for a volunteer to read them. Have students read the exercise items and then reread the selection independently. As students read, they can underline words or information in the reading that will help them to complete the exercise. Allow students a set period of time to refer to the reading as necessary to complete the exercise individually, in pairs, or in small groups. Have students check their work with a partner, have pairs or groups check their work with another pair or group, or review answers as a class. For a challenge, have students practice reading the selection out loud in small groups.

Extra reading comprehension activities. 🌀 If you want more extensive comprehension questions than the ones that appear in the Student's Book, you can print them out from the Teacher's Resource Disk. The Extra Reading Comprehension Activities contain both traditional comprehension and critical thinking questions.

Learning strategies for reading. 🌀 If you want students to learn the reading strategies of skimming, scanning, and vocabulary building, as well as others, you can print out a Learning Strategies worksheet from the Teacher's Resource Disk. Many students need encouragement to approach readings in this way.

LISTENING COMPREHENSION. Listening Comprehension activities in Lessons 3 and 4 provide the core listening practice of the unit, containing language at students' productive level as well as at the more challenging +1 level. Receptive-level language is comprehensible to students through context, intonation, and similarity to language they already know.

Point out to students that a major cause of lack of comprehension is the natural panic that occurs when learners hear unknown words. Explain that it is not necessary to understand every word to understand the selection. To maximize the effectiveness of these activities, avoid providing students with explanations of new language beyond any vocabulary that was taught prior to the Listening. If a student specifically asks about a new word, give the meaning, but do not spend a lot of time on it. Exposure to receptive-level language promotes students' language development and prepares students to communicate in the world outside the classroom.

In general, it is suggested that students listen to the selection the first time with books closed. (In some cases, the Lesson Plans provide an alternative approach.) In this way, students can focus on the "big picture" without the distraction of completing the exercise. Read out loud the portion of the directions that provides information about the speakers, setting, or situation. Alternatively, you might prefer to ask (after the first listening) *Who's talking? Where are the people? What are the people doing?* If students are not forthcoming with answers to those questions, you can restate the question, providing two answers from which to choose. The value of this practice is to convince students that they have, in fact, understood a good deal, even if they have not understood everything. This is an essential listening skill for foreign language learners.

Before students listen again and complete the exercise, have them look at the exercise to focus their attention on the specific listening task, such as listening for occupations or times. Play the audio as many times as necessary for students to complete the activity. Do not approach these exercises as "tests." Repeated exposure to each listening sample has substantial instructional value. Increasing students' exposure to challenging language enhances their comprehension and confidence. Review answers in open class, or have students check answers with a partner.

Note that the Listening Comprehension exercises are not on the Student's Take-Home Audio CD. If you do not have the Class Audio Program, read the audioscript in the Lesson Plans out loud to your students.

Accented speakers. In order to accustom students to listening to English in the real world, the *Top Notch* audio program includes a number of non-native speakers of English as well as native speakers with regional variations of both American and British English. The Lesson Plans provide the language background of each accented speaker, information which may be interesting or informative to your class.

Note that accented speakers in *Top Notch* are heard only in receptive listening texts, not in productive models that students repeat.

TOP NOTCH INTERACTION. Both Lessons 3 and 4 culminate in an activity labeled *Top Notch* Interaction. The goal of this activity is to engage students in free and open-ended discussions, role plays, debates, presentations, and writing.

Free discussion is the goal of all language learners. But foreign language students often have difficulty with free communication because the combination of gathering their thoughts and remembering the language they know is too challenging and often leads to silent panic. Students need to move beyond the controlled safety of models and info-gaps to more extensive self-expression. However, the nature of the foreign language setting makes success at free discussion elusive. The *Top Notch* Interactions are deliberately constructed to provide prepared opportunities for students to experiment and succeed, because each task elicits language that is known.

A series of steps prepares students so they will be successful. Notepad activities prompt students to make notes that organize their ideas and provide speaking or writing points for the discussions, presentations, or writing activities that follow. Students often compare notes with classmates for additional input. They also fill out surveys, answer questions, and look at a variety of visual stimuli such as menus, headlines, and bills. When it is time to actually discuss a topic, they already have the language and the ideas laid out in front of them.

An important feature of many *Top Notch* Interactions is *Need Help?* The *Need Help?* feature lists language that students have "in their pockets"—language learned in the current and previous units that students can use in the *Top Notch* Interactions. Massive opportunities for recycling language occur throughout *Top Notch*.

WRITING. Many *Top Notch* Interactions contain a writing activity. The Student's Book often contains an example to get students started, and there are suggestions in the Lesson Plans as well.

Writing process worksheets. 💿 For activities that emphasize the process of writing, print out Writing Process Worksheets. These worksheets provide brainstorming and peer-editing activities related to specific writing tasks. Through these activities, which provide an opportunity to take initiative in correcting their own work, students become better writers. An icon alerts you that a worksheet is available.

▶ *Checkpoint*

The Checkpoint reviews the essential content of the unit and offers students the opportunity to check their progress. It also allows you to identify any areas of particular difficulty that may require additional practice. The Checkpoint page begins with a listening comprehension exercise and generally ends with a writing task. The Lesson Plans suggest ways to start students writing and often offer examples of what they are able to write. The Checkpoint page also includes exercises that review vocabulary, grammar, and social language from the unit.

Have students work individually to complete the Checkpoint exercises. Circulate to offer help as needed. Review the correct answers as a class. Note any areas of difficulty and provide additional instruction and practice as necessary.

Top Notch Project. Every *Top Notch* unit contains a project idea that is related to the unit's content. Projects allow students to use the language they have learned along with information from outside the classroom to complete real-life tasks such as making and sharing a family scrapbook or planning travel arrangements. The Lesson Plans give detailed instructions on how to prepare students to complete the project. Provide students with the opportunity to present their completed projects to the class.

Top Notch Companion Website. The website contains resources for teachers and online activities for students to accompany each unit. These activities are appropriate for use at the end of each unit.

Top Notch Pop Song. 💿 Five *Top Notch Pop* songs recycle language and make it both memorable and motivating. The *Top Notch Pop* songs are available in both traditional and karaoke versions on the Class Audio Program and in the traditional version only, on the Student's Take-Home Audio CD. The *Top Notch TV* video contains the karaoke in classic visual form. Lyrics for the songs appear on the last page of the Student's Book. Activities to accompany each song can be printed out from the Teacher's Resource Disk. An icon alerts you that a *Top Notch Pop* song activity is available.

UNIT WRAP-UP. A special feature of the *Top Notch* series is the full-page illustration at the end of each unit. Open-ended activities are designed to elicit from students language they know—vocabulary, social language, and grammar. The picture provides a clear visual context for practice and helps bridge the gap between language practice and authentic language use.

The bulleted vocabulary, grammar, social language, and writing activities on the Student's Book page prompt students to find and name items in the picture, ask and answer questions about the picture, create conversations between people in the picture, tell stories about people or situations in the picture, and more.

Specific suggestions for getting much more out of each illustration are given in the Lesson Plans. Depending on the focus of the Unit Wrap-Up, the Lesson Plans also provide lists of vocabulary items that can be found in the picture; examples of questions or sentences your students can produce to practice the unit's grammar; conversations for the people who are interacting in the picture; and stories your students can tell, using the language they know.

Have students work in pairs or small groups. Circulate and offer help as needed. To encourage the risk-taking and improvisation that are the major goals of these activities, avoid interrupting students with corrections. Instead, take notes on common student mistakes and review them as a class at the end of the activity. Encourage students to say as much as they can and to extend the suggested tasks as much as possible.

An optional oral assessment activity based on the full-page picture is provided in the Lesson Plans. These individual oral progress checks were designed to take no more than five minutes per student in order to make it possible to check class progress quickly. Note that the Complete Assessment Package provides complete Speaking Tests after Unit 5 and Unit 10.

Some options for the Unit Wrap-Up are the following:

➤ Allow students to look at the picture for one minute. Then have students close their books and write down all the vocabulary items they can remember from the picture. See who remembers the most items.

➤ In pairs, students write three true statements and three false statements about the picture. Regroup students into groups of four. One pair reads their statements, in random order, to the other pair, who replies *true* or *false*.

➤ One group (or pair) begins by saying a sentence about the picture, and the next group follows by saying another sentence. Groups that can no longer say anything are eliminated until only one group remains.

➤ Give students one minute to study the picture and remember all they can about it. Then have students close their books and form small groups. Ask questions about the picture and keep a record of the correct answers. After each question, allow the groups time to discuss and write down an answer. Review as a class, and see which group has the most correct answers.

➤ Working in pairs, students write one line of conversation for each person in the picture. Then each pair of students joins another pair. Pairs take turns reading their lines and guessing who in the picture is speaking.

➤ Have volunteers act out one of their conversations in front of the class. Students listen and guess which people in the picture are being portrayed.

➤ Have two volunteers act out their conversation in front of the class. The class listens and tries to remember exactly what was said. Working in pairs, students try to re-create the exact conversation they heard.

➤ In pairs, students write their conversation in dialogue form. Each pair then writes each line of its conversation on a separate slip of paper, mixes up the order of the slips, and gives them to another pair. The other pair must then put the conversation back in the correct order.

➤ Choose one of the example conversations from the Lesson Plans. Write all the lines from the conversation on the board in random order. Students try to re-create the conversation by putting the lines in order.

➤ Have students choose one person in the picture and write his or her biography. The details of the person's life should be based on what's in the picture, but students will have to make up much of the information. Have volunteers read their biographies to a group or to the class and have students guess who in the picture is being described.

NOW I CAN... The last item on the page is a box that reiterates the four lesson goals from the unit. Note that all the goals are stated on the first page of the unit, and then stated one by one at the beginning of each of the four numbered lessons. Students can check the goals off at the end of the unit, demonstrating to themselves how much they've learned. Alternatively, they can check each one off at the end of each lesson.

We sincerely hope you enjoy *Top Notch* and that you and your students find it an effective course.

TOP NOTCH

English for Today's World

1

Joan Saslow ■ Allen Ascher

With *Top Notch Pop Songs and Karaoke*
by Rob Morsberger

PEARSON
Longman

Scope and Sequence OF CONTENT AND SKILLS

GRAMMAR BOOSTER

UNIT	Vocabulary*	Social language	Grammar	

1 **Getting Acquainted** *Page 4*	• Titles
	• Occupations
	• Nationalities
		• Exchange personal information
		• Clarify and confirm information
		• Offer to introduce someone
		• Introduce someone
		• Shift to informality
			• The verb <u>be</u>:
			  <u>Yes</u> / <u>no</u> questions
			  Contractions
			  Information questions
			• Possessive nouns and adjectives
				• Further explanation of usage and form: <u>be</u>
				• Further explanation of form: possessive adjectives

2 **Going Out** *Page 16* *Top Notch* Song: "Going Out"	• Entertainment events
	• Kinds of music
	• Locations and directions
		• Offer, accept, and decline invitations
		• Talk about likes and dislikes
		• Ask for and give directions
			• The verb <u>be</u>:
			  Questions with <u>When</u>, <u>What time</u>, and <u>Where</u>
			  Contractions
			• Prepositions of time and place: <u>On</u>, <u>in</u>, <u>at</u>
				• Further explanation of usage: prepositions of time and place

3 **Talking about Families** *Page 28*	• Family relationships • Ways to describe similarities and differences • Marital status and relationships	• Ask about and describe families • Compare family members	• The simple present tense: Statements <u>Yes</u> / <u>no</u> questions Information questions	• Further explanation of usage and form: the simple present tense
4 **Coping with Technology** *Page 40*	• Descriptive adjectives • Electronics • Ways to sympathize • Machines at home and at work • Machine features • Ways to state a complaint	• Express surprise when meeting someone by chance • Ask for and make suggestions • Express frustration and sympathy	• The present continuous: for actions in progress and the future	• Spelling rules for the present participle • Further explanation of form: the present continuous
5 **Eating in, Eating out** *Page 52* *Top Notch* Song: "The World Café"	• Menu items • Categories of food • What to say to a waiter or waitress • Food and health	• Discuss what to eat • State preferences in food • Order a meal • Ask for the check • Pay for a meal	• Count and non-count nouns / <u>there is</u> and <u>there are</u> • <u>A</u>, <u>an</u>, <u>the</u>	• Categories of non-count nouns • Verb agreement: non-count nouns • Expressing quantities: non-count nouns • <u>How much</u> / <u>How many</u> • Spelling rules: plural nouns • <u>Some</u> / <u>any</u>

*In *Top Notch*, the term *vocabulary* refers to individual words, phrases, and expressions.

Speaking activities	Pronunciation	Listening	Reading	Writing
• Learn classmates' names • Introduce classmates to each other • Information gap: identify people • Interview a partner	• Rising and falling intonation for questions	• Conversations about people Task: listen for names, occupations, and nationalities	• Short introductions of people who travel for their jobs • Student descriptions	• Introduce a classmate • Introduce yourself
• Describe the time and place of a concert • Compare musical tastes • Invite someone to an event • Give directions • Role play: make plans to see events	• Repetition to confirm information	• Invitations to events Task: identify the events and times • Phone calls to a box office Task: identify events, times, and ticket prices	• Newspaper entertainment listings • Arts festival website • People's descriptions of their musical tastes • Music survey	• Describe your own musical tastes
• Describe family relationships • Compare people in your family • Compare small and large families	• Blending sounds: Does + he / Does + she	• Descriptions of family members Task: listen for people's marital status or relationship • An interview about a brother Task: determine similarities and differences • Descriptions of families Task: determine size of family and number of children	• Article about different family sizes • Article comparing a brother and sister	• Compare two people in your own family • Compare two siblings in another family
• Suggest a brand or model • Explain reasons to purchase a machine • Describe features of machines you own • Role play: make complaints to a hotel front desk clerk • Assess seriousness of mechanical problems	• Rising and falling intonation for questions: review	• Complaints about machines Task: identify the machines • Radio advertisements Task: listen for adjectives that describe machines • Complaints to a hotel front desk Task: identify the problem and room number • Problems with machines Task: write the problem	• Ads from electronics catalogs	• Describe one of your own machines • Describe all the problems in a picture
• Discuss what to eat and make food choices from a menu • Role play: discuss a menu, order, and pay for a meal • Describe your own diet • Discuss the healthfulness of the food you eat	• Pronunciation of the before consonant and vowel sounds	• Conversations about food Task: listen for and classify food items • Conversations in a restaurant Task: predict a diner's next statement • Conversations while eating Task: determine the location of the conversation	• Menus • Nutrition website	• Describe a traditional food in your own country • Write a story based on a picture

Scope and Sequence OF CONTENT AND SKILLS

GRAMMAR BOOSTER

UNIT	Vocabulary	Social language	Grammar	
6 **Staying in Shape** *Page 64* *Top Notch* Song: "A Typical Day"	• Physical and everyday activities • Places for sports and games • Talking about health habits	• Suggest an activity • Plan to get together • Provide an excuse • Describe routines	• <u>Can</u> and <u>have to</u> • The simple present tense and the present continuous • Frequency adverbs • Time expressions	• Further explanation of form: <u>can</u> / <u>have to</u> • Non-action verbs • Further explanation of usage and form: frequency adverbs / time expressions
7 **Finding Something to Wear** *Page 76*	• Categories of clothing • Clothing described as "pairs" • Types of clothing and shoes • Interior locations and directions • Describing clothes	• Ask for a different item • Offer an alternative • Agree to buy something • Ask about form of payment • Agree to a request • Ask for and get directions within a building	• Comparative adjectives • Object pronouns: as direct objects and in prepositional phrases	• Further explanation of spelling and usage: comparative adjectives • Further explanation of usage: direct and indirect objects
8 **Getting Away** *Page 88* *Top Notch* Song: "My Dream Vacation"	• Types of vacations • Adjectives for travel conditions • Adjectives to describe vacations • Travel problems	• Greet someone arriving from a trip • Describe travel conditions • Offer help • Describe a vacation • Complain about travel problems	• The past tense of <u>be</u> • The simple past tense: regular and irregular verbs	• Further explanation of usage and form: the past tense of <u>be</u> • Further explanation of usage and form: the simple past tense • Spelling rules: regular verbs in the simple past tense
9 **Taking Transportation** *Page 100*	• Tickets and trips • Travel services • Airline passenger information • Means of transportation • Transportation problems	• Talk about transportation schedules • Ask for advice • Suggest alternatives • Book travel arrangements • Discuss plans	• <u>Could</u> and <u>should</u> • <u>Be going to</u> for the future	• Further explanation of meaning: <u>can</u>, <u>should</u>, <u>could</u> • Explanation of form: modals • Comparison of ways to express the future
10 **Shopping Smart** *Page 112* *Top Notch* Song: "Shopping for Souvenirs"	• Money and travel • Electronic products • Handicrafts • Talking about prices	• Ask for a recommendation • Recommend something within a budget • Bargain for a lower price • Accept an offer	• Superlative adjectives • <u>Too</u> and <u>enough</u>	• Contrasting the comparative and the superlative • Spelling rules for superlatives • Intensifiers <u>too</u>, <u>really</u> and <u>very</u>

Speaking activities	Pronunciation	Listening	Reading	Writing
• Discuss how many calories you burn in a day • Use your daily planner to make plans with a partner • Compare routines with a partner • Health survey: discuss exercise and diet • Interview: find out about a classmate's typical activities	• <u>Can</u> / <u>can't</u> • Third-person singular endings	• Conversations about immediate plans Task: identify destinations • Descriptions of exercise and diet routines Task: identify each person's health habits • Conversations about diet and exercise Task: complete the statement	• Graph showing calories burned by activity • Health survey • Article about Brooke Ellison's daily schedule	• Report about a classmate's typical day • Recount your own typical day
• Discuss where you shop for clothes • Ask a clerk for help shopping for clothes • Role play: pay for clothes • Role play: give and get directions in a store • Discuss culturally appropriate dress	• Contrastive stress for clarification	• Conversations about clothing needs Task: choose the clothing item • Directions in a store Task: mark the store departments • Conversations about clothes Task: determine the location of the conversation	• Clothing store website • Article about clothing tips for travelers • Personal dress code survey	• Give advice about clothing for visitors to your country • Plan clothing for a trip and explain reasons
• Discuss vacation preferences • Greet someone arriving from a trip • Talk about how you spent your free time • Tell about a past vacation	• Simple past-tense endings	• Descriptions of vacations Task: identify the vacation problems • Descriptions of travel experiences Task: choose the correct adjective	• Vacation ads • Travel agency brochure • Vacation survey • Student articles about vacations	• Describe a past vacation • Describe another person's vacation
• Discuss how often you fly • Discuss schedules and buy tickets • Book travel arrangements • Role play: discuss alternatives for an overbooked flight • Tell about transportation problems you had on a trip	• Intonation of alternatives	• Requests for travel services Task: identify the service requested • Airport announcements Task: listen for delays and cancellations • Conversations about transportation problems Task: complete the statement • Conversations about transportation problems Task: match the conversation with the picture	• Airport departure schedule • Travel survey • News clippings about transportation problems	• Recount transportation problems on a past trip • Imagine your next trip
• Discuss payment options • Ask for a recommendation • Bargain for a lower price • Discuss tipping customs • Discuss the best deals in your city • Discuss a story about a shopping experience	• Rising intonation to clarify information	• Recommendations of electronic products Task: identify the product • Shopping stories Task: listen for products and prices • Conversations about electronics purchases Task: check satisfactory or not satisfactory to the customer	• Travel guide about money and shopping • Article about tipping customs • Tipping survey • Story about a shopping experience	• Narrate a true story about a shopping experience • Create a shopping guide for your city

Acknowledgments

Top Notch International Advisory Board

The authors gratefully acknowledge the substantive and formative contributions of the members of the International Advisory Board.

CHERYL BELL, Middlesex County College, Middlesex, New Jersey, USA • **ELMA CABAHUG**, City College of San Francisco, San Francisco, California, USA • **JO CARAGATA**, Mukogawa Women's University, Hyogo, Japan • **ANN CARTIER**, Palo Alto Adult School, Palo Alto, California, USA • **TERRENCE FELLNER**, Himeji Dokkyo University, Hyogo, Japan • **JOHN FUJIMORI**, Meiji Gakuin High School, Tokyo, Japan • **ARETA ULHANA GALAT**, Escola Superior de Estudos Empresariais e Informática, Curitiba, Brazil • **DOREEN M. GAYLORD**, Kanazawa Technical College, Ishikawa, Japan • **EMILY GEHRMAN**, Newton International College, Garden Grove, California, USA • **ANN-MARIE HADZIMA**, National Taiwan University, Taipei, Taiwan • **KAREN KYONG-AI PARK**, Seoul National University, Seoul, Korea • **ANA PATRICIA MARTÍNEZ VITE DIP. R.S.A.**, Universidad del Valle de México, Mexico City, Mexico • **MICHELLE ANN MERRITT, PROULEX/** Universidad de Guadalajara, Guadalajara, Mexico • **ADRIANNE P. OCHOA**, Georgia State University, Atlanta, Georgia, USA • **LOUIS PARDILLO**, Korea Herald English Institute, Seoul, Korea • **THELMA PERES**, Casa Thomas Jefferson, Brasilia, Brazil • **DIANNE RUGGIERO**, Broward Community College, Davie, Florida, USA • **KEN SCHMIDT**, Tohoku Fukushi University, Sendai, Japan • **ALISA A. TAKEUCHI**, Garden Grove Adult Education, Garden Grove, California, USA • **JOSEPHINE TAYLOR**, Centro Colombo Americano, Bogotá, Colombia • **PATRICIA VECIÑO**, Instituto Cultural Argentino Norteamericano, Buenos Aires, Argentina • **FRANCES WESTBROOK**, AUA Language Center, Bangkok, Thailand

Reviewers and Piloters

Many thanks also to the reviewers and piloters all over the world who reviewed *Top Notch* in its final form.

G. Julian Abaqueta, Huachiew Chalermprakiet University, Samutprakarn, Thailand • **David Aline**, Kanagawa University, Kanagawa, Japan • **Marcia Alves**, Centro Cultural Brasil Estados Unidos, Franca, Brazil • **Yousef Al-Yacoub**, Qatar Petroleum, Doha, Qatar • **Maristela Barbosa Silveira e Silva**, Instituto Cultural Brasil-Estados Unidos, Manaus, Brazil • **Beth Bartlett**, Centro Colombo Americano, Cali, Colombia • **Carla Battigelli**, University of Zulia, Maracaibo, Venezuela • **Claudia Bautista**, C.B.C., Caracas, Venezuela • **Rob Bell**, Shumei Yachiyo High School, Chiba, Japan • **Dr. Maher Ben Moussa**, Sharjah University, Sharjah, United Arab Emirates • **Elaine Cantor**, Englewood Senior High School, Jacksonville, Florida, USA • **María Aparecida Capellari**, SENAC, São Paulo, Brazil • **Eunice Carrillo Ramos**, Colegio Durango, Naucalpan, Mexico • **Janette Carvalhinho de Oliveira**, Centro de Linguas (UFES), Vitória, Brazil • **María Amelia Carvalho Fonseca**, Centro Cultural Brasil-Estados Unidos, Belém, Brazil • **Audy Castañeda**, Instituto Pedagógico de Caracas, Caracas, Venezuela • **Ching-Fen Chang**, National Chiao Tung University, Hsinchu, Taiwan • **Ying-Yu Chen**, Chinese Culture University, Taipei, Taiwan • **Joyce Chin**, The Language Training and Testing Center, Taipei, Taiwan • **Eun Cho**, Pagoda Language School, Seoul, Korea • **Hyungzung Cho**, MBC Language Institute, Seoul, Korea • **Dong Sua Choi**, MBC Language Institute, Seoul, Korea • **Jeong Mi Choi**, Freelancer, Seoul, Korea • **Peter Chun**, Pagoda Language School, Seoul, Korea • **Eduardo Corbo**, Legacy ELT, Salto, Uruguay • **Marie Cosgrove**, Surugadai University, Saitama, Japan • **María Antonieta Covarrubias Souza**, Centro Escolar Akela, Mexico City, Mexico • **Katy Cox**, Casa Thomas Jefferson, Brasilia, Brazil • **Michael Donovan**, Gakushuin University, Tokyo, Japan • **Stewart Dorward**, Shumei Eiko High School, Saitama, Japan • **Ney Eric Espina**, Centro Venezolano Americano del Zulia, Maracaibo, Venezuela • **Edith Espino**, Centro Especializado de Lenguas - Universidad Tecnológica de Panamá, El Dorado, Panama • **Allen P. Fermon**, Instituto Brasil-Estados Unidos, Ceará, Brazil • **Simão Ferreira Banha**, Phil Young's English School, Curitiba, Brazil • **María Elena Flores Lara**, Colegio Mercedes, Mexico City, Mexico • **Valesca Fróis Nassif**, Associação Cultural Brasil-Estados Unidos, Salvador, Brazil • **José Fuentes**, Empire Language Consulting, Caracas, Venezuela • **Claudia Patricia Gutiérrez**, Centro Colombo Americano, Cali, Colombia • **Valerie Hansford**, Asia University, Tokyo, Japan • **Gene Hardstark**, Dotkyo University, Saitama, Japan • **Maiko Hata**, Kansai University, Osaka, Japan • **Susan Elizabeth Haydock Miranda de Araujo**, Centro Cultural Brasil Estados Unidos, Belém, Brazil • **Gabriela Herrera**, Fundametal, Valencia, Venezuela • **Sandy Ho**, GEOS International, New York, New York, USA • **Yuri Hosoda**, Showa Women's University, Tokyo, Japan • **Hsiao-I Hou**, Shu-Te University, Kaohsiung County, Taiwan • **Kuei-ping Hsu**, National Tsing Hua University, Hsinchu, Taiwan • **Chia-yu Huang**, National Tsing Hua University, Hsinchu, Taiwan • **Caroline C. Hwang**, National Taipei University of Science and Technology, Taipei, Taiwan • **Eunjeong Kim**, Freelancer, Seoul, Korea • **Julian Charles King**, Qatar Petroleum, Doha, Qatar • **Bruce Lee**, CIE: Foreign Language Institute, Seoul, Korea • **Myunghee Lee**, MBC Language Institute, Seoul, Korea • **Naidnapa Leoprasertkul**, Language Development Center, Mahasarakham University, Mahasarakham, Thailand • **Eleanor S. Leu**, Souchow University, Taipei, Taiwan • **Eliza Liu**, Chinese Culture University, Taipei, Taiwan • **Philippe Loussarevian**, Keio University Shonan Fujisawa High School, Kanagawa, Japan • **Jonathan Lynch**, Azabu University, Tokyo, Japan • **Thomas Mach**, Konan University, Hyogo, Japan • **Lilian Mandel Civatti**, Associação Cultural Brasil-Estados Unidos, Salvador, Brazil • **Hakan Mansuroglu**, Zoni Language Center, West New York, New Jersey, USA • **Martha McGaughey**, Language Training Institute, Englewood Cliffs, New Jersey, USA • **David Mendoza Plascencia**, Instituto Internacional de Idiomas, Naucalpan, Mexico • **Theresa Mezo**, Interamerican University, Río Piedras, Puerto Rico • **Luz Adriana Montenegro Silva**, Colegio CAFAM, Bogotá, Colombia • **Magali de Moraes Menti**, Instituto Lingua, Porto Alegre, Brazil • **Massoud Moslehpour**, The Overseas Chinese Institute of Technology, Taichung, Taiwan • **Jennifer Nam**, IKE, Seoul, Korea • **Marcos Norelle F. Victor**, Instituto Brasil-Estados Unidos, Ceará, Brazil • **Luz María Olvera**, Instituto Juventud del Estado de México, Naucalpan, Mexico • **Roxana Orrego Ramírez**, Universidad Diego Portales, Santiago, Chile • **Ming-Jong Pan**, National Central University, Jhongli City, Taiwan • **Sandy Park**, Topia Language School, Seoul, Korea • **Patrícia Elizabeth Peres Martins**, Instituto Brasil-Estados Unidos, Rio de Janeiro, Brazil • **Rodrigo Peza**, Passport Language Centers, Bogotá, Colombia • **William Porter**, Osaka Institute of Technology, Osaka, Japan • **Caleb Prichard**, Kwansei Gakuin University, Hyogo, Japan • **Mirna Quintero**, Instituto Pedagógico de Caracas, Caracas, Venezuela • **Roberto Rabbini**, Seigakuin University, Saitama, Japan • **Terri Rapoport**, Berkeley College, White Plains, New York, USA • **Yvette Rieser**, Centro Electrónico de Idiomas, Maracaibo, Venezuela • **Orlando Rodríguez**, New English Teaching School, Paysandu, Uruguay • **Mayra Rosario**, Pontificia Universidad Católica Madre y Maestra, Santiago, Dominican Republic • **Peter Scout**, Sakura no Seibo Junior College, Fukushima, Japan • **Jungyeon Shim**, EG School, Seoul, Korea • **Keum Ok Song**, MBC Language Institute, Seoul, Korea • **Assistant Professor Dr. Reongrudee Soonthornmanee**, Chulalongkorn University Language Institute, Bangkok, Thailand • **Claudia Stanisclause**, The Language College, Maracay, Venezuela • **Tom Suh**, The Princeton Review, Seoul, Korea • **Phiphawin Suphawat**, KhonKaen University, KhonKaen, Thailand • **Craig Sweet**, Poole Gakuin Junior and Senior High Schools, Osaka, Japan • **Yi-nien Josephine Twu**, National Tsing Hua University, Hsinchu, Taiwan • **Maria Christina Uchôa Close**, Instituto Cultural Brasil-Estados Unidos, São José dos Campos, Brazil • **Luz Vanegas Lopera**, Lexicom The Place For Learning English, Medellín, Colombia • **Julieta Vasconcelos García**, Centro Escolar del Lago, A.C., Mexico City, Mexico • **Carol Vaughan**, Kanto Kokusai High School, Tokyo, Japan • **Patricia Celia Veciño**, Instituto Cultural Argentino Norteamericano, Buenos Aires, Argentina • **Isabela Villas Boas**, Casa Thomas Jefferson, Brasilia, Brazil • **Iole Vitti**, Peanuts English School, Poços de Caldas, Brazil • **Gabi Witthaus**, Qatar Petroleum, Doha, Qatar • **Yi-Ling Wu**, Shih Chien University, Taipei, Taiwan • **Chad Wynne**, Osaka Keizai University, Osaka, Japan • **Belkis Yanes**, Freelance Instructor, Caracas, Venezuela • **I-Chieh Yang**, Chung-kuo Institute of Technology, Taipei, Taiwan • **Emil Ysona**, Instituto Cultural Dominico-Americano, Santo Domingo, Dominican Republic • **Chi-fang Yu**, Soo Chow University, Taipei, Taiwan, • **Shigeki Yusa**, Sendai Shirayuri Women's College, Sendai, Japan

To the Teacher

What is *Top Notch?*

- *Top Notch* is a six-level communicative English course for adults and young adults, with two beginning entry levels.
- *Top Notch* prepares students to interact successfully and confidently with both native and non-native speakers of English.
- *Top Notch* demonstrably brings students to a "Top Notch" level of communicative competence.

Key Elements of the *Top Notch* Instructional Design

Concise two-page lessons

Each easy-to-teach two-page lesson is designed for one class session and begins with a clearly stated communication goal and ends with controlled or free communication practice. Each lesson provides vocabulary, grammar, and social language contextualized in all four skills, keeping the pace of a class session lively and varied.

Daily confirmation of progress

Adult and young adult students need to observe and confirm their own progress. In *Top Notch*, students conclude each class session with a controlled or free practice activity that demonstrates their ability to use new vocabulary, grammar, and social language. This motivates and keeps students eager to continue their study of English and builds their pride in being able to speak accurately, fluently, and authentically.

Real language

Carefully exposing students to authentic, natural English, both receptively and productively, is a necessary component of building understanding and expression. All conversation models feature the language people really use; nowhere to be found is "textbook English" written merely to exemplify grammar.

Practical content

In addition to classic topical vocabulary, grammar, and conversation, *Top Notch* includes systematic practice of highly practical language, such as: how to ask for a restaurant check, how to ask whether the tip is included in the bill, how to complain when the air-conditioning in a hotel room doesn't work, how to bargain for a lower price—usable language today's students want and need.

Memorable model conversations

Effective language instruction must make language memorable. The full range of social and functional communicative needs is presented through practical model conversations that are intensively practiced and manipulated, first within a guided model and then in freer and more personalized formats.

High-impact vocabulary syllabus

In order to ensure students' solid acquisition of vocabulary essential for communication, *Top Notch* contains explicit presentation, practice, and systematic extended recycling of words, collocations, and expressions appropriate at each level of study. The extensive captioned illustrations, photos, definitions, examples, and contextualized sentences remove doubts about meaning and provide a permanent in-book reference for student test preparation. An added benefit is that teachers don't have to search for pictures to bring to class and don't have to resort to translating vocabulary into the students' native language.

Learner-supportive grammar

Grammar is approached explicitly and cognitively, through form, meaning, and use—both within the Student's Book units and in a bound-in Grammar Booster. Charts provide examples and paradigms enhanced by simple usage notes at students' level of comprehension. This takes the guesswork out of meaning, makes lesson preparation easier for teachers, and provides students with comprehensible charts for permanent reference and test preparation. All presentations of grammar are followed by exercises to ensure adequate practice.

English as an international language

Top Notch prepares students for interaction with both native and non-native speakers of English, both linguistically and culturally. English is treated as an international language, rather than the language of a particular country or region. In addition, *Top Notch* helps students develop a cultural fluency by creating an awareness of the varied rules across cultures for: politeness, greetings and introductions, appropriateness of dress in different settings, conversation do's and taboos, table manners, and other similar issues.

Two beginning-level texts

Beginning students can be placed either in *Top Notch 1* or *Top Notch Fundamentals*, depending on ability and background. Even absolute beginners can start with confidence in *Top Notch Fundamentals*. False beginners can begin with *Top Notch 1*. The *Top Notch Placement Test* clarifies the best placement within the series.

Estimated teaching time

Each level of *Top Notch* is designed for 60 to 90 instructional hours and contains a full range of supplementary components and enrichment devices to tailor the course to individual needs.

Components of *Top Notch 1*

Student's Book

The Student's Book contains a bound-in Grammar Booster and Student's Take-Home Audio CD with pronunciation/intonation practice and the *Top Notch Pop* songs.

Teacher's Edition and Lesson Planner

Complete yet concise lesson plans are provided for each class. Corpus notes provide essential information from the *Longman Spoken American Corpus* and the *Longman Learner's Corpus*. In addition, a free Teacher's Resource Disk offers the following printable extension activities to personalize your teaching style:

- Grammar self-checks
- *Top Notch Pop* song activities
- Writing process worksheets
- Learning strategies
- Pronunciation activities and supplements
- Extra reading comprehension activities
- Vocabulary cards and cumulative vocabulary activities
- Graphic organizers
- Pair work cards

Copy & Go: Ready-made Interactive Activities for Busy Teachers

Interactive games, puzzles, and other practice activities in convenient photocopiable form support the Student's Book content and provide a welcome change of pace.

Complete Classroom Audio Program

The audio program contains listening comprehension activities, rhythm and intonation practice, and targeted pronunciation activities that focus on accurate and comprehensible pronunciation.

Because *Top Notch* prepares students for international communication, a variety of native and non-native speakers are included to ready students for the world outside the classroom. The audio program also includes the five *Top Notch Pop* songs in standard and karaoke form.

Workbook

A tightly linked illustrated Workbook contains exercises that provide additional practice and reinforcement of language concepts and skills from *Top Notch* and its Grammar Booster.

Complete Assessment Package with *ExamView®* Software

Ten easy-to-administer and easy-to-score unit achievement tests assess listening, vocabulary, grammar, social language, reading, and writing. Two review tests, one mid-book and one end-of-book, provide additional cumulative assessment. Two speaking tests assess progress in speaking. In addition to the photocopiable achievement tests, *ExamView®* software enables teachers to tailor-make tests to best meet their needs by combining items in any way they wish.

Top Notch TV

A lively and entertaining video offers a TV-style situation comedy that reintroduces language from each *Top Notch* unit, plus authentic unrehearsed interviews with English speakers from around the world and authentic Karaoke. Packaged with the video are Student Video activity sheets, and a booklet with teaching suggestions and complete scripts.

Companion Website

A Companion Website at www.longman.com/topnotc provides numerous additional resources for students and teachers. This no-cost, high-benefit feature includes opportunities for further practice of language and content from the *Top Notch* Student's Book.

Welcome to Top Notch!

About the Authors

Joan Saslow

Joan Saslow has taught English as a Foreign Language and English as a Second Language to adults and young adults in both South America and the United States. She taught English and French at the Binational Centers of Valparaíso and Viña del Mar, Chile, and the Catholic University of Valparaíso. In the United States, Ms. Saslow taught English as a Foreign Language to Japanese university students at Marymount College and to international students in Westchester Community College's intensive English program as well as workplace English at the General Motors auto assembly plant in Tarrytown, NY.

Ms. Saslow is the series director of Longman's popular five-level adult series *True Colors: An EFL Course for Real Communication* and of *True Voices*, a five-level video course. She is author of *Ready to Go: Language, Lifeskills, and Civics*, a four-level adult ESL series; *Workplace Plus*, a vocational English series; and of *Literacy Plus*, a two-level series that teaches literacy, English, and culture to adult pre-literate students. She is also author of *English in Context: Reading Comprehension for Science and Technology*, a three-level series for English for special purposes. In addition, Ms. Saslow has been an author, an editor of language teaching materials, a teacher-trainer, and a frequent speaker at gatherings of EFL and ESL teachers for over thirty years.

Allen Ascher

Allen Ascher has been a teacher and teacher-trainer in both China and the United States, as well as an administrator and a publisher. Mr. Ascher specialized in teaching listening and speaking to students at the Beijing Second Foreign Language Institute, to hotel workers at a major international hotel in China, and to Japanese students from Chubu University studying English at Ohio University. In New York, Mr. Ascher taught students of all language backgrounds and abilities at the City University of New York, and he trained teachers in the TESOL Certificate Program at the New School. He was also the academic director of the International English Language Institute at Hunter College.

Mr. Ascher has provided lively workshops for EFL teachers throughout Asia, Latin America, Europe, and the Middle East. He is author of the popular *Think about Editing: A Grammar Editing Guide for ESL Writers*. As a publisher, Mr. Ascher played a key role in the creation of some of the most widely used materials for adults, including: *True Colors, NorthStar, Focus on Grammar, Global Links*, and *Ready to Go*. Mr. Ascher has an M.A. in Applied Linguistics from Ohio University.

Welcome to *Top Notch!*

A Read and listen. Then listen again and repeat in the pauses.

Hello. My name's Peter.

Hi. I'm Alexandra. But everyone calls me Alex.

More greetings
Good morning.
Good afternoon.
Good evening.

1. Introduce yourself.

What do you do?

I'm a student. And you?

I'm a student, too.

2. Tell someone what you do.

Alex, this is Emily. Emily, this is Alex.

Nice to meet you, Alex.

Nice to meet you, too.

3. Introduce someone.

Well, it was nice meeting you.

See you later.

Bye.

More ways to say good-bye
Good-bye.
Take it easy.
Take care.
Good night.

4. Say good-bye.

B GROUP WORK.
Get to know your classmates.

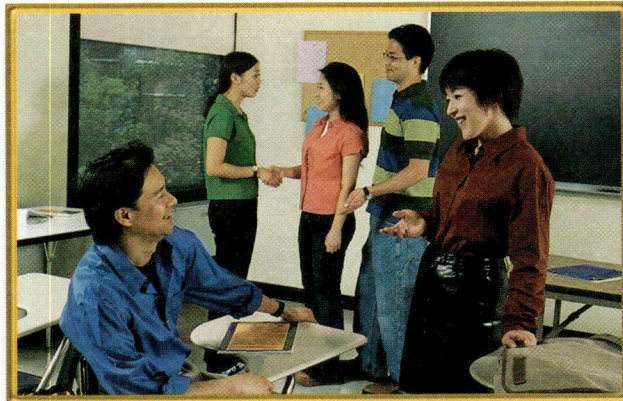

Introduce someone to your class.

Welcome to *Top Notch!*

Culture note: In many English-speaking countries, levels of formality are disappearing. Even at work, most North Americans address each other with first names, no matter what employment level. Similarly, there is no longer much distinction among greetings. Although *Good morning* (*afternoon,* or *evening*) are more formal than *Hi, Hi* has become acceptable in all situations.

In the EFL setting, however, you may wish to preserve the more traditional distinctions of formality to conform to local social and business customs.

The first day of class

- Start the first class with a simple introduction of yourself in English. Write on the board and say *Hello. I'm Miss / Mrs. / Ms. / Mr. ____* (or *Hello. My name's ____.*). If necessary, help students pronounce your name.

A 🎧 Read and listen . . .

Suggested teaching time:	10 minutes
Your actual teaching time:	_____

(See page T4 for a discussion of teaching time.)

- After students read and listen, point to the man in the first photo. Say:
  His name is . . . (Peter)
  He's a . . . (student)
  The class calls out the endings to the statements.
- Point to the woman in the first photo. Say:
  Her name is . . . (Alex / Alexandra)
  She's a . . . (student)
  Point to the woman in the third photo. Say:
  Her name is . . . (Emily)

🎧 More greetings

- If helpful, write times on the board to indicate the meanings of *morning, afternoon,* and *evening / night.* For example:
  morning: before 12:00 P.M.
  afternoon: 12:00 P.M.–6:00 P.M.
  evening / night: after 6:00 P.M.
- Ask the class *What time is it? Is it morning, afternoon, or evening / night?*
- After students listen and repeat, read the speech balloons in the first photo. Substitute *Good morning, Good afternoon,* or *Good evening* (depending on the time of day) for *Hello.*

🎧 More ways to say good-bye

- After students listen and repeat, read the speech balloons in the last photo again. Substitute *Good-bye,* *Take it easy,* or *Take care* for *See you later* and *Bye.* Only use *Good night* if your class meets in the evening.

Language note: While *night* and *evening* mean the same time of day, *Good evening* is a greeting and *Good night* is a way to say good-bye.

B GROUP WORK

Suggested teaching time:	10–15 minutes
Your actual teaching time:	_____

- Model the activity. Walk up to a student and extend your hand for a handshake. Say *Hello. My name's ____* (or *Hi, I'm ____.*). Encourage students to respond with *Hello. I'm ____* by pointing to the second speech balloon in the first photo or the sentence on the board. You may add short, simple responses such as *Nice to meet you.* Encourage students to respond with *Nice to meet you, too.*
- Ask the same student *What do you do?* Point to the second speech balloon in the second photo. Again, prompt the student to answer in the same way, changing the occupation if appropriate.
- Have students walk around the room and introduce themselves to their classmates. Encourage students to make eye contact and to shake hands. Students can also ask about what their classmates do.

Option: Create name tags for your students to make learning names easier. Have students display the cards where they will be visible to other students. Collect and redistribute the name tags for each class until the students become acquainted. **[+5 minutes]**

Option: Use the name tags in the first few classes as a quiz. Give a random name tag to a student. Ask the student to say the name on the card and then match the name to the correct student. Continue the procedure with different students until all the name tags are handed out. **[+10 minutes]**

Introduce someone to your class.

- Model the activity. Have the student who helped you model Exercise B stand. Introduce this student to the class. Say *Class, this is ____.* The class can respond *Nice to meet you, ____.*
- When you end your class, use one of the ways to say good-bye from Exercise A. Have students stand and say good-bye to each other before leaving.

Option: Students introduce two classmates to each other in front of the class. **[+5 minutes]**

Option: Have a contest to see who can remember the most names. **[+5 minutes]**

C 🎧 Read and listen ...

Suggested teaching time:	10–15 minutes
Your actual teaching time:	_____

- After students listen the second time, ask for volunteers to hold up objects from their desks or bags. Ask *What's this called in English?* See if any students know the answer. If not, say the name of the object. Have students repeat the name of the object, helping them pronounce it, if necessary.

- Make sure students understand *first* and *last name*. Write your full name on the board. Circle and label your first name. Then circle and label your last name. Ask the class:
  What's my last name?
  What's my first name?
  How do you say my last name?
  How do you spell my first name?

- Go around the classroom and ask different students the following questions. Be sure to ask a few students to repeat their response.
  What's your last name, please?
  What's your first name, please?
  How do you say your last name?
  How do you say your first name?
  How do you spell your last name?
  How do you spell your first name?

Option: If helpful, review the alphabet in English. Pronounce each letter and have students repeat. To practice, have students spell classmates' first names out loud. The student whose name is spelled raises his or her hand and then spells another classmate's name. **[+10 minutes]**

D 🎧 Listen to the conversations ...

Suggested teaching time:	10 minutes
Your actual teaching time:	_____

- To check their work, have students spell the names to a partner.

AUDIOSCRIPT

CONVERSATION 1 [F = Chinese*]
M: How do you spell your last name?
F: W-O-O-N.
M: W-O-N?
F: No, W-Oh-Oh-N.
M: And your first name?
F: It's Ming. M-I-N-G.
M: M-I-N-G?
F: That's right.

(**M** refers to a male speaker and **F** refers to a female speaker.)

CONVERSATION 2 [F = Russian]
M: What's your last name?
F: Margolina.
M: Could you spell that for me?
F: M-A-R-G-O-L-I-N-A.
M: Let me repeat that. M-A-R-G-O-L-I-N-A?
F: That's right.
M: And could I have your first name please?
F: Katya.
M: K-A-T-Y-A?
F: Yes.

E PAIR WORK

Suggested teaching time:	5–10 minutes
Your actual teaching time:	_____

- To check their work, students take turns asking and answering *What's this called in English?* with a partner.

- To review, point to each item and ask a different student *What's this called in English?* If students have difficulty pronouncing the names of the objects in English, you may want to say the name of each object and have students repeat.

Option: To check students' knowledge of the alphabet (both in producing the names of letters and understanding them when heard), choose one pair of students. Have one member of the pair (Student A) come up to the board. Ask the other partner (Student B) to spell the answer to the first item (C-H-A-L-K) out loud while Student A writes each letter of the word on the board. Continue the activity with a different pair of students for each of the other items. **[+10 minutes]**

Option: Provide a handout with simple drawings of ten common objects. Next to each object there should be a line for students to write the name of the object. Students write the names of the objects they know. Then they walk around and ask classmates *What's this called in English?* Give students five minutes to try to find the names of as many of the objects as they can. Make sure students know how to say *I don't know*. Remind students to use *Could you repeat that?* You may also want to present *How do you say it?* and *How do you spell it?* **[+10 minutes]**

---

* All recorded speakers are standard U.S., unless designated otherwise. These include: U.S. regional, varieties of British English, and non-native speakers of English. First language or country of origin is indicated for your information.

🎧 **Read and listen. Then listen again and repeat in the pauses.**

1.

What's this called in English?

A stapler.

A stapler?

Yes. That's right.

2.

What's your last name, please?

Choi.

I'm sorry. Could you repeat that?

Sure. It's Choi.

3.

How do you say your last name?

Yuan.

Yuan? Thanks.

4.

How do you spell your first name?

G-U-Y.

Thank you.

D 🎧 **Listen to the conversations. Then listen again and write the names.**

1. _____Ming_____   _____Woon_____
          first name   last name

2. _____Katya_____   _____Margolina_____
          first name   last name

E **PAIR WORK.** **What's this called in English? Use your dictionary.**

1. ___(a piece of) chalk___   **2.** ___a marker___   **3.** ___a pencil sharpener___   **4.** ___a map___

UNIT 1

Getting Acquainted

UNIT GOALS

1 Get to know someone
2 Offer to introduce someone
3 Talk about people
4 Interview a classmate

A **TOPIC PREVIEW.** Why are <u>you</u> studying English?

☐ **for business**

☐ **for travel**

☐ **for study**

☐ **to get to know people who don't speak my language**

B Enroll in *Top Notch*.

Mr. ☐
Mrs. ☐
Ms. ☐
Miss ☐

Last / Family Name

First / Given Name

Nationality

Occupation

🎧 **Titles**

Men	Women
Mr.	**Ms.** (married or single)
	Mrs. (married)
	Miss (single)

Use titles with family names, NOT first or given names.

Getting Acquainted

How to plan a *Top Notch* lesson

Suggested teaching times for the activities in each two-page lesson add up to a total teaching time of 45–60 minutes. To plan a class of approximately 45 minutes, use the shorter estimated teaching times when a range is shown. To plan a class of 60 or more minutes, use the longer estimated teaching times when a range is shown. Your actual teaching time will vary from the times suggested, according to your needs, your schedule, and the needs of your class.

Activities labeled "Option" or "Challenge" are additional to the 45–60 minutes, and the estimated teaching time for each is noted with the activity. Similarly, any time you spend in class on the Grammar Booster is additional to the 45–60 minutes.

In addition to the notes, options, and challenges, you will see icons indicating other possible extensions to the material on the Student's Book page. These of course will also increase the time allotted to the lesson:

An extension activity from the Teacher's Resource Disk in the back of this Teacher's Edition

An episode from the *Top Notch TV* Video

A test from the Complete Assessment Package

At the end of each lesson is an item labeled "Extras." These are optional activities that can be assigned as homework or class work. The activities include exercises from the Grammar Booster, exercises from the Workbook, interactive activities from Copy & Go, and Pronunciation Supplements from the Teacher's Resource Disk.

Regarding the *Top Notch* Projects, please see the Introduction to this Teacher's Edition. It is impossible to estimate the amount of class time individual projects will take as many teachers prefer to spread projects out over a number of lessons or assign them for homework.

The *Top Notch* authors strongly encourage you to view these teacher's notes and accompanying options, challenges, and extensions as a menu of possibilities in creating the best lesson plan for you. You may wish to construct your lesson entirely with the options, challenges, and extensions, or, to extend the lesson, to do all possible activities. The times are provided to help you do that.

A TOPIC PREVIEW

Suggested teaching time:	10–15 minutes
Your actual teaching time:	_____

- Students look at the photos and check the reason(s) they are studying English.

- Write the four reasons for studying English on the board.

- Ask *Who is studying English for business? Who is studying English for travel?* etc. Tell students to raise their hands when they hear the reason(s) they checked. Write the names of students under each reason.

- Circle the most popular reason and discuss. For example, ask *Where do you want to travel?* or *What do you study?* Elicit short answers. If students have difficulty, ask <u>yes</u> / <u>no</u> questions (*Do you want to travel to Paris? Do you study computers?*) and have students raise their hands in response.

B Enroll in *Top Notch*.

Suggested teaching time:	10–15 minutes
Your actual teaching time:	_____

- Write your full name, including a title, on the board. For example: *Mrs. Susan Miller** Label and talk about each part of your name. Explain why you use that title; for example, *I am a woman, and I am married. I use the title "Mrs."*

- If necessary, use a familiar symbol of marriage, such as a wedding ring, or a wedding photo, to demonstrate the meanings of *married* and *single*.

- Write your title with your first name and your title with your last name on the board. Ask *Which is correct?* Then cross out your title with your first name. Make sure students understand that a title is used with a full name (first and last name) or with just the family (last) name, but never with just the first name.

- Ask *Are you a man or a woman? Are you married or single?* Have students determine which title to use with their family name. Female students will have a choice of titles (see the *Culture note* on the next page).

- Make sure students understand the difference in pronunciation between *Ms.* (/ mɪz /) and *Miss* (/ mɪs /).

Option: Explain other titles students may come across. (*Dr.* [doctor], *Prof.* [professor])

- Tell the class where you are from and what you do; for example, *I am from Australia. I am a teacher.* Then write on the board:

  Nationality: *Australian*
  Occupation: *Teacher*

- Students fill in the chart with their own information. Tell students who don't work to write *student* as their occupation on the form. **[+5 minutes]**

---

* Here and throughout, substitute real names and information for examples provided.

Culture note: In some English-speaking countries, some women prefer the title *Ms.* because it does not draw attention to whether a woman is married or single. Use *Ms.* when you don't know if a woman is married or when you don't know which title she prefers.

Culture note: Forms generally ask for a person's family name first and given name second. This is because family names are used to keep records. So even though *Family Name* comes first on the form and *Given Name* comes last, we refer to the family name as the last name and the given name as the first name.

Culture note: In many Asian countries, the family name comes first, but it is still referred to as the person's last name.

⌖ C ⌒ SOUND BITES

Suggested teaching time:	10 minutes
Your actual teaching time:	_____

- Begin by having students look at the photos. Ask:
  How many people are in the photos? (four)
  How many are men? (one)
  How many are women? (three)
- After students read and listen to the conversation, check comprehension. Ask:
  What's the man's name? (Mr. Mills, Tom)
  What's his first (or given) name? (Tom)
  What's his last (or family) name? (Mills)
  What's his occupation? (teacher)
  Is Tom married or single? (married)
  What's his wife's first name? (Carol)

Option: On the board, write *Please call me _____.* Then walk around the classroom and introduce several students. Use students' title and family name. Look at Exercise B in students' open books or at your class list for help with names and titles. Say *Class, this is Mr. / Ms. / Mrs. / Miss [family name].* Prompt students to answer with *Please call me [first name or nickname].* **[+5 minutes]**

Language note: A nickname is a silly name or a shorter form of someone's real name, usually given by friends or family.

◆ D Complete each sentence.

Suggested teaching time:	10 minutes
Your actual teaching time:	_____

- Read item 1. Have students point to Mrs. Dare and Diana's teacher in the first photo. Say *Mrs. Dare says, "Nice to meet you . . ."* Elicit from the class *Mr. Mills.*
- Point out the informality of *Please call me Tom* and the continuation of formality in referring to the older woman as *Mrs. Dare.*

Culture note: In some English-speaking countries, when meeting someone for the first time, you should use a title and last name if the person is older or if you are in a professional / formal situation. If you're not sure, address the person formally and see if he or she responds *Please call me [first name].* As mentioned on page T2, this is customary in many English-speaking countries. It's not necessary to use titles with younger people or peers. When using English with people from non-English speaking countries, follow the customs of that particular country.

WHAT ABOUT **YOU?**

Suggested teaching time:	5–10 minutes
Your actual teaching time:	_____

- Before students complete the exercise, read the lines in the speech balloons out loud to the class.
- To review, have volunteers read the completed responses out loud.

Language note: While his Chinese name is Yao Ming, in English we refer to his given name (Ming) as his first name.

EXTRAS (optional)

Workbook: Exercises 1–3

C 🎧 **SOUND BITES.** Read along silently as you listen to a natural conversation.

DIANA: Mom, this is my teacher, Mr. Mills.

MRS. DARE: Nice to meet you, Mr. Mills. **CN**

MR. MILLS: Please call me Tom.

MR. MILLS: Let me introduce you to my wife, Carol.... Carol, Mrs. Dare and her daughter, Diana.

MRS. MILLS: Nice to meet you both.

D Complete each sentence.

1. Mrs. Dare calls Diana's teacher _____.
   a. Mr. Mills   **b.** Tom   **c.** Mr. Tom

2. Mr. Mills calls his wife _____.
   a. Carol   **b.** Mrs. Mills   **c.** Ms. Carol

3. Mr. Mills calls his student _____.
   a. Ms. Dare   **b.** Diana   **c.** Miss Dare

CN **Corpus Notes:**
"Good to meet you" and "Pleased to meet you" are also common ways of greeting someone, but "Nice to meet you" is by far the most frequent of the three in spoken American English.

WHAT ABOUT **YOU?**

Complete your response to each person.

1. Nice to meet you.

Josh   Groban
GIVEN NAME   FAMILY NAME
singer
OCCUPATION

Nice to meet you, _____.
a. Mr. Josh
b. Mr. Groban
c. Ms. Groban

2. Good to meet you.

Streep   Meryl
LAST NAME   FIRST NAME
actress
OCCUPATION

Good to meet you, _____.
a. Ms. Streep
b. Mr. Meryl
c. Ms. Meryl

3. Pleasure to meet you.

FAMILY NAME: Yao
FIRST NAME: Ming
OCCUPATION: basketball player

Pleasure to meet you, _____.
a. Mr. Yao
b. Mr. Ming
c. Ms. Yao

Get to Know Someone

🎧 CONVERSATION **MODEL** Read and listen.

A: Are you Bill?
B: No, I'm David. That's Bill over there.
A: Well, I'm Stacey. It's nice to meet you, David.
B: You, too.
A: Are you a student here?
B: As a matter of fact, I am.

🎧 **Rhythm and intonation practice**

Contractions

I'm	= I am
you're	= you are
he's	= he is
she's	= she is
we're	= we are
they're	= they are

A **GRAMMAR.** <u>Yes</u> / <u>no</u> questions and short answers with the verb <u>be</u> CN

Are you a student?	Yes, I am.	No, I'm not.	
Is he married?	Yes, he is.	No, he isn't.	[No, he's not.]
Is Claire from the U.S.?	Yes, she is.	No, she isn't.	[No, she's not.]
Are you in my class?	Yes, we are.	No, we aren't.	[No, we're not.]
Are they Canadian?	Yes, they are.	No, they aren't.	[No, they're not.]
Are your friends here?	Yes, they are.	No, they aren't.	[No, they're not.]

CN **Corpus Notes:**
The "he's not/she's not/we're not," etc. construction is much more common in American English than "he isn't/she isn't/we aren't," etc. This is true in both written and spoken English.

GRAMMAR BOOSTER

PAGE G1
For more ...

B Complete the questions and answers. Use contractions when possible.

___Are you___ from China?
1.

Yes, as a matter of fact,
___I am___.
2.

___Is___ he an athlete?
3.

No, ___he's not___.
4.
___He's___ an artist.
5.

LESSON 1 ▶ Get to Know Someone

🎧 CONVERSATION MODEL

Suggested teaching time:	5–10 minutes
Your actual teaching time:	_____

- After students read and listen, ask them to underline the names. *(Bill, David, Stacey)* Then have students read again and label the people in the photo.
- For comprehension, ask yes / no questions:
  Is she Stacey? [point to the second woman from the left] (no)
  Is he David? [point to the man standing] (yes)
  Is David a teacher? (no) *Is he a student?* (yes)

Culture note: Pointing visibly at another person is rude in many places. Note that Bill cannot see David pointing at him.

🎧 Rhythm and intonation practice

Suggested teaching time:	5 minutes
Your actual teaching time:	_____

- Have students repeat each line chorally. Make sure students:
  ○ use rising intonation for the two questions.
  ○ equally stress *You* and *too*.
  ○ use the following stress pattern:

STRESS PATTERN*

A: Are you Bill?

B: No, I'm David. That's Bill over there.

A: Well, I'm Stacey. It's nice to meet you, David.

B: You, too.

A: Are you a student here?

B: As a matter of fact, I am.

🔺A GRAMMAR

Suggested teaching time:	10–15 minutes
Your actual teaching time:	_____

- Show students how to form yes / no questions with *be*.

- Have students look again at the *What About You?* on page 5. On the board, write present tense, affirmative statements with *be* about the famous people pictured. For example, for Yao Ming:
  He is a basketball player. He is from China.
- Demonstrate how to make the statements into questions by moving the forms of *be* to the beginning and adding a question mark.
  Is he a basketball player? Is he from China?
- Tell students that yes / no questions are usually answered with short answers (*Yes, I am / No, I'm not*). Long answers are unnatural and rarely used.

Contractions

- Remind students that there are two ways to contract *is* and *are* in negative sentences (*isn't* or *'s not, aren't* or *'re not*). Both ways are equally acceptable.
- Pronounce each contraction and have students repeat.

Common error: Contractions should not be used with affirmative short answers. To demonstrate this point to students, write the following on the board:
  Are you a student? Yes, I am. NOT Yes, I'm.
  Is she Japanese? Yes, she is. NOT Yes, she's.

- After reviewing the examples in the Grammar box, ask the class some yes / no questions with *be*.
- Look at your list of students' names. Ask a few students *Are you [Name]?* Prompt students to answer *Yes, I am* or *No, I'm not*. You can also ask:
  Are you married / single?
  Are you [an occupation]?
  Are you from [city / neighborhood / country]?
- Check students' memory of their classmates' answers. Ask a few third-person yes / no questions with *be* (*Is he / she [name]? Is [name] married?*)

Option: Bring in photos of famous people. Ask yes / no questions with *be* about the people.
  Is she [Name]?
  Is she married / single?
  Is she [occupation]?
  Is she [nationality]? or *Is she from [country]?*

Prompt students to answer with the appropriate short answers from the box. Ask a mix of questions with *yes* and *no* answers. Emphasize the two different kinds of negative short answers. **[+10 minutes]**

💿 **Grammar Self-Checks**

🔺B Complete the questions ...

Suggested teaching time:	5 minutes
Your actual teaching time:	_____

- Remind students to capitalize the first letter of the first word when the answer comes at the beginning of a sentence, as in items 1, 2, 5, 6, and 9.

---

* The dots [•] and dashes [——] indicate the stress used in the recording. While there may be other correct ways to stress each of these utterances, what you see here is a representation of the stress you'll hear on the audio.

◆ PAIR WORK

Suggested teaching time:	5 minutes
Your actual teaching time:	_____

- To model the activity, have volunteers ask you yes / no questions with *be*. Write the questions on the board and then write your responses with short answers. Clarify negative short answers, as in the example in the Student's Book. If necessary, give students ideas about what to ask by writing the following items on the board:

  name:
  married / single:
  from:
  occupation:
  nationality:

Challenge: Students read their partner's answers. Then they tell the class two things about their partner; for example, *He's from Santos. He's single.* **[+5 minutes]**

CONVERSATION **PAIR WORK**

Suggested teaching time:	15–20 minutes
Your actual teaching time:	_____

- Write your name and your students' names on the board. You can also use the name tags from the first day of class.
- Model the activity with a more advanced student. Play the role of A. Choose a name from the board and ask the student *Are you _____?*
- Let the student respond. Then, as a class, think of different ways to answer the question, such as:
  Yes, I am.
  As a matter of fact, I am.
  No, I'm not.
  No, I'm [Name].
  That's [Name] over there.
- Continue modeling the conversation. If your students are ready, point out that in place of *It's nice to meet you,* they can also say *Nice to meet you, Good to meet you,* or *Pleasure to meet you* (from What About You? on page 5).
- Prompt the student playing the role of B to ask you a yes / no question with *be*. The student might ask:
  Are you from [Name of neighborhood]?
  Are you married / single?
  Are you [occupation]?
- Respond and then ask the student a yes / no question to demonstrate how to keep the conversation going.
- Have students work in pairs and practice the conversation out loud. Walk around the classroom, listening to students' conversations.
- If necessary, go over some common errors you heard students make as they worked in pairs.

🔵 **Pair Work Cards**

🔵 **Learning Strategies**

EXTRAS (optional)

Grammar Booster
Workbook: Exercises 4–9
Copy & Go: Activity 1

Oh, those are the new students. _Are they_ 6. from Canada?

No, _they're not_ 7. . I think _they're_ 8. from the U.K.

Hello. _Are you_ 9. Nancy and Ron?

No, _we're not_ 10. . I'm Jake and this is Patty.

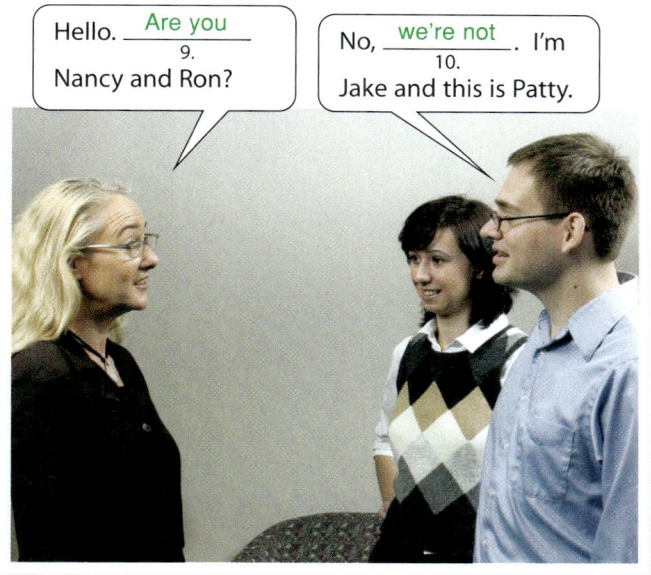

C **PAIR WORK.** Write questions for your partner. Then exchange questions. Write answers to your partner's questions.

Are you from São Paulo?

No, I'm not. I'm from Santos.

CONVERSATION **PAIR WORK**

Write all your classmates' names on the chalkboard. Then get to know your classmates. Use the guide, or create a new conversation.

A: Are you _____?

B: _____.

A: Well, I'm _____. It's nice to meet you, _____.

B: _____ …

Continue the conversation in your <u>own</u> way.

2 ▶ *Offer to Introduce Someone*

🎧 **CONVERSATION MODEL** **Read and listen.**

A: Who's that?
B: Over there? Her name's Kate. Come. I'll introduce you.
• • •
B: Lauren, I'd like you to meet Kate.
A: Nice to meet you, Kate.
C: Nice to meet you, too.

🎧 **Rhythm and intonation practice**

A **GRAMMAR.** **Information questions with be**

Who's that?	That's Park Su.
Who are they?	They're my classmates.
Where's he from?	He's from Tokyo.
What's your occupation?	I'm a student.
How old are they?	He's sixteen and his brother is ten.
What's your nickname?	Everyone calls me Susie.
What are their names?	Costas and Ahmed.
What's his e-mail address?	ted@kr.com [say "ted at k r dot com"]

Possessive nouns
the **teacher's** name
Peter's address

Possessive adjectives
I	= **my**	it	= **its**
you	= **your**	we	= **our**
he	= **his**	they	= **their**
she	= **her**		

Contractions 🄲🄽
Who's	= Who is
What's	= What is
Where's	= Where is
That's	= That is

GRAMMAR BOOSTER
PAGE G2
For more . . .

B **Complete the conversations. Use contractions when possible.**

1. **A:** <u>Who's</u> that over there?
   B: Oh, that <u>'s</u> Erol. He <u>'s</u> from Turkey.
   A: <u>How old</u> is he? He looks very young.
   B: I think he <u>'s</u> twenty-five.

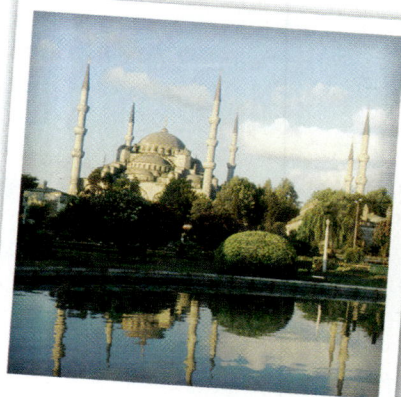

Istanbul, Turkey

🄲🄽 **Corpus Notes:**
In spoken American English, the contractions "who's," "what's," "where's," and "that's" are used more than seven times as often as "who is," "what is," "where is," and "that is."

LESSON

2 ▶ Offer to Introduce Someone

🎧 CONVERSATION **MODEL**

Suggested teaching time:	10 minutes
Your actual teaching time:	_____

* Before listening to the conversation, have students look at the main photo. Ask:
  How many people are in the photo? (three)
  How many are women? (two)
  How many are men? (one)

* After students read and listen, ask them to underline the names in the conversation *(Kate, Lauren).* Then have students read again and label the two women in the photo.

* Point to the appropriate people in the photo and ask:
  Does Lauren know him? (yes)
  Does Lauren know Kate? (no)
  Does he know Kate? (yes)

* Summarize. Point to the man and say *Lauren is his friend. Kate is his friend. He introduces Lauren to Kate.*

🎧 Rhythm and intonation practice

Suggested teaching time:	5 minutes
Your actual teaching time:	_____

* Have students repeat each line chorally. Make sure students:
  ○ use falling intonation in *Who's that?* and rising intonation in *Over there?*
  ○ pause after *Come* and *Lauren.*
  ○ stress *too* in *Nice to meet you, too,* but do not stress *Kate* in *Nice to meet you, Kate.*
  ○ use the following stress pattern:

┌─ **STRESS PATTERN** ────────────────────
│
│ **A:** Who's that?
│
│ **B:** Over there? Her name's Kate.
│
│ Come. I'll introduce you.
│
│ **B:** Lauren, I'd like you to meet Kate.
│
│ **A:** Nice to meet you, Kate.
│
│ **C:** Nice to meet you, too.
│
└──

🔺 GRAMMAR

Suggested teaching time:	5–10 minutes
Your actual teaching time:	_____

* Go over the examples in the box. Practice the meanings of *Who, What, Where,* and *How old.* Call out a person, thing, place, or age. The class responds with the appropriate question word. For example, call out *Kate* or *your mother,* and the class responds *Who.* For *What,* you can call out *name, title, nationality,* or *occupation.*

* Review the meaning of *nickname.* Read the example *What's your nickname? Everyone calls me Susie* again. Say *Susie is a nickname for Susan. Her name is Susan, but people call her Susie.* You may wish to give other examples of nicknames for common English names such as, *Tom—Thomas, Bill—William, Patty—Patricia, Kate—Katherine.*

* Point out that only *is* contracts with the question words and *that. Am* and *are* do not.

Possessive nouns

* Pick up a Student's Book (or some other belonging: pen, pencil, notebook, etc.). Say the student's name + *'s* and the name of the item *(Tim's book*).* Stress the possessive *'s.*

* Write on the board *[Name]'s book.*

* Walk around the room, picking up items from different students' desks. Have the class use the possessive to tell you whom the item belongs to.

Possessive adjectives

* Have students look at where you wrote *[Name]'s book* on the board.

* Cross out the possessive noun and write *his* or *her* in its place.

* Repeat some of the possessive nouns used previously to identify students' belongings. Elicit possessive adjectives in their place; for example, say *(Michael)'s book* and elicit *his book* from the class.

* Pick up an item belonging to you. Say *the teacher's (book).* Elicit *your book* from the class. Say *the students' classroom* and elicit *our classroom.*

🔵 Grammar Self-Checks

🔷 Complete the conversations . . .

Suggested teaching time:	5 minutes
Your actual teaching time:	_____

* Make sure students understand *that* and *over there.* Indicate different students who are sitting far away from you. Ask the class *Who's that?* To clarify, gesture toward a student and say *Over there.*

* Have students check answers with a partner. Then review as a class. For each item, have two different students read the roles of A and B.

_____
* Substitute real names of students in your class.

◆C PAIR WORK

Suggested teaching time:	5–10 minutes
Your actual teaching time:	_____

- Review question words from page 8 with students.
- To model the activity, have volunteers ask you information questions with *be*. Write a few of the questions on the board. Then answer with complete sentences.
- Your students might ask:
  Who are your friends?
  What's your nickname?
  What's your occupation?
  How old are you?

Culture note: In some cultures, asking a person's age is considered impolite. It's typically OK to ask a child or young person *How old are you?*

Option: To help students ask more questions with *Who*, introduce or review the word *favorite*. Students can ask *Who is your favorite teacher / singer / actress (actor) / athlete / artist?* [**+5 minutes**]

◆D 🎧 PRONUNCIATION

Suggested teaching time:	5 minutes
Your actual teaching time:	_____

- Before students listen, read the four items out loud. Model rising and falling intonation between the <u>yes</u> / <u>no</u> questions and the information questions. Write some examples on the board, using arrows to indicate rising and falling intonation.

Option: For more practice, read the questions in the Grammar box on page 6 with rising intonation. Have students repeat. Then read the questions in the Grammar box on page 8 with falling intonation. Have students repeat. [**+5 minutes**]

Option: Have students practice reading out loud the questions they wrote for Exercise C on pages 7 and 9. With a new partner, students read the questions from page 7 with rising intonation. Then have them read the questions from page 9 with falling intonation. Partners can answer the questions. [**+5 minutes**]

💿 **Pronunciation Activities**

CONVERSATION **PAIR WORK**

Suggested teaching time:	10–15 minutes
Your actual teaching time:	_____

- Model the conversation with a student. Play the role of B. Act out the conversation. Take the student playing the role of A over to meet the classmate he or she indicated.
- After the two students you've introduced shake hands and say *Nice to meet you (too)* to each other, ask the class for ideas about how the two can continue the conversation. For example, students can ask:
  Where are you from?
  What's your occupation?
  Are you married?

Option: Have the class stand. Pairs act out the conversation. Student B should take Student A over to meet the classmate he or she indicated. This new pair then continues talking. As students finish their part in a conversation, they should move on, find a new partner, and practice the conversation again. Make sure students switch roles when they change partners so they have practice with all parts of the conversation. [**+10 minutes**]

💿 **Pair Work Cards**

EXTRAS (optional)

Grammar Booster
Workbook: Exercises 10–14
Copy & Go: Activity 2

💿 **Pronunciation Supplements**

2. **A:** ___Is___ that your new neighbor?

   B: Yeah. ___Her___ name ___is___ Roberta.

   A: ___Where's___ she from?

   B: Costa Rica.

Costa Rican rainforest

Mieko and Rika

3. **A:** ___Who are___ they?

   B: Oh, ___they're___ my classmates.

   A: ___What are___ their names?

   B: That ___'s___ Mieko on the left, and that ___'s___ Rika on the right.

C **PAIR WORK.** Write questions for your partner. Then exchange questions. Answer your partner's questions.

| What's your father's name? | His name is Paul. |

D 🎧 **PRONUNCIATION.** **Intonation.** Use rising intonation in <u>yes</u> / <u>no</u> questions. Use falling intonation in information questions. Listen. Then listen again and repeat.

1. Is she French?
2. Who's that?
3. Are they married?
4. Where are they from?

CONVERSATION PAIR WORK

Offer to introduce your partner to other classmates. Use the guide, or create a new conversation.

A: Who's that?
B: Over there? _____ name's _____.
   Come. I'll introduce you.

   • • •

B: _____, I'd like you to meet _____.
A: _____ . . .

Continue the conversation in your <u>own</u> way.

Talk about People

A 🎧 **VOCABULARY.** Some occupations. Listen and practice.

a computer
programmer

a photographer

an interpreter

a musician

a manager

a chef

a salesperson

a flight attendant

a graphic designer

a pilot

B 🎧 **LISTENING COMPREHENSION.** Listen to the conversations about the people.
Then listen again. Write the occupation and the nationality.

1. Fumiko Ito
graphic designer
Japanese

2. Lee Hyuk
musician
Korean

3. Ilhan Ramic
computer programmer
Turkish

4. Ana Gutierrez
interpreter
Spanish

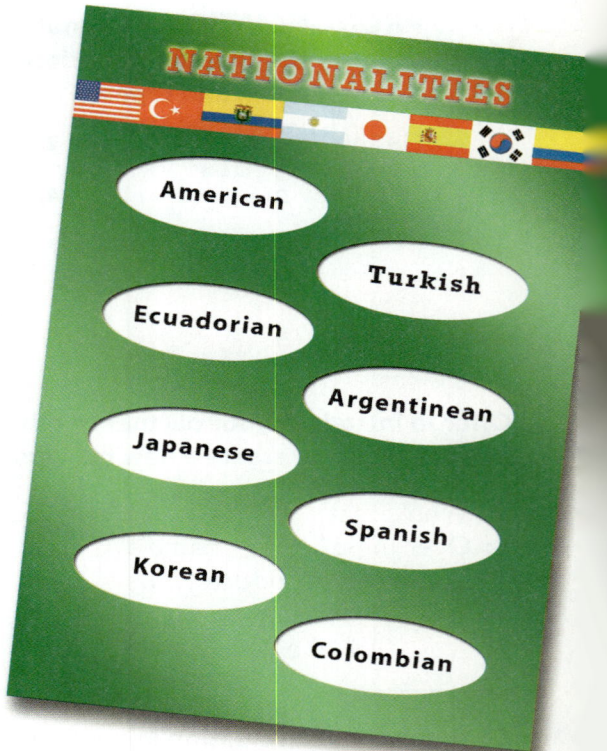

NATIONALITIES

American

Turkish

Ecuadorian

Argentinean

Japanese

Spanish

Korean

Colombian

LESSON 3 ▶ Talk about People

A 🎧 VOCABULARY

Suggested teaching time:	10–15 minutes
Your actual teaching time:	_____

• After students repeat in the pauses, talk about people you know who work in the occupations pictured; for example, *My neighbor is a computer programmer. My husband's friend is a chef. My friend Nicole is a salesperson.* Then have students write or talk to a partner about people they know in the different occupations.

Option: Ask questions about the people pictured. Tell students to look at the pictures and invent answers. Some questions you can ask are:
  How old is the manager?
  Where's the interpreter from?
  What is the pilot's name?
  Is the chef married?
[+5 minutes]

Challenge: Pairs choose one picture and write about the person. Students invent information about the person. To model the activity, ask the class about the computer programmer and write the answers on the board. Ask:
  What's his name?
  Where's he from?
  Is he married?
  How old is he?

Use the class's answers to the questions to write answers in complete sentences. Following is an example of what you might write:
  His name is (Dennis). He's a (computer programmer). He's from (England). He is (married). He's (thirty-one).
[+10 minutes]

🔘 **Vocabulary Cards**

B 🎧 LISTENING COMPREHENSION

Suggested teaching time:	15–20 minutes
Your actual teaching time:	_____

• Before listening to the conversations, read the nationalities out loud. Have students repeat.

• Ask students if they can name some other nationalities. Write their answers on the board.

• After students listen and complete the exercise, review as a class. Have students give answers in complete sentences; for example, *Her name is Fumiko Ito. She's a graphic designer. She's Japanese.*

Challenge: Pairs create a similar conversation about a classmate. [+10 minutes]

┌─ **Your students can say ...** ─────────┐
A: Who's that? B: Over there? That's _____.
A: Is he from _____? / Where's she from? / Is he married? / What's her occupation?
└──────────────────────────────────────┘

Challenge: Pairs create a similar conversation about a famous singer, actor / actress, athlete, or artist. [+10 minutes]

┌─ **Your students can say ...** ─────────┐
A: That's Penelope Cruz! B: Who's that? A: She's an actress. B: Where's she from? A: She's from Spain.
└──────────────────────────────────────┘

◀ AUDIOSCRIPT ▶

CONVERSATION 1
F: Who's that?
M: Oh, that's Fumiko Ito. She's a graphic designer.
F: Where's she from?
M: Nagoya, Japan. But she lives in New York now.

CONVERSATION 2
F: Oh, hey! That's Lee Hyuk!
M: Who's Lee Hyuk?
F: She's a musician. She's really excellent!
M: Where's she from?
F: I think she's from Korea.

CONVERSATION 3 [F = Spanish]
M: Who is that over there?
F: It's Ilhan Ramic. He's a computer programmer.
M: Really? Is he from around here?
F: No. He's from Turkey.

CONVERSATION 4
M: Who's that woman over there?
F: That's Ana Gutierrez. She's from Spain.
M: What does she do?
F: She's an interpreter for the president of Ecuador.

TOP NOTCH **INTERACTION**

Suggested teaching time: 20–25 minutes
Your actual teaching time: _____

- Partner B in each pair should turn his or her book upside down. Have students cover the bottom of the page with a sheet of paper so that they are looking only at their part.

- To identify whom they are talking about, students first use a name or possessive noun; for example:
  Where is Paul Melin from?
  What's Paul Melin's occupation?

- When it's clear whom they are asking about, students use a personal pronoun or possessive adjective; for example:
  How old is he?
  What's his e-mail address?

- To check their answers, partners take turns talking about the people; for example, Partner A talks about Paul Melin. He or she says:
  His name is Paul Melin. He's a chef. He's Canadian. (or: He's from Canada.) He's forty-three. His e-mail address is pmelin678@interlink.com.

EXTRAS (optional)

    Copy & Go: Activity 3

Partner A: Look at the top of the page.
Partner B: Look at the bottom of the page.
Ask questions and write the missing information.

PARTNER A

Name: Paul Melin
Occupation: Chef
Nationality: Canadian
Age: 43
E-mail address:
pmelin678@interlink.com

Name: Helena Da Silva
Occupation: Photographer
Nationality: Brazilian
Age: 36
E-mail address:
dasilva.helena@brasnet.com

Name: Chisoto Nakamura
Occupation: Musician
Nationality: Japanese
Age: 24
E-mail address:
nakamurac@genki.com.jp

Name: Georges Hayek
Occupation: Interpreter
Nationality: Lebanese
Age: 57
E-mail address:
hayek1435@lebworld.com

PARTNER B

Name: Georges Hayek
Occupation: Interpreter
Nationality: Lebanese
Age: 57
E-mail address: hayek1435@lebworld.com

Name: Chisoto Nakamura
Occupation: Musician
Nationality: Japanese
Age: 24
E-mail address: nakamurac@genki.com.jp

Name: Helena Da Silva
Occupation: Photographer
Nationality: Brazilian
Age: 36
E-mail address: dasilva.helena@brasnet.com

Name: Paul Melin
Occupation: Chef
Nationality: Canadian
Age: 43
E-mail address: pmelin678@interlink.com

4 ▸ Interview a Classmate

A ▸ **READING WARM-UP.** Do you know people who travel a lot for their jobs? Where? What are their occupations?

B ▸ 🎧 **READING.** *Top Notch* interviewed people who travel for their jobs. Read about them.

CRISTINA PETRIZZI

Meet Maria Cristina Petrizzi S. Ferreira, 38, an interpreter and translator from Brazil. She works for some well-known Brazilian and international companies. Ms. Petrizzi lives in São Paulo with her husband, Roberto, and their daughter, Natalia. But her hometown is Santos, a town on the coast. "My work is great because I travel and get to know lots of people." ■

HIDETAKA KAMIMURA

This is Dr. Hidetaka Kamimura and his family. Dr. Kamimura is a manager in a pharmaceutical company. He was born in Shizuoka, in central Japan, in 1951. Today he lives in Tokyo with his wife, Yumi, and their three children. "I travel overseas for my job several times a year," he says. "But I really like to travel with my family." ■

ARLYS DOCKENDORFF

Meet Arlys Dockendorff, 52, a photographer. Ms. Dockendorff lives near New York City, but she comes from the state of Iowa in the center of the United States. She takes photographs around the world. "I like to photograph interesting people," she says. "Musicians, artists, children, old people." You can see her photographs of Tibet on the Internet at www.echinaart.com. ■

SOURCE: authentic *Top Notch* interviews

C ▸ Read about the people again. Complete the chart. Fill in each person's occupation, age, city, and hometown.

	Occupation	Age	Lives in ...	Comes from ...
Ms. Petrizzi	interpreter and translator	38	São Paulo	Santos
Dr. Kamimura	manager	55	Tokyo	Shizuoka
Ms. Dockendorff	photographer	52	New York	Iowa

LESSON

4 ▶ Interview a Classmate

A READING WARM-UP

Suggested teaching time:	5–10 minutes
Your actual teaching time:	_____

- Have students look at the occupations on page 11 again. Ask *Which people probably travel a lot for their jobs?* (photographer, interpreter, musician, flight attendant, pilot)
- Have students answer the Reading Warm-Up questions in small groups. Students should only be expected to provide the name, occupation, and names of places. Some students will be able to say more; for example: *(Name)'s father is a pilot. He travels to (Santiago, Buenos Aires, and São Paulo).*

B 🎧 READING

Suggested teaching time:	15–20 minutes
Your actual teaching time:	_____

- After students read the interviews silently, have them close their books. On the board, write *Ms. Petrizzi, Dr. Kamimura, Ms. Dockendorff.*
- Pronounce each of the names and have students repeat. Then read the following sentences. Ask students to identify who the person is.
  He's married. (Dr. Kamimura)
  She's Brazilian. (Ms. Petrizzi)
  She's from the United States. (Ms. Dockendorff)
  His hometown is Shizuoka. (Dr. Kamimura)
  Her photographs are on the Internet.
   (Ms. Dockendorff)
  Her husband's name is Roberto. (Ms. Petrizzi)

Option: Ask students what they remember about each person. Say *Who's Cristina Petrizzi?* Write what the class remembers about her under her name. For example, *She's an interpreter. She's Brazilian. She's married. Her husband's name is Roberto.* Then students open their books and check the information on the board. **[+5 minutes]**

🌐 **Learning Strategies**

C Read about the people again . . .

Suggested teaching time:	10 minutes
Your actual teaching time:	_____

Language note: A *hometown* is the town or city where a person was born and lived as a child. It can also mean the place a person lives now.

- Tell the class the name of your hometown. Ask a few students about their hometowns, especially if you think students were born elsewhere.
- Go over the information students need to look for. Have students look at the chart. Say *What's the person's occupation? How old is he or she? What city does the person live in now? Where's the person from? / What's his or her hometown?* Students should not say the answers to these questions at this point.
- Have students underline this information as they read. After students read, they use the underlined information to fill in the chart.
- Review as a class. Have students read their answers out loud in complete sentences; for example:
   Ms. Petrizzi is an interpreter and translator. She's thirty-eight. She lives in São Paulo. She comes from Santos, Brazil.

Note: Students will have to subtract 1951 from the current year to determine Dr. Kamimura's age.

Language note: An *interpreter* changes spoken words from one language into another. A *translator* changes speech or writing into a different language.

🌐 **Extra Reading Comprehension Activities**

TOP NOTCH **INTERACTION**

Suggested teaching time:	15–20 minutes
Your actual teaching time:	_____

STEP 1

- After students read the articles silently, ask:
  What's Ms. Hirano's occupation? (international marketing manager)
  How old is she? (26)
  What's her hometown? (Tokyo, Japan)
  What's Mr. Paz's occupation? (businessman)
  How old is he? (40)
  What's his wife's name? (Margarita)
  What's his wife's occupation? (opera singer)

- Ask *Are Ms. Hirano and Mr. Paz students?* (Yes, they are.) Point out that this is a class newsletter.

STEP 2

- To model the activity, have the class interview you. Different volunteers ask you questions: *What's your name? What's your nickname?* etc. Another student writes the information on the board. Leave this information on the board to use in Step 3.

- As a class, think of other questions to ask. Possible questions include:
  Are you married?
  What is your husband / wife's name?
  What is your husband / wife's occupation?

- Make sure students interview different partners from the ones they exchanged questions with for Exercise C on pages 7 and 9.

STEP 3

- Have students look at the information about you that is on the board. To model the activity, ask volunteers to use this information to create sentences about you.

Note: To write their article about their partner, students only need to use *be* in the present tense. However, the article in Step 1 also uses *lives*. Stronger false beginners may spontaneously use *lives* and/or *comes from* in the articles they write.

Option: Read some of the articles out loud, but don't say the student's name. Ask the class to guess who you are reading about. **[+5 minutes]**

Option: Collect the articles, mix up their order, then pass them back out to the class. A volunteer reads the article he or she has out loud but doesn't say the student's name. The class guesses who it is. Then that student reads the article he or she has. Continue until several articles have been read out loud. **[+10 minutes]**

🌀 **Writing Process Worksheets**

EXTRAS (optional)

Workbook: Exercises 15–19

STEP 1.   Read the articles students wrote to introduce their classmates.

This is Kyoko Hirano. She is an international marketing manager. She is from Tokyo, Japan. Ms. Hirano is 26 years old. She lives near New York with her sister, Motoko.

Kyoko Hirano

Arturo Paz

Meet Arturo Paz. What's his occupation? Arturo is a businessman. He lives in Caracas, Venezuela. He is 40 years old and married. His wife, Margarita, is an opera singer.

STEP 2.   PAIR WORK.   Interview a classmate. Write his or her personal information on the notepad.

Name:

Nickname:

Occupation:

Hometown:

Age:

Other:

STEP 3.   WRITING. Write a short article about your classmate.

Francisco is my partner. He's a bank manager. His nickname is

CHECKPOINT

A 🎧 **LISTENING COMPREHENSION.** Listen to the conversations at an international conference. Listen again and write each person's occupation and country or hometown.

	Occupation	From . . .
1. Bill Anderson	computer programmer	Scotland
2. Penny Latulippe	musician	Vancouver
3. Mike Johnson	interpreter	San Diego
4. Margo Brenner	photographer	Peru

Australia
Scotland
Vancouver
the U.S.
San Diego
Peru

B Look at the pictures below. Write the occupations.

1. A _____chef_____ works in a restaurant.
2. A _computer programmer_ works in an office.
3. A _flight attendant_ works on an airplane.
4. A _salesperson_ works in a store.
5. A _teacher_ works in a school.

1.

2.

3.

4.

5.

C Complete each conversation in your own way.

1. "Are you Pat?"
   YOU _____.

2. "What's your name?"
   YOU _____.

3. "Are you a new student?"
   YOU _____.

4. **YOU** _____?
   "I'm from Paraguay."

5. **YOU** _____?
   "I'm a musician."

6. **YOU** _____.
   "Nice to meet you, too."

D **WRITING.** Write a paragraph about yourself. Use the questions as a guide.

- What's your first and last name?
- What's your nickname?
- How old are you?
- What's your hometown?
- What's your occupation?

TOP NOTCH PROJECT
Create a class newsletter with photos to introduce your classmates.

TOP NOTCH WEBSITE
For Unit 1 online activities, visit the *Top Notch* Companion Website at www.longman.com/topnotch.

UNIT 1
CHECKPOINT

A 🎧 LISTENING COMPREHENSION

Suggested teaching time:	10 minutes
Your actual teaching time:	_____

• Review answers as a class. Have students give answers in complete sentences.

Challenge: Ask questions such as *Where's San Diego?* (the U.S.) *Who's from Australia?* (Penny Latulippe's father) **[+5 minutes]**

Challenge: Say *I'm a teacher. What do you do?* Ask several students. Then ask different students to recall their classmates' occupations. Ask *What does [Name] do?* If some students are not originally from here, ask *Are you originally from [Name of city]?* Students can say *No. I'm originally from [Name of city].* **[+5 minutes]**

AUDIOSCRIPT

CONVERSATION 1
F: Is that David Evans?
M: No, that's Bill Anderson. David is over there.
F: Oh, what does Bill do?
M: He's a computer programmer.
F: Really? Where's he from?
M: He's from Scotland.

CONVERSATION 2
M1: Who's that over there?
M2: Her name's Penny Latulippe.
M1: What does she do?
M2: They say she's a musician.
M1: Is she from around here?
M2: No. She's from Vancouver.

CONVERSATION 3
F: Are you from around here?
M: No, I'm from San Diego, California. My name's Mike. Mike Johnson.
F: Nice to meet you, Mike. I'm Louise. What do you do?
M: I'm an interpreter. I work for PBC.

CONVERSATION 4 [F = Spanish]
M: Is that Margo Brenner?
F: Yes, it is.
M: I heard she's a photographer.
F: That's right.
M: Is it true that she's from Australia?
F: Her father is. But she's from Peru.

B Look at the pictures . . .

Suggested teaching time:	5 minutes
Your actual teaching time:	_____

• Say *Who works in a restaurant?* Elicit *A chef.*
• Students complete the exercise independently. Review answers as a class.

C Complete each conversation . . .

Suggested teaching time:	5–10 minutes
Your actual teaching time:	_____

• To check their work, have students practice the conversations with a partner. Students practice the conversations twice so that both partners can read their answers.

D WRITING

Suggested teaching time:	10–15 minutes
Your actual teaching time:	_____

Students write paragraphs very similar to the articles they wrote on page 13. However, here they should write in the first person.

Option: Have students rewrite the articles about Kyoko Hirano and Arturo Paz on page 13 in the first person; for example:

My name is Kyoko Hirano. I'm an international marketing manager. I'm from Tokyo, Japan. I'm 26 years old. I live near New York with my sister, Motoko.
[+10 minutes]

🔹 **Writing Process Worksheets**

***TOP NOTCH* PROJECT**

Idea: Students can change the first sentence of their article (from page 13) for inclusion in a class newsletter. Have students change *[Name] is my partner* to *This is [Name]* or *Meet [Name].*

Idea: With their permission, include students' e-mail addresses with their articles. If possible, make a copy of the newsletter for each student in the class to keep as a reference.

UNIT WRAP-UP

Suggested teaching time:	15–20 minutes
Your actual teaching time:	_____

Vocabulary

- Ask *Where are the people? What are their occupations? / What do they do?*

- Students point to and identify the different occupations they see: *They're flight attendants, He's a pilot*, etc.

Your students can say ...

flight attendants, a pilot, a photographer, a musician, a computer programmer, a driver, business people

---

Option: Find the occupation. Do the activity in reverse. One student says an occupation and the other points to the appropriate person in the picture. **[+5 minutes]**

Social language

- As a class, create names for the seven people in the foreground of the picture who are engaged in conversations.

Option: Guessing game. Have volunteers act out one of their conversations in front of the class. Have students listen and guess which people in the picture are being portrayed. **[+5 minutes]**

Option: Writing activity. Have students write their conversations in dialogue form. **[+5 minutes]**

Your students can say ...

(The three people at the top left of the picture)
A: _____, I'd like you to meet _____. / Let me introduce you to _____. **B:** Nice to meet you, _____. **C:** Nice to meet you, too. **B:** Are you (an occupation)? *or* Are you from (place)?

(The pair at the bottom left)
A: Are you _____? **B:** Yes, I am. *or* As a matter of fact, I am. **A:** Well, I'm _____. It's nice to meet you, _____. **B:** You, too.

(The pair at the bottom right)
A: Are you Ms. Smith? **B:** Yes, I am. Please call me _____. **A:** Where are you from, _____? *or* What do you do, _____?

Grammar

- Students can use <u>yes</u> / <u>no</u> questions and short answers with *be* to talk about the people's occupations; for example, *Are they flight attendants? Yes, they are.*

- Students can practice information questions with *be.*
  Who's that? (His / Her name's _____. He's / She's [an occupation].)
  What are their names?
  What's her occupation? / What does he do?

Option: Question prompts. Write on the board: *A flight attendant? A pilot? A musician? A photographer? From Italy? Gina?* Students use the words as prompts for questions. **[+5 minutes]**

Your students can say ...

Is he a pilot? Is she Gina? Are they from Italy? Is she a photographer?

Option: Students can make up additional information about the people pictured and ask:
  Where's she from? / What's his hometown?
  How old are they?
  What's her nickname?
  Is he married? What's his wife's name / occupation?
  What's her nationality?
  Where does he live?
[+5 minutes]

Individual oral progress check (optional)

Use the illustration on page 15 for an oral test. Have students point to and talk about three people in the picture. For example (pointing to the musician), *He is a musician.* Evaluate students on correctness, intelligibility, and completeness.

Cumulative Vocabulary Activities

You may wish to use the video for Unit 1 at this point. For video activity worksheets, go to www.longman.com/topnotch.

**Complete Assessment Package
Unit 1 Achievement Test**

- **Vocabulary.** Look at the people and guess the occupations.

- **Social language.** Create conversations for the people.

  A: Are you _____?   A: This is _____.
  B: _____.   B: _____.

- **Grammar.** Ask and answer questions about the people.

GATE 6

MS. SMITH

Now I can ...

☐ get to know someone.
☐ offer to introduce someone.
☐ talk about people.
☐ interview a classmate.

15

Going out

A **TOPIC PREVIEW.** Look at the newspaper entertainment page. Choose a concert. Circle the date of the concert on the calendar. Circle the location on the map.

THURSDAY, JUNE 19   THE GARNET CITY GAZETTE

WEEKEND LISTINGS

LATIN

Pilar Montenegro. Latin dance-pop music from Mexico. 8 p.m. June 22. Grant Park Band Shell, Grant Park (between First and Second Ave). $25 in advance/$35 on the day of show. Tickets: 622-4408.

CLASSICAL

Kyung-wha Chung. Korean violinist performs Debussy's Sonata for Violin and Piano. With pianist Radu Lupu. 7:15 p.m. June 20. Symphony Hall, 500 First Ave. (across from Grant Park). Tickets: $35–$75.
Box office: 622-6000.

ROCK

Guitar Wolf. Japanese Rock Showcase. 10:30 p.m. June 21. Maxwell's, corner of Second Ave. and Market St. Tickets: $8 in advance/ $10 at the door. Box office: 622-1736.

JAZZ

Sergio Mendes. The king of Bossa Nova jazz returns with his group, Brasil. 8:00 and 11:30 p.m. June 21. The Downbeat, 303 First Ave. Call for ticket prices: 622-1209.

Downtown Garnet City

SECOND AVE.
GRAND ST.
Band Shell
Maxwell's
Grant Park
PARK ST.
FIRST AVE.
The Downbeat
MARKET ST.
Symphony Hall

June

SUN	MON	TUE	WED	THU	FRI	SAT
1	2	3	4	5	6	7
8	9	10	11	12	13	14
15	16	17	18	19	20	21
22	23	24	25	26	27	28
29	30					

B **PAIR WORK.** Tell your partner about your choice. Where is it? When is it?

UNIT 2

Going Out

A TOPIC PREVIEW

Suggested teaching time:	10 minutes
Your actual teaching time:	_____

• Explain that in English-speaking countries *weekend* means the period beginning on Friday night, all of Saturday, and all of Sunday. The other days are called *weekdays*.

Option: If possible, bring in samples of Latin, classical, rock, and jazz music for students to listen to. Some artists you might look for are: Olga Tanon, Ricky Martin (Latin); Mozart, Yo-Yo Ma (classical); U2, the Beatles, (rock); Miles Davis, Billie Holiday (jazz). You can also ask students to bring in samples of the different musical types. [**+5 minutes**]

Culture note: *The Garnet City Gazette* is adapted from an authentic U.S. local newspaper. For that reason, prices are in U.S. dollars and phone numbers are typical U.S. style (7 digits made up for 2 sets, 3 plus 4). An entertainment listing based on an authentic international arts festival website is seen on pages 22 and 23.

B PAIR WORK

Suggested teaching time:	5 minutes
Your actual teaching time:	_____

• Write the following questions on the board:
  What's your choice?
  Where is it?
  When is it?

• Model questions for students and have them repeat.

• Partner A asks the questions from the board; and Partner B gives short answers (for example, *Sergio Mendes, the Downbeat / 303 First Ave., June 21*).

• To review, ask different students *What concert do you want to see this weekend?* Students answer with the name of the performer. Stronger false beginners may produce full sentences with the simple present tense.

Option: On the board, draw a chart like the one that follows. As a class, fill in the information for Pilar Montenegro. Then have students work with their partners to complete the rest of the chart. [**+10 minutes**]

Performer / group	Pilar Montenegro	Kyung-wha Chung	Guitar Wolf	Sergio Mendes
Kind of music	Latin	Classical	Rock	Jazz
Performer's nationality	Mexican	Korean	Japanese	?
Date	June 22	June 20	June 21	June 21
Time	8 p.m.	7:15 p.m.	10:30 p.m.	8:00 p.m. and 11:30 p.m.
Ticket prices	$25 in advance $30 day of show	$35–$75	$8 in advance $10 at the door	?
Telephone number	622-4408	622-6000	622-1736	622-1209

Graphic Organizer

C 🎧 SOUND BITES

Suggested teaching time:	10 minutes
Your actual teaching time:	_____

- To check understanding, ask:
    Does Mike want to see Guitar Wolf? (no)
    Does he want to see Sergio Mendes? (yes)
    Does Mike want to go at 11:30? (no)
    Does he want to go at 8:00? (yes)

D Match the sentences . . .

Suggested teaching time:	5–10 minutes
Your actual teaching time:	_____

- Read the letter choices out loud. Have students underline these sentences in the conversation. Then students read the conversation again and complete the exercise independently.
- To review, say:
    1. *Does Mike want to see Guitar Wolf? Why not? What does he say?* (That's not for me. I'm not really a rock fan.) *So "That's not for me" is the same as . . . ?* (a. I don't think I want to go to that.)
    2. *Does Mike want to see Sergio Mendes? Why? What does he say?* (Now that's more my style.) *So "That's more my style" is the same as . . . ?* (b. I like that better.)
    3. *Does Mike want to go at 11:30? Why not? What does he say?* (That's past my bedtime.) *So "That's past my bedtime" is the same as . . . ?* (c. That's too late.)

E Read the Garnet City weekend listings . . .

Suggested teaching time:	5–10 minutes
Your actual teaching time:	_____

Option: Have students change items 1, 2, and 4 to make them true. [+**5 minutes**]

1. Pilar Montenegro is playing at the **Grant Park Band Shell** *or* **Sergio Mendes** is playing at the Downbeat.
2. **Pilar Montenegro** tickets cost $25 (on the day of the show).
4. Guitar Wolf plays **rock** music *or* **Kyung-wha Chung** plays classical music.

WHAT ABOUT **YOU?**

Suggested teaching time:	10–15 minutes
Your actual teaching time:	_____

- To make sure the meaning of *fan* is clear, say:
    Mike is not a rock fan. He doesn't like rock.
    Mike is a jazz fan. He likes jazz.
- Model the activity. Say *I like [Latin] and [jazz].* Then ask a student *Are you a [Latin] fan? Are you a [jazz] fan? What kind of music do you like?*
- Ask a few pairs to share their answers with the class; for example, *I'm a Latin fan. My partner is a classical fan.*

Option: Learn about your students' other interests. On the board, write:
    I'm a [soccer] fan. What about you, [Name]?

Model the activity by telling class what kind of music you like and asking a student *What about you, [Name of student]?* That student answers and then asks another student. Students can fill in the blank with anything that they like—a kind of music, a sport, the name of a famous person, etc. Continue until several students have had the opportunity to respond. [+**10 minutes**]

EXTRAS (optional)

Workbook: Exercises 1–3

C 🎧 **SOUND BITES. Read along silently as you listen to a natural conversation.**

EVAN: Do you want to see a concert Saturday? Guitar Wolf's at Maxwell's.

MIKE: Well, thanks, but that's not for me. I'm not really a rock fan.

EVAN: What about Sergio Mendes? He's playing Saturday at the Downbeat.

MIKE: Now that's more my style!

EVAN: Great! There's a show at eleven thirty.

MIKE: Eleven thirty? That's past my bedtime!

EVAN: No problem. There's an early show at eight. **CN**

MIKE: Perfect. See you then.

D Match the sentences with the same meaning.

___c___ **1.** "That's past my bedtime."   **a.** I don't think I want to go to that.

___a___ **2.** "That's not for me."   **b.** I like that better.

___b___ **3.** "That's more my style."   **c.** That's too late.

CN Corpus Notes:
"No problem" is used very frequently in spoken and informal American English.

E Read the Garnet City weekend listings on page 16 again. Check ☑ <u>true</u>, <u>false</u>, or <u>no information</u>.

	true	false	no information
1. Pilar Montenegro is playing at the Downbeat.	☐	☑	☐
2. Sergio Mendes tickets cost $25.	☐	☐	☑
3. Symphony Hall is on First Avenue.	☑	☐	☐
4. Guitar Wolf plays classical music.	☐	☑	☐

WHAT ABOUT YOU?

Are you a music fan? What kind of music do you like? Check the boxes.

☐ Latin   ☐ Rock   ☐ Other _____
☐ Classical   ☐ Jazz

PAIR WORK. Compare your choices. Do you like the same kind of music?

1 ▶ Accept or Decline an Invitation

🎧 **CONVERSATION MODEL** Read and listen.

A: Are you free on Friday? *Married on Main Street* is at the Film Forum.

B: Really? I'd love to go. What time?

A: At seven ten.

To decline . . .

B: Really? I'd love to go, but I'm busy on Friday.

A: Too bad. Maybe some other time.

🎧 **Rhythm and intonation practice**

A ▶ **GRAMMAR.** Prepositions of time and place **CN**

When's the concert? What time's the movie?

Prepositions of time

on	in	at
on Saturday	in May	at 8:30
on June 7th	in 2003	at noon
on Saturday, June 5th	in the summer	at midnight
on Friday morning	in the morning	

Where's the play?

Prepositions of place

on	in	at
on Fifth Avenue	in Mexico	at the Film Forum
on the corner	in Osaka	at work
on the street	in the park	at school
	in the neighborhood	at the theater

CN **Corpus Notes:**
Be sure students don't mix up prepositions of time. For example, it is common for students to use "in" with days of the week and "on" with months.

Contractions
When's = When is
What time's = What time is
Where's = Where is

0291172

GRAMMAR BOOSTER
PAGE G3
For more . . .

B ▶ **Complete the e-mail message with prepositions of time and place.**

From: val670@telcalm.net
To: hiroko_une@global.jp
Subject: African music concert

Hi Hiroko: Are you busy __on__ Monday night? There's a free concert of African music right near your office __at__ the Stern Art Center. Sounds like a great show! It starts __at__ 7:30. I'll be __at__ work until 5:00, but I could meet you __at__ 5:15 or 5:30 __on__ the corner of Grand and Crane. We could have something to eat before the concert. What do you think? The price is right! —Val

LESSON

1 Accept or Decline an Invitation

🎧 CONVERSATION MODEL

Suggested teaching time:	10 minutes
Your actual teaching time:	_____

- After students read and listen, ask:
  What's the name of the movie? ("Married on Main Street")
  Where's the movie? (at the Film Forum)
  When's the movie? (on Friday, at 7:10)

- Have students listen again. Pause between the models of how to accept and how to decline an invitation.
  After the *accept* model, ask *Does she want to go to the movie?* (yes) After the *decline* model, ask *Can she go to the movie?* (no)

- Ask a few students *Are you free on Friday, or are you busy?*

Culture note: In most English-speaking countries it is essential to provide a reason when declining a social invitation.

🎧 Rhythm and intonation practice

Suggested teaching time:	5 minutes
Your actual teaching time:	_____

- Have students repeat each line chorally. Make sure students:
  ○ use rising intonation in *Are you free on Friday?* and *Really?*
  ○ use falling intonation in *What time?*
  ○ use the following stress pattern:

---STRESS PATTERN---

A: Are you free on Friday? *Married on Main Street* is at the Film Forum.

B: Really? I'd love to go. What time?

A: At seven ten.

To decline . . .

B: Really? I'd love to go, but I'm busy on Friday.

A: Too bad. Maybe some other time.

🔶 A GRAMMAR

Suggested teaching time:	5–10 minutes
Your actual teaching time:	_____

- Review the contracted question words. Read each word and have students repeat.

- To model the use of prepositions of time and place, talk about when and where your class meets; for example:
  Our class is on (Mondays and Wednesdays).
  It's in (the afternoon).
  It's at (3:30).
  Our class is at (name of your school).
  (Name of your school) is on (your street).
  (Name of your school) is in (your city or town).

  Be sure to substitute your own information for the information in parentheses above.

Option: Bring to class information about a couple of events near you this weekend. Write the information about the event on the board; for example:

  Vivaldi concert
  Saturday
  7:30
  Water Street
  Pacific City

Students write sentences about when and where each event is (*It's on Saturday. It's at 7:30.*, etc.) **[+10 minutes]**

🔷 Grammar Self-Checks

🔷 B Complete the e-mail message . . .

Suggested teaching time:	5 minutes
Your actual teaching time:	_____

- To check their work, have students read the e-mail message out loud with a partner.

- To check students' understanding of the e-mail message, ask:
  When's the concert? (on Monday night)
  What time? (at 7:30)
  Where's the concert? (at the Stern Center)
  What kind of music is it? (African)
  What are the ticket prices? (free) [or *How much is a ticket?*]

Language note: The word *free* is used in two different ways on page 18. In *Are you **free** on Friday?*, *free* means *not busy* or *having nothing to do*. In *There's a **free** concert . . .*, *free* means *not costing any money.*

C ∩ VOCABULARY

Suggested teaching time:	5 minutes
Your actual teaching time:	_____

• After students listen and repeat, ask questions:
 Is Blues Explosion *a movie?* (No, it's not.)
 Is Hamlet *a play?* (Yes, it is.)
 Is the talk on Tuesday? (No it's not.)

• In the illustration for *a movie,* point out the place where tickets are sold. Say *This is the box office.* Write the word on the board.

Option: Bring in the entertainment listing from the local paper. Write the following questions on the board:

 What movie would you love to see?
 What play would you love to see?
 What concert would you love to see?
 What talk would you love to go to?
 What art exhibit would you love to see?

Students write short answers to the questions. Then have students ask and answer the questions with a partner. Do not expect productive use of "would love to." Students can just answer with name of the event.
[+10 minutes]

◉ **Vocabulary Cards**

D PAIR WORK

Suggested teaching time:	5 minutes
Your actual teaching time:	_____

• Walk around the classroom while students ask and answer questions. Check for correct use of prepositions of time and place: *on* with the day(s) of the week, *at* with the venue and time.

• If necessary, go over some common errors you heard students make as they worked in pairs.

> **Language note:** *The* is used with proper names of theaters, galleries, and museums: *at **the** Film Forum, at **the** Reed Theater, at **the** Beekman Gallery.* It is generally not used with proper names of a park or store/shop: *at Elliot Park, at Book World.*

E ∩ LISTENING COMPREHENSION

Suggested teaching time:	5–10 minutes
Your actual teaching time:	_____

• Before listening to the conversations, tell students to listen for the type of event and the time of the event.

Challenge: Copy the chart from Exercise E on the board. Add another column to the chart with the heading "Yes / No / Maybe." Ask *Does the person want to go?* Have students listen to the conversations again. After each conversation, ask a volunteer to come to the board and write either yes, no or maybe in the new column. (Answers: 1. yes, 2. no, 3. maybe, 4. yes)
[+10 minutes]

◖AUDIOSCRIPT◗

CONVERSATION 1
M: Are you free on Sunday at 11:30? Nick Hornby's going to be at the City Nights bookstore.
F: Nick Hornby? I love his books. What's he doing there?
M: Giving a talk about his new novel *How to Be Good.* Want to go?
F: Absolutely.

CONVERSATION 2 [F1 = Australian]
F1: What's playing at the Classic Film Center?
F2: There's an old Audrey Hepburn movie showing at 7:10—*Roman Holiday.* Interested?
F1: Not really. I'm not an Audrey Hepburn fan.

CONVERSATION 3 [M = Spanish: Mexico]
F: Oh, look. *Oedipus Rex* is at the Theater in the Circle.
M: What's *Oedipus Rex*?
F: It's a famous Greek play. It's great. There's a performance tonight at eight o'clock. Do you want to go?
M: At eight? Maybe.

CONVERSATION 4
M1: I'm in the mood for a good concert. Is the festival still in town?
M2: Only the São Paulo Symphony. They're playing Brahms's First tonight.
M1: Well, that sounds great. What time?
M2: At 7:45. Let's do it.

CONVERSATION PAIR WORK

Suggested teaching time:	5–10 minutes
Your actual teaching time:	_____

• Have students look at the Melbourne entertainment listings. For each venue, ask students whether or not to use *the* (the Cine Metro, The Garage, Book City, the Cameo Theater).

• If Student B at first declines Student A's invitation, A can say *What about _____?* and suggest another event or day.

Challenge: If your students are ready, point out that they can also use language from the Sound Bites on page 17. **[+5 minutes]**

Option: Have students bring in local entertainment listings. Students then practice the conversation using these listings. **[+10 minutes]**

◉ **Pair Work Cards**

EXTRAS (optional)

Grammar Booster
Workbook: Exercises 4–8
Copy & Go: Activity 5

🎧 **VOCABULARY.** **Entertainment events.** **Listen and practice.**

THE FILM FORUM PRESENTS MARRIED ON MAIN STREET Friday night only! 7:10	HAMLET THURSDAY AND FRIDAY 7:30 PM REED THEATER	BLUES EXPLOSION THIS SATURDAY AT 12:00 ELLIOT PARK	BOOK WORLD / BRAD McFEE AUTHOR OF "TRAVELING ALONE" THURSDAY AT 5:30	BEEKMAN GALLERY "ART OF THE SIXTIES" OPENING RECEPTION TUESDAY 8:00 PM
a movie	**a play**	**a concert**	**a talk**	**an art exhibit**

D **PAIR WORK.** Ask and answer questions about the events in the pictures above. Use **When**, **What time**, and **Where**.

❝ Where's the movie? ❞

❝ It's at the Film Forum. ❞

E 🎧 **LISTENING COMPREHENSION.** Listen to the conversations about entertainment events. Then listen again and complete the chart.

	Kind of event	Time of event
1.	a talk	11:30
2.		
3.		
4.		

CONVERSATION PAIR WORK

Invite your partner to an event. Use these events or other events in **your** town.

A: Are you free _____? _____ is at _____.

B: _____ ...

Continue the conversation in your own way.

Melbourne
WEEKEND ENTERTAINMENT

MOVIES *Like Water for Chocolate,* Cine Metro, Sat. / Sun. 8:55

MUSIC **The Noyz Boyz,** The Garage, Fri. Midnight

TALKS **Novelist Toni Morrison:** "Love," Book City, Mon. 8:00

THEATER *My Fair Lady,* Cameo Theater, Every night 8:00

CONTROLLED PRACTICE

Ask for and Give Directions

🎧 CONVERSATION MODEL Read and listen.

A: Excuse me. I'm looking for The Bell Theater. **CN**

B: The Bell Theater? Do you know the address?

A: Yes. It's 101 Harper Street.

B: Oh. That's right around the corner, on the left side of the street.

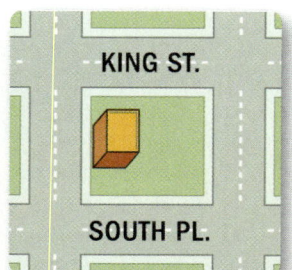

A: Thanks.

If you don't know . . .

B: The Bell Theater? I'm sorry, I'm not from around here.

A: Thanks, anyway.

🎧 **Rhythm and intonation practice**

CN **Corpus Notes:**
Some people say "Pardon me" when trying to get someone's attention, but "Excuse me" is more than six times as common in spoken American English.

A 🎧 **VOCABULARY.** Locations and directions. Listen and practice.

on Clark Street

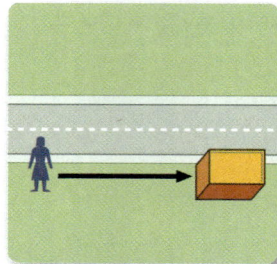

down the street

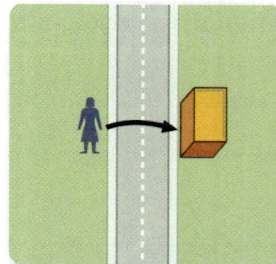

across the street

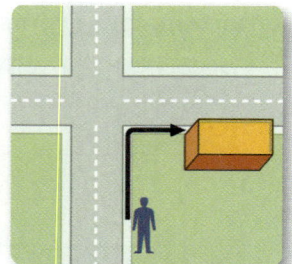

around the corner

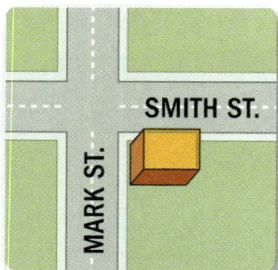

on the corner of Smith and Mark

on the right side of the street

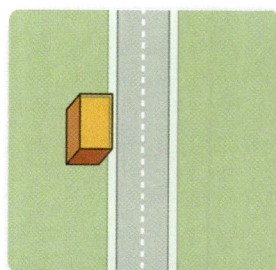

on the left side of the street

between King Street and South Place

B Tell your partner where your house or apartment is. Use the vocabulary.

> My house is on Grove Street, between Dodd Street and Park Street.

LESSON

2 ▶ *Ask for and Give Directions*

🎧 CONVERSATION **MODEL**

Suggested teaching time:	10 minutes
Your actual teaching time:	_____

- After students read and listen, ask *What's the address of The Bell Theater?* (101 Harper Street) Say *So, The Bell Theater's on Harper Street.* Then point to the pair in the photograph and ask *Are they on Harper Street?* (no)

- On the board, draw a map like the one that follows. Have students read the conversation again and look at where the man in the photograph is pointing. Ask a volunteer to come to the board and draw The Bell Theater on the map.

- To review, point to the theater building on the map and say *The Bell Theater is on Harper Street. It's on the left side of the street.* Trace the path from the two stick figures to The Bell Theater and say *The theater is around the corner.*

🎧 Rhythm and intonation practice

Suggested teaching time:	5 minutes
Your actual teaching time:	_____

- Have students repeat each line chorally. Make sure students:
  - pause after *Excuse me, Yes,* and *Oh.*
  - use rising intonation for *The Bell Theater?* and *Do you know the address?*
  - pause after *That's right around the corner* and *I'm sorry.*
  - use the following stress pattern:

STRESS PATTERN

A: Excuse me. I'm looking for The Bell Theater.

B: The Bell Theater? Do you know the address?

A: Yes. It's one-oh-one Harper Street.

B: Oh. That's right around the corner, on the left side of the street.

A: Thanks.

If you don't know . . .

B: The Bell Theater? I'm sorry, I'm not from around here.

A: Thanks, anyway.

A 🎧 VOCABULARY

Suggested teaching time:	5–10 minutes
Your actual teaching time:	_____

- After students listen and repeat, ask *Where is our school?* or *What's the address of our school?* After students answer, say *So our school is on [street name].* Then ask:
  - *What's across the street from our school?*
  - *What's down the street?*
  - *What's around the corner?*

Language note: There are variations in the way people describe locations. For example, *on the corner of Smith and Mark* can also be stated as *on the corner of Smith Street and Mark Street* or *on the corner of Smith and Mark Streets. Between King Street and South Place* can also be stated as *between King and South.*

💿 **Vocabulary Cards**

💿 **Learning Strategies**

B Tell your partner . . .

Suggested teaching time:	5 minutes
Your actual teaching time:	_____

- To model the activity, describe the location of your school; for example, *Our school is on [street name], between [street name] and [street name].*

Option: Describe the locations of familiar places or landmarks in your town and have students guess the places you describe. To give more details, use *across the street, around the corner,* and *down the street;* for example, *It's down the street from the Italian restaurant.* **[+5 minutes]**

◆C PAIR WORK

Suggested teaching time:	5–10 minutes
Your actual teaching time:	_____

Note: When it's necessary to use *the* with a place, it's included here in the place name. Students don't need to determine whether or not to use *the* with the different places on the map.

Language note: *Blvd.* is the abbreviation of the word *Boulevard.* A boulevard is a wide road in a town or city and means the same as *street.*

- Have students look at the map. Ask *What city is this?* (Piermont)
- Have students locate the two people in the bottom, right corner of the map (You are here). Say *You are here.* *With your partner, ask for and give directions to different places on the map.*
- To ask for directions, students can say *Where's (name of place)?* or *I'm looking for (name of place).* To respond, students can say:

    For The Bell Theater: *It's around the corner, on the left side of the street.*
    For The Film Forum: *It's down the street, on the right side.*
    For The Dance Palace: *It's on the corner of Second Avenue and Clark Street.*
    For Taft Symphony Hall: *It's on First Avenue, between Harper Street and Holly Boulevard.*
    For Moonbucks Coffee 1: *It's on the corner of Holly Boulevard and First Avenue.*
    For Moonbucks Coffee 2: *It's across the street.*
    For the Piermont Museum of Art: *It's on Holly Boulevard, between First Avenue and Second Avenue.*

◆D 🎧 PRONUNCIATION

Suggested teaching time:	5 minutes
Your actual teaching time:	_____

- Review Exercise D and model using rising intonation to confirm information.
- Have students ask you about the places on the map in Exercise C. Repeat each place name to confirm the information. Use rising intonation. For example:

    Student: *Where's The Film Forum?*

    Teacher: *The Film Forum?*

- Give directions or describe the location of each place so students can check their own responses from Exercise C.

    Teacher: *The Film Forum? It's down the street, on the right side.*

🔵 **Pronunciation Activities**

CONVERSATION 1
M: I'm looking for the public library.
F: The public library?
M: Yes, that's right.

CONVERSATION 2
F: Excuse me. I'm looking for 200 Main Street.
M: 200 Main Street? That's right across the street.

CONVERSATION 3
M: Excuse me. Where's the mall?
F: The mall? I'm sorry. I don't know.

CONVERSATION **PAIR WORK**

Suggested teaching time:	10–15 minutes
Your actual teaching time:	_____

- Remind students to use rising intonation in B's first line and to use falling intonation on the information questions.
- If students use the Piermont map, point out that there are address numbers on the buildings. Say *The Film Forum is at 127 First Avenue.*
- To give directions, Student B can use *It's . . .* or *That's . . .*

Option: Have students draw a simple map of the neighborhood around the school and have them practice the conversation using their maps.
[+10 minutes]

🔵 **Pair Work Cards**

EXTRAS (optional)

Workbook: Exercises 9–12
Copy & Go: Activity 6

🔵 **Pronunciation Supplements**

PAIR WORK. Practice asking about these locations and giving directions.

- The Bell Theater
- The Film Forum
- Book World
- The Dance Palace
- Taft Symphony Hall
- Moonbucks Coffee 1
- Moonbucks Coffee 2
- The Piermont Museum of Art

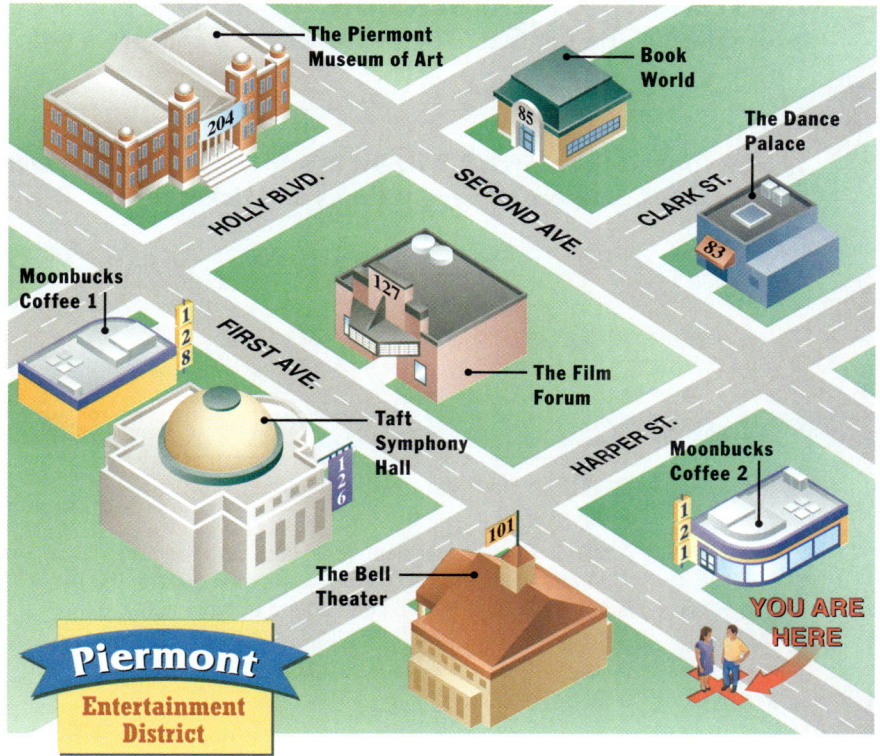

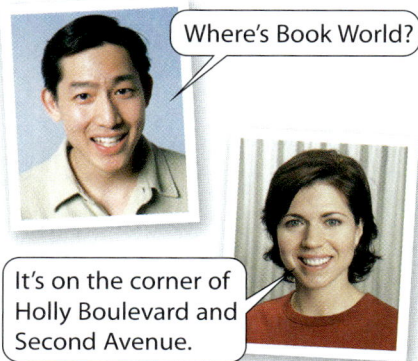

Where's Book World?

It's on the corner of Holly Boulevard and Second Avenue.

The Piermont Museum of Art

Book World

The Dance Palace

HOLLY BLVD.

SECOND AVE.

CLARK ST.

204

85

83

Moonbucks Coffee 1

128

FIRST AVE.

127

The Film Forum

Taft Symphony Hall

126

HARPER ST.

Moonbucks Coffee 2

121

The Bell Theater

101

YOU ARE HERE

Piermont
Entertainment District

D ☊ **PRONUNCIATION.** Rising intonation to confirm information. Repeat information with rising intonation to be sure you understand. Listen. Then listen again and repeat.

The public library?   200 Main Street?   The mall?

CONVERSATION
PAIR WORK

Ask for and give directions. Use the Piermont map or a map of <u>your</u> town or neighborhood. Start like this:

A: Excuse me. I'm looking for _____.
B: _____? _____ …

Continue the conversation in your <u>own</u> way.

CONTROLLED PRACTICE

Make Plans to See an Event

A 🎧 **LISTENING COMPREHENSION.** Listen to the phone calls about events at an international arts festival. Then write either <u>a concert</u>, <u>a talk</u>, or <u>a play</u>.

1. _____a concert_____ 2. _____a play_____ 3. _____a talk_____

B 🎧 Now look at the March 9th event listings on the festival website. Listen to the phone calls again. Complete the event times and ticket prices.

Barrington International Arts Festival

Barrington International Arts Festival

login | update me

Saturday, March 9

Indian Ocean
INDIA

A blend of Indian classical, rock, jazz, and reggae. When traditional Indian music meets rock guitars, the result is Indian Ocean—the unique sound of India today.

when 8:30 pm
where Barrington Festival Main Stage
price US $ 39.00

Copenhagen
NEW ZEALAND

Harborview Theater presents Michael Frayn's Tony Award–winning play. *Copenhagen* explores the impact of scientific progress on modern life.

"This tremendous new play is a piece of history, an intellectual thriller, and a psychological investigation." —*Sunday Times*, UK

when 4:30 pm and 7:00 pm
where Harborview Theater
price US $ 25.00

John Banville
IRELAND

Irish author John Banville talks about his new novel, *The Untouchable*, about British spy Anthony Blunt. "Brilliant"... "exquisitely written." —*Scotland on Sunday*, UK

when 1:00 p.m.
where Ambassador Theater
price US $ 0.00

BARRINGTON FESTIVAL
MAP KEY

① Main Stage
② Harborview Theater
③ Ambassador Theater
④ Prescott Park Pavilion
ⓘ Festival Information
Ⓟ Parking

FIRST STREET
PRESCOTT AVENUE
AMBASSADOR AVENUE
HARBORVIEW DRIVE
SECOND STREET
Prescott Park
THIRD STREET

RPX0507 GA G021014 C 00 ERPX0507
RPX0507 GA
*** Indian Ocean ***
MAR 9 SAT MAR 9 8:30 PM
PCOMP
1014
quickticket

3 ▶ *Make Plans to See an Event*

A 🎧 LISTENING COMPREHENSION

Suggested teaching time:	15 minutes
Your actual teaching time:	_____

• Say *Listen to the phone calls. Is the call about a concert, a talk, or a play?*

• After students listen to the phone calls, ask:
  What kind of event is Indian Ocean? (a concert)
  What's Copenhagen? (a play)
  What kind of event is John Banville? (a talk)

B 🎧 Now look at . . .

Suggested teaching time:	15–20 minutes
Your actual teaching time:	_____

• Before students listen again and complete the missing information, ask a few questions about each event:
  Indian Ocean:
  Where are they from? (India)
  What kind of music is it? (classical, rock, jazz, and reggae)
  Where's the show? (at the [Barrington Festival] Main Stage)
  Are you a (classical, rock) music fan?

  Copenhagen:
  Where's the play from? (New Zealand)
  Where's the show? (at the Harborview Theater)
  Do you want to see the play?

  John Banville:
  What's his nationality? (Irish)
  What's the name of his book? (*The Untouchable*)
  Where's the talk? (at the Ambassador Theater)

• After students listen and complete the activity, have them look at the map. Tell students to describe the locations of the events to a partner. To model the activity, say *Indian Ocean is at the Barrington Festival Main Stage. Where's the Main Stage?* (It's on Harborview Drive.)

┌─ **Your students can say . . .** ─────────
Copenhagen's at the Harborview Theater. It's on First Street, between Ambassador Avenue and Harborview Drive.

John Banville's at the Ambassador Theater. It's on Ambassador Avenue, between First and Second.
└───

AUDIOSCRIPT

CONVERSATION 1 [F = Portuguese]
M: Barrington Festival. Can I help you?
F: Yes, please. What are tonight's concerts?
M: We have two concerts tonight at the Barrington Festival Main Stage: Indian Ocean and Latin Jam.
F: Indian Ocean? Is that new age?
M: Let's see . . . No, Indian Ocean is a blend of Indian classical, rock, jazz, and reggae. Their show starts at eight-thirty.
F: Sounds good. How much are tickets?
M: Tickets are thirty-nine dollars.
F: Thanks.

CONVERSATION 2 [M2 = Chinese]
M1: Harborview Theater box office.
M2: Hello. I'm calling about today's play.
M1: *Copenhagen*?
M2: Yes, thanks. How much are tickets?
M1: They're twenty-five dollars.
M2: And what time is the show?
M1: Let me check . . . There are two shows today: at four-thirty and again at seven o'clock.

CONVERSATION 3 [F = French]
M: Ambassador Theater. How can I help you?
F: I'm calling for information about today's Barrington Festival events.
M: OK. We have a talk this afternoon at one o'clock by author John Banville. He's reading from his novel *The Untouchable*.
F: How much are tickets?
M: The talk is free.
F: Great. Thanks very much.

TOP NOTCH **INTERACTION**

Suggested teaching time:	20–25 minutes
Your actual teaching time:	_____

STEP 1

• After students look at event listing, ask:
  Is Latin Jam a movie, a play, a concert, a talk, or an art exhibit? (a concert)
  What about the Maori Workshop? (an art exhibit)

Option: Students use the event listings on pages 22 and 23 to practice prepositions. For each event, students create sentences with *from, on,* and *at.* Students can write the sentences or take turns talking about the events with a partner; for example:
  *Indian Ocean is **from** India.*
  *The concert is **on** Saturday, March 9.*
  *It's **at** 8:30 P.M.*
  *It's **at** the Main Stage.*
  *The Main Stage is **on** Harborview Drive.*
[+10 minutes]

STEP 2

• Divide the class into pairs. Have each student choose an event to invite his/her partner to. Student A should choose an event on Saturday and Student B should choose an event on Sunday.

• Encourage students to create long conversations. Remind them to talk about:
  kind of event
  date
  time
  place
  location
Some students may also be able to ask about where the artists are from and how much tickets are. If your students are ready, have them add *Where are they from? / Where is he/she from?* and *How much are tickets?* to the list of questions they can ask about the event.

• Model the activity with a more confident student. Have the student invite you to an event. Ask questions about the kind of event, date, time, etc. Decline the invitation. Encourage the student to offer an alternative.

• Remind students to refer to NEED HELP? in their role play.

Option: Have students make plans to go to a Saturday event with a partner. Then have students make plans to go to a Sunday event with a different partner.
[+15 minutes]

EXTRAS (optional)

  Copy & Go: Activity 7

STEP 1. Look at some event listings for March 10.

Barrington International Arts Festival

Latin Jam
CUBA

The Cuban ensembles Cutumba and Baobab play with local musicians for a high-energy performance of Latin music and dance. This has something for everyone.

when	10:00 pm
where	Barrington Festival Main Stage
price	US $39.00

Maori Workshop
NEW ZEALAND

Traditional works of art by Maori and other indigenous artists. During the exhibition, visitors watch the artists create traditional paintings and sculpture.

when	from 10:00 am to 5:00 pm
where	Prescott Park Pavilion
price	US $8.00 / $5.00 students

STEP 2. PAIR WORK. Now make plans with a partner for the weekend of Saturday, March 9 and Sunday, March 10 at the arts festival.

NEED HELP? **Here's language you already know:**

Invitations

Do you want to see
_____ on _____?
Are you free on _____?
There's a [show] at _____.

07251968

Accept and decline

I'd love to go.
Perfect!
See you then.
I'd love to go, but I'm busy on _____.
Maybe some other time.

07251969

Ask for information

What about _____?
What time's the _____?
Where is it?

07251971

Likes and dislikes

I'm a _____ fan.
I'm not really a _____ fan.
That's past my bedtime.
That's not for me.
That's more my style.

07251972

4 ▶ Talk about Musical Tastes

A ▶ **READING WARM-UP.** Is music important in your life?

B ▶ 🎧 **READING.** *Top Notch* interviewed people about music. Read what they said.

Music Makes the World Go 'Round!

ALFREDO LOPEZ
Mexico, sales manager

▶ I'm really into music. I listen to it all the time, especially when I travel. Mexico City is my hometown, but I live and work in Veracruz. My favorite music is pop. I prefer CDs to cassettes because the sound quality is good—better than cassettes. But most of all, I like live concerts.

KYUNG-AH SON
Korea, mother and student of English

▶ I'm a 32-year-old housewife and mother from Seoul. My daughters Han-na and Su-ji keep me very busy all day long, so I don't have much time to listen to music. I listen when they go to sleep. I like dance music, but I don't have much time to dance!

SANDRA PIKE
Canada, managing editor

▶ I'm from St. Johns, Newfoundland, but I live in New York right now. I'm a big rock fan. I also love choral music and R&B, but I always come back to rock. At work, I listen to music, quietly, if the work isn't too complicated. I recently went to a Rolling Stones concert in New York. It was fantastic!

SOURCE: authentic *Top Notch* interviews

C ▶ Read about the people again. Check ☑ each statement <u>true</u>, <u>false</u>, or <u>no information</u>. Then explain your answers.

	true	false	no information
1. Mr. Lopez likes cassettes better than CDs.	☐	☑	☐
2. Mrs. Son listens to music all day long.	☐	☑	☐
3. Ms. Pike doesn't like classical music.	☐	☐	☑

D ▶ **WHAT ABOUT YOU?** Who are you like—Mr. Lopez, Mrs. Son, or Ms. Pike?

> ❝ I'm like Alfredo Lopez. I'm really into music. ❞

LESSON

4 ▶ *Talk about Musical Tastes*

A ◆ READING WARM-UP

Suggested teaching time:	10–15 minutes
Your actual teaching time:	_____

- Model the activity by answering the question yourself. Tell students what kind of music you listen to and when you listen to music; for example: *Music is important in my life. I listen to music at home. I like classical music, and I love jazz.*

- Allow students to say what they can. You can use yes / no questions to get students to say more: *Do you listen to music on the bus? On the train? At work? At home? In the morning? In the afternoon?*

B ◆ 🎧 READING

Suggested teaching time:	15 minutes
Your actual teaching time:	_____

- Before students read the interviews, read the title "Music Makes the World Go 'Round!" out loud. Explain that if something is said to *make the world go 'round,* it means that it is something very important in people's lives. In this expression, *'round* is short for *around.*

- After students read and listen, have them read again independently. Ask students to underline the kinds of music the people like and when they listen to music. (Mr. Lopez: pop, all the time; Mrs. Son: dance music, when they [her daughters] go to sleep; Ms. Pike: rock, choral music, R&B, at work)

Language note: Choral music is music sung by a group of people known as a *chorus* or *choir.* It can be many different kinds of music (classical, religious, jazz, show tunes). R&B is the abbreviation for *rhythm and blues,* another type of music. R&B is a combination of blues and jazz that was developed in the United States by African-American musicians. It is an important precursor of rock and roll.

Option: Draw the chart that follows on the board, without the answers. As a class, fill in the information about Mr. Lopez. Have students copy the chart and complete the information for Mrs. Son and Ms. Pike. [+10 minutes]

	Mr. Lopez	Mrs. Son	Ms. Pike
Occupation	sales manager	housewife and mother	managing editor
Lives in	Veracruz, Mexico	Seoul, Korea	New York, USA
Favorite music	pop	dance music	rock, choral, R&B
Listens to music	all the time	at night	at work

Option: Have students add a column to the chart and write in the same information about themselves. [+5 minutes]

🔘 **Graphic Organizer**

🔘 **Learning Strategies**

C ◆ Read about the people again . . .

Suggested teaching time:	5–10 minutes
Your actual teaching time:	_____

- Have students circle the information that supports their answers.

- Review as a class. Then ask: *When does Mrs. Son listen to music?* (when her daughters go to sleep) *What kind of music does Ms. Pike like?* (rock, choral music, R&B)

Challenge: Ask students the following questions: *Why doesn't Mr. Lopez like cassettes?* (The sound quality isn't good / isn't as good as CDs.) *Do you think Mrs. Son goes to concerts?* (No. / Probably not.) *Why?* (She's too busy taking care of her daughters.) *Do you think Ms. Pike would rather go to a rock concert or an R&B concert?* (a rock concert) *Why?* (It's her favorite music.) [+10 minutes]

🔘 **Extra Reading Comprehension Activities**

D ◆ WHAT ABOUT YOU?

Suggested teaching time:	5 minutes
Your actual teaching time:	_____

- Model the activity. Tell the class which person you are most like; for example, *I'm like Mrs. Son. I don't have much time to listen to music.*

- Following are examples of what your students can say: *I'm like Mr. Lopez. I listen to music all the time. I'm like Mrs. Son. I like dance music. I'm like Ms. Pike. I listen to music at work. / I'm a rock fan.*

Language note: To *like* something means you enjoy it or think it's nice. If someone *is like* someone else, it means they are similar in some way(s) to each other.

Option: With a partner, students answer the question and talk about their favorite kind of music. Then have each student tell the class what his or her partner's favorite music is; for example, *Rosa's favorite music is Latin.* Make sure students use the possessive. [+10 minutes]

TOP NOTCH **INTERACTION**

Suggested teaching time:	25 minutes
Your actual teaching time:	_____

STEP 1

• After students complete the survey, review by asking each question to a different student.

• Read the second question (*What's your favorite kind of music?*) out loud. On the board, list the possible responses (rock, pop, jazz, R&B, Latin, classical, rap / hip-hop, and other). Ask students if they have other kinds of music to add to the list. As you read down the list of choices, students raise their hands when they hear their favorite kind of music. Record the number of students next to each kind of music. See which music type is most popular in your class.

STEP 2

• With a partner, students take turns asking and answering the questions on the survey.

• Students can make an (✗), or some other mark on the survey to note their partner's responses.

• To remind students of the different expressions with *be* from this unit, write the following language on the board:

> *I'm / She's / He's not really a _____ fan.*
> *I'm / She's / He's a _____ fan.*
> *I'm / She's / He's really into _____.*
> *I'm / She's / He's not really into _____.*

• Using the verb *be*, all students should be able to write sentences about the first, second, and last items on the survey; for example:

> *I'm not really a music fan. She's really into music.*
> *My favorite kind of music is pop. Her favorite music is rap.*
> *I'm twenty-five years old. He's twenty.*

• Your students can also write something like:

> *Concerts are not for me.*
> *I'm (not) really into concerts.*

• Stronger false beginners may also be able to write simple present-tense sentences about the third through sixth items on the survey. They may also use Sound Bites language in their answers. For example:

> *I listen to music when I drive. She listens to music all the time.*
> *I don't go to concerts. She goes to concerts.*
> *I listen to CDs. He listens to CDs.*
> *I have forty CDs. She has more than 100 CDs.*
> *Rock music's not my style. He loves rock music.*

Note: The simple present tense is presented in Unit 3.

STEP 3

• Say *I'm a [rock] fan. What about you?* Keep asking individual students until you find someone who is also a fan. Then say *We're both [rock] fans.*

• Do the same with a few other questions; for example, *I listen to the radio. Do you listen to the radio? . . . We both listen to the radio.*

• Each pair tells the class something they have in common; for example, *My partner and I are both pop fans.*

• Pairs tell the class something about themselves and their partner that is different.

EXTRAS (optional)

Workbook: Exercises 13–16
Copy & Go: Activity 8

STEP 1. Take the music survey.

TOP NOTCH — MUSIC SURVEY

Are you a music fan?
○ yes ○ no

What's your favorite kind of music?
○ rock ○ pop ○ jazz
○ R&B ○ Latin ○ classical
○ rap / hip-hop ○ other _____

When do you listen to music?
○ all the time ○ when I study
○ when I drive ○ when I work
○ other _____

Do you go to concerts?
○ yes ○ no

How do you listen to music?
○ cassettes ○ CDs ○ Internet
○ radio ○ other

How many CDs or cassettes do you own?
○ none ○ 1–50 ○ 50–100
○ 100–200 ○ more than 200

Your age [optional]
○ under 20 ○ 20–30
○ 31–40 ○ over 40

STEP 2. PAIR WORK. Compare surveys with your partner. Summarize your answers and your partner's answers on the notepad.

About me	About my partner
I'm a hip-hop fan.	Her favorite music is hip-hop.

STEP 3. DISCUSSION. Use your notepad to tell the class about yourself and your partner.

My partner and I are both hip-hop fans.

A 🎧 LISTENING COMPREHENSION. Listen to the conversations about events. Complete the chart.

Kind of event	Time of event
1. an art exhibit	7:00
2. a concert	10:00
3. a play	8:00

B Complete each sentence with the name of the event.

1. This ____play____ is the most popular of the season.

2. Whose paintings are at the ____art exhibit____ ?

3. Tonight's ____concert____ is the Mexico City String Quartet.

4. Dr. Benson is giving a _____talk_____ on the native plants of the desert. Do you want to go?

5. I'm watching my favorite ____movie____. It just came out on DVD!

C Complete the answers.

1.

2.

3.

4.

1. Where's the bookstore? It's ____on Bank St____.
2. Where's the art exhibit? It's ____at the Smith Gallery____.
3. Where's the movie theater? It's ____around the corner____.
4. Where's the house? It's ____across the street____.

D WRITING. Write about yourself and <u>your</u> tastes in music.

My name is Kazu Sato. I'm from Nagoya.
I'm a classical music fan. I love Mozart.

🎵 **TOP NOTCH SONG**
"Going Out"
Lyrics on last book page.

TOP NOTCH PROJECT
Bring in the entertainment page of your local newspaper. Choose an event. Then write a short note or e-mail message to a classmate inviting him or her to the event. Describe the location of the event.

TOP NOTCH WEBSITE
For Unit 2 online activities, visit the *Top Notch* Companion Website at www.longman.com/topnotch.

UNIT 2
CHECKPOINT

A ⌑ LISTENING COMPREHENSION

Suggested teaching time:	10 minutes
Your actual teaching time:	_____

- Before listening to the conversations, have students look at the chart. Point out that they need to listen for the kind of event and the time of the event.

- After students complete the chart, review the answers:
    What's at the Pine Street Gallery? (an art exhibit)
    What time's the exhibit? (at 7:00)
    What's at the Tip Top? (a concert)
    What kind of music is it? (rap / hip-hop)
    What time's the concert? (at 10:00)
    What's Much Ado About Nothing? (a play)
    What time's the play? (at 8:00)

AUDIOSCRIPT

CONVERSATION 1
F: Hey. There's a new art exhibit opening today at the Pine Street Gallery.
M: Really? Who's the artist?
F: Jessica Miller-Smith. I love her paintings.
M: Me too. What time's the opening?
F: Seven o'clock. What do you think?
M: Let's go.

CONVERSATION 2 [M1 = Arabic]
M1: I feel like some loud music tonight.
M2: Like what?
M1: How about some rap or hip-hop? There's a great concert at the Tip Top.
M2: Hip-Hop at the Tip Top? You're kidding. Who's playing?
M1: Old School.
M2: Oh yeah? What time is the show?
M1: Ten o'clock.

CONVERSATION 3 [F2 = Russian]
F1: What are you doing tonight at eight?
F2: Nothing much. Why?
F1: Well, I've got an extra ticket to *Much Ado About Nothing.*
F2: *Much Ado about Nothing?* What's that?
F1: It's a play ... by Shakespeare. Do you want to go?
F2: Sounds like fun! What time did you say?
F1: Eight o'clock.

B Complete each sentence ...

Suggested teaching time:	5 minutes
Your actual teaching time:	_____

Challenge: Write the following sentences on the board:
  a. *The painter is Diego Rivera.*
  b. *What's the title of the film?*
  c. *No, thanks. Maybe some other time.*
  d. *I'd love to go, but I'm busy tonight.*
  e. *I'm not really a theater fan.*

Tell students to match each sentence in the exercise with a sentence from the board. Students write the letter of the correct match next to the picture on the Student's Book page. (Answers: 1. e 2. a 3. d 4. c 5. b) [+5 minutes]

Option: Ask students about events around town and about themselves; for example:
  What movie is the most popular of the season?
  What's your favorite DVD / play / rock band?
  Where do you go to hear talks?
  Where do you go to see art exhibits / movies?
[+5 minutes]

C Complete the answers

Suggested teaching time:	5–10 minutes
Your actual teaching time:	_____

- Students can ask and answer the questions with a partner.

D WRITING

Suggested teaching time:	10–15 minutes
Your actual teaching time:	_____

- To model the activity, talk about yourself and your tastes in music.

- Write the following on the board:
    Your favorite kind of music:
    Kind of music you're not really into:
    Singers / bands you're a fan of:
    When you listen to music:
    Concerts you go to:

Have the students copy the list and make notes before they begin the writing task.

💿 **Writing Process Worksheets**

💿 *Top Notch Pop* **Song Activities**

***TOP NOTCH* PROJECT**

Idea: Write the following list on the board:

Kind of event:	*Place:*
Date:	*Location:*
Time:	*Ticket prices:*

After students choose an event, have them copy the list and fill in the information that is available. Students use their list to write the note or e-mail message.

- Remind students to use the language listed under NEED HELP? on page 23.

- Students can use the e-mail message on page 18 as a model for their note or e-mail.

Idea: Students exchange notes or send their e-mail messages and respond to their classmates' invitations.

Unit Wrap-Up

Suggested teaching time:	15–20 minutes
Your actual teaching time:	_____

Vocabulary

> **Your students can say . . .**
> two movies (*Past my Bedtime, Lethal Noise*), a talk (*Tina Truffle*), a classical music concert (*Saint Louis Symphony Orchestra*), a rock concert (*Electric Mayhem*), a play (*Phantom of the Opera*)

Ask if students can name one of the movies from the ads (*Past My Bedtime, Lethal Noise*).

Grammar

> **Your students can say . . .**
> *Where's the classical concert?* (It's at Powell Symphony Hall.) *When's Phantom of the Opera?* (It's at 8:55.) *What time's the talk?* (It's at 6:45.)

Option: True or False? Working in pairs, students produce a set of true and false statements about the ads (where they're playing, what time they are, etc.). Regroup students into groups of four. One pair reads their statements to the other pair, who says *True* or *False*. **[+10 minutes]**

Social language

- Before students practice with a partner, have them read the entertainment page. Students decide which events they would like to go to and which events they are not interested in.
- Draw the following chart on the board:

I'd love to go.	That's not for me.

  Students copy the chart and write each event on one side of the chart.
- Refer students to the language listed under NEED HELP? on page 23 for support.
- While following are a couple of examples of what your students can say, students should be encouraged to answer in their *own* way.

> **Your students can say . . .**
> **A:** Do you want to see a movie tonight? *Past My Bedtime's* at the Bedford Movie Theater. **B:** I'm not really into plays. **A:** What about *Lethal Noise?* **B:** That's more my style! **A:** There's a show at 9:30. **B:** Perfect.
>
> **A:** Electric Mayhem's playing at the Cat Club tonight. **B:** I'm not really into rock music. I like jazz. **A:** Well, what about a play? *Phantom of the Opera's* at the Metroplex. **B:** Great!

Challenge: Students compete to see who can produce the longest conversation. **[+10 minutes]**

Option: Competition. Divide students into small groups. One group begins by saying a word or sentence about the picture, and each group follows by saying something more. Groups that can no longer say anything are eliminated until only one group remains. Students can make up information about addresses, locations, and directions as long as their answers are intelligible and complete. **[+10 minutes]**

> **Your students can say . . .**
> a movie, a talk, a play, a concert; *Past My Bedtime* is at the Bedford Movie Theater. It's at 7:00, 9:05, and 11:10. The rock concert is at The Cat Club.

> **Individual oral progress check (optional)**
> Use the illustration on page 27 for an oral test. Have students ask you questions about one of the events. For example, the student could ask *Where is the movie* Lethal Noise? You could answer *It's at the Plaza Theater.* Evaluate students on correctness, intelligibility, and completeness of the questions they ask.

Cumulative Vocabulary Activities

You may wish to use the video for Unit 2 at this point. For video activity worksheets, go to www.longman.com/topnotch.

Complete Assessment Package
Unit 2 Achievement Test

UNIT WRAP-UP

- **Vocabulary.** Look at the ads. Then close your book and write the events you remember.

- **Grammar.** Ask and answer questions with <u>Where</u>, <u>When</u>, and <u>What time</u>.

- **Social language.** Make plans, suggestions, and invitations. Discuss your likes and dislikes.

✓ *Now I can ...*

- ☐ accept or decline an invitation.
- ☐ ask for and give directions.
- ☐ make plans to see an event.
- ☐ talk about musical tastes.

27

UNIT 3

Talking about Families

UNIT GOALS

1 Describe your family
2 Ask about family members
3 Compare people
4 Talk about small families and large famili

A ▷ **TOPIC PREVIEW.** Do you have lots of photos?
Look at Linda's photo album.

I'm Linda. This is my family.

grandparents

grandfather: Cliff   grandmother: Helen

parents

in-laws

uncle: Jack   aunt: Sally

mother: Mary   father: Mark

mother-in-law: Fran   father-in law: Dan

cousins: Pete and Pam

husband: Tom

brother-in-law: Paul

sister-in-law: Rita   brother: Bill

sister: Jane

nephew: Evan   niece: Kim

children

son: Kevin   daughter: Kaye

B 🎧 **VOCABULARY.** Family relationships. Listen and practice.   ❝Who is Pam?❞

❝Pam is Linda's cousin.❞

C ▷ **PAIR WORK.** Ask and answer questions about Linda's family.
Use the vocabulary of family relationships.

UNIT 3

Talking about Families

A TOPIC PREVIEW

Suggested teaching time: 5 minutes
Your actual teaching time: _____

- Model the activity by answering the question yourself; for example:
  Yes. I have lots of photos of my children, Joe and Brianna. Joe is eight years old, and Brianna is ten. I have lots of travel photos of my vacations, too. I have photos of Spain and Turkey. I have photos of my friends at Grant Park in the summer.

- Ask:
  Do you have lots of photos of your family?
  Do you have lots of photos of your friends?
  Do you have lots of photos of your vacations?

- After students look at the photo album, ask:
  Is Linda married or single? (married)
  What's her husband's name? (Tom)

B 🎧 VOCABULARY

Suggested teaching time: 5–10 minutes
Your actual teaching time: _____

- After students listen and repeat the family relationships, pronounce the names and have students repeat.

- Ask the class a few <u>yes</u> / <u>no</u> questions with *be* about Linda's family:
  Is Mark Linda's father? (Yes, he is.)
  Is Jane Linda's daughter? (No, she's not.)
  Is Fran Linda's mother-in-law? (Yes, she is.)
  Is Fran Tom's mother? (Yes, she is.)

- To make sure the meaning of *in-law* is clear, say *Dan is Tom's father. Tom and Linda are married. So Dan is Linda's father-in-law.*

  Another example you can give students: *Bill is Linda's brother. Bill and Rita are married. So Rita is Linda's sister-in-law.*

Option: Using the photo album, introduce other vocabulary for family relationships, such as *granddaughter, grandson, daughter-in-law, son-in-law, great-grandmother,* and *great-grandfather.* For example, say *Linda is Fran and Dan's daughter-in-law. Tom is Mary and Mark's son-in-law.* **[+5 minutes]**

Language note: We refer to a spouse's cousins and aunts/uncles as *my wife's cousin* or *my husband's aunt.* A *great-grandmother* and *great-grandfather* are the grandparents of one of your parents. A *great-granddaughter* and *great-grandson* are the children of one of your grandchildren. *Great great-grandmother* is the mother of your great-grandmother. *Sibling* is another way to refer to your brother or sister.

🔊 **Vocabulary Cards**

C PAIR WORK

Suggested teaching time: 5 minutes
Your actual teaching time: _____

Option: Students ask for the names of Linda's family members; for example, *What's her sister's name?* (Jane)
[+5 minutes]

Challenge: Ask students about Tom's family:
  Who is Tom's father-in-law? (Mark)
  Who is Tom's brother-in-law? (Bill)
  Who is Tom's brother? (Paul)
  Who is Tom's father? (Dan)
  Who is Tom's niece? (Kim)
[+5 minutes]

Option: Students choose three of Linda's family members. For each person, students write three sentences about how that family member is related to other family members; for example:
  Kaye is Kevin's sister. She's Jane's niece. She's Evan's cousin.
[+10 minutes]

D ⌑ SOUND BITES

Suggested teaching time:	5–10 minutes
Your actual teaching time:	_____

Note: The accented speaker in this Sound Bites is Chinese.

- Before students read and listen, have them look at the photo. Point to the first woman. Say *This is Anna.* Point to the second woman. Say *This is May.*
- Ask *What does May have?* (a book, a photo album) If students answer *a book*, have them read the description under Sound Bites.
- After students read and listen, ask:
    Who are the people in May's photos? (her older brother, her sister's kids, her sister)
    Does May have nieces and nephews? (Yes.)

Language note: The word *kids* means the same as *children*. It is used only in informal spoken language but is very commonly used.

- Have students look at the photo album on page 28. Point to Linda's children. Say *Kevin is Kaye's older brother. Kaye is Kevin's younger sister.* Then say *Look at Linda and at her sister Jane. How old do you think Linda is? How old do you think Jane is? Who's older?* (Linda) *Who's younger?* (Jane)

E Check ☑ true, false, or no information.

Suggested teaching time:	5 minutes
Your actual teaching time:	_____

- Students complete the exercise independently.
- Review as a class.
    Where does May's brother live? (in London)
    Where does her sister live? (in Hong Kong)

WHAT ABOUT YOU?

Suggested teaching time:	20–25 minutes
Your actual teaching time:	_____

Language note: A *stepmother* is a woman who is married to your father but who is not your mother. A *stepfather* is a man who is married to your mother but who is not your father. A *stepson* or *stepdaughter* is a child that your husband or wife has from a relationship before your marriage.
    A *half-brother* or *half-sister* is a brother or sister who is the child of only one of your parents. It's common to call half-brothers, *brothers* and half-sisters, *sisters*.

- After students complete the chart, model the activity. Tell the class about your family. For your children or nieces and nephews, you can also give ages; for example:
    My parents are Karen and Robert. I have one brother, Gary. My husband's name is Andrew. I have two children. Marina is five years old, and Evan is two.
- Students should be able to tell the class the name and relationship of their family members. More advanced students may give the ages of their family members.

Common error: When giving ages, students may make the error of saying *She has seven years old* instead of *She is seven years old.* Focus on the message rather than the accuracy of their response. Repeat students' answers in the correct form; for example:
    Student: *She has seven years old.*
    Teacher: *Oh, really? She's seven?*

EXTRAS (optional)

Workbook: Exercises 1–3

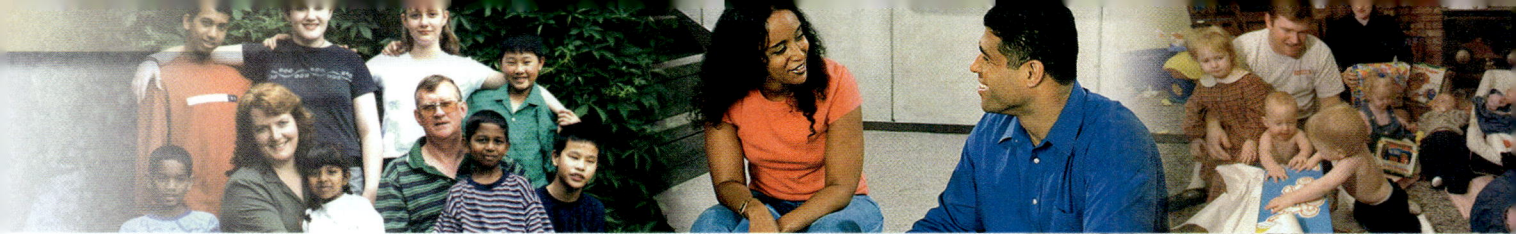

D 🎧 **SOUND BITES.** Read along silently as you listen to a natural conversation.

ANNA: What are you up to?

MAY: I have some photos of my family. Come take a look.

ANNA: Oh great! Let me see.

• • •

ANNA: Who's that guy? **CN**

MAY: That's my older brother. He works for World Tech in London.

ANNA: Really! And who are those two? They're really cute!

MAY: Oh, those are my sister's kids. That's her right here. They live in Hong Kong.

CN **Corpus Notes:**
Native speakers are about twenty times more likely to use the word "guy" than English learners (non-native speakers typically use the word "man"). This word is used quite often in informal American English.

E Check ☑ **true**, **false**, or **no information**.

	true	false	no information
1. Anna has a large family.	☐	☐	☑
2. May has a husband.	☐	☐	☑
3. May's older brother lives in Hong Kong.	☐	☑	☐
4. May is an aunt.	☑	☐	☐
5. Anna thinks May's sister's kids are cute.	☑	☐	☐

WHAT ABOUT **YOU?**

Complete the chart with names of people in your family.

grandparents	
parents	
in-laws	
sisters and brothers	
nieces and nephews	
husband or wife	
children	
aunts and uncles	
cousins	

Tell the class about your family.

❝ My parents are Blanche and Herbert. I have two brothers, David and Paul. ❞

1 Describe Your Family

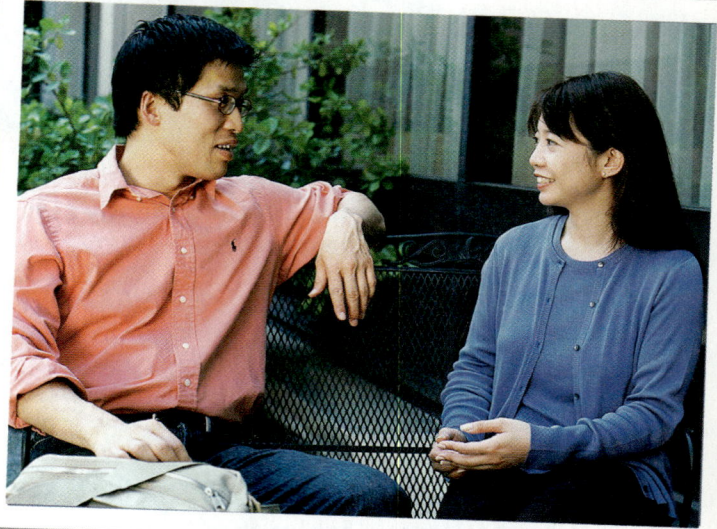

🎧 **CONVERSATION MODEL** Read and listen.

A: Tell me something about your family.

B: Sure. What do you want to know?

A: Well, do you have any brothers or sisters?

B: I have two older brothers and a younger sister.

A: Do they look like you?

B: Not really.

🎧 **Rhythm and intonation practice**

A **GRAMMAR.** The simple present tense

Affirmative statements

I **live** in Rio.   He **lives** in Tokyo.
We **have** two children   She **has** four sisters.
They **work** in a school.   Sam **works** in an office.

Negative statements

I **don't live** in Japan.   She **doesn't live** in Mexico.

Yes / no questions   **Short answers**

Do you **have** any nieces and nephews?   Yes, I do. / No, I don't.
Does he **live** near her parents?   Yes, he does. / No, he doesn't.

GRAMMAR BOOSTER
PAGE G4
For more . . .

B **Complete the questions and answers with the simple present tense.**

1. (have) **A:** __Does__ your cousin __have__ any children?

   B: Yes, she __does__. She __has__ a son and a daughter.

2. (live) **A:** __Do__ your grandparents __live__ in Vancouver?

   B: No, they __don't__. They __live__ in Seattle.

3. (work) **A:** __Does__ your father __work__ in Caracas?

   B: Yes, he __does__. He __works__ at a bank.

4. (look) **A:** __Do__ your sisters __look__ like you?

   B: No, they __don't__. They __look__ like our father.

5. (like) **A:** __Does__ your brother __like__ rock music?

   B: Yes, he __does__. He __likes__ rock music very much.

1 ▶ *Describe Your Family*

🎧 CONVERSATION **MODEL**

Suggested teaching time:	10 minutes
Your actual teaching time:	_____

Language note: If we say someone "looks like" someone, it means that they are similar in some way (*I have blond hair. My sister has blond hair. I look like my sister.*)

• After students read and listen, ask:
  Does the woman have any brothers and sisters? (yes)
  How many brothers and sisters does she have? (two brothers and one sister)
  Do her brothers and sisters look like her? (no / not really)

Culture note: In some cultures it is not polite to ask about other peoples' families. However, in English-speaking countries and many others, it is not only OK to ask about family, but it is expected in friendly conversation.

🎧 Rhythm and intonation practice

Suggested teaching time:	5 minutes
Your actual teaching time:	_____

• After students listen again and repeat, have them underline the questions in the conversation. Ask them what kind of intonation they should use with each question. Make sure they remember to use rising intonation with <u>yes</u> / <u>no</u> questions and falling intonation with information questions.

• Have students repeat each line chorally. Make sure students:

  ○ pause after *Well*.

  ○ use rising intonation with *two older brothers* and falling intonation with *and a younger sister*.

  ○ use the following stress pattern:

┌─**STRESS PATTERN**────────────────────┐

A: Tell me something about your family.

B: Sure. What do you want to know?

A: Well, do you have any brothers or sisters?

B: I have two older brothers and a younger sister.

A: Do they look like you?

B: Not really.

└───────────────────────────────────────┘

🔺 A GRAMMAR

Suggested teaching time:	5–10 minutes
Your actual teaching time:	_____

• Emphasize adding *s* to the base form of the verb for third-person singular. Ask *Where do you live?* Students should answer in the first person; for example, *I live in (name of neighborhood).* Then write on the board *(Name) lives in (name of neighborhood).* Continue until you have statements about several students on the board.

• Point out that we say *I have*, but *he / she / it* **has** (not *haves*).

Option: Ask students to write three simple present tense statements about themselves; for example *I have two sisters. I live in Caracas. I study English.* Then have students write three simple present tense statements about a family member; for example *My sister, Ana, has three kids. She lives in Lima. She's an artist.* **[+5 minutes]**

Option: On the board, write the following verbs:
  live, have, work, study, speak, like, look like

Make a negative statement about yourself, using one of the verbs from the board; for example, *I don't speak French.* Ask a volunteer to change your statement to the third person *[Teacher's name] doesn't speak French.* Have the same student then make a negative statement and have another student change the statement to the third person. Continue until all students have participated. **[+5 minutes]**

Option: Write the questionnaire that follows on the board. On a sheet of paper, students answer the questions with *Yes, I do* or *No, I don't.* Students then switch papers and tell the class or another pair about their partner. Alternatively, students can write about their partner.

  Questionnaire
  1. Do you have a big family?
  2. Do you have any children?
  3. Do you have lots of photos?
  4. Do you work?
  5. Do you speak French?
  6. Do you like Indian food?
  7. Do you like classical music?
  8. Do you look like your mother?
  9. Do you go to concerts?
  10. Do you travel a lot?
[+10 minutes]

🔵 **Grammar Self-Checks**

🔺 B Complete the questions and answers . . .

Suggested teaching time:	10–15 minutes
Your actual teaching time:	_____

• Point out that *do* and *don't* are used with *I, you, we,* and *they. Does* and *doesn't* are used with *he* and *she*.

C ⌂ VOCABULARY

Suggested teaching time:	5 minutes
Your actual teaching time:	_____

Option: Students use the vocabulary to describe their own family members. They can write sentences or tell a partner. Model the activity by writing a sentence about one of your family members on the board. For example:

My cousin (name) is (an only child).

Examples of what students may write are as follows:

My sister (Jae) is single.
My brother (Tim) is married.
My uncle (Ed) is divorced.
My grandmother (Rose) is widowed.
My cousins (Kevin and Kirk) are twins.

[+5 minutes]

◉ **Vocabulary Cards**

D ⌂ LISTENING COMPREHENSION

Suggested teaching time:	10 minutes
Your actual teaching time:	_____

• Point out that students should use one of the vocabulary words to complete the statements.

AUDIOSCRIPT

CONVERSATION 1
F: Nice photos. Who are they?
M: Well, that's my wife, Linda. And those are my in-laws.

CONVERSATION 2 [F = Russian]
M: These two make a cute couple. Who are they?
F: That's my aunt and her ex-husband.
M: Her ex-husband?
F: Yes, they divorced last year.
M: Oh, that's too bad.

CONVERSATION 3
F: Is that your sister?
M: Yes, it is.
F: She's very pretty. Is she married?
M: Not yet.

CONVERSATION 4 [F = Portuguese]
M: Are those your brothers?
F: Actually, no. Those are my cousins. I don't have any brothers or sisters.

CONVERSATION 5
F1: Eddie, I'd like you to meet my sister, Iris.
F2: Nice to meet you, Eddie.
M: Wow! Iris looks just like you! I mean exactly!
F1: Didn't I tell you I had a twin sister?

CONVERSATION 6
F: Is this your brother?
M: Yes, that's my brother Jim.
F: He looks like you. Is he married?
M: Unfortunately, his wife died in 1998.
F: Oh, I'm sorry to hear that.

Language note: When a person gets a divorce, the husband or wife is called an *ex-husband* or *ex-wife*. Two people who are going to be married are *engaged*. The man is the woman's *fiance*, and the woman is the man's *fiancee*.

CONVERSATION **PAIR WORK**

Suggested teaching time:	10–15 minutes
Your actual teaching time:	_____

• Model the conversation with a more advanced student. Play the role of Student A.

• In the first blank, Student B can say *Sure. No problem* or *OK.*

• Student A can ask *Well, do you have any brothers and sisters / children / aunts and uncles / nieces and nephews?*

• To continue the conversation, Student A can use the ideas on the note to ask about other family members. They can also ask questions about the family members already mentioned; for example
  Do they (or Does he / she) look like you?
  Do they (or Does he / she) live in _____? / Where do they (or Where does he / she) live?
  What are their names? or What is his / her name?
  How old are they? or How old is he / she?
  What do they do? or What does he / she do?

Option: Ask a few students to tell what they remember about their partner's family. Say *Tell me something about [Name's] family.* Make sure they use the third-person singular verb forms. **[+10 minutes]**

◉ **Pair Work Cards**

EXTRAS (optional)

Grammar Booster
Workbook: Exercises 4–9
Copy & Go: Activity 9

C 🎧 **VOCABULARY.** **Marital status and relationships.** **Listen and practice.**

They're **single**.

They're **married**.

They're **divorced**.

She's **widowed**.

He's **an only child**. **CN**

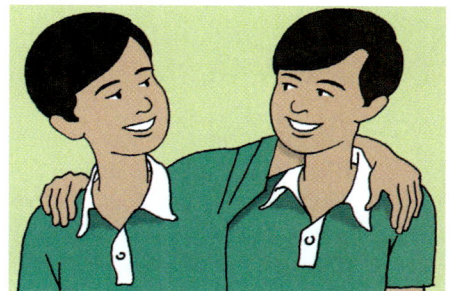

They're **twins**.

D 🎧 **LISTENING COMPREHENSION.** **Listen to the conversations carefully.**
Use the vocabulary to complete the statements about the people.

1. He's ___married___.

2. They're ___divorced___.

3. She's ___single___.

4. She's ___an only child___.

5. They're ___twins___.

6. He's ___widowed___.

CONVERSATION
PAIR WORK

**Describe your family. Use the guide,
or create a new conversation.**

A: Tell me something about your family.

B: _____. What do you want to know?

A: Well, do you have any _____?

B: _____ …

Continue the conversation in your <u>own</u> way.

To continue:
How about children?
Aunts and uncles?
Nieces and nephews?

CN **Corpus Notes:**
Many English learners make the mistake of saying
"He's **the** only child" instead of "He's **an** only child."

2 Ask about Family Members

🎧 CONVERSATION MODEL Read and listen.

A: So what does your sister do?
B: She's a graphic designer. She works at Panorama Designs.
A: That's great! How about your brother?
B: He doesn't have a job right now. He's a student.

🎧 **Rhythm and intonation practice**

A GRAMMAR. The simple present tense: information questions

What does your younger brother **do**?   He works in a bank.
What do your parents **do**?   They're artists.
Where do your grandparents **live**?   They live near me.
Where does your sister **live**?   She lives in Toronto.
When do you **see** your cousins?   We visit them every summer.
How many children **do** you **have**?   I have two—a boy and a girl.
Who works at Panorama?   My sister does.

GRAMMAR BOOSTER
PAGE G5
For more . . .

B Complete the conversations with the simple present tense.

1. **A:** My father ___works___ in a restaurant.
   B: Really? _What does_ he do?
   A: He's a chef.

2. **A:** My brother ___lives___ with his family in Sydney.
   B: _How many_ kids ___does___ he have?
   A: Three. I've got three nephews.
   B: That's great!

Sydney, Australia

3. **A:** _Where does_ your sister live?
   B: She ___lives___ in Bangkok with her family.
   A: _When do you_ see them?
   B: I visit them every year.

Bangkok, Thailand

LESSON
2 ▶ *Ask about Family Members*

🎧 CONVERSATION **MODEL**

Suggested teaching time:	10 minutes
Your actual teaching time:	_____

- After students read and listen, point to the man in the photo. Ask:
  Does he have any brothers or sisters? (Yes, he does. He has a sister and a brother.)
  What's his sister's occupation? (She's a graphic designer.)
  Where does she work? (Panorama Designs)
  Does his brother work? (No, he doesn't. He's a student.)

🎧 Rhythm and intonation practice

Suggested teaching time:	5 minutes
Your actual teaching time:	_____

- Ask students to underline the questions in the conversation and indicate what kind of intonation they should use with them. (Both are information questions with falling intonation.)
- Have students repeat each line chorally. Make sure students:
  ○ accurately imitate the intonation for *That's great!*
  ○ use the following stress pattern:

STRESS PATTERN

A: • — • • — •
So what does your sister do?

B: — • • • — • • • — •
She's a graphic designer. She works at
— • — • • —
Panorama Designs.

A: — — • • • — •
That's great! How about your brother?

B: — • • — • • • • — • — •
He doesn't have a job right now. He's a student.

🔺A GRAMMAR

Suggested teaching time:	5–10 minutes
Your actual teaching time:	_____

- To make it clear how to form information questions in the simple present tense, write the following on the board:

  question word + do / does + subject + base form
  of verb

Write the first sentence from the Grammar box on the board, putting each part of the sentence under the appropriate heading.

- If necessary, make the meaning of *How many?* clear. Ask:
  How many students are in this class?
  How many pages are in our book?
  How many days are in (this month)?

- After reviewing the examples in the Grammar box, ask each information question to a different student; for example, *Do you have a younger brother? What does your younger brother do?* Students should respond with their own answers, not the answers in the Grammar box.

Option: Do a quick drill to practice *do* vs. *does*. Call out subjects and have the class respond with *do* or *does* and the correct pronoun; for example:
  your daughter (What does she do?)
  his parents (What do they do?)
  you (What do you do?)
  her mother-in-law (What does she do?)
  Tom (What does he do?)
  Tom and Linda (What do they do?)
  his ex-wife (What does she do?)
  they (What do they do?)
[+5 minutes]

Option: Write the following questions on the board:
  What do you do?
  Where do you live?
  When do you go out?
  What time do you go to bed?
  How many languages do you speak?

In pairs, students ask and answer questions. Make sure students answer in complete sentences. After both students have asked and answered all the questions, have them write sentences about their partner, using their partner's answers: *My partner works with children. She lives in . . .* , etc. [+10 minutes]

🔵 Grammar Self-Checks

🔶B Complete the conversations . . .

Suggested teaching time:	5 minutes
Your actual teaching time:	_____

- Point out that students will need to write more than one word in some of the spaces.

- To check their work, have students read each conversation with a partner.

C > PAIR WORK

Suggested teaching time:	5–10 minutes
Your actual teaching time:	_____

- Following are examples of questions your students can write:

  Yes / no questions:

  Do you have any brothers or sisters / children / aunts and uncles / nieces and nephews?
  Do you look like your parents / brothers or sisters?
  Do you have a big family?
  Do you live in (your town)?
  Do you work?
  Do you like _____ music?

  Information questions:

  What do you do?
  What does your (family member) do?
  Where do you live?
  Where does your (family member) live?
  When do you see your (family member)?
  What time do you go to work / school?
  How many children / brothers and sisters / nieces and nephews / cousins do you have?

Option: Do the Pair Work in two steps. First have students write only the three yes / no questions first. Students exchange papers, write answers, and return the paper to their partner. Then, based on their partner's answers, students write the three information questions. This way students can ask information questions about their partners' family members. **[+10 minutes]**

D > 🎧 PRONUNCIATION

Suggested teaching time:	5 minutes
Your actual teaching time:	_____

Option: For more practice blending sounds, have students read out loud the questions in the Grammar boxes on pages 30 and 32. **[+5 minutes]**

🔘 **Pronunciation Activities**

CONVERSATION **PAIR WORK**

Suggested teaching time:	10–15 minutes
Your actual teaching time:	_____

- Have students practice the conversation with the same partner as in the Conversation Pair Work on page 31 or with someone whose family they already know something about.
- After students ask about family members' occupations, they can ask other questions about the same family members. For example:

  Where does your _____ live?
  When do you see your _____?
  How many children does your _____ have?

🔘 **Pair Work Cards**

🔘 **Learning Strategies**

EXTRAS (optional)

Grammar Booster
Workbook: Exercises 10–15
Copy & Go: Activity 10

🔘 **Pronunciation Supplements**

4. **A:** _____What do_____ your in-laws do?

B: They both _____work_____ at City Hospital. They're doctors.

A: Really? Is your wife a doctor, too?

B: No, she _____works_____ in an office.

5. **A:** My older sister and my younger brother both _____have_____ kids.

B: _____How many_____ nieces and nephews _____do_____ you _____have_____?

A: I have six. Four nieces and two nephews.

6. **A:** Where _____does_____ your husband _____work_____?

B: He works at Harry's Shoes, on Franklin Street.

A: Oh, I know that place! What _____does_____ he _____do_____ there?

B: He's a manager.

◆ **C** ▷ **PAIR WORK.** On a separate sheet of paper, write three <u>yes</u> / <u>no</u> questions and three information questions for your partner. Write answers to your partner's questions.

> Do you have any brothers or sisters?

> Yes, I do. I have three older brothers
>
> and two younger sisters.

◆ **D** ▷ 🎧 **PRONUNCIATION.** **Blending sounds.** Listen and repeat the questions.

/dʌʃi/
1. <mark>Does she</mark> have any children?

/dʌʃi/
What <mark>does she</mark> do?

/dʌzi/
2. <mark>Does he</mark> live near you?

/dʌzi/
What <mark>does he</mark> do?

CONVERSATION
PAIR WORK

Ask about your partner's family. Use the guide, or create a new conversation.

A: So what does your _____ do?

B: _____.

A: _____. How about your _____?

B: _____ …

Continue the conversation in your <u>own</u> way.

3 *Compare People*

A 🎧 **VOCABULARY.** **Similarities and differences.** **Listen and practice.**

How are you <u>alike</u>?

We **look alike**.

We wear **similar** clothes.
CN

We **both** like basketball.
She likes basketball, and
I do **too**.

She doesn't like fish,
and I don't **either**.

How are you <u>different</u>?

We **look different**.

We wear **different** clothes.

He likes rock music,
but I like classical.

He likes coffee,
but I don't.

CN **Corpus Notes:**
Students frequently misspell "similar." They often spell it "simillar"
or "simmilar." Be sure students don't make this common error.

B 🎧 **LISTENING COMPREHENSION.** **Listen to Frank Pascal talk
about himself and his brother, Philippe. Listen for their similarities
and differences. Check ☑ the statements that are true.**

Frank and Philippe ...	
1. ☐ live in the same country	☑ live in different countries
2. ☐ look alike	☑ look different
3. ☑ have similar occupations	☐ have very different occupations
4. ☑ like the same music	☐ like different music
5. ☐ read the same things	☑ read different things
6. ☐ like the same kinds of movies	☑ like different kinds of movies

LESSON

3 ▸ *Compare People*

A 🎧 VOCABULARY

Suggested teaching time:	5–10 minutes
Your actual teaching time:	_____

Language note: To *be like* someone means that you are very similar. (*I am like him. She is like me.*)

- As a class, give names to the four people pictured; for example, *Krista, Trista, Alexander,* and *Joe.* Ask:
  Does [Krista] like basketball? (Yes, she does.)
  Does [Trista] like basketball? (Yes, she does.)
  Does [Krista] like fish? (No, she doesn't.)
  Does [Trista] like fish? (No, she doesn't.)
  Does [Joe] like rock music? (Yes, he does.)
  Does [Alexander] like rock music? (No, he doesn't.)
  What kind of music does [Alexander] like? (He likes classical.)
  Does [Joe] like coffee? (Yes, he does.)
  Does [Alexander] like coffee? (No, he doesn't.)

Challenge: Students find one thing they have in common with each person in the class. Students pair up and ask each other questions until they find some way that they are alike. They write a sentence and then move on to ask and answer questions with another classmate. For example:
A: *How many brothers and sisters do you have?*
B: *I have two sisters. How about you?* **A:** *I have one brother.* **B:** *Do you like hip-hop music?* **A:** *Yes, I do.*
B: *I do too!*

Students A and B write (*Partner's name*) *and I both like hip-hop music.*

To vary the activity, you can have students find one way they are different from each person in the class instead. **[+10 minutes]**

💿 **Vocabulary Cards**

B 🎧 LISTENING COMPREHENSION

Suggested teaching time:	15–20 minutes
Your actual teaching time:	_____

- Have students look at the Vocabulary. Point to the first picture under *How are you alike?* Say *They both wear glasses.* Then point to the first picture under *How are you different?* Ask *Do they both wear glasses?* (no) Point and say *He wears glasses, but he doesn't.*

- Students read the list of statements before listening to the interview. The first time through, tell students to listen only for how Frank and his brother Philippe are alike and have them take notes.

- Tell students to listen the second time only for how Frank and Philippe are different. Students should again take notes.

After students complete the exercise, ask some questions about the interview:

1. *Where does Frank live?* (He lives in the U.S.) *Where does Philippe live?* (He lives in France.)

2. *What color hair does Frank have?* (He has brown hair.) *What color hair does Philippe have?* (He has blond hair.)

3. *What kind of work do they do?* (They work in education.)

4. *What kind of music do they like?* (They like rock.)

5. *What does Frank read?* (He reads books.) *What does Philippe read?* (He reads newspapers and magazines.)

6. *What kind of movies does Frank like?* (He likes American movies.) *What kind of movies does Philippe like?* (He likes French movies.)

🌐 **Learning Strategies**

AUDIOSCRIPT

[M = French]
F: We're talking today with Frank Pascal about his family. Thank you, Frank, for taking the time to talk with us today.
M: Thank *you.* It's my pleasure.
F: So Frank, you're from France originally, right?
M: That's right. My family lives in France—in Normandy. But I live in the U.S. now.
F: So how many brothers and sisters do you have in all?
M: I have one brother and two sisters.
F: Well that's a pretty big family, isn't it?
M: In France it is.
F: Frank, let's talk first about you and your brother. What's his name?
M: Philippe.
F: Philippe. Does he look like you?
M: Not really. He's a lot taller and bigger than me. And he has blond hair. My hair is brown.
F: Is that all?
M: And he wears glasses. I don't.
F: How about the work you do? Similar or different?
M: Quite similar, actually. Philippe started as a teacher, and so did I. And today, we both still work in education.
F: How else are you alike?
M: Well, we both like rock music. But neither of us likes really loud music. Both of us are big basketball fans. And soccer. And we both play basketball, too.
F: Anything else?
M: Our personalities are pretty similar. We both enjoy humor. He likes to joke and laugh a lot and so do I.
F: And how are you different?
M: Well, I like to read books. But he reads newspapers and magazines mostly. Also, Philippe likes French movies and I prefer American movies.

T34

TOP NOTCH **INTERACTION**

Suggested teaching time:	25–30 minutes
Your actual teaching time:	_____

STEP 1

• Model the activity by comparing yourself to one of your family members. Copy the notepad on the board, filling in your information; for example:

Person's name: *Isabel*
Relationship to you: *sister*

How are you alike? / How are you different?
We wear similar clothes. / *We look different.*
We both like coffee. / *She likes baseball, but I don't.*
She speaks two languages, / *She's single, but I'm married.*
and I do too.

STEP 2

• In their conversations, students focus on the family member they wrote about in Step 1.

• Model the activity with a more advanced student. Tell something about the family member you wrote about in Step 1.

• Remind students to refer to NEED HELP? to support them in their role play.

STEP 3

• Students choose two people in their families to compare.

• Have students make notes about how the two are alike and how they are different.

Option: To get started comparing the two people in their family, students can make notes on a Venn diagram. In the area where the circles overlap, students write how the two people are alike. In the areas to the left and right, students write how each person is different; for example:

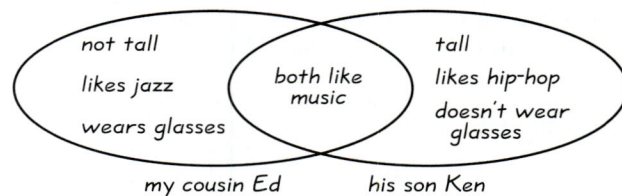

not tall
likes jazz
wears glasses

both like music

tall
likes hip-hop
doesn't wear glasses

my cousin Ed   his son Ken

[**+10 minutes**]

Writing Process Worksheets

EXTRAS (optional)

Copy & Go: Activity 11

STEP 1. On the notepad, write sentences comparing yourself to one member of your family.

The person's name and relationship to you:

How are you alike?   How are you different?

STEP 2. PAIR WORK. First tell your partner about the person you wrote about. Then discuss other people in your families.

" My brother and I are different ... "

NEED HELP? Here's language you already know:

Ask about families

Tell me about your ____.
Do you have any ____?
How many ____ do you have?
How about ____?

How old ____?
What do / does your ____ do?
Where do / does your ____ live?

Similarities and differences

How are you alike?
How are you different?
Do you look alike?
Do you both ____?

STEP 3. WRITING. Write a paragraph comparing two people in your family.

My cousin Ed and his son Ken are very different. They don't look the same. Ken is very tall, but Ed isn't. They don't like the same music. Ken likes hip-hop, and he plays music very loud. Ed likes jazz, but Ken says jazz is boring.

FREE PRACTICE

4 ▶ Talk about Small Families and Large Families

A ▶ **READING WARM-UP.** Do you come from a small family or a large family?

B ▶ 🎧 **READING.** Read about large and small families.

Families Come in All Sizes

On November 18, 1997, Bobbi and Kenny McCaughey of the United States were the happy parents of one child—their daughter Mikayla. The next day, they had eight children. Bobbi gave birth to septuplets—three more daughters and four new sons. At first it was very hard. They lived in a very small house and they needed lots of help. Now it is better. They live in a big house and the children help with the housework.

Barry and Julia Rollings of Canberra, Australia started with just two daughters: Alix and Briony. Then, between 1991 and 1998, they adopted six more children—five sons and one daughter. Barry also has four adult children from his first marriage. People always ask them, "How many kids do you have now?"

Julia says, "I love my family and my life!" And she adds, "Barry likes housework."

In traditional Chinese culture, families were very large. But in mainland China today, with a population of over 1,000,000,000 people, the government has a one-child policy: in most places, a family can have only one child. In the future, there will be no aunts, uncles, or cousins. Why? Because there will be no sisters or brothers.

Many people don't agree with the one-child policy. But all agree that one advantage of a small family is that parents have more money for their children.

SOURCE: www.geocities.com/juro/madhouse and www.msnbc.com

C ▶ **Now read the following statements. Figure out if they are true or false, based on the information in the reading.**

	true	false	no information given
1. Septuplets are seven children born at the same time.	✓	☐	☐
2. Alix and Briony Rollings are twins.	☐	☐	✓
3. Julia Rollings is Barry's first wife.	☐	✓	☐
4. The traditional Chinese family was a one-child family.	☐	✓	☐

LESSON

4 — Talk about Small Families and Large Families

A — READING WARM-UP

Suggested teaching time:	5 minutes
Your actual teaching time:	_____

• Model the activity by answering the question yourself. Also, describe the size of your family; for example:

  I come from a small family. I have four people in my family: my mother, my father, me, and my younger brother.

• Go around the classroom and ask students if they come from a small family or a large family. Ask *How many people are in your family?*

B — 🎧 READING

Suggested teaching time:	10–15 minutes
Your actual teaching time:	_____

• Before reading, have students look at the photos. Point to each photo and ask *How many children do they have?* (McCaughey family: 8; Rollings family: 8; Chinese family: 1)

• After reading, ask:

  Where is each family from? (the U.S., Australia, China)
  How many sons do the McCaugheys have? (four)
  How many daughters do the McCaugheys have? (four)
  How many of the Rollings' children are adopted? (six)
  Do people have large families in China today? (no)
  How many children do Chinese families usually have? (one)

🔵 **Learning Strategies**

C — Now read the following statements . . .

Suggested teaching time:	5–10 minutes
Your actual teaching time:	_____

• Have students underline the sentences in the reading that show that items 3 and 4 are false. (3. Barry also has four adult children from his first marriage.; 4. In traditional Chinese culture, families were very large.)

Challenge: After students complete the exercise, ask some questions about each family:

  When is the McCaughey septuplets' birthday?
   (November 18, 1997)
  How many children does Barry Rollings have?
   (twelve)
  Does everyone like the one-child policy in China? (no)
  Why do you think people don't like the one-child policy?
   (they want to have more than one child)
[+5 minutes]

Challenge: Ask the class *Which family would you want to be a member of? Why?* **[+5 minutes]**

Language note: *Septuplets* are seven children born at the same time to the same mother. *Triplets* are three children born at the same time to the same mother; also: *quadruplets* (four), *quintuplets* (five), *sextuplets* (six), *octuplets* (eight).

🔵 **Extra Reading Comprehension Activities**

◆D〉 According to the reading . . .

Suggested teaching time:	10 minutes
Your actual teaching time:	_____

• To make sure students understand *advantage* and *disadvantage*, write the following on the board:
> flight attendant
> *1. They can travel. They can see lots of places.*
> *2. They don't see their families a lot.*

Then ask *Which one is an advantage of work as a flight attendant?* (item 1) *Which one is a disadvantage?* (item 2)

TOP NOTCH **INTERACTION**

Suggested teaching time:	15–20 minutes
Your actual teaching time:	_____

STEP 1

• Before students look at the *Top Notch* Interaction, have them close their books. Ask the class the following questions and write one answer for each on the board:
> *What's an advantage of a small family?*
> *What's a disadvantage of a small family?*
> *What's an advantage of a large family?*
> *What's a disadvantage of a large family?*

Students use ideas suggested by the class and their own ideas to complete the notepad. Some, but not all, students might produce *can / can't / there is / there are* on their notepad.

STEP 2

• Model the activity by telling the class what kind of family you prefer. Explain why.

Following is a list of things your students might say. Not all students will be able to produce the full utterances:

┌─ **Your students can say . . .** ─────────┐
I prefer a small family because . . .
. . . parents have more time / money for the children.
. . . there are not too many people in the house.
. . . small families can travel and go to movies, concerts, restaurants, etc.

I prefer a large family because . . .
. . . the children can help with the housework.
. . . large families have lots of aunts, uncles, and cousins.
. . . families with lots of children are happy.
└──────────────────────────────────────┘

Option: Take a poll. Ask *Who prefers a small family? Who prefers a large family?* Have students raise hands to indicate which one they prefer. Write the results on the board. Next, ask the students who prefer a small family: *Who comes from a small family?* Of the students who prefer a large family, ask *Who comes from a large family?* Write the results on the board. **[+10 minutes]**

Challenge: Ask the class *Do people usually prefer the same kind of family as the one they came from or a different kind of family?* **[+5 minutes]**

EXTRAS (optional)

> **Workbook:** Exercises 16–19
> **Copy & Go:** Activity 12

D **According to the reading, what are the advantages and disadvantages of small and large families? Match the information in the two columns.**

<u>a</u> **1.** an advantage of a small family

<u>d</u> **2.** an advantage of a large family

<u>c</u> **3.** a disadvantage of a small family

<u>b</u> **4.** a disadvantage of a large family

a. Families have more money.

b. There are too many people in the house.

c. Children don't have brothers, sisters, aunts, uncles, or cousins.

d. Children help their parents with the housework.

TOP NOTCH INTERACTION • *Small or Large?*

STEP 1. Write some more advantages and disadvantages of small and large families on the notepad.

A Small Family

Advantages	Disadvantages

A Large Family

Advantages	Disadvantages

STEP 2. DISCUSSION. What kind of family do you prefer: a small family or a large family? Tell your class why.

I prefer a small family because the parents have more time for the children.

I disagree. I think a large family is better. A family with lots of children is a happy family.

UNIT 3
CHECKPOINT

A 🎧 **LISTENING COMPREHENSION.** Listen carefully to the people talking about their families. Check ☑ if the person has a big or small family.

		big family	small family
1.	Hassan	☑	☐
2.	Karen	☐	☑
3.	Andrew	☐	☑
4.	Sandra	☑	☐

B 🎧 **Listen again.** How many children are there in each family?

1. _____eight_____   2. _____one_____   3. _____two_____   4. _____seven_____

C **Complete the sentences with the correct word or words.**

1. Jason doesn't have any brothers and sisters. He's an ___only child___ .

2. Harry is Henry's brother. They have the same birthdate. They are ___twins___ .

3. Nick's sister has three daughters. They are Nick's ___nieces___ .

4. Gary is Teresa's husband. Gary's parents are Teresa's ___in-laws___ .

5. Randy's mother has a niece and a nephew. They are Randy's ___cousins___ .

6. John and Carl are brothers. John's wife is Carl's ___sister-in-law___.

7. Oliva is Ellen's mother. Alice is Ellen's daughter. Oliva is Alice's ___grandmother___.

D **WRITING.** Read about Susan and Peter Wolf. Then write about them. How are they different? How are they similar?

> Susan Wolf, 28, is the manager of a clothing store in Chicago. She is short and blonde and she wears glasses. Susan is a big fan of classical music. She goes to classical concerts and has lots of classical music CDs. She likes some other kinds of music, too, but she doesn't like hip-hop or rock.
>
> Peter Wolf, 24, is Susan's younger brother. He is a rock musician and lives in Seattle. Peter has blond hair. He is tall and he wears glasses. Peter loves rock music. He doesn't like any other kind of music. He goes to rock concerts and has lots of CDs of rock musicians.

Peter is a rock music fan, but Susan likes classical music.

They both have blond hair.

TOP NOTCH PROJECT
Make a family scrapbook. Bring in photos from home. Tell your class about your family.

TOP NOTCH WEBSITE
For Unit 3 online activities, visit the *Top Notch* Companion Website at www.longman.com/topnotch.

UNIT 3
CHECKPOINT

A 🎧 LISTENING COMPREHENSION

Suggested teaching time:	10 minutes
Your actual teaching time:	_____

• Point out that *large* and *big* have the same meaning.

B 🎧 Listen again . . .

Suggested teaching time:	5 minutes
Your actual teaching time:	_____

Challenge: Students listen for one disadvantage of a large family and one disadvantage of a small family. [+10 minutes]

AUDIOSCRIPT

1. HASSAN [M = Arabic]
   M: Hi. My name is Hassan. I come from a pretty large family. There are actually ten of us, if you can believe it. There's my mom and dad, of course. And I've got seven brothers and sisters. It was a little crowded around the house sometimes, and sometimes I really wanted to be an only child. But all in all, it was great.

2. KAREN
   F: My name's Karen. And I'm the daughter of Harry and Betty Halter of Long Beach, California. My father is a teacher and my mom's a homemaker. I was an only child. It was a little lonely sometimes, but I had lots of friends, and my parents loved me. And now I'm a teacher, too.

3. ANDREW [M = Chinese]
   M: You want my name first? OK. My name is Andrew. Andrew Yee. I have a younger brother, James. That's it. He's a computer programmer. He lives in Spain right now so I don't see him much. What else? Um, my father is retired—he stopped working last year. And my mom works at a department store.

4. SANDRA [F = Spanish]
   F: My name's Sandra. You want to hear about my family? OK, let me see. Well, there's, uh-whew!—there are a lot of us. Let's see. Uh, Juan, Marta, Ana, and me. I'm in the middle. Arturo, Enrique, and Isabella. OK, that's seven kids in all. But you know something? We're a very happy family.

C Complete the sentences . . .

Suggested teaching time:	5–10 minutes
Your actual teaching time:	_____

• To review, have students read their answers out loud.

D WRITING

Suggested teaching time:	10–15 minutes
Your actual teaching time:	_____

• If helpful, have students write one paragraph about how the brother and sister are alike and one paragraph about how they are different.

Your students can say . . .

Susan and Peter Wolf look alike. They both have blond hair and wear glasses. Susan likes music, and Peter does too. They both go to concerts and have lots of CDs.

Susan and Peter Wolf are different. She's short, but he's tall. She's a manager, but he's a musician. Susan is a classical music fan, but Peter likes rock. She likes some other kinds of music, but her brother doesn't.

Option: Students use a Venn diagram to compare Susan and Peter Wolf. They write how they are alike in the area where the circles overlap. In the non-overlapping areas, they write how each is different. [+10 minutes]

28
a manager
short
likes classical music
likes some other kinds of music

wear glasses
blond hair
go to concerts
have lots of CDs

24
a musician
tall
likes rock music
doesn't like other kinds of music

Susan Wolf   Peter Wolf

TOP NOTCH PROJECT

• To talk about their photos, students can say *That's . . .* for one person and *Those are . . .* for two or more people.

Idea: Model the activity. Bring in your own photos and tell the class about your family. For example:
   That's my sister. Her name is Julia. That's her husband, Jack. They live in New York. Those are their two children. Sophia is five years old, and Sam is three. Sophia looks like her father . . .

Idea: Write the questions that follow on the board. Say *Tell the class about the people in your photos. Use the questions on the board for ideas.*
   What are their names? How old are they?
   Where do they work? / What do they do?
   Where do they live?
   Are they married, single, divorced, or widowed?
   Do they have any children?
   Who do they look like?
   What do they like?

UNIT WRAP-UP

Suggested teaching time:	15–20 minutes
Your actual teaching time:	_____

- On the board, write *Kirk Douglas*, *Michael Douglas*, and *Catherine Zeta-Jones*.
- Find out if students know who those three people are. Ask *Who are they?* (They're actors.)
- If you think your students will know, ask if they know any movies the three actors have been in.
- Students write movie titles on the board.

Vocabulary

- If necessary, review the terms *ex-husband* and *ex-wife*. Use the Douglas family tree. For example, *Diandra Douglas is Michael Douglas's ex-wife.*
- Point out that to make *Douglas* or *Jones* possessive, you add *'s* /ɪz/: *Douglas's, Jones's.* Pronounce each of these and have students repeat.

Your students can say . . .
Diana Dill is Michael Douglas's mother. David Jones is Catherine Zeta-Jones's father. Michael Douglas has one brother and two half-brothers*. Catherine is Cameron Douglas's stepmother. Carys Douglas is Michael and Catherine's daughter.

Option: Identification. Students work in pairs. One student points to a person or people in the picture. The other makes statements. For example:
> *He's an actor.*
> *She has two brothers.*
> *They're divorced.*
> *He's an only child.*

This can also be done in reverse. One student makes a statement, and the other points to the appropriate picture. **[+10 minutes]**

Option: Name Game. Have students write two sentences about one person in the family tree. For example, students could write *She is married. She had two brothers* about Catherine Zeta-Jones. Students then pass the sentences to a partner who must write the name of the person described. **[+10 minutes]**

Grammar

Your students can say . . .
Does (name) have any (brothers or sisters / children / aunts and uncles?)
How many brothers and sisters does he / she have?
How many children do (names) have?
What does (name) do?
Where does Catherine Zeta-Jones come from? (Wales)
Where does Catherine-Zeta-Jones live? (in the U.S.)
When is Michael Douglas's / Catherine Zeta-Jones's birthday? (September 25)

Option: Competition. Divide class into two teams. To begin, a student from Team A holds up the textbook and points to any person on the page. This student then points to a student on Team B who must make a sentence about the person. If the sentence is grammatically correct, Team B is awarded one point. If the statement is incorrect, Team A has a chance to correct the sentence for one point. The teams then reverse roles. **[+10 minutes]**

Writing

Your students can say . . .
Kirk Douglas is Michael Douglas's father. Cameron Douglas is Michael Douglas's son. Kirk, Michael, and Cameron have the same occupation. They are actors.
   Michael Douglas is married. His wife is Catherine Zeta-Jones. She's an actress. She's from Wales, but she lives in the U.S. Michael and Catherine have the same birthday. They have two children, Dylan Michael and Carys. Cameron is Catherine's stepson.

Individual oral progress check (optional)
Use the family tree on page 39 for an oral test. Point to a person on the page and have individual students make a statement about that person. For example, if you point to Diandra Douglas students could say *She has a son. Michael Douglas is her ex-husband.* Evaluate students on correctness, intelligibility, and completeness.

Cumulative Vocabulary Activities

You may wish to use the video for Unit 3 at this point. For video activity worksheets, go to www.longman.com/topnotch.

**Complete Assessment Package
Unit 3 Achievement Test**

---

* Michael Douglas's half-brother, Eric, died July 2004.

UNIT WRAP-UP
- **Vocabulary.** Look at the Douglas family tree. Talk about the family relationships.
  Kirk Douglas is Michael Douglas's father ...
- **Grammar.** Ask and answer questions.
  Does Michael Douglas have any brothers or sisters?
- **Writing.** Write about the Douglas family.

The Douglas Family

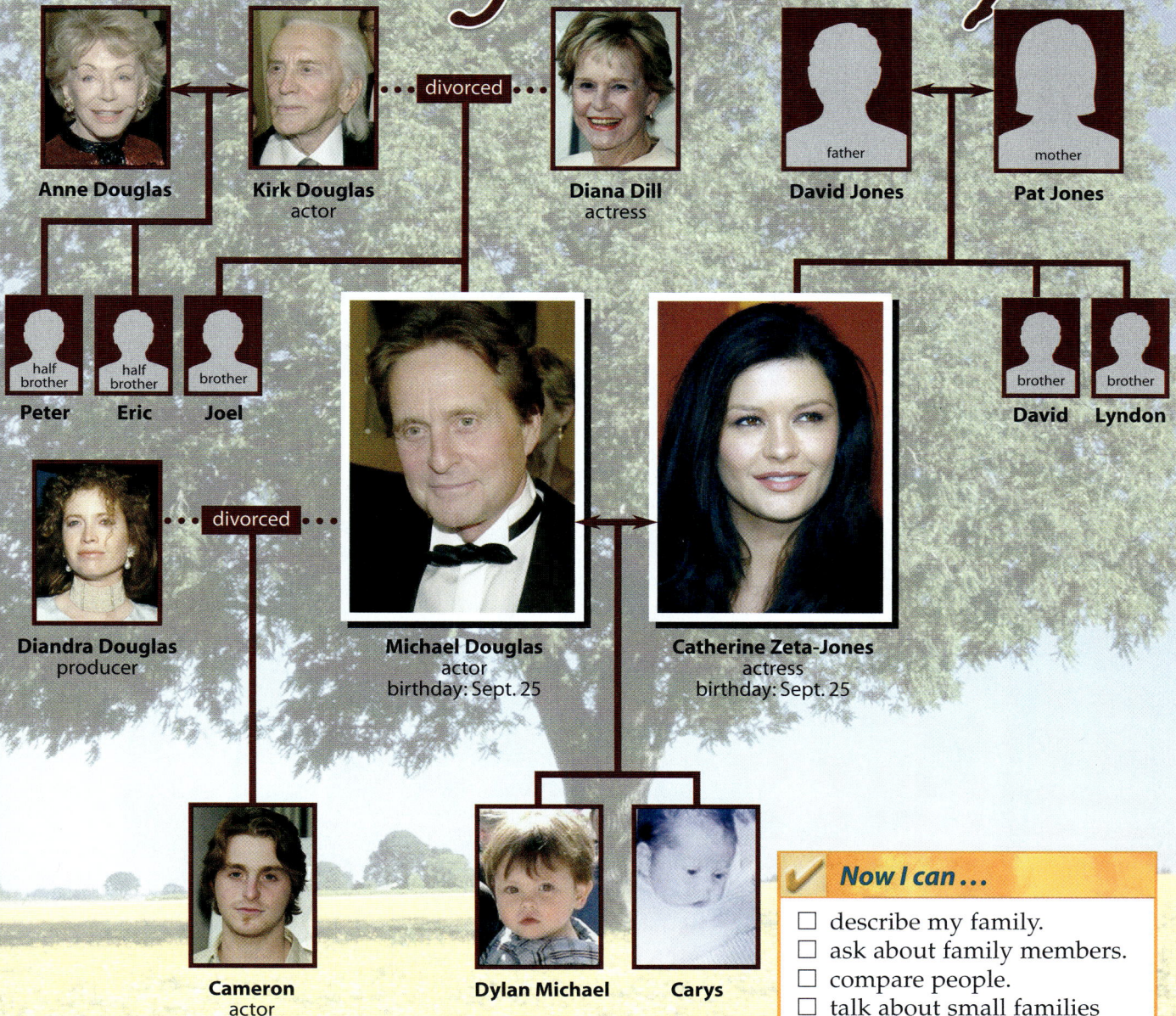

Anne Douglas

Kirk Douglas
actor

... divorced ...

Diana Dill
actress

father
David Jones

mother
Pat Jones

half brother
Peter

half brother
Eric

brother
Joel

brother
David

brother
Lyndon

Diandra Douglas
producer

... divorced ...

Michael Douglas
actor
birthday: Sept. 25

Catherine Zeta-Jones
actress
birthday: Sept. 25

Cameron
actor

Dylan Michael

Carys

SOURCE: www.michaeldouglas.com

✔ Now I can ...
- ☐ describe my family.
- ☐ ask about family members.
- ☐ compare people.
- ☐ talk about small families and large families.

39

Coping with Technology

UNIT GOALS

1 Suggest a brand or model
2 Express frustration about a machine
3 Describe features of machines
4 Complain when things don't work

A **TOPIC PREVIEW.** Look at the ad from a shopping catalog. Do you like catalogs that sell electronic gadgets?

THE COMMUNICATOR

สวัสดี
HELLO

RM2000

THE COMMUNICATOR
Pocket electronic talking translator

- Translates from English to eight other world languages.
- Displays text on screen AND correctly pronounces words and phrases.
- Makes world travel a breeze!

COM445 . . . .
see page 46

B **DISCUSSION.** Is The Communicator a good product? Would you like to have one? Why or why not?

" It's great for me. I like to travel. "

" It's not a good way to learn English. "

UNIT 4

Coping with Technology

A TOPIC PREVIEW

Suggested teaching time:	10 minutes
Your actual teaching time:	_____

- Ask the class questions about the ad:
  What's the name of the gadget? (The Communicator)
  Does The Communicator "talk"? (yes)
  Can you see the word on the screen? (yes)
  Is The Communicator good for travel? (yes)

- To model the activity, answer the question yourself; for example:
  Yes, I do. I love electronic gadgets.
  Yes, I do. I'm really into electronic gadgets.
    Or:
  No, I don't. Electronic gadgets are not for me.
  No, I don't. Electronic gadgets are not my style.
  No, I don't. I'm not really an electronic gadgets fan.

B DISCUSSION

Suggested teaching time:	5–10 minutes
Your actual teaching time:	_____

- After students discuss in pairs or small groups, ask the class *Who thinks The Communicator is a good product? Why?* Write some reasons on the board. Then ask *Who wouldn't like to have a Communicator? Why?* Write the reasons on the board.

Your students can say . . .

Reasons it's a good product:
    It "speaks" nine languages.
    It spells words for you.
    It says words for you.
    It's good for travel.

Reasons I wouldn't like to have one:
    I don't like gadgets.
    I don't travel.

Option: Bring in some catalogs that sell electronic gadgets for students to look at. You can also have students look at electronic gadgets online. Have students look for one gadget that they think is a good product. In small groups, students tell why they would like to have the product.
[+10 minutes]

C ◯ SOUND BITES

Suggested teaching time:	10–15 minutes
Your actual teaching time:	_____

- Before students listen, ask questions about the photo. Point to the woman on the left. Ask *Does she look happy?* (No, she doesn't.)

- After students read and listen, ask:
  Where are they? (in an office)
  What machine are they talking about? (the printer)
  What's the problem? (It's not working. / It won't print.)
  Does she know why it won't print? (no)

Language note: If something is called *"a lemon,"* it means that it has a lot of problems and doesn't work correctly. The term is usually used to describe a car or a piece of machinery.

D ▷ Read the conversation . . .

Suggested teaching time:	10 minutes
Your actual teaching time:	_____

Option: For items 1 and 2, have students find and underline the sentences in the conversation that show that they are true (1. This printer's driving me crazy! 2. It's not working again. It won't print.). For item 4, have students change the statement to make it true (A lemon is a bad machine.) **[+5 minutes]**

WHAT ABOUT **YOU?**

Suggested teaching time:	10–15 minutes
Your actual teaching time:	_____

- After students read the directions, say *What machines do you have or use that drive you crazy?* Students write down their machines on the notepad.

- Ask different students to share one machine from their lists. Write students' responses on the board. Then read each item on the list out loud and have the class repeat.

- Say *Do you have any lemons on your list?* Have students circle the machines on their lists that are lemons.

Option: Ask for volunteers to act out using different machines from the list on the board. The class guesses the machine. **[+10 minutes]**

PAIR WORK

- Students can ask each other *Do you have a/an [name of machine] on your list?*

- Each pair can report to the class. For example:
  Our lists are the same. We both have our computers and our PDAs on our lists.
  Our lists are different. My cell phone is a lemon. His fax machine is a lemon.

EXTRAS (optional)

Workbook: Exercises 1–3

🎧 **SOUND BITES.** Read along silently as you listen to a natural conversation.

> **CLAIRE:** This printer's driving me crazy!
> **MARIE:** What do you mean?
> **CLAIRE:** It's not working again. It won't print.
> **MARIE:** What's wrong with it?
> **CLAIRE:** I don't know. It's just a lemon!

D Read the conversation carefully. Then check ☑ each statement <u>true</u>, <u>false</u>, or <u>no information</u>.

	true	false	no information
1. The printer is not printing.	☑	☐	☐
2. It's a new printer.	☐	☐	☑
3. Marie doesn't have a printer.	☐	☐	☑
4. A lemon is a good machine.	☐	☑	☐

WHAT ABOUT **YOU?**

What machines drive <u>you</u> crazy? Make a list. Use a dictionary if necessary.

my laptop

my cell phone

PAIR WORK. Compare your lists. Are they the same or different?

Suggest a Brand or Model

🎧 CONVERSATION MODEL Read and listen.

A: Hey, Bob! What are *you* doing here?

B: Hi, Louis. I'm looking for a laptop. Any suggestions?

A: What about a Pell? The X340 is great.

B: Really?

A: Yes. And it's inexpensive. **CN**

🎧 **Rhythm and intonation practice**

CN Corpus Notes:
"Cheap" is used about six times as frequently as "inexpensive." Both mean "not expensive" but "cheap" can also mean that something is not of good quality.

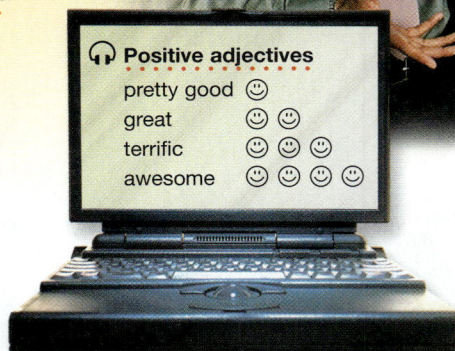

🎧 **Positive adjectives**
pretty good ☺
great ☺ ☺
terrific ☺ ☺ ☺
awesome ☺ ☺ ☺ ☺

Ⓐ GRAMMAR. The present continuous

Use the present continuous for actions in progress now and for some future actions.
Form the present continuous with **be** and a present participle (base form + **-ing**).

I'm looking for a laptop. (action in progress now)

Tomorrow **I'm going** to Technoland. (future action)

Questions	Answers
Are you looking for a cell phone?	Yes, I am. / No, I'm not.
Is he using the computer?	Yes, he is. / No, he's not.
Are they buying the X340?	Yes, they are. / No, they're not.
What are you doing?	We're getting a new printer.
Who's buying a new cell phone?	My brother is.

GRAMMAR BOOSTER
PAGES G5–G7
For more . . .

Ⓑ Read the sentences and questions. Check ☑ Action in progress or Future action.

	Action in progress	Future action
1. What are you doing this weekend?		✔
2. I'm busy right now. I'm answering my e-mails.	✔	
3. He's leaving in thirty minutes. Hurry!		✔
4. Beth is at the library. She's studying for an exam.	✔	
5. Josh isn't home right now. He's shopping for a laptop.	✔	

1 ▶ *Suggest a Brand or Model*

🎧 CONVERSATION **MODEL**

Suggested teaching time:	5–10 minutes
Your actual teaching time:	_____

- Before students read and listen, ask some pre-listening questions:
  What do you see in the photo? (laptops, computers)
  Where do you think the men are? (in a store)
- After students read and listen, ask:
  What does Bob want to buy? (a laptop)
  What kind of laptop does Louis say is good?
  (a Pell X340)
  Does the Pell X340 cost a lot? (no)
- Explain that Pell is a brand and that X340 is a model. Ask *What brands do you think are good?*

🎧 Positive adjectives

Option: Students choose something they're interested in, such as movies, rock bands, artists, or places to travel. They make a list and then rate each item of their list as *pretty good, great, terrific,* or *awesome.* Then walk around the classroom so that you can look at students' papers. Say *I'm looking for a [movie, a rock CD, etc.].* Any suggestions? **[+10 minutes]**

🎧 Rhythm and intonation practice

Suggested teaching time:	5 minutes
Your actual teaching time:	_____

- Write *What are you doing here?* on the board. Explain that Louis is surprised to see Bob. Read the question with emphasis on *you.* Have students repeat.
- Have students repeat each line chorally. Make sure students:
  ○ use correct intonation on Hey, Bob! Any suggestions? What about a Pell? Really?
  ○ use the following stress pattern:

STRESS PATTERN

A: — — • • • — • • •
Hey, Bob! What are *you* doing here?

B: — — • • • — • • — • • • • — •
Hi, Louis. I'm looking for a laptop. Any suggestions?

A: • • • • — • — • — • • —
What about a Pell? The X-three forty is great.

B: — •
Really?

A: — — • • • — •
Yes. And it's inexpensive.

🔶 A ▷ GRAMMAR

Suggested teaching time:	5–10 minutes
Your actual teaching time:	_____

- After students read the information in the Grammar box, have them look for two examples of the present continuous in the Conversation Model (What are you doing here? I'm looking for a laptop.)
- On the board, write *Actions in progress now.* Ask *Why is Bob at the computer store right now?* (He's looking for a laptop) Then ask *What are we doing right now?* Write their answers on the board under the heading.

Your students can say . . .

We're studying the present continuous / English.
We're speaking English.
We're listening to the teacher.
We're reading *Top Notch.*

- On the board, write the heading *Future actions.* Ask several students *What are you doing tomorrow?* Write students' responses under the heading.

Your students can say . . .

I'm working.
I'm watching the basketball game.
I'm going to an art exhibit.

Option: Have students write about what they think their family members are doing right now. Students write sentences in the present continuous. For example:

My brother is sleeping.
My mother is cooking.
My father is working.
My grandmother is reading.

[+5 minutes]

💿 Grammar Self-Checks

🔶 B ▷ Read the sentences and questions . . .

Suggested teaching time:	5 minutes
Your actual teaching time:	_____

- Have students underline any words that tell them whether the item is an action in progress or a future action. (1. this weekend 2. right now 3. in thirty minutes 5. right now; Note: There is nothing to underline in item 4.)

Option: Write the first item on the board. Have students answer the question. Students can make notes and then talk to a partner, or they can write complete sentences. For example:

Friday night: go to a concert at the Lagoon
Saturday: visit my grandmother
Saturday night: watch a DVD
Sunday: study
On Friday night I'm going to a concert at the Lagoon.
On Saturday I'm visiting my grandmother . . .

[+5 minutes]

C 🎧 VOCABULARY

Suggested teaching time:	5 minutes
Your actual teaching time:	_____

Language note: Students may confuse the photo of a CD burner with a CD-ROM drive. If helpful, point out that a CD burner is a machine that records data on a compact disc.

Option: With a partner, students can talk about which electronics items they have and what brands they are; for example:

┌─ **Your students can say . . .** ─────────
A: Do you have a PDA? **B:** Yes, I do. **A:** What brand is it? **B:** It's a Datacomp.
└─────────────────────────────────

[+5 minutes]

💿 **Vocabulary Cards**

D Complete each conversation . . .

Suggested teaching time:	5 minutes
Your actual teaching time:	_____

• To review, have students read the completed conversations with a partner.
• Have students check their spelling of the present participles in items 2 and 3. With *leave* and *take*, students need to drop the *-e* before adding *-ing*: *leaving, taking*. With *shop*, they need to double the *-p* before adding *-ing*: *shopping*. If necessary, have students review the spelling rules on pages G5–G6 of the Grammar Booster.

Option: Have students identify which items are actions in progress (3 and 4) and which are future actions (1 and 2). [+5 minutes]

E 🎧 PRONUNCIATION

Suggested teaching time:	5 minutes
Your actual teaching time:	_____

• Model rising and falling intonation. Say:

    Is your laptop a Pell?

    What brand is your laptop?

Have students repeat each question, practicing the correct intonation.

• After students complete the activity, have them look back at Exercise D on page 9. Ask:
    Do <u>yes</u> / <u>no</u> *questions have rising or falling intonation?* (rising intonation)
    Do information questions have rising or falling intonation? (falling intonation)

Then have students check their answers.

• With a partner, have students practice reading the questions on page 9 with correct intonation.

Option: For more practice, students can read the conversations in Exercise D with the correct intonation. Students can also read out loud the questions in the Grammar box on page 42. [+5 minutes]

💿 **Pronunciation Activities**

CONVERSATION **PAIR WORK**

Suggested teaching time:	10–15 minutes
Your actual teaching time:	_____

• Model the activity with a student. Play the role of A.
• For the last line of the conversation, your students can say:
    Yes. And it's [on sale / fast / small / inexpensive / great / terrific].

Options: Have students bring in electronics store ads. Students can use the ads—with actual brands, models, and prices—to practice the conversation. [+10 minutes]

💿 **Pair Work Cards**

EXTRAS (optional)

Grammar Booster
Workbook: Exercises 5–10
Copy & Go: Activity 13

💿 **Pronunciation Supplements**

C 🎧 **VOCABULARY.** **Electronics.** Listen and practice. Which machines do you have? Which machines are you looking for?

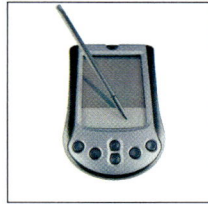

| a TV | a laptop | a PDA | a printer | a cell phone | a CD burner |

D Complete each conversation with the present continuous.

1. **A:** <u>Is Marian going</u> to Technoland this afternoon?
   Marian / go
   B: Yes, <u>she's buying</u> a new CD burner.
   she / buy

2. **A:** What time <u>are you leaving</u> tomorrow?
   you / leave
   B: <u>I'm taking</u> the 5:30 train.
   I / take

3. **A:** <u>Is Jim looking</u> for a new laptop?
   Jim / look
   B: No, <u>he's not</u>. <u>He's shopping</u> for a PDA.
   he / not   *He / shop*

4. **A:** <u>Are you doing</u> anything right now?
   you / do
   B: Yes, <u>I'm cleaning</u> the house.
   I / clean

E 🎧 **PRONUNCIATION.** Intonation of <u>yes</u> / <u>no</u> and information questions. Listen and check ☑ the boxes for rising or falling intonation.

| | ☑ | 1. What time are you leaving? | | ☑ | 3. When is she returning? |
| ☑ | | 2. Are you going today? | ☑ | | 4. Is Julie buying a laptop? |

CONVERSATION
PAIR WORK

Suggest a brand or a model. Use the pictures and the guide, or create a new conversation.

A: Hey, _____! What are *you* doing here?
B: Hi, I'm looking for _____. Any suggestions?
A: What about _____? The _____ is _____.
B: Really?
A: Yes. And it's _____.

On sale
Super brand Model 260

Printmore **brand** *Great* Model GX 200

Fast! **Pell** Model 2400

DataWhiz Model M211 *Terrific!*

43

CONTROLLED PRACTICE

Express Frustration about a Machine

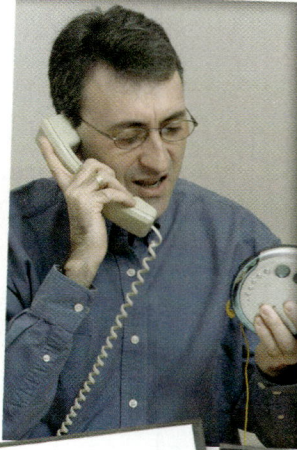

🎧 CONVERSATION MODEL Read and listen.

A: Hello?
B: Hi, Ed. How's it going? **CN**
A: Fine, thanks. But my CD player's not working. It's driving me crazy!
B: I'm sorry to hear that. What brand is it?
A: A Tunebox. It's awful.

🎧 **Rhythm and intonation practice**

CN Corpus Notes: "How's it going?" is used as a way to greet someone in spoken American English. "How are you?" is twelve times more common, though.

🎧 **Ways to sympathize**
I'm sorry to hear that.
That's too bad.
That's a shame.

🎧 **Negative descriptions**
pretty bad
terrible
a piece of junk
awful
a lemon

A 🎧 VOCABULARY. Machines at home and at work. Listen and practice.

  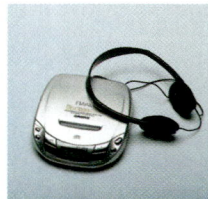 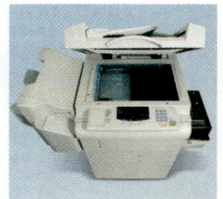

a microwave oven **a coffee maker** **a hair dryer** **a CD player** **a fax machine** **a photocopier**

B Complete each statement with the name of a machine from the vocabulary.

1. You use a <u>photocopier</u> to make copies of documents and pictures.
2. I just got a new battery-operated <u>CD player</u> so I can listen to music outside.
3. I love my new <u>microwave</u>. It can cook a chicken in minutes!
4. You use a <u>fax machine</u> to send a copy of your document to someone else over the telephone line.
5. This <u>hair dryer</u> is making a funny sound. Maybe I'll just go out with wet hair.

C 🎧 LISTENING COMPREHENSION. Listen to the conversations. Write the name of each machine. Do <u>you</u> have problems with one of these machines too? Tell your partner.

	Machine			Machine
1.	CD player		**4.**	microwave
2.	hair dryer		**5.**	photocopier
3.	coffee maker		**6.**	fax machine

LESSON 2

Express Frustration about a Machine

🎧 CONVERSATION **MODEL**

Suggested teaching time:	10 minutes
Your actual teaching time:	_____

- Before students read and listen, ask questions about the picture. Ask *What are they doing?* (They're talking on the phone.). Point to the man on the left and ask *What does he have?* (a CD player) *Does he look happy?* (No, he doesn't.)

- After students read and listen, ask:
  What's wrong with Ed's CD player? (It's not working.)
  What brand is his CD player? (Tunebox)
  Is Tunebox a good brand? (No, it's not.)

> **Language note:** *How's it going? How are you?* and *How are you doing?* are similar to *hello* or *hi* in English. English speakers respond to these questions as greetings, not as actual questions. They usually answer *Fine, thanks* or *Not so good* automatically. They don't usually give long explanations of how they are doing.

🎧 Ways to sympathize / Negative descriptions

- Point out that:
  - *terrible* and *awful* both mean very bad.
  - *a piece of junk* and *a lemon* are both words to describe something that's not useful. *A piece of junk* is usually bad because it's old or very inexpensive. *A lemon* can be a new machine or a good brand, but it breaks a lot.
  - *pretty bad* is not as strong as the other negative descriptions.

Option: Students can talk about any bad machines or electronics they have; for example: *I have a car. It's a Monsoon Sport. It's ten years old. It's a piece of junk.* [+5 minutes]

🎧 Rhythm and intonation practice

Suggested teaching time:	5 minutes
Your actual teaching time:	_____

- Walk around the room and greet several students. Say *Hello* (with falling intonation) and shake hands. Then act out picking up a telephone receiver and model the rising intonation of *Hello?* Have students practice the different intonation of *Hello?* to answer the phone and *Hello* to greet someone.

- Have students repeat each line chorally. Make sure they:
  - use falling intonation in *How's it going?* and *What brand is it?*
  - accurately imitate the intonation of *It's driving me crazy! I'm sorry to hear that,* and *It's awful.*
  - use the following stress pattern:

STRESS PATTERN

A: Hello?

B: Hi, Ed. How's it going?

A: Fine, thanks. But my C-D player's not working. It's driving me crazy!

B: I'm sorry to hear that. What brand is it?

A: A Tunebox. It's awful.

A 🎧 VOCABULARY

Suggested teaching time:	5 minutes
Your actual teaching time:	_____

- After students listen and repeat, ask a few students *Do you have a _____?* If the students say yes, ask some follow-up questions such as:
  What brand is it?
  Is it a good product?
  Does it work?
  Does it drive you crazy?
  Was it expensive or inexpensive?
  How old is it?

💿 **Vocabulary Cards**

💿 **Learning Strategies**

B Complete each statement . . .

Suggested teaching time:	5 minutes
Your actual teaching time:	_____

Challenge: Have students read items 1 and 4 again. Students write similar sentences to define the electronics on page 43; for example: *You use a PDA to store phone numbers, addresses, and your calendar.* [+5 minutes]

C 🎧 LISTENING COMPREHENSION

Suggested teaching time:	5–10 minutes
Your actual teaching time:	_____

Challenge: Have students listen again. For items 1, 2, 4, and 6, students write what the machine *won't* do:
  1. The CD player won't start.
  2. The hair dryer won't blow hot air.
  4. The microwave won't heat anything.
  6. The fax machine won't fax.
[+10 minutes]

> **Language note:** In spoken English, it is very common to delete "Do you" in <u>yes</u> / <u>no</u> questions, as in "Want to hear it?"

(Audioscript is on page T45.)

T44

AUDIOSCRIPT

CONVERSATION 1
M: I just got this great CD. Want to hear it?
F: You bet.
[sound of CD being placed inside a Discman]
M: What's happening?
F: I have no clue. The CD player just won't start. Let me check the batteries.

CONVERSATION 2
F1: This hair dryer is such a piece of junk!
F2: What's wrong?
F1: It only blows cold air. My hair'll never dry!

CONVERSATION 3
M: I don't believe it.
F: What's the matter?
M: The coffee maker's broken.
F: Again? What a lemon!
M: You can say that again.

CONVERSATION 4 [F1 = Spanish]
F1: What's wrong with the microwave?
F2: I have no idea. Isn't it working?
F1: No. It just won't heat anything.
F2: That's awful. I wanted to make some soup.

CONVERSATION 5 [M2 = British English]
M1: Why is all that paper on the floor?
M2: It's from the photocopier.
M1: You mean it's not working again?
M2: It's a disaster.

CONVERSATION 6 [M = Polish]
M: The fax machine won't work.
F: How old is it?
M: About six months old.
F: You're kidding.
M: It's a piece of junk!

D VOCABULARY BUILDING

Suggested teaching time:	5–10 minutes
Your actual teaching time:	_____

Note: Students know the words for some of the machines and appliances pictured. Others are new. Have students look up words they don't know in English in their dictionaries.

• To encourage students to add machines and appliances they have in their own homes, talk about machines and appliances you have. For example, say:
  In my kitchen, I have a toaster. In my living room, I have a stereo . . .

CONVERSATION **PAIR WORK**

Suggested teaching time:	10–15 minutes
Your actual teaching time:	_____

• Students can talk about machines from the Vocabulary on page 43 or 44 or from the lists they made in Exercise D. Encourage students to use actual brand names.

• As students practice, circulate and listen. Make sure A uses 's when he or she says *But my [machine]'s not working.*

Pair Work Cards

EXTRAS (optional)

Workbook: Exercises 11–14
Copy & Go: Activity 14

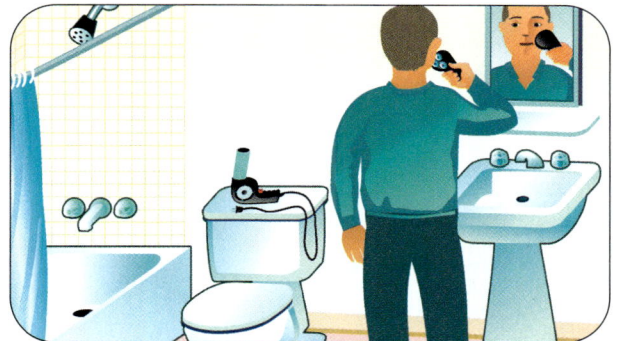

D **VOCABULARY BUILDING.** Make a list of the machines and appliances in the pictures. Add machines and appliances you have in <u>your</u> house. Use a bilingual dictionary for words you don't know in English.

in the kitchen

a microwave oven	a refrigerator
a coffee maker	a dishwasher
a sink	an oven

in the living room

a TV
a CD player
a DVD player

in the bedroom

a laptop	a cell phone
a printer	
a fax machine	

in the bathroom

a hair dryer	a toilet
an electric razor	a sink
a shower	a bathtub

CONVERSATION PAIR WORK

Express frustration about a machine. Use your own brands. Use the guide, or create a new conversation.

A: Hello?

B: Hi, _____. How's it going?

A: Fine, thanks. But my _____ not working. It's driving me crazy!

B: _____. What brand is it?

A: _____. It's _____.

Describe Features of Machines

A ▷ **READING WARM-UP.** Do you like electronic gadgets? Where do you buy them?

B ▷ 🎧 **READING.** Read and listen to the ad. Then close your book and write two sentences about the Communicator.

THE COMMUNICATOR

The pocket electronic talking translator!!

Translates to AND from English and eight other world languages. Displays text on screen and correctly pronounces words for you.

FEATURES

- It's **convenient**. Makes reading and speaking a foreign language easy and fast. Just press a button and get a translation. Save time!
- It's **popular**. Used by more travelers than any other pocket translator.
- It's **portable**. Lighter and smaller than a dictionary. Just put the Communicator in your pocket or purse and carry it anywhere.
- It's **guaranteed**. Use The Communicator for one full year. If you are not happy with our product, just return it and we will refund your money!

Battery operated. Uses 2 AAA batteries (included). Weighs just 5.5 oz. (.15 kg.)

46

C ▷ 🎧 **LISTENING COMPREHENSION.** Listen to the radio ads. Then listen again. Check the adjectives.

1	2	3
"The Sleeper"	"Cool as a Cucumber"	"The Scribbler"
☐ convenient ☑ portable	☑ convenient ☑ portable	☑ convenient ☐ portable
☑ popular ☐ guaranteed	☐ popular ☐ guaranteed	☐ popular ☑ guaranteed

D ▷ **PAIR WORK.** Which product would _you_ like to have? Why?

LESSON 3

Describe Features of Machines

A. READING WARM-UP

Suggested teaching time:	5–10 minutes
Your actual teaching time:	_____

- After students answer the questions, review by asking a few students about places to buy electronic gadgets. Say *I'm looking for a CD burner. I don't know where to go. Any suggestions?* Students can answer:
  What about _____?
  _____ is pretty good / great / terrific / awesome.
- To continue ask one of the following questions:
  Where is it?
  What brands do they have?
  Are they expensive?

B. 🎧 READING

Suggested teaching time:	10 minutes
Your actual teaching time:	_____

- After students read and listen, ask some comprehension questions about The Communicator:
  Is The Communicator . . .
    . . . fast or slow? (fast)
    . . . easy or difficult to use? (easy to use)
    . . . large or small? (small)
    . . . heavy or light? (light)
  What does The Communicator do?

Challenge: Ask the following questions:
  Who might buy The Communicator? Why?
  Do you think The Communicator is better than a dictionary? Why or why not?
[+5 minutes]

- Pronounce each adjective and have students repeat.
- Review the meanings of the adjectives in bold. Talk about a machine that it describes. For example:
  *Microwaves are **convenient**. They heat food fast—in just minutes, or even seconds.*
  *Cell phones are **popular**. Lots of people have them.*
  *PDAs are **portable**. They're small and light. You can take them wherever you go.*
  *Most laptops are **guaranteed**. If you buy a lemon, you can take it back to the store and get your money back.*

- Have students underline words in the reading that define each adjective:
  for **convenient**: *easy, fast, Save time!*
  for **popular**: *Used by more travelers*
  for **portable**: *lighter, smaller, carry it anywhere*
  for **guaranteed**: *If you are not happy with our product, just return it and we will refund your money.*

Option: Write the sentences that follow on the board. Have students complete the sentences with a machine, appliance, or electronic gadget.

  _____ are convenient.
  _____ are popular right now.
  _____ are portable.
  _____ are usually guaranteed for one year.
[+5 minutes]

💿 **Extra Reading Comprehension Activities**

💿 **Learning Strategies**

C. 🎧 LISTENING COMPREHENSION

Suggested teaching time:	10 minutes
Your actual teaching time:	_____

- Tell students to listen for the adjectives *convenient, popular, portable,* and *guaranteed.* Tell students to also listen for words that mean the same thing, such as *easy and fast, light and small.*

Challenge: Write the following questions on the board:
  Is [Name of product] a good product? Would you like to have one? Why? / Why not?

Have students listen to the radio ads again. Students ask and answer the questions in pairs or small groups.
[+10 minutes]

AUDIOSCRIPT

ADVERTISEMENT 1
F: Having trouble sleeping? Thinking about taking sleeping pills? Try *The Sleeper!* Our portable CD player plays relaxing sounds of nature to help you fall asleep. But you'll have to move fast! This popular gadget is on everybody's gift list for the holidays.

ADVERTISEMENT 2
M: Are you considering air conditioning your home or office? Stop! Before spending all that money, ask to see *Cool as a Cucumber,* the amazing portable air conditioner you WEAR! Yes, you heard right. You wear *Cool as a Cucumber* around your neck. And it's so small you can take it anywhere—to the beach, to the office, even on the bus! So stay cool with *Cool as a Cucumber.*

ADVERTISEMENT 3
F: Be the first person in your school or office to have *The SCRIBBLER!* The world's first electric pencil. Just plug *The Scribbler* into any outlet and start writing: notes, ideas, plans, memos. Makes writing so easy and fast, you'll save hours every day! And it's guaranteed for a full year. If you don't love your *Scribbler,* we'll give you your money back!

D. PAIR WORK

Suggested teaching time:	5–10 minutes
Your actual teaching time:	_____

- In pairs, students discuss which product they would like to have and why.

Option: Take a poll. Write the name of each product on the board. Have students raise their hands for the one they would like to have. Tell students they can only choose one of the products. **[+5 minutes]**

E Complete each sentence . . .

Suggested teaching time:	5 minutes
Your actual teaching time:	_____

- To review, have volunteers read the sentences out loud.

TOP NOTCH **INTERACTION**

Suggested teaching time:	15–20 minutes
Your actual teaching time:	_____

STEP 1

- Point to the woman in the car. Ask *What is she doing?* (She's driving.)
- Have students read the ads independently. Then put students in small groups to discuss the ads. Write the following questions on the board to prompt discussion:

  When do you use it?

  What does it do?

  Is it guaranteed?

  Do you like the product? Why or why not?

- When students talk about whether they like the products, they might say:

  The Driver Alarm's not good for me. I don't drive.
  The Spotlight Pen is awesome. I study late at night.

STEP 2

- Draw the chart from the Student's Book on the board. Ask volunteers to share some of their answers with the class. Write their information on the board.

STEP 3

- Students talk about the items on their lists. Following is an example of what your students can say:

  I have an electric teapot. It's a Quick-T. It's fast and convenient. What do you have?

- Remind students to refer to NEED HELP? to support them in their discussions.

EXTRAS (optional)

Copy & Go: Activity 15

E **Complete each sentence with an adjective from the reading and listening.**

1. If this hair dryer stops working, you can get your money back. It's _guaranteed_.
2. This TV is _portable_; it's so small and light you can carry it anywhere!
3. This new cell phone is very _popular_. Everybody wants one.
4. I use the Coffee Pro 200 to make coffee at home. It's easy and it saves time. It's _convenient_.

TOP NOTCH
INTERACTION • *It's the Latest Thing!*

STEP 1. **DISCUSSION.** **Read and discuss the ads. Do you like these products? Why? Why not?**

DRIVER ALARM

Avoid accidents. Alarm rings if you start to fall asleep while you are driving. Battery powered. Guaranteed to keep you awake.

SPOTLIGHT PEN

When it's too dark to see what you're writing, it's not too dark for the Spotlight Pen. The amazing Spotlight Pen lights up your paper. Won't disturb those who are sleeping nearby. Guaranteed.

STEP 2. **Write your own machines, gadgets, and appliances on the notepad.**

	Item	Brand	Description
	electric teapot	Quick-T	It's fast and convenient.
1.			
2.			
3.			

STEP 3. **GROUP WORK.** **Tell your classmates about your machines. Write your lists on the board. Discuss the products.**

NEED HELP? **Here's language you already know:**

pretty bad	awful
terrible	a lemon
a piece of junk	
☹	

great	terrific
awesome	fast
popular	convenient
guaranteed	pretty good
☺	

Complain When Things Don't Work

A 🎧 **VOCABULARY.** Ways to state a complaint. **Listen and practice.**

The window **won't open / close**.

The iron **won't turn on**.

The air-conditioning **won't turn off**.

The fridge is **making a funny sound**.

The toilet **won't flush**.

The sink **is clogged**.

B 🎧 **LISTENING COMPREHENSION.** Listen to the conversations between hotel guests and the front desk. Then listen again and write the room number for each complaint.

GUEST COMPLAINT LOG

InterGlobal HOTEL

DATE: June 24

ROOM	PROBLEM
203	The toilet won't stop flushing.
608	The fridge isn't working.
723	The sink is clogged.
1417	The air-conditioning won't turn off.

C **DISCUSSION.** Look at the vocabulary pictures and the problems on the Guest Complaint Log. Which are bad problems? Which are not so bad? Explain.

LESSON

4 Complain When Things Don't Work

A ∩ VOCABULARY

Suggested teaching time:	5–10 minutes
Your actual teaching time:	_____

- Explain that *won't* is the short form of *will not*.
- Say *Use "won't" to describe a problem with something. When something isn't working, tell what it **won't** do. For example: The printer won't print; the CD player won't start; the microwave won't heat.*
- Have students label *the window, the iron, the air conditioner, the fridge, the toilet,* and *the sink* in each picture.
- Use a door to demonstrate *open* and *close*. Use a light switch to demonstrate *turn on* and *turn off*.

Language note: *The air conditioning* is the system that makes the air in a room cool. The machine or piece of equipment that creates air conditioning is called *an air conditioner*. *Fridge* is an abbreviation for *refrigerator*.

💿 **Vocabulary Cards**

B ∩ LISTENING COMPREHENSION

Suggested teaching time:	10–15 minutes
Your actual teaching time:	_____

- Tell students that the conversations are not in order. Tell them to listen for the problem and then write the room number.

AUDIOSCRIPT

CONVERSATION 1 [M = Korean]
- **F:** Front desk.
- **M:** This is Mr. Lee. There's a serious problem with my room.
- **F:** I'm sorry to hear that. What is it?
- **M:** It's the toilet. It won't stop flushing.
- **F:** It won't STOP flushing?
- **M:** Yes, that's right. And it's making a lot of noise.
- **F:** What room are you in?
- **M:** Uh . . . 203

CONVERSATION 2 [M = Arabic]
- **M:** Front desk. This is Ahmed.
- **F:** Yes. This is Mrs. Johnson in 732. I have an emergency.
- **M:** What kind of emergency?
- **F:** It's the sink in the bathroom. It's clogged and there's water all over the floor.
- **M:** Don't worry, Mrs. Johnson. I'll send a plumber right away.

CONVERSATION 3
- **M1:** Front desk. How can I help you?
- **M2:** This is Mr. Prentice in room 1417. I have a problem.
- **M1:** Yes, Mr. Prentice. What seems to be the problem?
- **M2:** It's the air conditioning. It's freezing in here.
- **M1:** Have you tried shutting it off?
- **M2:** Of course. That's why I'm calling you.

CONVERSATION 4 [F2 = Spanish]
- **F1:** Front desk. Marlene speaking. How may I direct your call?
- **F2:** This is Ms. Rios in room 608.
- **F1:** Excuse me. What room did you say you were in?
- **F2:** 608.
- **F1:** Certainly. How can I help you?
- **F2:** There's a problem with my fridge.
- **F1:** Not working?
- **F2:** Yes, that's right. Everything's warm.
- **F1:** I'm sorry. I'll have someone look at it right away.

C DISCUSSION

Suggested teaching time:	10 minutes
Your actual teaching time:	_____

- On the board, write the headings *bad* and *not so bad*. Have students look at Exercise A again. Students say whether the problem is bad or not so bad. Write the problem under the appropriate heading.
- Ask students to explain why they think the problem belongs in that column.

TOP NOTCH **INTERACTION**

Suggested teaching time: 25 minutes
Your actual teaching time: _____

STEP 1

- On the board, write the titles from the notepad (*Room* and *Problem*).
- To model the activity, identify the first problem as a class. Point to the woman with the hair dryer. Ask *What room is she in?* (210). Write the room number on the board.
- Next ask *What's the problem?* (The hair dryer is making a funny sound.) Write the problem on the board.
- After students complete the activity, ask:
  Is there another problem in the hotel? (yes)
  What's the problem? (The elevator is stuck. /
    The elevator won't open.)

STEP 2

- Pairs use their notepads to role-play telephone conversations.
- Partners take turns playing the roles of the front desk clerk and the guest. Remind students to refer to NEED HELP? to support them in their role play.

Option: Provide additional language for the front desk clerk to use. On the board, write the following:
    How can I help you?
    What room are you in?
    I'm sorry. I'll have someone look at it right away.
    I'm sorry. I'll send someone right away.
[**+5 minutes**]

Option: After each conversation, have students pair up with a different classmate and practice a new conversation. [**+10 minutes**]

EXTRAS (optional)

   Workbook: Exercises 15–19
   Copy & Go: Activity 16

INTERACTION • *"Front Desk, Can I Help You?"*

STEP 1. Find all the problems in the hotel. Write them on the notepad.

Room or place	Problem
Bathroom (Room 100)	The sink is clogged.
Room 211	The door won't open.
Bathroom (Room 210)	The hair dryer is making a funny sound.
Bedroom (Room 100)	The air-conditioner won't turn on.
Kitchen (Room 210)	The coffee maker isn't working.

STEP 2. PAIR WORK. Role-play conversations between the hotel guests and the front desk clerk.

> " Front desk. Can I help you? "

> " This is room 211. Our door won't open. "

NEED HELP? Here's language you already know:

Telephone language

Hello?
This is room ___.
Can I call you back?
Bye.

State a problem

won't open / close
won't turn on / off
won't stop flushing
isn't working
is clogged
is making a funny sound
is driving me crazy

Respond

What's the problem?
I'm sorry to hear that.

UNIT 4
CHECKPOINT

A 🎧 **LISTENING COMPREHENSION.** Listen to the conversations about problems with machines. Then listen again. Write the problem.

1. The cell phone isn't working.
2. The computer is making a funny sound.
3. The air conditioner won't turn on.

The printer is making a funny sound.

B **Write a question in the present continuous.**

☐ 1. he / talk / on the phone Is he talking on the phone ?

☐ 2. Who / use / the computer / right now Who is using the computer right now ?

☑ 3. When / Laura / leave When is Laura leaving ?

☑ 4. we / go / to work tomorrow Are we going to work tomorrow ?

☑ 5. When / you / buy / the tickets When are you buying the tickets ?

☑ 6. What time / you / leave / for the concert What time are you leaving for the concert ?

C **Check ☑ the questions in exercise B that have __future__ meaning.**

D **Write your __own__ answer to each question with real information. Use the present continuous. Use contractions.**

1. Where are you going tomorrow? (YOU) _____.

2. Where are you eating dinner tonight? (YOU) _____.

3. What are you doing tomorrow? (YOU) _____.

4. What are you doing right now? (YOU) _____.

E **Complete each statement with an adjective.**

1. Lots of people are buying it. It's _____popular_____.

2. It's small enough to fit in your pocket. It's very _____portable_____.

3. It only takes a few seconds to do the job. It's _____convenient_____.

4. It doesn't cost too much. It's very _____inexpensive_____.

5. If it stops working, you can get your money back.
   It's _____guaranteed_____.

F **WRITING.** Write a paragraph about a machine that you own. Use your notes on page 47 for ideas.

▶ **TOP NOTCH PROJECT**
Write and design ads for the best products. Include pictures or photographs. Use the ads in Unit 4 as a model.

▶ **TOP NOTCH WEBSITE**
For Unit 4 online activities, visit the *Top Notch* Companion Website at www.longman.com/topnotch.

UNIT 4
CHECKPOINT

A 🎧 LISTENING COMPREHENSION

Suggested teaching time:	5–10 minutes
Your actual teaching time:	_____

• Tell students to listen for the kind of machine.

Option: Have students listen again for the problem with each machine. Students write what's wrong with the machine to the right of each item (1. It isn't working. 2. It's making a funny sound. 3. It won't turn on.) **[+10 minutes]**

AUDIOSCRIPT

CONVERSATION 1
F: This thing is such a lemon!
M: What thing?
F: The cell phone. It isn't working!

CONVERSATION 2
M: My computer is driving me crazy.
F: Why?
M: It makes a funny sound when I use it, and I don't know what's wrong.

CONVERSATION 3 [F1 = Australian]
F1: It's hot in here.
F2: Well, no wonder. The air conditioner is off.
F1: I know. But it won't turn on.

B Write a question . . .

Suggested teaching time:	5 minutes
Your actual teaching time:	_____

• Remind students to place the verb *be* before the subject. If helpful, have students underline the subject in each item (1. he 2. Who 3. Laura 4. we 5. you 6. you) In item 2, *Who* is the subject even though identity is not known; *be* is placed after *Who*.

• Have students check their spelling of *using* in item 2 and *leaving* in items 3 and 6.

C Check ☑ the questions . . .

Suggested teaching time:	5 minutes
Your actual teaching time:	_____

• Explain that items 3, 5, and 6 have future meaning because asking *When* or *What time* implies that the action is not in progress right now.

D Write your own answer . . .

Suggested teaching time:	5 minutes
Your actual teaching time:	_____

• To review, students can take turns reading the questions and their answers with a partner.

E Complete each statement . . .

Suggested teaching time:	5 minutes
Your actual teaching time:	_____

• To review, have different students read each completed sentence out loud.

F WRITING

Suggested teaching time:	5–10 minutes
Your actual teaching time:	_____

• To help students get started, write the following questions on the board:
  What is it?
  What brand is it?
  What model is it?
  Is it a good product? Why or why not?
  What does it do?
  What adjectives describe it?
  What room in your home is it in?
  Is it working?
  Does it drive you crazy?
  How old is it?

Your students can say . . .

I love my new PDA. It's a Blueberry 7500. It's a great product. It stores phone numbers, addresses, and my calendar. It's a cell phone and web browser too. I can check my e-mail anywhere. It's small and very light. It's fast too. It's really convenient and guaranteed for one year.

💿 **Writing Process Worksheets**

***TOP NOTCH* PROJECT**

Idea: Groups choose one or two good products from the charts they completed on page 47. Have groups list adjectives to describe the product(s).

Idea: Have groups answer these questions:
  What does it do?
  When do you use it?
  Why is it a good product?

Idea: Ask groups to look at the ads on pages 40, 46, and 47 before they design their own ads. You may also want to bring in an electronics flyer.

T50

UNIT WRAP-UP

Suggested teaching time: 15–20 minutes
Your actual teaching time: _____

Vocabulary

Option: Find the machines. In pairs, have students point to and identify the different machines they see. You can also have students do the activity in reverse. One student says a machine and the other points to the appropriate machine in the picture. **[+5 minutes]**

> **Your students can say ...**
> two telephones, a TV, a remote control, a refrigerator / (fridge), a dishwasher, a stove, an oven, a microwave, a hairdryer, a computer, a CD player

Grammar

• Point out to students that the people in the picture are a family. Students can use *mother, father, grandmother, grandfather, daughter,* and *son* to identify the people when they ask questions.

> **Your students can say ...**
> What is the mother doing? (She's calling about the TV.)
> Is the father reading? (No, he isn't.)
> Who's listening to music? (the son)
> What are the grandparents doing? (They're using the computer. / They're looking at family pictures on the computer.)
> Some students may be able to produce the following:
> What is the daughter doing? (She's complaining about her hair dryer.)
> What is the father doing? (He's fixing the clogged sink.)

Option: Create conversations. Have students work in pairs to create conversations for the people in the picture. **[+10 minutes]**

Option: Role-play. Have students write the conversations in dialogue form and then role-play their conversation in front of the class. **[+10 minutes]**

Writing

• Students write sentences about the problems in the picture.

> **Your students can say**
> The TV's not working.
> The sink is clogged.
> The daughter's hair dryer isn't working.

Challenge: Students write about the problem with the TV or the hair dryer in the first person. For example, My new hair dryer's not working. It's driving me crazy. It's a good brand, but it's just a lemon! I'm taking it back to the store tomorrow. **[+5 minutes]**

Option: Competition. Divide the class into groups of four. One group begins by saying a word or sentence about the picture, and each other group follows by saying something more. Groups that can no longer say anything are eliminated until only one group remains. **[+10 minutes]**

🔘 **Writing Process Worksheets**

> **Individual oral progress check (optional)**
> Use the illustration on page 51 for an oral test. Ask students questions about the pictures, such as: What's wrong with the sink? What are the grandparents doing? Who's listening to music? Evaluate students on correctness, intelligibility, and completeness.

🔘 **Cumulative Vocabulary Activities**

📼 You may wish to use the video for Unit 4 at this point. For video activity worksheets, go to www.longman.com/topnotch.

📒 **Complete Assessment Package**
Unit 4 Achievement Test

- **Vocabulary.** Look at the picture. Then close your books. Write all the machines you remember.

- **Grammar.** Ask and answer questions about what the people are doing. Use the present continuous.

- **Writing.** Write about the problems in the picture.

We fix anything

Joe

Guaranteed

✔ *Now I can...*

☐ suggest a brand or model.
☐ express frustration about a machine.
☐ describe features of machines.
☐ complain when things don't work.

51

Eating in, Eating out

UNIT GOALS

1 Discuss what to eat
2 Make food choices
3 Order and pay for a meal
4 Discuss food and health

A ▸ **TOPIC PREVIEW.** Read the menu. Which foods do you like? Which foods do you dislike?

World Café
Chef and Owner: Ronald Gebert

"The Best Food in the World!" Max Reed, *Journal News*, April 22

Appetizers
Thai grilled shrimp
Mexican black bean soup

Entrées
Brazilian steak
Fried fish Chinese style
Roast chicken

Salads
Mixed green salad
Tomato salad

Desserts
Ice cream
Apple pie
German chocolate cake

Beverages
Coffee • Tea • Soft drinks • Fruit juice
Bottled water

B ▸ Look at the menu again. Check ☑ the information you can find.

- ☑ 1. food choices
- ☑ 2. beverage choices
- ☐ 3. prices
- ☑ 4. the name of the restaurant owner
- ☐ 5. the names of the waiters and waitresses
- ☑ 6. the name of the chef
- ☑ 7. a restaurant review

Eating in, Eating out

A. TOPIC PREVIEW

Suggested teaching time:	10 minutes
Your actual teaching time:	_____

• After students read the menu ask:
 What's the name of the restaurant? (World Café)
 What is the chef and owner's name / first name?
  (Ronald Gebert)

• Ask a few students *What foods on this menu do you like? What foods do you dislike?*

Language note: *Soft drinks* are carbonated non-alcoholic beverages. Depending on where a person is from there are variations of the term *soft drinks*. Some are: soda, pop, soda pop. In British English they are called *fizzy drinks*.

• To check students' understanding of the beverages, ask questions such as:
 Do you like coffee or tea?
 Do you drink soft drinks?
 What's your favorite soft drink?
 What type of fruit juice do you like?

• Have students look at the pictures on the menu. In pairs, ask them to match the names of the menu items with the pictures. Point out that beverages are not pictured. Review the names of each pictured menu item as a class.

• With a partner, have students talk about which menu items they like and dislike. Have several pairs report to the class a like or dislike they have in common; for example, *We both like ice cream, He doesn't like fish, and I don't either.*

Option: If your class is ready, ask students to name other foods they like and dislike. Write some of the foods students mention on the board. [+**5 minutes**]

Option: Have students look again at the foods listed on the board. Ask *Are there any appetizers? Are there any entrees?* For each category on the menu, ask students to find examples on the board. [+**5 minutes**]

Challenge: Ask students to find three words on the menu that describe how the food is prepared (*fried, grilled, roast[ed]*). Some students may be able to explain the meaning of each (*fried* = cooked in hot oil; *grilled* = cooked on a hot surface, such as a pan; *roast[ed]* = cooked in a hot, dry oven). [+**5 minutes**]

B. Look at the menu again . . .

Suggested teaching time:	5–10 minutes
Your actual teaching time:	_____

• Have students complete Exercise B independently.

• Review as a class. For each item that can be found on the menu, ask students to give examples. (1. food choices: potato soup, grilled steak, tomato salad . . .)

Option: Talk about the information that cannot be found on the menu. For item 3, ask *What do you think the price of the fried fish at the World Café is? How much are entrees at your favorite restaurant?* For item 5, ask *Do you know the name of a waiter or waitress at your favorite restaurant?* For item 7, ask *Do you read restaurant reviews before going to a restaurant?* [+**5 minutes**]

C 🎧 SOUND BITES

Suggested teaching time:	10 minutes
Your actual teaching time:	_____

Note: The accented speaker in this Sound Bites is Sri Lankan.

- Before students read and listen to the conversation, ask some questions about the photo:
    Where are they? (in a restaurant)
    What's the man's occupation? (waiter)
    What is the woman doing? (She's ordering food from the menu.)
- After students listen and read, ask:
    Does the customer order an appetizer? (Yes, she does.)
    What appetizer does she order? (She orders black bean soup.)

Continue in a similar manner for each course.

- Have students listen to the conversation again. Tell students to circle three items the customer orders on the menu on page 52. Students should circle black bean soup, roast chicken, bottled water. It is also acceptable if students circle one of the salad choices.

Language note: This authentic conversation uses a number of shortened phrases that are typical of spoken English. "The carrots, please." is short for "I'll have the carrots, please." "Anything to drink?" is short for "Would you like anything to drink?" It is not expected that students will produce such constructions yet, but it is important for them to observe them, which will greatly increase their comprehension and begin to prepare them to produce them later.

D Read the conversation . . .

Suggested teaching time:	5–10 minutes
Your actual teaching time:	_____

- Have students complete Exercise D independently.
- Have students check answers with a partner. Ask them to change the false sentence to make it true. (2. The customer doesn't order [fish] *or* The customer [does] order [soup].)

Challenge: Ask *What do entrees come with at your favorite restaurant?* **[+5 minutes]**

WHAT ABOUT **YOU?**

Suggested teaching time:	15–20 minutes
Your actual teaching time:	_____

Language note: One of the separate parts of a meal (appetizer, salad, entree, etc.) is called a *course*. The word *entree* sometimes means "first course" and sometimes means "second course" or "main course," depending on the country or region in which the restaurant is located.

- Read the courses listed on the notepad and have students repeat. Give students a minute to study the menu on page 52. Then ask them to close their books. Name different foods on the menu and have the class call out the course. For example, you say *apple pie*, and the class responds *dessert*.
- Have students independently complete the notepad with their food choices.

Option: Have students add their favorite foods that are not found on the menu on page 52 to the notepad. **[+5 minutes]**

PAIR WORK

- With a more advanced student, model how to compare choices. Say *I'd like the grilled shrimp. What about you?*

EXTRAS (optional)

    Workbook: Exercises 1, 2

🎧 **SOUND BITES.** Read along silently as you listen to a natural conversation.

WAITER: Are you ready to order? Or do you need some more time?

CUSTOMER: I'm ready. I think I'll start with the black bean soup. Then I'll have the roast chicken. That comes **CN** with salad, doesn't it?

WAITER: Yes, it does. And there's also a choice of vegetables. Tonight we have carrots or grilled tomatoes.

CUSTOMER: The carrots, please.

WAITER: Certainly. Anything to drink?

CUSTOMER: I'll have bottled water, no ice.

D Read the conversation carefully again. Then write **true** or **false**.

<u> true </u> **1.** The customer orders carrots.

<u> false </u> **2.** The customer doesn't order soup.

<u> true </u> **3.** The chicken comes with salad.

<u> true </u> **4.** The chicken comes with a vegetable.

CN Corpus Notes:
When ordering food or drinks, "I'll have the…" is almost three times more common than "I'd like the…" in spoken American English.

WHAT ABOUT **YOU?**

Look at the menu from the World Café again. Write the items that you would like to order.

appetizer:
salad:
entrée / main course:
dessert:
beverage:

PAIR WORK. Compare your choices. Are they the same or different?

1 ▶ Discuss What to Eat

🎧 **CONVERSATION MODEL** Read and listen.

A: What is there to eat?
B: Not much. Cheese, bread, . . . eggs.
A: Is that all? I'm in the mood for seafood.
B: Sorry. You're out of luck. Let's go out!
A: Good idea!

🎧 **Rhythm and intonation practice**

A ▶ **GRAMMAR.** Count and non-count nouns / **there is** and **there are** **CN**

Count and non-count nouns

Count nouns name things you can count. They are singular or plural.

singular count noun	plural count noun
an **egg**	ten **eggs**

Non-count nouns name things you can not count. They are not singular or plural. Don't use a, an, or a number with non-count nouns.

rice   NOT ~~a rice~~   NOT ~~rices~~

There is and there are

Use there is with non-count nouns and singular count nouns.
Use there are with plural count nouns.

There's milk and an apple in the fridge.

There are oranges, too. But **there aren't** any vegetables.

Use there is with something, anything, or nothing.

Is there anything to eat? No, **there isn't** anything.

count nouns
an appetizer   an onion
an apple   an orange
a cookie   a sandwich
an egg   a vegetable

non-count nouns
bread   juice   rice
candy   lettuce   salt
cheese   meat   seafood
chocolate   milk   soup
coffee   pasta   sugar
fruit

GRAMMAR BOOSTER

PAGES G7–G9
For more . . .

B ▶ **Complete each sentence or question with a form of there is or there are.**

1. __Is there__ anything in the fridge?
2. __Are there__ any cookies?
3. I hope __there is__ no chocolate in this cake. I'm allergic.
4. __Is there__ anything to eat in this house? I'm hungry.
5. __There are__ eggs in the fridge. We could make an omelette.
6. I don't think __there are__ any vegetables on the menu.
7. __There is__ too much sugar in this coffee.
8. __Is there__ enough lettuce to make a salad?

CN **Corpus Notes:**
Learners often use "there are" incorrectly, such as before a list of items. For example, "There are a bedroom, a bathroom, and a kitchen."

LESSON

▶1 *Discuss What to Eat*

🎧 CONVERSATION **MODEL**

Suggested teaching time:	10 minutes
Your actual teaching time:	_____

- Before students read and listen, have them look at the photo. Ask some easy and some analytical questions:
  Where are the people? (in the kitchen)
  What is the woman doing? (She's opening the fridge.)
  What do you think their relationship is? (husband and wife)
  Do you think they have children? (yes / probably)
  Why? (There are pictures on the fridge.)

- After students read and listen, ask comprehension questions:
  What's in the fridge? (cheese, bread, eggs)
  Does the man want cheese, bread, or eggs? (no)
  What does he want? (seafood)
  Is there seafood in the fridge? (no)
  Are they going to eat at home? (no)
  Where are they going? (out to eat, to a restaurant)

- Write on the board *What do you want for dinner tonight? I'm in the mood for _____.* Have students ask and answer the question with several classmates.

- To demonstrate the meaning of *You're out of luck,* ask individual students what they want for dinner tonight. Following is an example conversation:
  Teacher: What do you want for dinner tonight?
  Student: I'm in the mood for [steak].
  Teacher: Sorry. There isn't any [steak] in the fridge. You're out of luck.

🎧 Rhythm and intonation practice

Suggested teaching time:	5 minutes
Your actual teaching time:	_____

- Point out that the woman is looking in the fridge and saying each food item as she sees it. Read Student B's first line out loud. Pause between each food item listed. Model the extended pause between bread and eggs that's indicated by the ellipsis (. . .) Have students repeat.

- Have students repeat each line chorally. Make sure students:

  ○ use falling intonation with *What is there to eat?* and rising intonation with *Is that all?*

  ○ pause after *Not much.*

  ○ use the following stress pattern:

STRESS PATTERN

A: What is there to eat?

B: Not much. Cheese, bread, . . . eggs.

A: Is that all? I'm in the mood for seafood.

B: Sorry. You're out of luck. Let's go out!

A: Good idea!

🅐 GRAMMAR

Suggested teaching time:	5–10 minutes
Your actual teaching time:	_____

Language note: The word *fridge* is a shortened form of the word *refrigerator*. It is used only in informal spoken language but is very commonly used.

- Have students make a list of five foods that are in their refrigerators right now. Then have them read the explanation in the Grammar box.

- On the board, draw a two-column chart with the headings *Count* and *Non-count*. Ask individual students *What's in your fridge?* and have them tell you one food from their list. Ask whether each food is a count or a non-count noun before writing it on the chart.

- Have students use their lists to write sentences with *there is* and *there are*; for example, *There are tomatoes in my fridge. There is / There's juice in my fridge.*

- When students finish, they can use their sentences to ask and answer *Is there anything to eat?* with several classmates and check each other's work at the same time; for example, *Is there anything to eat? There are tomatoes.*

- Have students list five foods that are not in their refrigerators right now and then write sentences with *there isn't* and *there aren't*. Point out that with plural nouns and non-count nouns, it's necessary to use *any* before the noun in negative sentences; for example, *There aren't any tomatoes* or *There isn't any juice.* (*Some* and *any* are taught extensively and productively later in *Top Notch*. *Any* is included here simply to familiarize students with this indefinite in a formulaic way. Students of this level are not yet ready to master *some* and *any*.)

💿 Grammar Self-Checks

🅑 Complete each sentence . . .

Suggested teaching time:	5 minutes
Your actual teaching time:	_____

- Have students check answers with a partner, or review as a class.

- *Cookies, chocolate,* and *lettuce* are new food words that appear in this exercise. Discuss whether they are count (cookies) or non-count (chocolate, lettuce), and add them to the chart on the board.

T54

C 🎧 VOCABULARY BUILDING

Suggested teaching time:	5–10 minutes
Your actual teaching time:	_____

- Before students read and listen to the categories of food, have them cover the words under the pictures with a sheet of paper so that they are looking only at the pictures. With a partner, have students name as many of the foods pictured as they can. Review any foods students don't know. Point out that the words that are in plural form are count and the others are non-count.

- After students complete the activity, write the categories of food on the board. Elicit from the class examples of additional foods for each category and list them under the appropriate category on the board. Have students write down any food words that are new to them, creating individualized vocabulary lists.

Language note: In British English, candy, cookies, french fries, and chips are called *sweets, biscuits, chips,* and *crisps* respectively. In American English, biscuits are a kind of small bread.

Option: Students plan their meals for tomorrow. Have students copy the chart from the board. Students fill in what they are having for each meal, writing the foods in the appropriate row according to the category they belong to. For example, if a student is having cereal with milk and bananas for breakfast tomorrow, he or she would write that information in the breakfast column. After students complete their charts, have them ask and answer questions in pairs. *(What are you having for lunch tomorrow? Are you having any vegetables for dinner?)* Point out that *have* can be used in the present continuous when it refers to eating or drinking instead of possession.

	breakfast	lunch	dinner	snacks
fruit				
vegetables				
meat				
seafood				
grains				
dairy products				
sweets				

[+10 minutes]

🔘 **Graphic Organizer**

🔘 **Vocabulary Cards**

🔘 **Learning Strategies**

D 🎧 LISTENING COMPREHENSION

Suggested teaching time:	10 minutes
Your actual teaching time:	_____

- After students listen the first time, tell them to listen for the food that is talked about in each conversation. Point out that students will write the category the food belongs to, not the food itself. To demonstrate this, pause after the first conversation and ask *What food or drink are they talking about?* (milk) *What category of food is milk?* (dairy products)

AUDIOSCRIPT

CONVERSATION 1
M: I'm going shopping. Need anything from the supermarket?
F: Yeah. Could you pick up a gallon of milk?
M: No problem.

CONVERSATION 2
F: Are we out of bread?
M: No, we aren't. There's bread on the table.

CONVERSATION 3
F: What's for supper tonight?
M: I don't know. I'm in the mood for chicken.

CONVERSATION 4
M: Are there any apples?
F: No, there aren't. But there are bananas.

CONVERSATION 5
M: Are you ready to order?
F: Yes. I am. What's the special?
M: Fried shrimp.
F: Sounds good. I'll have that.

CONVERSATION 6 [M1 = U.S. regional]
M1: Excuse me, waiter. Can I have carrots instead of broccoli?
M2: No problem.

CONVERSATION PAIR WORK

Suggested teaching time:	5–10 minutes
Your actual teaching time:	_____

- Model the activity with a more advanced student. Play the role of Student B. Demonstrate continuing the conversation in a way that is slightly different from the model; for example, *Want to go out?* or *Let's go to Ronald's.* Encourage Student A to ask you a question in response to keep the conversation going; for example, *Any suggestions? Do you know a good (seafood, pasta, etc.) restaurant? What about (restaurant name)?* or *Where's the restaurant? Is it expensive?* Students can also use *Great!* and *Perfect!* in their conversations.

- When students practice the conversation, have them take turns playing the roles of Student A and Student B.

- Ask volunteers to present their conversations to the class.

🔘 **Pair Work Cards**

EXTRAS (optional)

Grammar Booster
Workbook: Exercises 3–6
Copy & Go: Activity 17

C 🎧 VOCABULARY BUILDING. Categories of food. Add another food you know to each list. Then listen and practice. (Answers will vary, but may include the following:)

fruit
① apples ② bananas
③ grapes ④ oranges

mangoes

vegetables
⑤ carrots ⑥ peppers
⑦ broccoli ⑧ onions

spinach, green beans

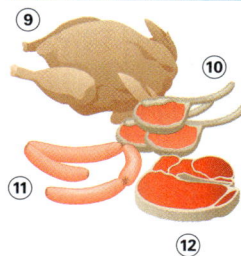

meat
⑨ chicken ⑩ lamb
⑪ sausage ⑫ beef

pork, turkey

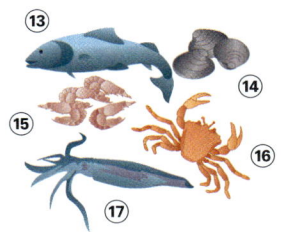

seafood
⑬ fish ⑭ clams
⑮ shrimp ⑯ crab
⑰ squid
salmon

grains
⑱ pasta ⑲ rice
⑳ noodles ㉑ bread
cereal, tortilla

dairy products
㉒ butter ㉓ cheese
㉔ milk ㉕ yogurt
cream, margarine

oils
㉖ corn oil ㉗ olive oil
㉘ coconut oil
sesame oil

sweets
㉙ candy ㉚ pie
㉛ cake ㉜ cookies
ice cream, soft drinks

D 🎧 LISTENING COMPREHENSION. Listen to the conversations. Then listen again. Classify the foods in each conversation.

1. *dairy products*
2. grains
3. meat
4. fruit
5. seafood
6. vegetables

CONVERSATION PAIR WORK

Discuss what to eat. Use foods __you__ like and eat. Use the guide, or create a new conversation.

A: What is there to eat?
B: _____.
A: Is that all? I'm in the mood for _____.
B: _____ . . .

Continue the conversation in your __own__ way.

Make Food Choices

🎧 CONVERSATION MODEL Read and listen.

A: I'll have the pasta for my main course, please. What does that come with?

B: It comes with soup or a salad.

A: What kind of soup is there? **CN**

B: There's tomato soup or chicken soup.

A: I think I'll have the salad.

B: Certainly. And to drink?

A: Water, please.

🎧 **Rhythm and intonation practice**

Ⓐ GRAMMAR. A / an / the

a / an

It comes with **a salad** and **an appetizer**.

---

the

Use the to name something a second time.

A: It comes with a salad.
B: OK. I'll have **the salad**.

Also use the to talk about something specific.

A: Would you like an appetizer? [not specific]
B: Yes. **The fried clams** sound delicious. [specific: they're on the menu]

GRAMMAR BOOSTER

PAGES G9–G10
For more . . .

Ⓑ 🎧 PRONUNCIATION. The. Compare the pronunciation of the before consonant and vowel sounds. Read and listen. Then repeat.

/ə/(before consonant sounds)
the chicken
the soup
the juice
the hot appetizer
the fried eggs

/i/(before vowel sounds)
the orange juice
the onion soup
the apple juice
the appetizer
the eggs

CN Corpus Notes:
"Kind of" is much more common than "type of" – in both spoken and written American English – and is almost always used when talking about food or drinks.

LESSON

2 ▶ Make Food Choices

🎧 CONVERSATION **MODEL**

Suggested teaching time:	10 minutes
Your actual teaching time:	_____

- Check comprehension using the notepad on page 53. Have students copy the course names onto a sheet of paper and then close their books. Play the conversation two more times. The first time, instruct students to make a check mark next to the courses the customer orders (salad, main course, beverage). The second time, have students write what he orders for each course, if known (main course: pasta; beverage: orange juice).

Option: On the board, write the lines from the conversation in random order, numbering them from 1 to 7. Have students try to determine who says each line. On a sheet of paper, have students number from 1 to 7 and write either *customer* or *waitress* for each item. **[+10 minutes]**

🎧 Rhythm and intonation practice

Suggested teaching time:	5 minutes
Your actual teaching time:	_____

- Have students repeat each line chorally. Make sure students:
  - use falling intonation on *What does that come with?* and *What kind of soup is there?*.
  - use rising intonation with *And to drink?*.
  - accurately imitate the intonation of these sentences: *It comes with soup or a salad* and *There's tomato soup or chicken soup.* Students should use rising intonation before *or* and falling intonation after *or*.
  - use the following stress pattern:

┌─ **STRESS PATTERN** ──────────────────┐

A: I'll have the pasta for my main course, please.

What does that come with?

B: It comes with soup or a salad.

A: What kind of soup is there?

B: There's tomato soup or chicken soup.

A: I think I'll have the salad.

B: Certainly. And to drink?

A: Water, please.

└──────────────────────────────┘

🔶 GRAMMAR

Suggested teaching time:	5–10 minutes
Your actual teaching time:	_____

- Have students read the information in the Grammar box.
- On the board, write: *I'm in the mood for an appetizer.* Ask *How many appetizers do I want?* (one) Then cross out *appetizer* and change it to *soup*. Circle the indefinite article and ask *Do I use* a *or* an *with soup?* (no) *Why?* (Because *soup* is non-count; you can count bowls of soup but not soup itself.)
- Have students read the soup and appetizer specials from the menu at the bottom of page 57. Ask each student *What would you like?* Prompt students to answer in a complete sentence and use *the* before their choices; for example, *I'd like the seafood salad.*
- Make sure students understand that:
  - the first time a singular noun is mentioned, we use the article *a* or *an*.
  - the first time a plural noun or a non-count noun is used, no article is used.
  - the second time a noun (singular or plural or a non-count noun) is mentioned or to talk about something specific, use *the*.

Option: On the board, draw the inside of a refrigerator with three shelves (a rectangle with three horizontal lines). Make the drawing as large as possible. Label the shelves *top shelf, middle shelf, bottom shelf*. Say *Tell me what to put on the shelves in the fridge.* Students direct you to draw different foods and beverages. (*Put an onion on the top shelf. Put some milk on the bottom shelf.*) Make sure students use *a/an* with singular nouns and *some* with noncount or plural nouns. After a few items are in the refrigerator, say *You can also tell me to move something that is already in the fridge.* Erase and redraw items according to students' directions. Make sure students use *the* when telling you to move an item; for example, *Move the milk to the top shelf.* With pencil and paper, students can do the same activity with a partner. **[+10 minutes]**

💿 **Grammar Self-Checks**

🔶 🎧 PRONUNCIATION

Suggested teaching time:	5–10 minutes
Your actual teaching time:	_____

- Before students listen, have them look at the two lists of words. Ask *How are the words in the first list alike?* (They all start with consonants.) Then do the same for the second list. (They all start with vowel sounds.) Explain that *the* is pronounced differently before consonants and vowel sounds. If students don't know the terms vowel and consonant, refer them to page G7 in the Grammar Booster.

💿 **Pronunciation Activities**

C Write a, an, or the.

Suggested teaching time: 10 minutes
Your actual teaching time: _____

- After students complete the exercise, have them check their answers by reading the conversation in groups of three. Group members should discuss any different answers they have. Remind students to practice the correct pronunciation of *the*.
- Review as a class. Ask volunteers to read the conversation out loud to the class.
- Ask:
  What does the man order? (tortilla soup and Thai chicken)
  What does the woman order? (tortilla soup and the seafood special)
- Have students circle the picture of hot pepper sauce. Explain that when a food is said to be spicy, it means it has a strong taste and gives you a pleasant burning feeling in your mouth.
- Ask:
  What other types of food are spicy? (Mexican, Korean, Indian)
  Do you like spicy food?
  What is a spicy dish that you like?
  Do you put hot sauce on your food?

Challenge: Have students number the three rules [1 (for *a* or *an*), 2 (for *the* to name something a second time), and 3 (for *the* to talk about something specific)] in the Grammar box on page 56. For each answer in Exercise C, ask students to indicate which rule applies by writing a 1, 2, or 3 next to it. **[+5 minutes]**

CONVERSATION **PAIR WORK**

Suggested teaching time: 10–15 minutes
Your actual teaching time: _____

- Review the items on the menu board. Talk about any items students may not understand.
- Model the activity with a more advanced student. Play the role of Student A. In Student A's second line, use *appetizers* instead of *soup* and emphasize *are* in *What kind of appetizers are there?*
- As a class, brainstorm responses other than *Certainly* for Student B's last line, such as *OK, Sure, Great, Absolutely.*
- In pairs, students practice ordering from the menu. Have students switch roles to practice both parts.

Option: Have pairs create their own menu board with tonight's specials. Students then trade boards with another pair and practice the conversation again. **[+10 minutes]**

 Pair Work Cards

EXTRAS (optional)

Grammar Booster
Workbook: Exercises 7–10
Copy & Go: Activity 18

 Pronunciation Supplements

T57

C **Write _a_, _an_, or _the_.**

HUSBAND: What do you feel like eating tonight?

WIFE: Well, __the__ seafood special sounds delicious. I think I'll order that. What about you?

HUSBAND: I'm not sure. I'm really in the mood for __a__ spicy dish.

WIFE: Well, what about __the__ Thai chicken? Thai food is usually spicy.

HUSBAND: Sounds good.

HUSBAND: Excuse me! We're ready to order.

WAITER: Certainly. Would you like to start with __an__ appetizer or soup? Our soup of the day is tortilla soup—that's __a__ Mexican specialty.

HUSBAND: Is __the__ tortilla soup spicy?

WAITER: Not very. But we can give you hot pepper sauce to put into it if you'd like.

HUSBAND: OK. I'll have __the__ tortilla soup—with the hot sauce on the side.

WIFE: I'll have the same thing, please.

WAITER: And for your main course? We have __a__ nice seafood special on __the__ menu tonight.

WIFE: Good. I'll have __the__ seafood special.

HUSBAND: Hmm. I love Thai food. I'll have __the__ Thai chicken.

WAITER: You won't need hot sauce with that, sir!

CONVERSATION
PAIR WORK

**Make food choices from the menu with a partner.
Use the guide, or create a new conversation.**

A: I'll have the _____ for my main course, please. What does that come with?

B: _____.

A: What kind of _____ there?

B: _____.

A: I think I'll have the _____.

B: _____. And to drink?

A: _____, please.

Tonight's Specials

Soup   tomato soup
        beef noodle soup

Appetizers
        seafood salad
        grilled vegetables

Main Courses   all come with soup
                or an appetizer
        grilled chicken
        pasta with clam sauce
        roast lamb

Beverages
        fruit juices   coffee
        bottled water   tea

Order and Pay for a Meal

A 🎧 **VOCABULARY.** **What to say to a waiter or waitress.** **Listen and practice.**

Excuse me!

We're ready to order.

We'll take the check, please. **CN** ↓

Is the tip included?

Do you accept credit cards?

B 🎧 **LISTENING COMPREHENSION.** **Listen to the conversations in a restaurant.** **Then listen again and predict the next thing the customer will say to the waiter or waitress.**

1. ☑ Is the tip included in the check? ☐ We'll take the check, please.
2. ☐ Is the tip included? ☑ We're ready to order.
3. ☐ Excuse me! ☑ No, thanks. We'll take the check, please.
4. ☐ Is the tip included? ☑ Do you accept credit cards?
5. ☑ I'll have the seafood soup, please. ☐ Excuse me!

C **PAIR WORK.** **Imagine you're in a restaurant.** **Practice asking and answering the questions. Write the answers. Then reverse roles and do it again.**

Your questions   **Your partner's answers**

1. What do you feel like eating for an appetizer? _____

2. What do you want for a main course? _____

3. What would you like for a beverage? _____

4. How about a dessert? What are you in the mood for? _____

CN **Corpus Notes:**
In restaurants and bars, some people refer to "the check" and some people refer to "the bill." They are equally common in spoken American English.

3 ▸ Order and Pay for a Meal

A 🎧 VOCABULARY

Suggested teaching time:	5 minutes
Your actual teaching time:	_____

- Students read and listen to the vocabulary, then repeat each phrase.
- To check students' understanding, ask about each picture and vocabulary item. For example, for *We're ready to order,* you can ask *Do they know what they want to eat?* (yes) For *We'll take the check, please,* have students point out the check in the following picture.

Language note: A *tip* is the extra money you give a waiter or waitress.

- Tell students to think about their favorite restaurant. Ask questions about the restaurant:
  What is the name of the restaurant? Where is it?
  What do you usually order?
  Is the tip included in the check?
  How much do you usually give for a tip?
  Do they accept credit cards?

Challenge: For each vocabulary item, have students create a response for the waiter. For example, for *Excuse me!* the waiter might respond, *Are you ready to order?* For *We're ready to order,* the waiter might respond *Certainly. What would you like?* **[+5 minutes]**

💿 **Vocabulary Cards**

💿 **Learning Strategies**

B 🎧 LISTENING COMPREHENSION

Suggested teaching time:	10–15 minutes
Your actual teaching time:	_____

- Tell students that they will listen to conversations between people in a restaurant. Play or read the conversations twice.
- Before students listen the second time, have them read the answer choices.
- After students complete the exercise, review the answers. Then have students listen a third time, pausing after each conversation. Ask a few questions about the conversation before eliciting the answer. For example, for Conversation 1, ask *Do they have the check or do they need the check? Were their meals expensive or inexpensive? What does the customer want to know?*

AUDIOSCRIPT

CONVERSATION 1 [M2 = Chinese]
M1: Can you believe this check?
M2: What do you mean?
M1: It's more than I earn in a week!
M2: I wonder if that includes a tip.

CONVERSATION 2 [F1 = U.S. regional]
F1: What are you in the mood for?
F2: Something fast. I don't have much time.
F1: Well, why don't you order soup? They have your favorite, black bean.
F2: Good idea. That's probably ready.

CONVERSATION 3
M: Excuse me. Are you finished with your meal?
F: Yes, thanks. It was delicious.
M: Would you care for some dessert or some coffee? Or an after-dinner drink?

CONVERSATION 4 [F1 = Sri Lankan]
F1: I don't have enough cash to pay for this. Do you think they take credit cards?
F2: They probably accept plastic. Just ask.

CONVERSATION 5 [M = British English]
M: Good evening. I'm John, and I'll be your server. Would you like to hear about tonight's specials?
F: Actually, no, thanks. We're ready to order.
M: Certainly.

C ◁ PAIR WORK

Suggested teaching time:	10–15 minutes
Your actual teaching time:	_____

- Model the activity with a more advanced student. Ask the first two questions and write the student's answers on the board. Have the student ask you the next two questions and write your own answers on the board.

Option: Write each of the questions that follow on a small slip of paper. Pass one question out to each student. (If you have more than fourteen students, repeat some of the questions.) Tell students to pretend they're in a restaurant in their town. Students pair up, ask each other their questions, and then trade slips of paper and move on to find another partner. Continue until students have had the opportunity to ask and answer several different questions. **[+10 minutes]**

What are you in the mood for?
What do you feel like eating?
What do you want for an appetizer?
What would you like for an entree?
What would you like to drink?
Are you having soup or salad?
What about the _____?
Why don't you order the _____?
Do you want some dessert or some coffee?
Want to share an appetizer?
Any suggestions?
Do you know what's in the _____?
What's good here?
Is the _____ spicy?

TOP NOTCH **INTERACTION**

Suggested teaching time:	20–25 minutes
Your actual teaching time:	_____

- To prepare for the activity, have students circle on the menu what they would like for each course.

- Put students into groups of three. Students practice discussing the menu, ordering, and paying. Each person in the group should take a turn playing the role of server.

- Have volunteers present their conversations to the class.

- Remind students to refer to NEED HELP? to support them in their role play.

Note: All language in this menu is known, though words from the menu on page 52 have been combined in different ways. If students have difficulty, write the following words on the board:

> fried
>
> pie
>
> salad
>
> spicy
>
> mixed
>
> grilled

Ask students to find these words in the menu on page 52.

Option: Tell each group to create their own menu. Then have groups exchange menus and practice discussing and ordering from the menus, and paying for their meals. **[+10 minutes]**

Challenge: Ask students to combine the food and food preparation words to make the largest possible list of dishes. **[+5 minutes]**

EXTRAS (optional)

Copy & Go: Activity 19

ROLE PLAY. Form groups of diners and servers at tables. Practice discussing the menu and ordering and paying for food.

LAND AND SEA

All Entrées include
Bread • Pasta or Salad • Vegetable
Coffee or Tea

APPETIZERS
Fried clams • Mini vegetable pies (2) • Shrimp salad

SOUP
French onion • Beef vegetable • Spicy fish

ENTRÉES
Steak • Chicken and rice • Mixed grilled seafood

Children's menu available

DESSERTS
Chocolate cake • Carrot cake

NEED HELP? Here's language you already know:

Discuss food

What do you feel like eating?
I'm in the mood for ____.
There's ____ on the menu.
The ____ sound(s) delicious!
What about ____?

Serve food

Are you ready to order?
Do you need more time?
That comes with ____.
Would you like ____?
Anything to drink?
And to drink?
And for your main course /
    dessert / beverage?

Order food

Excuse me!
I'm / We're ready.
I'd like to start with ____.
I think I'll have ____.
And then I'll have ____.
Does that come with ____?
What kind of ____ is there?

Pay for food

I'll / We'll take the check,
    please.
Is the tip included?
Do you accept credit
    cards?

4 *Discuss Food and Health*

A 🎧 VOCABULARY. Food and health. Listen and practice.

healthy (or healthful)   good for your body
> Take care of your body! Choose foods that are healthy.

fatty   containing a lot of fat or oil
> Some fatty foods are meat, fried foods, and cheese.

a portion   the amount of a food that you eat at one time **CN**
> Eat at least five portions of fruit and vegetables every day.

a meal   breakfast, lunch, or dinner
> Many people eat three meals a day.

a snack   food you eat between meals
> Raw vegetables are a healthy low-calorie snack, but
> many people prefer high-fat snacks like potato chips and nuts.

in moderation   not too much
> Eat sweets in moderation. Small portions are better.

"Veggies"

B READING WARM-UP. Is eating healthy food important to you?

CN Corpus Notes:
The word "portion" is followed by the word "of" 82% of the time in American English.

C 🎧 READING. Read the tips from the nutrition website. Which tip do you think is the most important?

Healthy Eating Tips

search [   ] [go]

| Home | Healthy Eating | Kid-Friendly Snacks | Food Shopping Tips | Eat Out, Eat Smart |

Here are some tips for healthy eating at home, work, and elsewhere.

Try some of these ideas.

- Start your day off right! Eat breakfast.
- Take a piece of fruit to munch on during your commute. It tastes great, is filling, and provides energy.
- Use "lite" dairy products, which are low-fat and better for your health.

- If you like to eat meat, trim all visible fat.
- Fried foods? Snacks? Desserts? Sweets? They taste great but are not great for you. They are high in calories and can be high in fat, salt, and sugar.
- Pack your own snacks of raw veggies. Buy healthy snacks like pretzels.
- Cut down on portion size so you don't eat too much unhealthy food.
- Eat everything in moderation.

Home
About
FAQ's
Links
Contact

E-Mail This Page ✉   Print This Page 🖥   Next Page ➡

SOURCE: http://www.nlm.nih.gov/medlineplus/

LESSON

4 *Discuss Food and Health*

A 🎧 VOCABULARY

Suggested teaching time:	5 minutes
Your actual teaching time:	_____

- On the board, draw a two-column chart with the headings *Healthy* and *Not healthy / Unhealthy.* Before students read or listen to the vocabulary, ask *What foods are good for your body? What foods are not good for your body?* Record students' answers on the chart.

Language note: *Healthful* is the more traditional way to describe foods; *healthy* is more traditional for describing a person's health. It is more common today, however, to hear *healthy* for both meanings.

- Have students read or listen to the vocabulary, definitions, and examples. Then read and discuss the vocabulary as a class. For each vocabulary item, ask a question:
    Do you usually eat healthy foods?
    What is your favorite fatty food?
    How many portions of fruit and vegetables do you eat in a day?
    How many meals do you eat a day?
    What do you eat for snacks?
    Do you eat fatty foods in moderation?
    What about sweets?

Option: Have students write down everything they ate yesterday. Then have them classify those foods according to the following categories: *cereals and grains; fruits and vegetables; dairy products; meat, seafood, beans and eggs; sweets, oils, and fats.* For each category, students determine how many portions they ate. **[+10 minutes]**

Language note: *Veggies* is an informal word meaning vegetables.

🔵 **Vocabulary Cards**

B READING WARM-UP

Suggested teaching time:	5 minutes
Your actual teaching time:	_____

- To model, answer the question yourself.
    Eating healthy is important to me. It gives me energy.

Language note: *Healthy* (an adjective) is used here as an adverb. This is non-traditional but acceptable in informal speech and writing.

- Ask the class for some reasons why eating healthy food is important to them. Write these on the board.

C 🎧 READING

Suggested teaching time:	10–15 minutes
Your actual teaching time:	_____

- After students read and listen, discuss each tip as a class. For each tip, ask students if it is something they already do. For example, after the first tip, ask *Do you eat breakfast?* For each bulleted item, have students make a checkmark if it's something they usually do. If it's something they don't do, have them circle the item.

- For the other bulleted items, you might ask:
    Do you take fruit to eat in the car / on the train / on the bus?
    Do you use low-fat dairy products?
    Do you cut the fat off meat?
    Do you eat foods that are low in fat, salt, and sugar?
    Do you take healthy snacks to work / school with you?
    Do you eat small portions?

- Have students look at the items they circled. Ask:
    Do you want to make any changes to your eating habits?
    What do you think you want to do?

Option: Have students look for healthy eating tips on the Internet or in newspapers or magazines. Encourage students to bring in what they find and share it with the class. **[+10 minutes]**

🔵 **Learning Strategies**

D UNDERSTANDING MEANING FROM CONTENT

| Suggested teaching time: | 5–10 minutes |
| Your actual teaching time: | _____ |

- Have students read the underlined words and phrases. Tell students to find and circle these words and phrases in the reading on page 60. Students read each bulleted item that contains an underlined word or phrase again.
- Review the answers as a class. Substitute each answer choice as described previously. Then ask *Which one is correct?*

Extra Reading Comprehension Activities

TOP NOTCH INTERACTION

| Suggested teaching time: | 20–25 minutes |
| Your actual teaching time: | _____ |

STEP 1

- For each food students marked with an (✗), ask them why they think the food is not healthy. (high in calories / fat / salt / sugar)
- Have students compare answers and discuss any different answers they have. Students may disagree about which foods are healthy (see the *Culture note* that follows).

STEP 2

- If necessary, review the meanings of *spicy, fatty, salty,* and *sweet*. For *spicy*, refer students to the pictures of hot sauce on page 57. For *fatty*, refer students to the definition and examples on page 60. For *salty*, point out the salt shaker in the photo on page 56. For *sweet*, have students look at the sweets category on page 55.
- After students classify the foods from the pictures, review the answers as a class.

Option: Write as headings on the board *Spicy, Fatty, Salty, Sweet*. Have students look back through the pages of this unit to find other foods that are spicy, fatty, salty, or sweet. List these on the board. (Spicy: Thai chicken, hot pepper sauce, garlic bread; Fatty: cheese, corn oil, fried seafood; Salty: pretzels; Sweet: chocolate cake, fruit pie, candy) **[+5 minutes]**

STEP 3

- Model the activity by answering the questions yourself.
  I like beef, rice and broccoli. I also like spicy food. I try to eat healthy food every day. I eat sweets in moderation.
- In answering the first question, students can use the categories from Step 2 and those from page 55.

Culture note: People in different places around the world have different ideas about healthy eating. Some people count calories. They try to eat small portions and choose foods that are low in sugar and fat. Other people follow a low-fat, high-fiber diet (avoid fatty foods and eat a lot of grains, fruits, and vegetables). Recently, many people have been trying diets that are high in protein and low in carbohydrates. These people eat a lot of meat, seafood, and nuts. They don't eat bread, rice, pasta, noodles, or even many high-carbohydrate fruits and vegetables.

EXTRAS (optional)

Workbook: Exercises 11, 12
Copy & Go: Activity 20

UNDERSTANDING MEANING FROM CONTEXT. Use each sentence to help you understand the meaning of each underlined word or phrase.

1. Take a piece of fruit to <u>munch on</u> during your commute.
   - ☑ eat
   - ☐ buy

2. If you like to eat meat, <u>trim</u> all visible fat.
   - ☐ eat
   - ☑ cut off

3. Use "<u>lite</u>" dairy products which are low-fat and better for your health.
   - ☐ fatty
   - ☑ not fatty

4. <u>Cut down on portion size</u> so you don't eat too much unhealthy food.
   - ☐ Eat larger portions
   - ☑ Eat smaller portions

TOP NOTCH
INTERACTION • *What's Good?*

STEP 1. PAIR WORK. Together write a check mark ✔ next to the foods you think are healthy. Write an ✗ next to the foods you think are not healthy. Do you agree or disagree?

_____ rice   _____ french fries   _____ peppers and garlic   _____ ice cream

_____ nuts and chips   _____ chicken   _____ salad   _____ pasta with sauce

STEP 2. On the notepad, classify the foods from the pictures.

spicy:	*peppers and garlic*
fatty:	
salty:	
sweet:	

STEP 3. DISCUSSION. What kind of food do you like? Do you eat healthy foods? What do you eat in moderation? Discuss with your classmates.

FREE PRACTICE

UNIT 5
CHECKPOINT

A 🎧 **LISTENING COMPREHENSION.** Listen critically to the conversations. Are they in a restaurant or at home? Check ☑ the boxes.

	Restaurant	Home
1.	☑	☐
2.	☐	☑
3.	☑	☐
4.	☐	☐

B Classify foods. Complete the chart with some foods in each category.

Fruit	Vegetables	Meat	Dairy products	Seafood	Grains
apples	carrots	chicken	butter	fish	pasta
bananas	peppers	lamb	cheese	clams	rice
grapes	broccoli	sausage	milk	shrimp	noodles
oranges	onions	beef	yogurt	crab	bread

C Write four questions you can ask a waiter or a waitress.

1. What does that come with ?
2. What kind of soup is there ?
3. Do you accept credit cards ?
4. Is the tip included ?

D Complete with a form of <u>there is</u> or <u>there are</u>.

1. _There is_ too much pepper in the soup.

2. I hope _there is_ not too much sugar in the cake. Sugar isn't good for you.

3. I'm looking for a good restaurant. _Are there_ any restaurants near you?

4. _Are there_ any low-fat desserts on the menu?

5. _Is there_ an inexpensive restaurant nearby?

6. You should eat some fruit. _There are_ some oranges on the kitchen table.

7. _Is there_ enough cheese in the fridge for two sandwiches?

8. I'm in the mood for soup. What kind of soup _is there_ on the menu?

E **WRITING.** On a separate piece of paper, write information about food in this country for the readers of a travel newsletter.

🎧 **TOP NOTCH SONG**
"The World Café"
Lyrics on last book page.

TOP NOTCH PROJECT
- In groups, choose traditional dishes to describe to a visitor to this country.
- Practice describing the dishes and their ingredients, and how they taste.

TOP NOTCH WEBSITE
For Unit 5 online activities, visit the *Top Notch* Companion Website at www.longman.com/topnotch.

UNIT 5
CHECKPOINT

A 🎧 LISTENING COMPREHENSION

Suggested teaching time:	5–10 minutes
Your actual teaching time:	_____

- Before students listen, ask *What words would you use or hear when talking about food in a restaurant?* (menu, appetizer, entree, "I'll have," check) *What words would you use or hear when talking about food at home?* (fridge, kitchen, cook)
- Review answers as a class.

AUDIOSCRIPT

CONVERSATION 1 [M = British English]
M: Do you think the price of the entree includes a salad and dessert?
F: The menu doesn't say. Just ask.

CONVERSATION 2
F1: There's nothing in this fridge but veggies. I want something bad for me tonight!
F2: Well, you could just put a lot of salt and oil on the veggies!

CONVERSATION 3 [F = U.S. regional]
F: What do *you* feel like eating?
M: Actually, I feel like seafood tonight.
F: Well, there's a mixed seafood special with shrimp, clams, and crab. What about that?
M: Perfect.

CONVERSATION 4
M: There's cheese, eggs, butter, and some nice lettuce.
F: We could make a cheese omelette and a salad.
M: Sounds great. Let's start cooking.

B Classify foods . . .

Suggested teaching time:	5 minutes
Your actual teaching time:	_____

Option: Have students put a (✓) next to the foods in the chart they like and an (✗) next to the foods they don't like. **[+5 minutes]**

C Write four questions . . .

Suggested teaching time:	5 minutes
Your actual teaching time:	_____

Option: Have students practice asking and answering their questions with a partner. **[+5 minutes]**

D Complete with a form . . .

Suggested teaching time:	5 minutes
Your actual teaching time:	_____

- Explain that students will use *there is, there are, is there,* or *are there.*
- If students have trouble, have them underline the noun in each sentence. *(pepper, sugar, restaurants, low-fat desserts, restaurant, oranges, cheese, soup)* Make sure students know if the noun is not plural, the answer is *there is* (or *is there,* if the sentence is a question).

E WRITING

Suggested teaching time:	10–15 minutes
Your actual teaching time:	_____

- Before students write, generate ideas. Ask *What is the food like in this country?* Write students' ideas on the board.

💿 **Writing Process Worksheets**

💿 *Top Notch Pop* **Song Activities**

TOP NOTCH PROJECT
Idea: Write the following on the board:
What's the name of the dish?
What's in it?
How does it taste?
Is it for breakfast, lunch, or dinner?
Is it healthy? Why or why not?
What restaurants serve the dish?
Is it usually expensive or inexpensive?

Each group chooses a traditional dish. They practice describing it by answering the questions on the board. To describe how the dish tastes, students can use *spicy, salty, sweet, delicious.*

Idea: Each group describes its dish to the class without telling the name of the dish. The class guesses what dish the group is describing.

UNIT WRAP-UP

Suggested teaching time:	15–20 minutes
Your actual teaching time:	_____

Vocabulary

Your students can say . . .

cheese, milk, juice, eggs, cookies, chips, apples, pears, bananas, grapes, salad, chicken, bread, cake, potatoes, pasta

Option: Have students list the foods they remember by category (fruit, vegetables, etc.). Then have students put a (✓) next to the foods they like and an (✗) next to the foods they dislike. Read down the list and ask whether each food is healthy or unhealthy. **[+5 minutes]**

Grammar

• With non-count and plural nouns, students can use *some* in their statements; for example, *There is some bread.*

Option: In pairs, one student looks at his or her statements while the other looks at the picture on page 63. The student looking at the statements checks his or her memory of the foods in the picture by making the statements into questions. *(Is there any bread?)* The student looking at the picture answers *Yes, there is / are* or *No, there isn't / aren't.* **[+10 minutes]**

Challenge: True / false statements. In pairs, students write five *true / false* statements with *There is* or *There are* about the picture. Divide the class into groups of four. One pair reads their statements to the other pair, who say *True* or *False.* For example, A: *There are eggs in the picture.* B: *True.* A: *There are three waiters in the picture.* B: *False. There aren't three waiters in the picture. There are two waiters in the picture.* **[+10 minutes]**

Social language

• Students can create a conversation for the two people looking into the fridge, among the waiter and family members sitting at the table, and/or between any of the pairs of diners.

Option: Writing activity. Have students write their conversations in dialogue form. **[+10 minutes]**

Option: Guessing game. Have students act out one of their conversations in front of the class. Have students listen and guess which people in the picture are being portrayed. **[+10 minutes]**

Challenge: Have pairs copy each line of their conversation onto a slip of paper. Tell them to include a label for the speaker; for example, *wife, husband, daughter, son, woman, man, waiter.* Students then mix up the order of the slips and give them to another pair. The other pair must put the conversation back in the correct order. Each pair then reads the conversation they put in order to the pair who wrote the conversation. **[+10 minutes]**

Your students can say . . .

(For the family in the kitchen)
Wife: What is there to eat? **Husband:** Not much. Cheese and eggs. **Wife:** Is that all? I'm in the mood for chicken. Let's go out! **Husband:** Good idea.

(For the family in restaurant)
Waiter: Are you ready to order? **Woman:** Yes, I'm ready. I'll have the grilled chicken. **Waiter:** Certainly. It comes with soup or salad. **Woman:** I'll have the salad. **Waiter:** OK. And to drink? **Woman:** Tea, please.

(For the couple at the table)
Man: Excuse me! **Waitress:** Yes? **Man:** We'll take the check, please. **Waitress:** Certainly.

Writing

• Point to the picture at the top of the page and ask questions. Write some of the students' answers on the board so they can use the information when they write their stories. Ask: *Who are the people? / What is their relationship? Where are they? What time is it? What are the husband and wife doing? What's the son doing? Is there anything to eat?*

• Point to the family at the bottom of the picture. Ask: *Where are they now? What time is it? What are they doing? What do you think each family member is ordering?*

Option: Ask volunteers to read their story out loud to the class. **[+10 minutes]**

Your students can say . . .

The [Clark] family is in their kitchen. It is 6:10. The mother is looking for something to eat in the fridge. The son is eating cookies. There's some cheese, eggs, juice, and milk in the fridge.

The [Clark] family goes to a restaurant. It is 7:30. They are ordering food from the waiter. There's some bread on the table. The mother is asking about the appetizers. The father wants pasta.

Individual oral progress check (optional)

Use the illustration on page 63 for an oral test. Have students point to people and items in the illustration and ask questions. For example, students could ask *Is there any milk in the fridge?* You could then answer *Yes, there is.* Evaluate students on correctness, intelligibility, and completeness of the questions they ask.

Cumulative Vocabulary Activities

You may wish to use the video for Unit 5 at this point. For video activity worksheets, go to www.longman.com/topnotch.

Complete Assessment Package
Unit 5 Achievement Test
Review Test 1
Speaking Test 1

UNIT WRAP-UP

- **Vocabulary.** Look at the pictures. Then close your book and write the names of all the foods you remember.

- **Grammar.** Write statements with <u>there is</u>/<u>there are</u> for the foods.

- **Social language.** Create conversations for the people.

- **Writing.** Write a story about the family.

LATER

Menu

✔	*Now I can ...*
☐ discuss what to eat.
☐ make food choices.
☐ order and pay for a meal.
☐ discuss food and health.

63

Staying in Shape

UNIT GOALS

1 Plan an activity with someone
2 Talk about daily routines
3 Discuss exercise and diet
4 Describe your typical day

A ▶ **TOPIC PREVIEW.** Look at the graphs. Which activities do you do regularly?

How Many Calories Can a Person*
BURN IN ONE HOUR?
*Based on a person weighing 150 pounds/68.2 kilograms.

PHYSICAL ACTIVITIES

Number of calories burned

Activity	Calories
lift weights	214
go walking	250
go dancing	322
play golf	322
do aerobics	429
go bike riding	500
play tennis	501
play soccer	501
go swimming	572
go running	572
play basketball	572

EVERYDAY ACTIVITIES

Number of calories burned

Activity	Calories
sleep	64
watch TV	71
read	71
talk on the phone	71
work in an office	107
study English	128
go shopping	164
cook dinner	179
clean the house	179
play the guitar	214
take a shower	248

SOURCE: www.msnbc.com

B ᛡ **VOCABULARY.** Activities. Listen and practice.

C ▶ **DISCUSSION.** Do you burn a lot of calories every day? Who in your class burns more than 1500 calories a day?

UNIT 6

Staying in Shape

A TOPIC PREVIEW

Suggested teaching time:	5–10 minutes
Your actual teaching time:	_____

- Have students look at the graphs. Ask:
  What three physical activities can you do to burn a lot of calories? (go swimming, go running, play basketball)
  What four physical activities don't burn a lot of calories? (go walking, go dancing, play golf, lift weights)
  What four everyday activities can you do to burn a lot of calories? (cook dinner, clean the house, play the guitar, take a shower)
  What four everyday activities that you do don't burn a lot of calories? (sleep, watch TV, read, talk on the phone)

Note: These calorie charts are based on a calorie calculator from an authentic source. You and your students may be surprised at some of the information. You may want to ask your students if they are surprised.

- Have students put a checkmark next to the activities they do every day or most days.

- Have students compare their activities with a partner's; for example, *I go walking. Do you?*

Option: Take a poll to find out the most popular physical and everyday activities. On the board, write down the physical and everyday activities from the graphs. Ask *Who likes to go walking? Who likes to go dancing?* Continue in the same manner for all the physical and everyday activities listed. Students raise their hands when they hear the activities they do. Count the number of students who respond to each item and write the number next to the activity name on the board. **[+10 minutes]**

Language note: In British English, *soccer* is called *football*. In American English, *football* is a different game, which is called *American football* in British English.

B VOCABULARY

Suggested teaching time:	10 minutes
Your actual teaching time:	_____

Option: Have a volunteer act out one of the activities. The class guesses what the student is doing. To make a guess, students should use the present continuous; for example, *Are you cleaning the house? Are you going swimming?* The student who guesses correctly then acts out a different activity. **[+10 minutes]**

 Vocabulary Cards

C DISCUSSION

Suggested teaching time:	10 minutes
Your actual teaching time:	_____

- Have students look at their checkmarks on the graphs. Students add up the number of calories they usually burn in a day. If students do an activity for more than one hour, they should multiply the number of calories burned by the number of hours they engage in the activity. For example, if a student rides his or her bike two hours every day, then that student burns 1000 calories (500 × 2).

- Ask *Who burns more than 1500 calories a day?* Students raise their hands in response.

Option: Ask *What can you do to burn more calories?* Have students make a weekly exercise plan. For example:

Monday	Wednesday	Friday	Saturday
7:00–8:00 A.M.	4:00–6:00 P.M.	7:00–8:00 A.M.	10:00 A.M.
go running	play soccer	go running	go bike riding

[+10 minutes]

D ⌂ SOUND BITES

Suggested teaching time:	5–10 minutes
Your actual teaching time:	_____

- Have students look at the photos. Ask *What two activities do you see?* (play tennis, watch TV) For a challenge, ask students to find a third activity. (go shopping)
- After students read and listen, ask some comprehension questions:
  Where's Jane going? (She's going to the park.)
  When does Jane play tennis? (every weekend)
  Does Sue play tennis? (Yes, she does.)
  Does Jane's husband, Ed, play tennis?
    (No, he doesn't.)
  Why not? (He's a couch potato.)
  Does Sue's husband play tennis? (Yes, he does.)
  Does he like tennis a lot or a little? (A lot. He's crazy about tennis.)

Challenge: Ask students the following questions:
  Who's burning a lot of calories today? (Jane)
  Why? (because she's playing tennis)
  Who's not burning a lot of calories today? (Ed)
  Why? (because he's watching TV)
[+5 minutes]

Option: Write the following questions on the board:
  Are you a couch potato?
  Do you know any couch potatoes?
  What are you crazy about?
  What are your family members crazy about?
First, model the activity by answering the questions yourself. (*I'm not a couch potato. My sister, Kristen, is a couch potato. I'm crazy about soccer. My father is crazy about basketball.*) Then have students discuss in small groups. [+10 minutes]

Culture note: It's always more polite to provide a reason for declining an invitation in English. (*Sorry, I can't. I have to meet my sister at the airport.*)

Language note: *That sounds great* is an acceptance of the invitation.

E UNDERSTANDING MEANING FROM CONTEXT

Suggested teaching time:	5 minutes
Your actual teaching time:	_____

- Remind students to look back at Exercise D for help understanding the items in Exercise E.
- Have students check answers by reading each item with a partner.

WHAT ABOUT **YOU?**

Suggested teaching time:	10–15 minutes
Your actual teaching time:	_____

- To make sure students understand the frequency terms, draw the chart on the board and fill in the first row yourself. Explain how often you do each activity. For example:
  I take a shower every day—Monday, Tuesday, Wednesday, Thursday, Friday, Saturday, and Sunday.
  I play golf every weekend—every Saturday or Sunday.
  I clean the house once a week—every Friday.
  I play tennis once in a while—maybe one time a month.
  I never do aerobics. I don't like aerobics.
- Students can use the activities on page 64 and their own activities to complete the chart.
- To review, ask a few students *What do you do every day? What do you do every weekend?* etc. Point out that students should place the frequency expression at the end of the sentence; for example, *I go swimming every Saturday. I talk on the phone every day.* Encourage students to come up with other activities. Write any new activities on the board.
- Read the activities on the board out loud and have students repeat.

Option: Introduce the terms *twice a week* and *three times a week.* [+5 minutes]

EXTRAS (optional)
  Workbook: Exercises 1, 2

D ⌒ SOUND BITES. Read along silently as you listen to a natural conversation.

SUE: Hey, Jane! Where are you off to?

JANE: I'm on my way to the park.

SUE: You play tennis? How often?

JANE: Just about every weekend. **CN**
Do you want to play together
sometime?

SUE: That would be great.

SUE: What about your husband?
Does he play?

JANE: Ed? No way. He's a
couch potato.

SUE: Too bad. My husband's
crazy about tennis. **CN**

E UNDERSTANDING MEANING FROM CONTEXT. Use the conversation to help you choose
the correct response.

1. "Where are you off to?"
   ☑ I'm going to work.
   ☐ I play tennis.

2. "Do you lift weights?"
   ☐ No kidding.
   ☑ No way.

3. "Does your daughter play golf?"
   ☑ Yes. She's crazy about golf.
   ☐ Yes. She's a couch potato.

4. "How often do you play tennis?"
   ☐ Well, let's play together some time.
   ☑ I don't. I'm a couch potato.

CN Corpus Notes: "Just about"
and "almost" mean the same thing,
but "almost" is used much more
frequently, especially in written
American English.

CN Corpus Notes: English
learners almost always use "crazy
about" to talk about something they
really like. Native speakers are much
more likely to say they are not "crazy
about" something.

WHAT ABOUT YOU?

Write about your activities.

Every day	Every weekend	Once a week	Once in a while	Never
I study English.				

Preview **65**

1 Plan an Activity with Someone

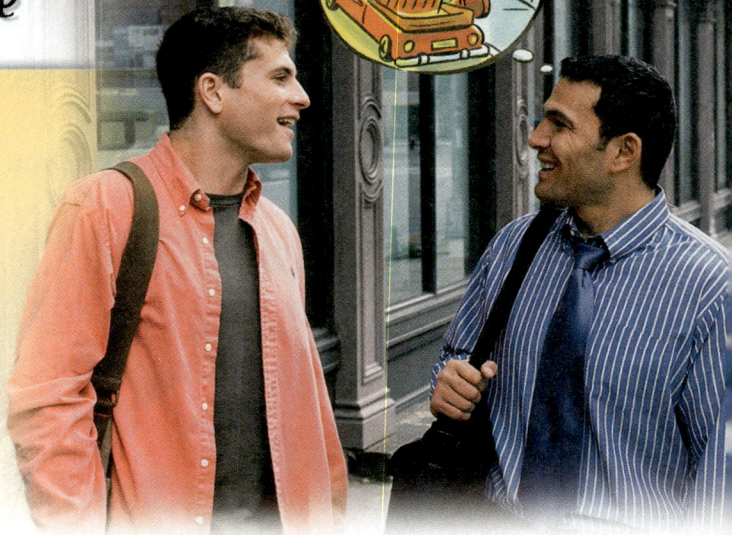

🎧 **CONVERSATION MODEL** Read and listen.

A: Hey, Paul. Why don't we play basketball sometime?

B: Great idea. When's good for you?

A: Tomorrow at three?

B: Sorry, I can't. I have to meet my sister at the airport.

A: How about Wednesday at five?

B: That sounds great.

🎧 **Rhythm and intonation practice**

A ▸ GRAMMAR. Can and have to

can

Use can + the base form of a verb for ability or possibility.

I **can speak** English, but I **can't speak** Italian.

I **can't play** golf today. I'm too busy.

Yes / no questions	**Short answers**
Can you **come** for dinner this evening?	Yes, I can. / No, I can't.

can't = {can not / cannot}

have to

Use have to + the base form of a verb for obligation.

I can't go running tomorrow. I **have to meet** my cousin after class.

She can't come for dinner. She **has to work** late.

Dave can sleep late. He **doesn't have to go** to work.

Relax! You **don't have to drive** to the airport until 10:00.

Yes / no questions	**Short answers**
Do you **have to work** tomorrow?	Yes, I do. / No, I don't.
Does she **have to go** to school today?	Yes, she does. / No, she doesn't.

don't = do not
doesn't = does

GRAMMAR BOOSTER

PAGES G10–G12
For more . . .

B ▸ Complete the sentences with can or have to.

1. Vicky __can't come__ for dinner tonight. She __has to finish__ a report for her boss.
   _{not / come} _{finish}

2. I __can meet__ you at 6:00. I __to work__ late tonight.
   _{meet} don't have _{not / work}

3. My brother __can't play__ soccer today. He __has to go__ to the doctor.
   _{not / play} _{go}

4. I want to see a movie, but I have an exam tomorrow. I __have to study__ tonight.
   _{study}

5. __Can__ Nick __play__ golf with us next Wednesday?
   _{play}

1 Plan an Activity with Someone

🎧 CONVERSATION MODEL

Suggested teaching time:	5–10 minutes
Your actual teaching time:	_____

- After students read and listen, ask:
  What are the two men planning to do?
    (play basketball)
  Is Paul free to play basketball tomorrow at 3:00?
    (No, he isn't.)
  Why not? What's he doing at that time?
    (He's meeting his sister at the airport.)
  Is he free to play Wednesday at 5:00? (Yes, he is.)

- Point out that *Why don't we . . .?* is similar to *Do you want to . . . ?*

🎧 Rhythm and intonation practice

Suggested teaching time:	5 minutes
Your actual teaching time:	_____

- Have students repeat chorally. Make sure they:

  ○ use falling intonation for *Why don't we play basketball sometime?* Use rising intonation for *When's good for you?* and *How about Wednesday at five?*

  ○ use rising intonation for *Tomorrow at three?* This is a shortened version of *Is tomorrow at three OK?*

  ○ pause after *Sorry, I can't.*

  ○ pay special attention to stress and rhythm of the sentence *I have to meet my sister at the airport* with primary stress on *have, sister,* and *airport.*

  ○ use the following stress pattern:

STRESS PATTERN

A: Hey, Paul. Why don't we play basketball sometime?

B: Great idea. When's good for you?

A: Tomorrow at three?

B: Sorry, I can't. I have to meet my sister at the airport.

A: How about Wednesday at five?

B: That sounds great.

🔺 GRAMMAR

Suggested teaching time:	10 minutes
Your actual teaching time:	_____

can: ability

- After students read the information in the Grammar box, ask them to circle a statement of possibility or ability in the Conversation Model. *(Sorry, I can't.)*

- Ask several students questions about their abilities.
  Can you play [golf]?
  Can you play the [guitar]?
  Can you speak [Russian]?
  Can you order and pay for a meal in English?

- Ask *What can you do? Tell me something about your abilities.*

Option: To see if students can remember their classmates' responses, have them write as many sentences as they can about what their classmates can do. **[+10 minutes]**

Option: Have students look back at the activities on page 64. With a partner, students talk about which activities they can and can't do well. **[+5 minutes]**

can: possibility

- Say to a student *Can you go shopping on [the day and time your next class meets]?* The student should answer *No, I can't.* Ask *Why not?* (*I have to come to class.*)

- Say *Imagine that I am new to [your town]. Answer my questions about where to go for different activities.* Then ask:
  Where can I go dancing?
  Where can I go swimming?
  Where can I do aerobics?
  Where can I eat good seafood?
  Where can I buy a PDA?
  Where can I see a play?

Option: Have students suggest activities for visitors to your town. Students write sentences using *can.* For example:
  You can go dancing at [Club 21]. It's on [Lake Avenue], across from the [bookstore].
  You can go swimming at [the park on Mountain Street].
[+5 minutes]

have to

- Ask students to underline the statement of obligation in the Conversation Model. *(I have to meet my sister at the airport.)*

- Tell the class what your obligations are this week. *I have to teach on Monday, Wednesday, and Friday. I have to clean the house. I have to cook dinner for my in-laws on Sunday.*

- On the board, write *What do you have to do this week?* In pairs, students ask each other about their obligations.

- Have each student tell the class about one of their partner's obligations; for example, *[Name] has to work every day this week.*

🔵 Grammar Self-Checks

🔶 B Complete the sentences . . .

Suggested teaching time:	5 minutes
Your actual teaching time:	_____

- Ask different students to read each sentence out loud.

T66

C 🎧 PRONUNCIATION

Suggested teaching time:	5 minutes
Your actual teaching time:	_____

Option: Have students practice the pronunciation and stress of <u>can</u> and <u>can't</u> by reading out loud the sentences in the Grammar box on page 66. **[+5 minutes]**

Option: Have students tell a partner three things they can do and three things they can't do, using the correct pronunciation and stress of <u>can</u> and <u>can't</u>. For example:

I can speak Swahili.	*I can't speak Russian.*
I can play golf.	*I can't play basketball.*
I can cook Italian food.	*I can't cook French food.*

[+5 minutes]

💿 **Pronunciation Activities**

AUDIOSCRIPT

1. I can play the guitar.
2. I can't cook.
3. I can play tennis at six-thirty.
4. I can't play tennis at ten.
5. I can go swimming on Saturday.
6. I can't go swimming on Sunday.

D PAIR WORK

Suggested teaching time:	5–10 minutes
Your actual teaching time:	_____

• If helpful, have students review prepositions of time on page 18 before they write their invitations. Students can also use *this afternoon, tonight, tomorrow, tomorrow night, this weekend, next week, next weekend.*

• Following are some examples of invitations your students can write:

> *Can you play soccer on Wednesday at 4:00?*
> *Can you go out tonight?*
> *Can you go bike riding this weekend?*

• Before students exchange papers, make sure they know to respond that they aren't able to go and to explain why. *(I have to . . .)* You may want to remind students of other language they know, such as:

> *I'd love to go, but . . .*
> *Maybe some other time.*
> *Thanks, anyway.*

CONVERSATION **PAIR WORK**

Suggested teaching time:	10–15 minutes
Your actual teaching time:	_____

• Students fill in their plans for this Friday, Saturday, and Sunday on the daily planner. Students should leave some boxes blank.

• Before they practice the conversation, ask a few students about their plans for the weekend: *What are you doing on [Saturday] at [11:00]?*

• Remind students to use *Hey, Hi,* or *How's it going?* to greet their classmates.

• Students consult their daily planners as they make plans with classmates. To agree on an activity or on a time and place, students can say:

> *Great!*
> *Perfect.*
> *See you then.*
> *I'd love to go.*
> *Sure.*
> *Sounds good / great.*
> *That would be great.*

• To review, ask a few students to tell you about their plans. Your students can say, for example, *[David] and I are [going bike riding] on [Saturday] at [9:00].*

Language note: In British English, *schedule* is pronounced /ˈʃedjuːl/. In American English it is /ˈskedʒʊl/.

💿 **Pair Work Cards**

EXTRAS (optional)

Grammar Booster
Workbook: Exercises 3–7
Copy & Go: Activity 21

💿 **Pronunciation Supplements**

🎧 **PRONUNCIATION.** <u>Can</u> / <u>can't</u>. **Listen to the pronunciation and stress of <u>can</u> and <u>can't</u> in sentences. Then listen again and repeat.**

/kən/

I can **call** you tomorrow.

/kænt/

I **can't** call you tomorrow.

🎧 **Now listen carefully and check <u>can</u> or <u>can't</u>. Then listen again and repeat.**

1. ☑ can ☐ can't
2. ☐ can ☑ can't
3. ☑ can ☐ can't
4. ☐ can ☑ can't
5. ☑ can ☐ can't
6. ☐ can ☑ can't

D **PAIR WORK.** **Write three invitations using <u>can</u>. Then read your partner's invitations and write excuses.**

Can you go swimming tomorrow?

Sorry, I can't. I have to work.

	FRIDAY	SATURDAY	SUNDAY
9:00	go running	visit Mom	

CONVERSATION PAIR WORK

Write your schedule for this weekend in the daily planner.

GROUP WORK. **Talk to at least three different classmates. Plan an activity together this weekend. Use your daily planner.**

A: _____. Why don't we _____ sometime?

B: Great idea. When's good for you?

A: _____?

B: _____ …

Continue the conversation in your <u>own</u> way.

Daily Planner

	FRIDAY	SATURDAY	SUNDAY
9:00			
11:00			
1:00			
3:00			
5:00			
7:00			

Talk about Daily Routines

🎧 CONVERSATION MODEL Read and listen.

A: Janet! What are <u>you</u> doing here?

B: Hi, Lisa. I always go to the gym on Saturday 🆑 morning. You too?

A: Actually, I usually go in the evening. But not today.

B: How come?

A: I'm going to the theater tonight.

B: Well, have a great time.

🎧 **Rhythm and intonation practice**

🆑 **Corpus Notes:**
Many students place "always" incorrectly by saying or writing something like "I go always to the gym." Learners often misspell this word "allways" or "all ways."

🅰 GRAMMAR. The simple present tense and the present continuous

The simple present tense

Use the simple present tense to describe frequency, habits, and routines.

How often **do** you **play** basketball?	I **play** basketball at least once a week.
When **does** Paula **do** aerobics?	She **does** aerobics on Tuesdays.
When **do** you usually **go** to the gym?	I usually **go** in the evening.

Frequency adverbs
100% always
        almost always
        usually / often
        sometimes
        hardly ever
0%   never

The present continuous

Use the present continuous for actions in progress now or for future plans.

She**'s talking** on the phone.   Paul and Judy **are going** running tomorrow.

Don't use the present continuous with frequency adverbs.
    Don't say: ~~She's usually talking on the phone.~~
Don't use the present continuous with <u>have</u>, <u>want</u>, <u>need</u>, or <u>like</u>.
    Don't say: ~~She's liking the gym.~~

GRAMMAR BOOSTER

PAGES G12–G13
For more . . .

🅱 Complete the sentences. Use the simple present tense or the present continuous.

1. How often ___do you go___ running?
   _{you / go}

2. I'm sorry. ___Paul is studying___ right now.
   _{Paul / study}

3. ___I'm going___ to the track this afternoon.
   _{I / go}

4. ___I lift___ weights three times a week.
   _{I / lift}

5. ___Tim is cooking___ lunch. Can he call you back?
   _{Tim / cook}

6. How often ___do you play___ the guitar?
   _{you / play}

7. ___I play___ tennis every day.
   _{I / play}

2 ▸ *Talk about Daily Routines*

🎧 CONVERSATION **MODEL**

Suggested teaching time:	5–10 minutes
Your actual teaching time:	_____

- Have students look at the picture. Ask *Where are the women?* (They're at the gym.)
- After students read and listen, ask:
  When does Janet go to the gym? (on Saturday mornings / every Saturday morning)
  When does Lisa usually go to the gym? (in the evening)
  Why is Lisa going to the gym in the morning today? (because she's going to the theater tonight)

Language note: In the Conversation Model, *today* refers to *this day* and includes the evening.

🎧 Rhythm and intonation practice

Suggested teaching time:	5 minutes
Your actual teaching time:	_____

- Have students find and underline *always* and *usually* in the conversation. Point out that they are stressed. Read each sentence out loud, stressing the two frequency adverbs. Have students repeat.
- Have students repeat each line chorally. Make sure they:
  - use rising intonation with *You too?* (a shortened version of *Do you always go to the gym on Saturday morning too?*)
  - use rising intonation with *How come?*
  - use the following stress pattern:

STRESS PATTERN

A: Janet! What are *you* doing here?

B: Hi, Lisa. I always go to the gym on Saturday
morning. You too?

A: Actually, I usually go in the evening. But not today

B: How come?

A: I'm going to the theater tonight.

B: Well, have a great time.

🔶 A GRAMMAR

Suggested teaching time:	10 minutes
Your actual teaching time:	_____

- After students read the information in the Grammar box, read the frequency adverbs out loud and have students repeat.
- To practice the frequency adverbs, write on the board the list of activities that follows. Have students tell a partner how often they do each activity—*always, almost always, usually, never,* etc. Point out that the frequency adverb should be placed before the verb. (*I **always** eat breakfast.*)
  eat breakfast
  read the newspaper in the morning
  cook dinner
  watch TV in the evening
  go out on Saturday nights
  sleep late on the weekends
  order dessert in restaurants
  listen to music when I study
  drink coffee in the afternoon
  take a shower at night
- On the board, write the headings *simple present tense* and *present continuous.* Ask the class *When do you use the simple present tense? When do you use the present continuous?* List students' responses under the appropriate heading.

simple present tense	present continuous
frequency	actions in progress now
habits	future plans
routines	
with <u>have</u>, <u>want</u>, <u>need</u>, or <u>like</u>	

- In pairs, have students write an example sentence for each item on the list. Your students might write:
  simple present tense
  frequency: We almost always go shopping once a week.
  habits: Anna never eats junk food or sweets.
  routines: Elizabeth goes walking every day
  at 4:00 P.M.
  with have, want, need, *or* like: We don't like seafood.

  present continuous
  actions in progress: We're writing sentences right now.
  future plans: We're playing soccer after class.

🔷 **Grammar Self-Checks**

🔷 B Complete the sentences ...

Suggested teaching time:	5–10 minutes
Your actual teaching time:	_____

- Have students underline any frequency words or time expressions in the sentences (*right now,* etc.) that indicate whether to use the simple present tense or the present continuous.

C. ⌂ VOCABULARY

Suggested teaching time:	5 minutes
Your actual teaching time:	_____

- After students listen and repeat, ask students to name one activity you can do in each place; for example, *You can go walking at the park.*
- Have students tell a partner how often or when they go to each place. Circulate and check that students are using the simple present tense (*I go . . .*), placing frequency adverbs before *go* (*I **hardly ever** go . . .*), and placing frequency or time expressions at the end of the sentence (*I go to the gym **twice a week**.*).

Language note: A *gym* can be a building with weights, other exercise equipment, and rooms for aerobics and other exercise classes (also called a *healthclub* or *fitness center*). A *gym* can also be a building for indoor sports such as basketball (also called a *gymnasium*).

◉ **Vocabulary Cards**

◉ **Learning Strategies**

D. ⌂ LISTENING COMPREHENSION

Suggested teaching time:	10 minutes
Your actual teaching time:	_____

AUDIOSCRIPT

CONVERSATION 1 [F = Australian]
M: Where's John?
F: Oh, he's at the golf course.
M: Today? But it's raining!

CONVERSATION 2
F: I'm heading for the track to go running. Want to come?
M: Sure. Can you give me a minute to get ready?
F: No problem.

CONVERSATION 3 [M = Arabic]
M: We're going to the athletic field. Want to join us?
F: Maybe some other time, OK?

CONVERSATION 4
F: Hank, I'm off to the gym.
M: OK. What are you going to do today?
F: Lift some weights, run on the treadmill. The usual.

CONVERSATION 5 [M = Spanish]
M: Is the pool open today?
F: Yeah. Why?
M: I feel like swimming. Want to join me?

CONVERSATION 6
F: Tennis anyone?
M: Are you kidding? It's late. The tennis courts will be closed.
F: They're open till nine. Come on.

CONVERSATION 7
M: Where are you off to?
F: The park. Want to come along?
M: Sure. I need some fresh air.

CONVERSATION **PAIR WORK**

Suggested teaching time:	5–10 minutes
Your actual teaching time:	_____

Note: For the conversation to make sense, Student B will have to say that he or she usually does the activity that Student A chooses at a later time of day.

- As students practice the conversation, circulate and listen. Make sure that students use the simple present tense after *always* and *usually*. Make sure they use the present continuous to talk about a future action in the last blank.

◉ **Pair Work Cards**

EXTRAS (optional)

Grammar Booster
Workbook: Exercises 8–13
Copy & Go: Activity 22

C 🎧 **VOCABULARY.** **Places for physical activities.** **Listen and practice.**

a park

a gym

a track

a pool

an athletic field

a golf course

a tennis court

D 🎧 **LISTENING COMPREHENSION.** **Listen to each conversation. Match the conversation with the place.**

    __f__ **1.**   **a.** a park

    __c__ **2.**   **b.** a gym

    __e__ **3.**   **c.** a track

    __b__ **4.**   **d.** a pool

    __d__ **5.**   **e.** an athletic field

    __g__ **6.**   **f.** a golf course

    __a__ **7.**   **g.** a tennis court

CONVERSATION
PAIR WORK

Talk about daily routines. Use the guide, or create a new conversation.

A: _____ ! What are _you_ doing here?

B: Hi, _____ . I always _____ on _____ .
You too?

A: Actually, I usually _____ . But not today.

B: How come?

A: _____ …

Continue the conversation in your _own_ way.

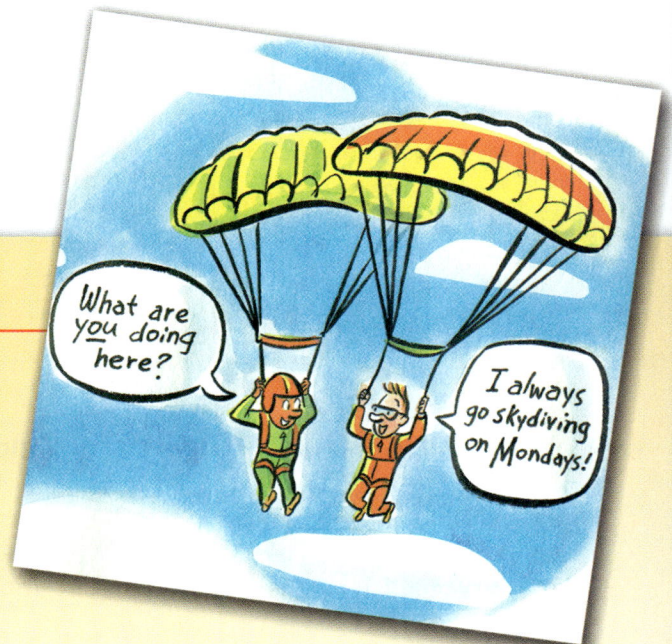

What are you doing here?

I always go skydiving on Mondays!

CONTROLLED PRACTICE

3 Discuss Exercise and Diet

A 🎧 VOCABULARY. Talking about health habits. Listen and practice.

be in shape **CN**   be out of shape   eat junk food   avoid sweets   have a sweet tooth

B Practice the new vocabulary. Complete each statement.

1. I hardly ever exercise, and I usually don't feel healthy. I'm really _____.
   - **a.** in great shape
   - **(b.)** out of shape
   - **c.** a sweet tooth

2. I generally try to eat healthy foods. I avoid _____.
   - **(a.)** fatty foods
   - **b.** vegetables
   - **c.** fruits

3. My son has a real sweet tooth. He loves _____.
   - **a.** fish
   - **(b.)** candy
   - **c.** meat

CN Corpus Notes:
"In shape" is most often used with the verbs "get," "keep," and "stay" ("get in shape," "keep in shape," "stay in shape").

C 🎧 LISTENING COMPREHENSION. Listen to people talk about their health habits. Then listen again and check the statements that are true.

1. Juan Reyneri:
- ☑ generally eats small meals.
- ☐ generally eats large meals.
- ☐ usually drinks soft drinks.
- ☑ usually drinks a lot of water.
- ☑ exercises regularly.
- ☐ doesn't exercise regularly.

2. Naomi Sato:
- ☐ exercises regularly.
- ☑ doesn't exercise regularly.
- ☑ eats fish once a week.
- ☐ hardly ever eats fish.
- ☑ eats fruits and vegetables every day.
- ☐ hardly ever eats fruits and vegetables.

3. Matt Lemke:
- ☑ exercises regularly.
- ☐ doesn't exercise regularly.
- ☑ generally avoids fatty foods.
- ☐ doesn't avoid fatty foods.
- ☑ always drinks a lot of water.
- ☐ always drinks soft drinks.

D 🎧 PRONUNCIATION. Third-person singular -s. Listen. Then repeat.

/s/	/z/	/ɪz/
sleep**s**	goe**s**	watch**es**
eat**s**	play**s**	exercis**es**
work**s**	avoid**s**	munch**es**

LESSON

3 ▶ Discuss Exercise and Diet

A 🎧 VOCABULARY

Suggested teaching time:	5 minutes
Your actual teaching time:	_____

• Make sure students understand the vocabulary. Ask:
If you exercise regularly and eat healthy foods, are you in shape *or out of shape?* (in shape)
Junk food is not healthy because it has lots of oil or sugar. What are some junk foods? (french fries, potato chips, soft drinks, candy)
If you avoid sweets, *do you eat sweets or not eat sweets?* (You don't eat sweets.)
If you have a sweet tooth, *do you like sweets or not like sweets?* (You like sweets.)

Option: Write the questions that follow on the board. Students then write answers or discuss questions with classmates.
1. *Are you in shape or out of shape?*
2. *Do you eat junk food? What junk foods do you like?*
3. *Do you have a sweet tooth? What are your favorite sweets?*
4. *Do you eat sweets or do you avoid them? What other kinds of foods do you avoid?*
[+10 minutes]

Challenge: Ask the class *What can you do to be in better shape?* [+5 minutes]

Culture note: In some cultures, it is considered impolite to talk about a person's weight. The words *fat* and *skinny* may be considered offensive. Words like *thin* and *heavy* are more polite.

💿 **Vocabulary Cards**

B ▶ Practice the new vocabulary …

Suggested teaching time:	5–10 minutes
Your actual teaching time:	_____

C 🎧 LISTENING COMPREHENSION

Suggested teaching time:	15–20 minutes
Your actual teaching time:	_____

• Have students read the statements below each person's photo before they listen.

Option: On a sheet of paper, have students write the title *My Health Habits*. Then have them draw two columns, with the headings *Good habits* and *Bad habits*. Students look at the statements under the photos and choose a few that describe their health habits. Students decide whether the items they pick are good habits or bad habits and write a sentence in the first person in the appropriate column on their paper. For example:

My Health Habits

Good habits	Bad habits
I generally eat small meals.	*I usually drink a lot of soda.*

[+10 minutes]

Option: Ask *What do you do to stay in shape?* Students can write sentences or tell a partner. Make sure students use the simple present tense in their answers; for example: *I play basketball on Mondays, Wednesdays, and Fridays. I avoid sweets. I eat vegetables every day.*
[+10 minutes]

💿 **Learning Strategies**

AUDIOSCRIPT

1. JUAN REYNERI
M: I'm Juan Reyneri. What do I do to stay in shape? Well, I generally try to eat right. I actually eat five or six small simple meals a day rather than two or three big ones. So you'll always see me munching on something. I generally avoid soft drinks and sweets, and I drink a large glass of water with each meal. I eat pretty healthy food six days a week and then on Sundays I pig out on junk food—pizza, burgers, ice cream—just about anything that I want. As far as exercise goes, I lift weights on Mondays, Wednesdays, and Fridays, and I run on Tuesdays, Thursdays, and Saturdays.

2. NAOMI SATO
F: Hi. Naomi Sato here … Exercise? Well, truth is I generally don't exercise at all. I occasionally go for walks with my daughters, but … I really don't have time for it. As far as eating goes, I try to eat right. We eat salmon or some other kind of fish at least once a week and we eat lots of salads. We try to eat fruits and vegetables every day. Luckily my daughters love vegetables, especially broccoli. Unfortunately, I have a sweet tooth—I love cookies. I make cookies with my daughters every weekend.

3. MATT LEMKE
M: I'm Matt Lemke … To stay in good shape, I ride my mountain bike with my friends at least three times a week. We go riding up and down the steep hills near my home—so it's pretty challenging. But it doesn't feel like exercise—it's a lot of fun. I also go to the gym four times a week to lift weights. With so much exercise, I can actually eat a lot of food and still stay thin! Even so, I am still careful to avoid fried foods or any type of food that's high in fat. I also drink a lot of water every day. And I try to get enough sleep.

D 🎧 PRONUNCIATION

Suggested teaching time:	5 minutes
Your actual teaching time:	_____

Option: After students listen and repeat, have them choose one word from each list and write a sentence. (*My brother works every day.*) Students then practice reading their sentences to a partner and pronouncing the third-person singular *-s* correctly. [+5 minutes]

💿 **Pronunciation Activities**

TOP NOTCH **INTERACTION**

Suggested teaching time:	15–20 minutes
Your actual teaching time:	_____

Language note: A *couch potato* is someone who spends a lot of time sitting and watching television, and who doesn't really exercise a lot.

STEP 1

• To make sure students understand item 2, ask a couple of students *How much sleep do you need?* or *How many hours of sleep do you get?* Then rephrase the question. Ask a couple other students *How much sleep is enough for you?*

• Using the scoring chart on the right side of the survey, students determine the point value for each of their answers and then add up their score.

STEP 2

• Talk about your answers to the first few survey questions. Model elaborating on each answer. For example:
  I lift weights regularly. I go to the gym every morning at 8:00 A.M.
  I sometimes don't get enough sleep. I have a two-month-old daughter.

• Encourage students to elaborate on their answers.

STEP 3

• Write the first item from the chart on the board. Then write *Do you . . . ?* Elicit the class's help in changing item 1 to a question. Cross off the *–s* on *eats*. Then write *Do you eat a lot of junk food?*

• To model the activity, ask the question to different students until you get a positive response. When a student answers *Yes, I do*, write his or her name next to item 1. Remind students that they can ask their classmates *How do you spell your first name?*

• Encourage students to ask each other to elaborate on their answers. Some questions students can ask include *How often do you [activity]? What kind of junk food do you eat? Why don't you get enough sleep?*

• Circulate as students ask questions. Make sure they are not using the third-person *–s* when they ask their classmates questions.

STEP 4

• Have several students tell the class about one of their classmates.

Option: Give students a minute to review their chart. Then have them close their books. Volunteers tell the class what they remember about one of their classmates; for example, *Charles eats a lot of junk food.* To confirm that the student remembered correctly, check with the student talked about; for example, *Charles, do you eat a lot of junk food?* **[+10 minutes]**

EXTRAS (optional)

Copy & Go: Activity 23

Pronunciation Supplements

INTERACTION • *Are You a Couch Potato?*

STEP 1. Take the health survey.

TOP NOTCH HEALTH SURVEY

Check the statements that are true for you. Then add up your total score.

1
- ☐ **a.** I exercise regularly.
- ☐ **b.** I don't have time to exercise regularly.
- ☐ **c.** I don't want to exercise regularly.

2
- ☐ **a.** I always get enough sleep.
- ☐ **b.** I sometimes don't get enough sleep.
- ☐ **c.** I never get enough sleep.

3
- ☐ **a.** I always eat vegetables.
- ☐ **b.** I sometimes eat vegetables.
- ☐ **c.** I never eat vegetables.

4
- ☐ **a.** I avoid fatty foods.
- ☐ **b.** I sometimes eat fatty foods.
- ☐ **c.** I eat lots of fatty foods.

5
- ☐ **a.** I hardly ever eat sweets.
- ☐ **b.** I sometimes eat sweets.
- ☐ **c.** I have a sweet tooth.

Score
Each **a** answer = 10 points.
Each **b** answer = 5 points.
Each **c** answer = 0 points.

Total points: ☐

40–50 points =
You're in terrific shape!

30–35 points =
Not bad. Keep it up!

20–25 points =
Come on. Try harder!

0–15 points =
You're a couch potato!

STEP 2. PAIR WORK. Compare your survey answers and scores. Then compare your exercise and diet habits.

> " Do you exercise at home? How often? "

STEP 3. PAIR WORK. Walk around your classroom and ask questions. Write your classmates' names on the chart.

Find someone who ...	Name
1. eats a lot of junk food.	
2. lifts weights regularly.	
3. doesn't have time to exercise.	
4. exercises at home.	
5. never eats sweets.	
6. doesn't get enough sleep every night.	
7. goes running regularly.	

STEP 4. GROUP WORK. Tell your class about some of your classmates.

> " Frank exercises at home every day. "

4 ▶ Describe Your Typical Day

A **READING WARM-UP.** Look at the photo. What do you think is the relationship between the two women? What do you think they are doing?

B 🎧 **READING.** Read the article about Brooke Ellison. How is her day different from yours?

With her mother's help, Brooke Ellison remains active

In June 2000, Brooke Ellison graduated from Harvard University. And now she is continuing her studies as a full-time graduate student. Brooke is a quadriplegic—she can't move her arms or legs. She spends all her time in a wheelchair, and she can't breathe without a special machine. A terrible accident at the age of 11 changed her life—she was hit by a car on her way home from school. But she stays active every day.

On a typical morning, it takes most people about a half hour to get up, get dressed, and have breakfast. For Brooke, it usually takes about four hours. Her mother, Jean, wakes her early in the morning and exercises her arms and legs. Then she gives her a bath, combs her hair, and brushes her teeth. After that, she dresses her and lifts her into her wheelchair. By late morning, Brooke is ready for breakfast. In the afternoon, Brooke goes to her classes and listens carefully. Her mother goes to classes with her and takes notes. For a lot of activities, such as using a calculator, Brooke uses her mouth, instead of her hands and legs. She can move her wheelchair by blowing into a tube.

At night, she does her homework and reads her e-mail, and she often phones her brother or sister to talk. To use a computer, she uses her voice—she tells the computer what to do. At about 8:00, she gets ready for bed—it usually takes about two hours. Her mother undresses her, bathes her, and exercises her arms and legs again.

When she can, Brooke gives speeches to young people. She tells them about her life and teaches them to always be active.

SOURCES: *Miracles Happen*, Brooke and Jean Ellison, 2001, Hyperion and *The Brooke Ellison Story*, directed by Christopher Reeve, 2004

C ▶ Read the article again. Complete each statement with <u>can</u>, <u>can't</u>, or <u>has to</u>.

Brooke Ellison:

1. __can't__ walk.

2. __has to__ use a wheelchair.

3. __can't__ breathe without a special machine.

4. __has to__ get up early every day.

5. __can__ use a computer.

6. __can__ use a calculator.

7. __can't__ use her hands.

8. __can__ read her e-mail.

LESSON

4 ▶ *Describe Your Typical Day*

A READING WARM-UP

Suggested teaching time:	5 minutes
Your actual teaching time:	_____

• Point to Brooke. Ask:
  Can she walk? Can she use her arms?

• Point to the mother. Ask:
  Is she a friend? Is she her sister? Is she her mother?

• Point to both women. Ask:
  Are they going to work? Are they going to class?

B 🎧 READING

Suggested teaching time:	10–15 minutes
Your actual teaching time:	_____

• Have students read the article independently.

• Have students listen to and read the article again. Pause after each paragraph and ask some comprehension questions. Encourage students to find and read the answers from the text:

Paragraph 1
What school did Brooke Ellison graduate from in 2000? (Harvard University)
How old was she when the accident happened? (eleven)
What's wrong with Ellison? (She can't move her arms and legs. She can't breathe without a machine.)

Paragraph 2
How much time does it take Ellison to get ready each morning? (About four hours.)
Who helps her exercise, bathe, and dress? (her mother / Jean Ellison)
When does Ellison go to classes? (in the afternoon)
Why does Jean Ellison go to classes with her daughter? (to take notes)
What does Ellison do to move here wheelchair? (She blows into a tube.)

Paragraph 3
What does Ellison do at night? (She does her homework. She checks her e-mail. She talks to her brother or sister on the phone.)
How does she use a computer since she can't type? (She uses her voice. She tells the computer what to do.)
How long does it take Ellison to get ready for bed? (About two hours.)
How often does she exercise? (twice a day)

Paragraph 4
What does Ellison do when she has some free time? (She gives speeches to young people to teach them how much a paraplegic can do.)

Option: Ask *How is Brooke Ellison still active? What does she do?* Have students make a list of all the activities Ellison does, both at school and at home. Following are examples of what your students can write:

She goes to (graduate) school.
She uses a calculator.
She uses a computer.
She makes phone calls.
She exercises twice a day
She reads her e-mail.
She gives speeches to young people.

[+ 10 minutes]

🌐 **Learning Strategies**

C Read the article again . . .

Suggested teaching time:	10 minutes
Your actual teaching time:	_____

Option: Ask students to find the source of the answer to each item in the reading.

◆D▷ Write what Brooke and Jean Ellison . . .

Suggested teaching time: 5–10 minutes
Your actual teaching time: _____

- Before students complete the exercise, have them find and underline the information in the article on page 72.
- Have students compare answers with a partner. Then review as a class. Ask questions like *What do they do in the morning? What do they do at night?*

 Extra Reading Comprehension Activities

TOP NOTCH **INTERACTION**

Suggested teaching time: 15–20 minutes
Your actual teaching time: _____

STEP 1

- Students answer questions independently.

STEP 2

- To get started, students can ask and answer the questions from Step 1. Then students can ask additional questions to fill in their charts completely. For example:
  Do you exercise in the morning?
  When do you take a shower?
  What do you do in the afternoon?

STEP 3

- Have volunteers stand up in front of the class and tell about their partner's typical day.

STEP 4

- Students use their notepads or a separate sheet of paper to write an article about their partners' typical day.
- Suggest that students write three paragraphs: one each about their partner's morning, afternoon, and evening activities.

 Writing Process Worksheets

EXTRAS (optional)

Workbook: Exercises 14–16
Copy & Go: Activity 24

D **Write what Brooke and Jean Ellison do each day.**

In the morning: _Brooke gets up early. Jean combs her hair._
Jean helps Brooke exercise her arms and legs. Jean dresses Brooke and lifts her into her
wheelchair. Brooke eats breakfast.

In the afternoon: Brooke goes to class. Jean goes to class with Brooke and takes notes.
Brooke uses a calculator. Brooke moves her wheelchair by blowing into a tube.

In the evening: Brooke does her homework. She reads her e-mail. Brooke phones her
brother or sister to talk. She uses a computer. Brooke gets ready for bed at 8:00. Jean
bathes Brooke. Jean exercises Brooke's arms and legs again.

TOP NOTCH
INTERACTION • *What About You?*

STEP 1. **Answer the questions about your typical day.**

1. What time do you usually get up? _____.
2. What do you do next? _____.
3. Do you usually eat breakfast? _____.
4. When do you usually have lunch? _____.
5. What do you do in the evening? _____.
6. What time do you go to bed? _____.

STEP 2. **PAIR WORK. Interview a partner about his or her activities on
a typical day. Use some or all of the questions in Step 1.
Take notes on the notepad.**

In the morning	In the afternoon	In the evening

STEP 3. DISCUSSION. **Tell your class about your partner's typical day.**

STEP 4. WRITING. **Write an article about your partner's typical day.**

In the morning, Nina usually gets up early and goes running. After that,
she eats breakfast. She usually has cereal and juice. After breakfast...

FREE PRACTICE

A 🎧 **LISTENING COMPREHENSION.** Listen carefully. Check ☑ the box to complete each statement. Then listen again to check your work.

1. She ___ eats breakfast. ☐ usually ☑ never ☐ almost always
2. Tony ___ goes swimming on Mondays. ☑ usually ☐ never ☐ hardly ever
3. He ___ eats healthy food. ☐ never ☑ almost always ☐ hardly ever
4. She goes running ___. ☑ daily ☐ once in a while ☐ three times a week

B What physical activities can you do in each of these places? Write sentences.

an athletic field

I can play soccer.
I can play baseball.
I can play football.

a gym

I can lift weights.
I can do aerobics.
I can exercise.

a park

I can go walking.
I can go running.
I can go bike riding.

C Choose the best response.

1. "Why don't we go to the pool next week?"
   ☐ Well, have a great time.
   ☑ Sorry, I can't. I have to study.

2. "Why don't we have dinner together tonight? How about at eight?"
   ☐ When's good for you?
   ☑ Sure. Sounds great.

3. "What are you doing here?"
   ☐ Sorry, I can't.
   ☑ I always have lunch here on Saturdays.

🎧 **TOP NOTCH SONG**
"A Typical Day"
Lyrics on last book page.

TOP NOTCH PROJECT
Vote to decide the five most important health habits. Make a poster for your class.

TOP NOTCH WEBSITE
For Unit 6 online activities, visit the *Top Notch* Companion Website at www.longman.com/topnotch.

D Answer the questions with real information.

1. How often do you go to your English class? **YOU**_____.
2. Are you going to your English class tomorrow? **YOU**_____.
3. What do you usually do on weekends? **YOU**_____.
4. What are you doing this weekend? **YOU**_____.

E **WRITING.** Write about **your** typical day.

Every morning, I get up at 6:30. I usually take a shower and ...

UNIT 6
CHECKPOINT

A · 🎧 LISTENING COMPREHENSION

Suggested teaching time:	5–10 minutes
Your actual teaching time:	_____

Language note: To *pig out* is to eat a lot of food, especially food that is bad for you (junk food). If something is said to be *gross*, it is disgusting to look at or think about.

AUDIOSCRIPT

CONVERSATION 1 [F = Chinese]
M: When do you usually eat breakfast?
F: Me? I never eat breakfast. No time.

CONVERSATION 2
F: Where's Tony? He usually goes swimming on Mondays, doesn't he?
M: Usually. But he has to pick up his mom from the airport tonight.

CONVERSATION 3 [F = U.S. regional]
F: Do you have to pig out on all that junk food? It's bad for you!
M: Hey, you know I almost always eat healthy stuff.
F: That's true. But it's really kind of gross.

CONVERSATION 4 [M = Lithuanian]
M: So how much time do you spend at the track?
F: Oh, I run for about thirty minutes or so.
M: Every day?
F: Yup.

B · What physical activities . . . ?

Suggested teaching time:	5 minutes
Your actual teaching time:	_____

• A variety of answers are possible. Students can use activities from page 64 or their own activities.

C · Choose the best response.

Suggested teaching time:	5 minutes
Your actual teaching time:	_____

• Have students check their answers by reading the conversations with a partner.

D · Answer the questions . . .

Suggested teaching time:	5–10 minutes
Your actual teaching time:	_____

• Make sure students use the simple present tense for items 1 and 3, and the present continuous for items 2 and 4.

• To review, have students take turns reading the questions and their answers with a partner.

E · WRITING

Suggested teaching time:	10 minutes
Your actual teaching time:	_____

• To get started, student can look back at their answers to the questions in Step 1 on page 73.

• Suggest that students write three paragraphs—one each about their morning, afternoon, and evening.

• Encourage students to use the frequency adverbs on page 68. Remind students to use the simple present tense.

Your students can say . . .

Every morning, I get up at 6:30. I usually take a shower and get ready for work. I almost always eat breakfast. I usually have coffee and toast. Sometimes I have eggs. I go to work at 7:30.

I come home at 12:30 in the afternoon. I eat lunch. Then I study. At 3:00, I go to my classes. I have two classes every afternoon. I often go to the gym after my classes. I lift weights and go swimming.

In the evening, I eat a small dinner at home. Then I study, read, or watch TV. I usually go to bed at 11:00.

Option: Have students read a classmate's paper to the group, changing *I* to the classmate's name and adding the third-person *–s* to the verbs as they read. **[+10 minutes]**

💿 **Writing Process Worksheets**

💿 *Top Notch Pop* **Song Activities**

TOP NOTCH PROJECT

Idea: Have small groups brainstorm five good health habits. One member of each group writes their group's health habits list on the board. As a class, look at the board and erase any duplicates.

Idea: Students vote on the five most important habits. Tell students to vote five times. Read each habit on the board and have students raise their hands for the ones they think are most important.

Some examples of good health habits are:
> *Exercise regularly.*   *Eat small meals.*
> *Avoid junk food.*   *Drink a lot of water.*
> *Avoid sweets.*   *Eat fish often.*
> *Avoid fatty foods.*   *Get enough sleep.*
> *Eat a lot of fruits and vegetables.*

• Have each group design a poster with the five health habits the class votes on.

T74

UNIT WRAP-UP

Suggested teaching time:	15–20 minutes
Your actual teaching time:	_____

Vocabulary and grammar

- With books closed, review all the language students know to talk about how often they do something. Your students have learned:

  regularly
  every day
  every morning / afternoon / evening / weekend
  once / twice / three times a week
  once in a while
  always

  almost always
  usually
  often
  sometimes
  hardly ever
  never

- Students talk about how often they do the activities pictured. They use the simple present tense and the frequency adverbs and expressions on the board; for example, *I hardly ever play tennis.*

- Students can talk about how often they:

  play tennis
  play basketball
  play (mini) golf
  go bike riding
  go walking
  play soccer
  go swimming
  lift weights

  go running (on the treadmill)
  talk on the phone
  watch TV
  cook dinner
  do aerobics
  clean the house
  play the guitar
  eat out

Social language

- Have students read or listen again to the Conversation Models on pages 66 and 68. In the conversations students create, the two men can talk about their daily routines, plan an activity together, or both.

┌─ **Your students can say . . .** ─────────────
A: Anthony, what are you doing here? **B:** I always go running in the park on Saturday afternoon. You too? **A:** I usually go on Sunday, but tomorrow I'm playing golf. **B:** Really? Where are you playing? **A:** At the golf course in Newtown. **B:** I'm crazy about golf. Why don't we play sometime? **A:** That would be great. Can you play on Friday morning? **B:** Sure. See you then.
└────────────────────────────────────

Writing

- Have students number the individuals, pairs, or groups of people participating in different activities in the picture. Then students write sentences about what the people are doing. The sentence numbers match the numbers in the picture. For example, students place a number 1 next to the people at the tennis court. They write:

  1. They're playing tennis.

Option: Have students use *There is* and *There are* to indicate who they are describing. Then students use the present continuous to describe what the people are doing. For example:

  There are two people on the tennis court. They are playing tennis.
  There's a woman in her apartment. She's in the kitchen. She's cooking dinner.

[+5 minutes]

┌─ **Your students can say . . .** ─────────────
A family is playing mini golf. [Name] and [Name] are playing tennis. Some kids are playing soccer. A boy and girl are swimming. A man is vacuuming. A woman is exercising. A group of people are having dinner at the Blue Moon Café.
└────────────────────────────────────

┌─ **Individual oral progress check (optional)** ─
Use the illustration on page 75 for an oral test. Point to the people in the picture and ask questions, such as: *What is she doing right now?* Students should make statements using the present continuous. Evaluate students on correctness, intelligibility, and completeness.
└────────────────────────────────────

Cumulative Vocabulary Activities

You may wish to use the video for Unit 6 at this point. For video activity worksheets, go to www.longman.com/topnotch.

**Complete Assessment Package
Unit 6 Achievement Test**

- **Vocabulary and grammar.** Talk about how often you do the activities in the picture.

- **Social language.** Create a conversation for the two men.

- **Writing.** Write about the people.
  A woman is cooking.

Mini Golf

Total Fitness

Blue Moon Café

✓ *Now I can . . .*

- ☐ plan an activity with someone.
- ☐ talk about daily routines.
- ☐ discuss exercise and diet.
- ☐ describe my typical day.

UNIT 7

Finding Something to Wear

UNIT GOALS

1 Shop for clothes
2 Pay for clothes
3 Give and get directions in a store
4 Discuss culturally appropriate dress

A **TOPIC PREVIEW.** Look at the store website. What department would <u>you</u> click on?

Shop at Home Online Department Store

Large selection of fine brand-name clothes FOR THE WHOLE FAMILY!

shop at home ONLINE DEPARTMENT STORE

"... Just click your mouse. Stay in your house."®

SIGN IN | REGISTER | MY ACCOUNT | CUSTOMER SERVICE | CHECKOUT | VIEW CART

DEPARTMENTS

Women's

Men's

Teens'

Kids'

Athletic Wear

Outerwear
(coats and jackets)

Sleepwear

Lingerie

Hosiery

Shoes

Bags and
Accessories

SEARCH GO

| SPECIALS | OUTERWEAR | HOSIERY | SLEEPWEAR | BAGS and ACCESSORIES | ATHLETIC WEAR |

OUTERWEAR SALE
SAVE 30–50% on <u>jackets</u>

Arctic brand unisex windbreaker

HOSIERY CLEARANCE!

men's socks   women's tights

THIS WEEK'S
SPECIALS
Click on items for special prices and other details.

ALL SLEEPWEAR, UNDERWEAR, AND LINGERIE ON SALE!

men's boxers   men's pajamas   women's nightgowns   bathrobes

SAVE 40–50% on all
BAGS and ACCESSORIES

leather bags   belts

100+ brands all on sale!
ATHLETIC WEAR

running shoes   shorts   sweatpants

HOME | OTHER PRODUCTS & SERVICES | GIFT CARDS | CATALOGS | ABOUT US | CONTACT US

B **DISCUSSION.** Where do you shop for clothes? Do you ever shop online?

Finding Something to Wear

A TOPIC PREVIEW

Suggested teaching time:	10 minutes
Your actual teaching time:	_____

- Ask the class some questions about the website:
  What's the name of the store? (shop at home)
  What can you buy? (clothes, shoes, bags)

- Read the list of departments and have students repeat.

- Explain that *specials* means items you can get for a lower price than usual (sale price).

- Ask *What departments are having sales this week?* (outerwear, hosiery, sleepwear, underwear, lingerie, bags and accessories, athletic wear)

- Make sure students understand the meaning of the name of each department. Ask:
  How old are teens? (13 to 19 years old)
  When you play sports, do you wear sleepwear or athletic wear? (athletic wear)
  When do you wear sleepwear? (when you go to bed, when you sleep)

- To explain *lingerie*, point to the photo of men's boxers. Say *This is underwear. It's men's underwear. Lingerie is women's underwear.*

- In small groups, have students say what department they would click on.

- As a class ask a few students *What department would you click on?* If students choose one of the departments with specials this week, find out what item they might be shopping for. For example, if a student says he or she would click on *hosiery*, ask *Are you looking for socks? Are you looking for tights? What color are you looking for?*

Language note: A number of clothing items have different names in American English and British English. Refer to the *Longman Dictionary of Contemporary English* for equivalents.

B DISCUSSION

Suggested teaching time:	5–10 minutes
Your actual teaching time:	_____

- Model the activity by answering the questions yourself. Read the first question and answer *I shop for clothes at [Name of store].* Then read the second question. Answer *Yes, I do. I [always] shop for clothes online. I shop at [web address].* Or: *No, I don't. I [hardly ever] shop for clothes online.*

- In small groups, students talk about what clothing stores they like to shop at. Encourage students to also discuss what websites they use to shop for clothes online.

Option: Ask students *What are some popular websites for clothes?* Have each group decide on the website they think is best. Write the web address on the board. Read each site and have students raise their hands once for their favorite. **[+5 minutes]**

Option: Have students look up some of the websites the class suggested. Tell them to look for new department names (ones that aren't listed on the website in Exercise A). Students click on the new departments they find to see what they are. On the board, have one member of each group write the names of the new departments and draw simple pictures to define them. Read the list of departments and have students repeat. Talk about any that are unclear. **[+10 minutes]**

Language note: When saying the name of a web address, it's OK to leave off the *www*. A period in the address is called *dot*. The last part of the address is pronounced as a word, not spelled out. So, the web address www.shopathome.com is said *shop at home dot com.*

C 🎧 SOUND BITES

Suggested teaching time:	10 minutes
Your actual teaching time:	_____

Note: The accented speaker in this Sound Bites is Chinese.

- Have students look at the photos. Ask *Where are the women?* (at a clothing store)

- Point to the woman on the right. Ask *What's her occupation?* (She's a clerk.)

- After students read and listen, ask:
  What does the shopper want to buy? (a V-neck [sweater])
  What color is it? (red)
  What size is it? / Is it a small, a medium, or a large? (a medium)
  What's the price? How much is it? ($55)*
  Who is the sweater for? (her sister)
  Is it a gift? (yes)

- If helpful, demonstrate the meaning of *V-neck*. Draw two simple sweaters on the board. On one, draw an opening for the neck in the shape of the letter *V*. Label it *V-neck*. On the other, draw a small circular opening for the neck. Label it *crew neck*. Ask a few students *Do you prefer V-necks or crew necks?*

- Have students label the photo in the thought balloon *gift wrap*.

D ▷ Read the conversation . . .

Suggested teaching time:	5–10 minutes
Your actual teaching time:	_____

Option: Have students change items 1 and 2 to make them true. (Answers: 1. The <u>shopper</u> asks about the price; 2. The first sweater <u>isn't</u> the right size.) [+5 minutes]

E UNDERSTANDING MEANING FROM CONTEXT

Suggested teaching time:	5 minutes
Your actual teaching time:	_____

- Have students underline the three expressions in the conversation.

- If students have difficulty, demonstrate how to substitute each answer choice for the underlined expression in the conversation. Say *Can you help me? How much is that V-neck?* Then say *I don't understand. How much is that V-neck?* Ask which one is correct.

Challenge: Ask some analytical thinking questions:
  Do you agree with the shopper? Is $55 not too bad for a sweater? Or do you think $55 is expensive?
  If the second sweater is a larger size, what size was the first sweater? (a small)
[+5 minutes]

WHAT ABOUT **YOU?**

Suggested teaching time:	10–15 minutes
Your actual teaching time:	_____

- If helpful, explain that *selection* means many different brands, styles, sizes, colors, etc. from which a customer can choose. *Service* is the help that the clerks in a store give you. It can also be the help that servers in a restaurant or people who work in a hotel give you.

- To get students started, ask *When you decide where to go shopping, are prices not important, important, or very important to you?*

- Students complete the chart by filling in one of the circles in each row.

PAIR WORK

- With a partner, have students compare their charts.

- Your students can say: *Prices are very important to me. Brands are not important to me.*

- After students compare their opinions, ask a few students *What's most important to you—prices, brands, selection, or service?*

Option: Take a poll to find out which factors are most important to your students. On the board, draw the chart that follows. [+10 minutes]

	Prices	Brands	Selection	Service
Not Important				
Important				
Very Important				

Next, ask *Who thinks prices are not important? Who thinks prices are important? Who thinks prices are very important?* Students raise their hands when they hear the response that reflects their opinion. Write the number of students under the appropriate factor.

Option: To give students more to talk about, write the following questions on the board and have pairs discuss.
  What stores have the best prices?
  What stores have the best brands?
  What stores have the best selection?
  What stores have the best service?
[+10 minutes]

EXTRAS (optional)

Workbook: Exercises 1, 2

_____
* In *Top Notch*, where U.S. dollars are given, you may wish to substitute prices in more familiar local currency.

C 🎧 **SOUND BITES.** Read along silently as you listen to a natural conversation.

SHOPPER: Excuse me. How much is that V-neck?

CLERK: This red one? It's $55.

SHOPPER: That's not too bad. And it's really nice.

SHOPPER: Do you have it in a larger size?

CLERK: Here you go. This one's a medium. Would you like to try it on?

SHOPPER: No, thanks. It's for my sister. Would you be nice enough to gift wrap it for me? **CN**

CLERK: Of course!

D Read the conversation carefully and check ☑ the statements that are true. Then explain your answers.

- ☐ **1.** The clerk asks about the price.
- ☐ **2.** The first sweater is the right size.
- ☑ **3.** The sweater is a gift.
- ☑ **4.** The shopper buys the sweater.

E **UNDERSTANDING MEANING FROM CONTEXT.** Complete the statements.

1. When the shopper says, "Excuse me," she means _____.
   - **a.** Can you help me?
   - **b.** I don't understand.
2. When the shopper says, "That's not too bad," she means _____.
   - **a.** The sweater is nice.
   - **b.** The price is not too high.
3. When the clerk says, "Here you go," she means _____.
   - **a.** Here's a cheaper one.
   - **b.** Here's a larger one.

CN Corpus Notes:
"(Would you be) nice enough" and "(Would you be) kind enough" have the same meaning but English learners almost always use "kind enough." Students should be encouraged to vary their speech.

WHAT ABOUT **YOU?**

What's important to you when you choose a place to shop for clothes? Complete the chart.

	Not important	Important	Very important
Prices	○	○	○
Brands	○	○	○
Selection	○	○	○
Service	○	○	○

PAIR WORK. Compare your opinions.

1 ▶ *Shop for Clothes*

🎧 CONVERSATION MODEL Read and listen.

A: Excuse me. Do you have these gloves in a larger size?
B: No, I'm sorry. We don't.
A: That's too bad.
B: But we have a larger pair in brown. See if they are better.
A: Yes, they're fine. Thanks.

🎧 **Rhythm and intonation practice**

A ▸ GRAMMAR. Comparative adjectives

small → small**er**   large → larg**er**   heavy → heav**ier**   big → big**ger**
cheap → cheap**er**   loose → loos**er**   pretty → prett**ier**   hot → hot**ter**

Irregular forms
good → better
bad → worse

Use comparative adjectives to compare two people, places, or things.
Do you have these pants in a **larger** size? This pair is too tight.

Use more or less with adjectives that have two or more syllables and don't end in -y. 🄲🄽
Do you have a **more comfortable** pair of shoes?
Let's look for a **less expensive** suit.

Use than after the adjective when you compare two items.
Some people say that black is more flattering **than** white, but white looks better on me.

GRAMMAR BOOSTER
PAGES G13–G1
For more ...

B ▸ Complete each conversation with comparative adjectives. Use than if necessary.

1. **A:** I just love these gloves, but I wish they were ___warmer___.
     warm
   B: What about these? They look great, and they're much ___less expensive___.
     expensive

2. **A:** Don't take those pajamas to Hawaii! It's hot there. Take something ___lighter___.
     light
   B: Good idea.

3. **A:** What do you think of this red dress?
   B: Beautiful. It's ___prettier than___ the black one. And ___cheaper___, too.
     pretty   _cheap_

4. **A:** Excuse me. Do these pants come in a ___longer___ length? These are too short.
     long
   B: Let me see if I can find you something ___better___.
     good

🄲🄽 **Corpus Notes:** Students sometimes mistakenly use "more" with comparative adjectives that end in "–er," such as "more cheaper" and "more bigger."

1 ▶ *Shop for Clothes*

🎧 CONVERSATION **MODEL**

Suggested teaching time:	5–10 minutes
Your actual teaching time:	_____

- Before students read and listen, Ask:
  Where are the women? (in a department store)
  The woman with brown hair is a shopper. The blond woman is the . . . ? (clerk)

- After students listen and read, ask:
  What is the shopper looking for? (gloves)
  Is she buying black or brown gloves? (brown)
  Why? (because the black gloves are small / because the brown gloves are larger)

🎧 **Rhythm and intonation practice**

Suggested teaching time:	5 minutes
Your actual teaching time:	_____

- Point out that in this conversation *Excuse me* is used to ask for help or initiate a conversation. In this situation, *Excuse me* has falling intonation. Read Student A's first line out loud and have students repeat.

- Make sure students use falling intonation with *Do you have these gloves in a larger size?*

- Tell students to look at the picture. Ask *How are the gloves the clerk has different from the gloves the shopper is looking at?* (They're brown.) Have students find and circle *brown* in the conversation. Read the sentence *But we have a larger pair in brown* with stress on *brown*. Point out that *brown* is stressed to emphasize that the alternative choice is different. Have students repeat.

- Make sure students use the following stress pattern:

┌─ **STRESS PATTERN** ─────────────────────┐

  • —   •   •   —   •   •
A: Excuse me. Do you have these

  —   • • —   •   —
gloves in a larger size?

  —   •   — •   •   —
B: No, I'm sorry. We don't.

  —   •   —
A: That's too bad.

  • •   —   •   —   • •   —
B: But we have a larger pair in brown.

  —   •   —   •   —   •
See if they are better.

  —   •   —   —
A: Yes, they're fine. Thanks.

└──┘

🔶 GRAMMAR

Suggested teaching time:	10–15 minutes
Your actual teaching time:	_____

- After students read the information in the Grammar box, have them find and underline the comparatives in the Conversation Model (larger, larger, better).

- Ask questions using comparatives. Have students answer in complete sentences:
  Which is smaller, a laptop or a PDA? (A PDA is smaller than a laptop.)
  Which is bigger, a pool or an athletic field? (An athletic field is bigger than a pool.)
  Which is cheaper, a movie or a concert? (A movie is usually cheaper than a concert.)
  Which is hotter, Indian food or Thai food?
  Which is easier, tennis or golf?
  Which is more popular, hip-hop or rock music?

- Give students some adjectives that are similar in form to the examples in the Grammar box. Ask the class how to change them to comparatives. For example:
  long (Add *–er.*)   *fat* (Double the *–t* and add *–er.*)
  nice (Add *–r.*)   *popular* (Use *more* or *less.*)
  ugly (Change the *–y* to *i* and add *–er.*)

Option: Have students review adjectives. On the board, write the list of words that follow. Ask students to copy the list and then write the opposite of each adjective.

  small (large, big)   *ugly (pretty)*
  expensive (cheap, inexpensive)   *tight (loose)*
  light (heavy, dark)   *short (long, tall)*
[+10 minutes]

🔵 **Grammar Self-Checks**

🔶 **Complete each conversation . . .**

Suggested teaching time:	5 minutes
Your actual teaching time:	_____

- Before students start, remind them to use *than* after the adjective when comparing two items.

- To check their work, have students read the conversations with a partner.

- If helpful, explain that something *practical* is something that you can really use.

Option: Practice creating comparative forms using large flashcards. Write an adjective from the Grammar box on one side of the flashcard and the comparative form on the other. Hold up each adjective and elicit the correct comparative form from the class.
[+5 minutes]

Option: Practice comparative sentences with a transformation drill. Write on the board *This shirt is cheaper than that shirt.* Then say the adjective *large* and elicit from the class *This shirt is larger than that shirt.* Then point to a student and say *comfortable.* Elicit the sentence *This shirt is more/less comfortable than that shirt.* Continue saying adjectives from the Grammar box and eliciting comparative sentences from individual students. **[+10 minutes]**

C 🎧 VOCABULARY

Suggested teaching time:	5 minutes
Your actual teaching time:	_____

- Explain that *a pair* is two of something. For example, *a pair of gloves* (two gloves) or *a pair of socks* (two socks).

Language note: Some things are called *a pair* even though they are really only one item. Usually this is because they are made of two similar parts. For example, pantyhose, tights, pants, and shorts have two legs.

- After students listen and repeat, ask the questions that follow. Have students answer in complete sentences.
    Which are longer, pants or shorts? (Pants are longer than shorts.)
    Which are heavier, pantyhose or tights? (Tights are heavier than pantyhose.)
    Which are looser, boxers or briefs? (Boxers are looser than briefs.)
    Which are warmer, pajamas or boxers? (Pajamas are warmer than boxers.)
    Which are more comfortable, socks or pantyhose? (Socks are more comfortable than pantyhose.)

- Have student look back at the store website on page 76. Have them find the word *underwear*. Explain that underwear is clothing you wear next to your body under your clothes. Say *Panties, boxers, and briefs are underwear.*

- Students continue to look at page 76. Ask:
    What department would you find socks, pantyhose, and tights in? (hosiery)
    What department would you find gloves in? (accessories)
    What department are pajamas in? (sleepwear)

Challenge: Ask *Why do think pajamas are described as pairs?* (maybe because they have two legs; maybe because there are two parts, a top and a bottom) *Why do you think underwear is described as pairs?* (maybe because they have openings for two legs) **[+5 minutes]**

💿 **Vocabulary Cards**

💿 **Learning Strategies**

D 🎧 LISTENING COMPREHENSION

Suggested teaching time:	5 minutes
Your actual teaching time:	_____

Language note: The words *pantyhose* and *stockings* are now generally used interchangeably to mean the same thing. In the past, stockings were single or separate leg coverings for women, held up by garters. Another word commonly heard is *hose.*

AUDIOSCRIPT

CONVERSATION 1
M (Recording): Third floor. Ladies' gloves, hats, and purses.
F1: Let's get off here. I need a new pair of gloves.
F2: Me, too.

CONVERSATION 2
M: These pajamas aren't comfortable. They're too small.
F: Would you like me to get you a couple of new pairs when I go shopping?
M: That'd be great. Thanks.

CONVERSATION 3
F: Look at these great tights. They have pictures of animals on them. Don't you love them?
M: Not particularly. They're a little wild for my taste.

CONVERSATION 4
M1: Can I help you, sir?
M2: Yes, please. I'm looking for underwear.
M1: Certainly. Would you like briefs or boxers?
M2: Boxers, please.

CONVERSATION 5
F1: I don't have a single pair of pantyhose to wear to the office. And I have a big meeting today!
F2: Why don't you wear a nice pair of pants. That way you don't need stockings. You can wear socks.
F1: Good idea.

CONVERSATION **PAIR WORK**

Suggested teaching time:	10–15 minutes
Your actual teaching time:	_____

- Remind students to use *this* with singular items (*this jacket*) and *these* with plural items (*these bathrobes*). Point out that *these* is used with all clothing described as pairs (*these pants*).

- Have students look back at the store website on page 76 and label each item of clothing pictured with *this* or *these* and its name. (this windbreaker/jacket, this bag, this nightgown, this belt, these sweatpants) To review, read the correct labels and have students repeat.

- In the first blank in the conversation, students use *this / these* + an article of clothing + an idea from the list. To continue the conversation, Student B offers an alternative.

Language note: Variations in clothing sizes, colors, and styles always use the preposition *in.* For example, *Do you have this shirt in blue? Do you have these gloves in large? Do you have this jacket in size 40 (or in a 40)?*

💿 **Pair Work Cards**

EXTRAS (optional)

Grammar Booster
Workbook: Exercises 3–7
Copy & Go: Activity 25

C ⌒ VOCABULARY. Clothing described as "pairs." Listen and practice.

(a pair of) gloves

(a pair of) pajamas

(a pair of) socks

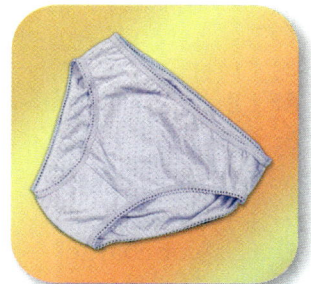

(a pair of) panties

(a pair of) boxers
(a pair of) briefs

(a pair of) pantyhose
(a pair of) tights

(a pair of) pants
(a pair of) shorts

D ⌒ LISTENING COMPREHENSION. Circle the clothing discussed in each conversation.

1. stockings   gloves
2. boxers   pajamas
3. tights   gloves
4. pajamas   boxers
5. pantyhose   panties

CONVERSATION
PAIR WORK

Role-play shopping for clothes. Start like this:

Excuse me.
Do you have _____?

Continue the conversation in your own way . . .

Ideas

in a smaller size
in a larger size
in another color
in [black]
in size [34]

CONTROLLED PRACTICE

Pay for Clothes

🎧 CONVERSATION MODEL Read and listen.

A: I'll take the loafers.
B: Certainly. How would you like **CN** to pay for them?
A: Excuse me?
B: Cash or charge?
A: Charge, please. And could you gift wrap them for me?
B: Absolutely.

🎧 **Rhythm and intonation practice**

CN **Corpus Notes:** "Certainly" is more formal than "sure" or "OK" and is used in conversation, especially by people such as sales clerks, waiters, and waitresses.

A 🎧 **VOCABULARY.** Types of clothing and shoes. **Listen and practice.**

casual clothes	sweaters and jackets	shoes

casual clothes
① jeans   ② a T-shirt
③ a sweatshirt   ④ a polo shirt
⑤ sweatpants

sweaters and jackets
① a crew neck   ② a cardigan
③ a turtleneck   ④ a V-neck
⑤ a windbreaker   ⑥ a blazer

shoes
① oxfords   ② loafers
③ sandals   ④ running shoes
⑤ pumps   ⑥ flats

B **GRAMMAR.** Uses of object pronouns

As direct objects

I want **the sweatshirt**.   →   I want **it**.
I love **these jeans**.   →   I love **them**.

In prepositional phrases

Give this hat **to Jane**.   →   Give this hat **to her**.
He's buying a bag **for his wife**.   →   He's buying a bag **for her**.

In sentences with both direct objects and object pronouns, the prepositional phrase comes last.

I want the sweatpants. Can you gift wrap **them for me**?

Object pronouns	
singular	**plural**
me	us
you	you
him	
her	} them
it	

GRAMMAR BOOSTER

PAGES G14–G15
For more . . .

LESSON

2 ▶ *Pay for Clothes*

🎧 CONVERSATION **MODEL**

Suggested teaching time:	5–10 minutes
Your actual teaching time:	_____

- To set the scene for the conversation ask *What department are they in?* (the shoe department)
- After students read and listen, ask:
  What is the shopper buying? (loafers/shoes)
  How is he paying? (charge)
  Are the shoes for him? (No, they're a gift.)
- To demonstrate *cash* and *charge*, hold up paper money and say *cash* and hold up a credit card and say *charge*.
- Ask a few students *Do you usually pay cash for clothes, or do you charge them?*

Option: Ask students the difference between *Excuse me* in the Sound Bites on page 77 and *Excuse me?* in the Conversation Model conversation. (The first is to ask for assistance in a shop. The second is to ask for clarification.) **[+5 minutes]**

🎧 Rhythm and intonation practice

Suggested teaching time:	5 minutes
Your actual teaching time:	_____

- Point out that in this conversation *Excuse me?* is used to ask for clarification or repetition. In this situation *Excuse me?* has rising intonation. Read Student A's second line out loud and have students repeat.
- Have students repeat each line chorally. Make sure they:
  - use falling intonation with *How would you like to pay for them?*
  - use rising intonation with *Cash or charge?* and *And could you gift wrap them for me?*
  - use the following stress pattern:

```
┌─ STRESS PATTERN ──────────────────────────
│      •   —   •   —   •
│  A:  I'll take the loafers.
│
│      —   •  •   •   •   •   •   •   —  •  •
│  B:  Certainly.  How would you like to pay for them?
│
│      —   —   •
│  A:  Excuse me?
│
│      —   •   •
│  B:  Cash or charge?
│
│      —   •  •   •   •   •
│  A:  Charge, please.  And could you
│
│      —   •   •   •
│  gift wrap them for me?
│
│      —   •   —   •
│  B:  Absolutely.
└───────────────────────────────────────────
```

🅐 🎧 VOCABULARY

Suggested teaching time:	5 minutes
Your actual teaching time:	_____

- Explain that *casual clothes* are informal clothes.
- Ask a few different students:
  Do you wear casual clothes . . .
  . . . to the park?
  . . . to the movies, concerts, plays?
  . . . to work?
  . . . to school?
  . . . to restaurants?
  Students can answer *Yes, I do* or *No, I don't* or with a frequency adverb. (*Yes, usually.*)
- Ask the class *Who's wearing a sweater today?* Then ask about the types of sweaters those students are wearing. For example, *OK, [Jane] is wearing a sweater. Is it a crew neck, a cardigan, a turtleneck, or a V-neck?*
- Ask several students *What type of shoes are you wearing today?*

Option: Ask the class *Who's wearing jeans today?* Choose one student who raises his or her hand. Using language your students know, describe everything that student is wearing. For example, you could say *[Name] is wearing jeans, a polo shirt, and oxfords.* Next, have that student describe what another classmate is wearing. Continue until several students have had a chance to participate. **[+5 minutes]**

💿 **Vocabulary Cards**

🅑 GRAMMAR

Suggested teaching time:	10 minutes
Your actual teaching time:	_____

- After students read the information in the Grammar box, have them find and circle the object pronouns in the Conversation Model. (them, them, me) Then ask *What does "them" refer to?* (the loafers)
- Bring in photos of clothing or use the clothing pictured in Exercise A on this page. Ask a student *Do you like [this blazer]?* Students answer using an object pronoun. (*Yes, I like **it*** or *No, I don't like **it**.)
- Put all the photos on the board. Say *It's [Name]'s birthday. What would you like to buy for him/her?* Tell students to begin with *I want to buy . . . ;* for example, *I want to buy the blue sweatshirt for him.* Continue addressing different students. Say *It's [Name]'s birthday.* Each student chooses an item from the board and says *I want to buy the (item from the board) for him/her.*

Challenge: Record or remember some of the gifts students say they would like to give. Ask those students *Why would you like to give the [blue sweatshirt] to [Joe]?* Have students answer in a complete sentence using object pronouns. For example, *I want to give **it** to **him** because he's always cold.* **[+5 minutes]**

💿 **Grammar Self-Checks**

T80

C ▸ Underline the direct object . . .

Suggested teaching time:	5–10 minutes
Your actual teaching time:	_____

• When you review, point out that the object pronoun for *that great pair of flats* in item 6 is *them*, not *it*.

Challenge: To allow students to hear and use object pronouns in quick succession, challenge students with a quick transformation drill. Say a short sentence and call on students to respond, using an object pronoun and changing the subject. Repeat the exercise, using a different object each time. For example:

T: *I'm teaching you.*   **S:** *You're teaching us.*
T: *You're listening to me.*   **S:** *We're listening to you.*

T: *I like the red jacket.*   **S:** *You like it.*
T: *I want the these running shoes.*   **S:** *You want them.*
T: *I don't need the green T-shirt.*   **S:** *You don't need it.*
T: *I'm buying the flats for [female classmate's name].*   **S:** *You're buying them for her.*
T: *I'm buying the black shirt for [male classmate's name].*   **S:** *You're buying it for him.*

D ▸ Write the words and phrases . . .

Suggested teaching time:	5 minutes
Your actual teaching time:	_____

• Copy Item 1 on the board. Point to the subject *I* and write the word on the board. Then point to the verb *am buying* and write it after the word *I*. Have the class finish the sentence by putting the remaining words in order.

• Remind students that the prepositional phrases come last. If helpful, have students circle the prepositional phrases before they complete the exercise.

CONVERSATION **PAIR WORK**

Suggested teaching time:	10–15 minutes
Your actual teaching time:	_____

• Students can choose an item of clothing from the Vocabulary on page 80, from the photos you brought in, or from a clothing catalog.

• As students practice their conversations, circulate and check that their object pronouns match the item of clothing they chose.

Option: Have students role play their conversations in front of the class. **[+10 minutes]**

🔵 **Pair Work Cards**

EXTRAS (optional)

Grammar Booster
Workbook: Exercises 8–11
Copy & Go: Activity 26

C ▸ **Underline the direct object in each sentence. Then rewrite the sentence, replacing the direct object with an object pronoun.**

1. They bought <u>the green sweatpants</u>.

   They bought them .

2. I love these <u>windbreakers</u>.

   I love them .

3. I'm buying <u>the crew neck</u>.

   I'm buying it .

4. Did you see <u>the blue polo shirts</u>?

   Did you see them ?

5. I don't need <u>the cardigan</u>.

   I don't need it .

6. Do you still have <u>that great pair of flats</u>?

   Do you still have them ?

7. They gave <u>the old jackets</u> to us.

   They gave them to us .

D ▸ **Write the words and phrases in the correct order.**

1. I / it / for her / am buying

   I am buying it for her .

2. They / them / for us / are getting

   They are getting them for us .

3. Please / it / to me / give

   Please give it to me .

4. for my son-in-law / I / them / need

   I need them for my son-in-law .

5. it / He / is gift wrapping / for me

   He is gift wrapping it for me .

CONVERSATION PAIR WORK

Role-play paying for clothes. Use the guide, or create a new conversation.

A: I'll take the _____.

B: _____. How would you like to pay for _____?

A: Excuse me?

B: Cash or charge?

A: _____, please. And could you gift wrap _____ for me?

B: _____.

CONTROLLED PRACTICE

Give and Get Directions in a Store

A 🎧 **VOCABULARY. Locations and directions.** Listen and practice.

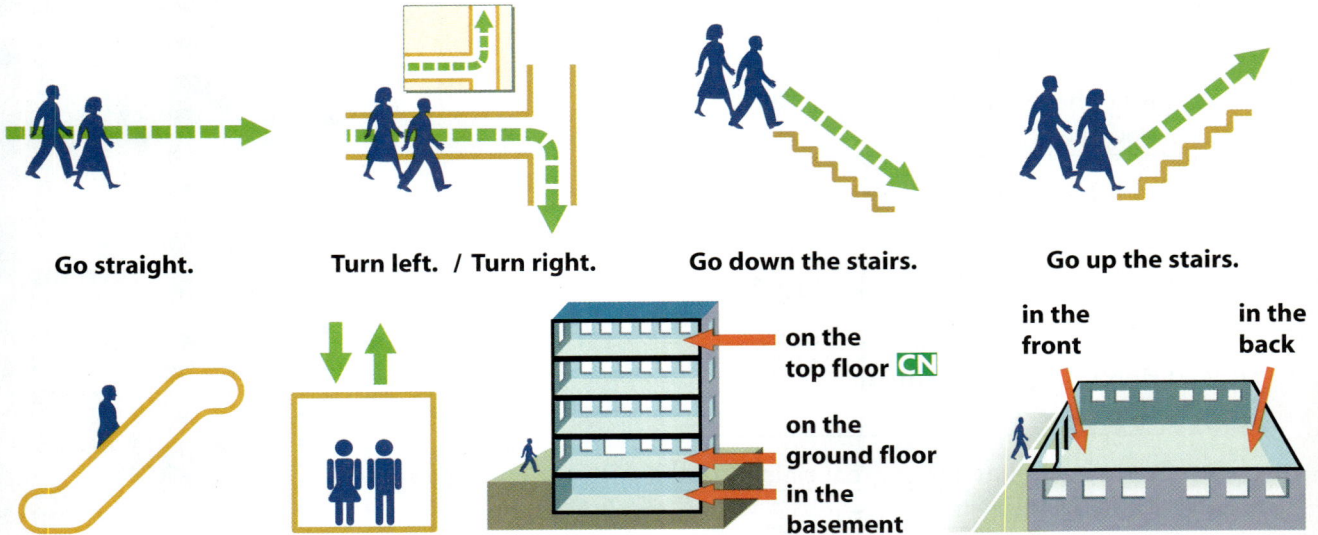

Go straight.

Turn left. / Turn right.

Go down the stairs.

Go up the stairs.

Take the escalator.   Take the elevator.

on the top floor **CN**

on the ground floor

in the basement

in the front

in the back

CN **Corpus Notes:**
English learners will sometimes make the mistake of saying "in the [top/ground] floor" and "on the basement.

B 🎧 **LISTENING COMPREHENSION. Listen to the directions at an information desk. Then listen again and write the number of each place on the diagrams.**

1	Coats	4	Lingerie
2	Children's shoes	5	Accessories
3	Coffee shop		

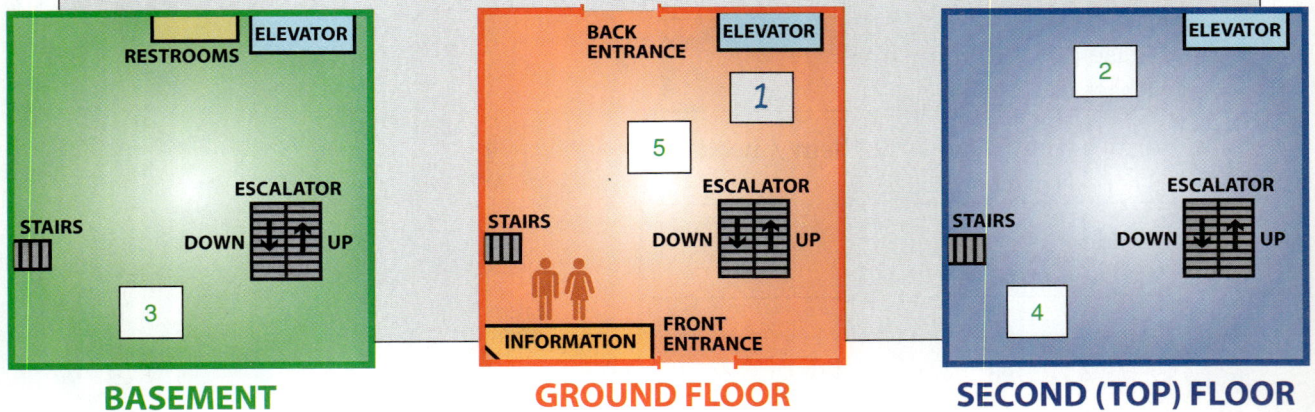

RESTROOMS   ELEVATOR

STAIRS

ESCALATOR
DOWN ↓↑ UP

3

BASEMENT

BACK ENTRANCE   ELEVATOR

1

5

STAIRS

ESCALATOR
DOWN ↓↑ UP

INFORMATION   FRONT ENTRANCE

GROUND FLOOR

ELEVATOR

2

STAIRS

ESCALATOR
DOWN ↓↑ UP

4

SECOND (TOP) FLOOR

C 🎧 **PRONUNCIATION. Contrastive stress for clarification.**
Read, listen, and repeat.

A: The shoe department is upstairs, on the third floor.

B: Excuse me? The first floor?

A: No. It's on the third floor.

LESSON

3 Give and Get Directions in a Store

A 🎧 VOCABULARY

Suggested teaching time:	10 minutes
Your actual teaching time:	_____

- After students listen and repeat, ask what the two floors between the top floor and the ground floor are called (third floor, second floor). Review ordinal numbers so students will be able to give directions in a multi-floor building. Ask *What floor is our classroom on?*

- Ask *Who's sitting in the front of the classroom? Who's sitting in the back of the classroom?*

Option: Have students write directions to your classroom from your building's entrance. Students who live in apartment buildings can write directions from their building's entrance to their apartment. **[+5 minutes]**

Culture note: In the U.K., the *first floor* is always called the *ground floor*. The next floor is called the *first floor*. In the U.S. and Canada, the *first floor* may be called the *ground floor* or the *first floor*. The next floor is called the *second floor*.

💿 **Vocabulary Cards**

💿 **Learning Strategies**

B 🎧 LISTENING COMPREHENSION

Suggested teaching time:	15–20 minutes
Your actual teaching time:	_____

- Before students listen to the conversations, tell them that they are looking at a diagram of a department store.

- Have students find the information desk. (on the ground floor, on the left side of the entrance)

- Have students look at the diagrams. Ask:
  Where are the elevators? (in the back of the store)
  Where are the escalators? (in the front of the store, on the right side)
  Where are the stairs? (on the left side of the store)

- Students start at the information desk. The places are talked about in the conversations in the same order as they are listed in the box.

Challenge: After students complete the activity, have them give directions from the information desk to the places on the diagrams. **[+5 minutes]**

AUDIOSCRIPT

CONVERSATION 1 [M = Spanish]
M: Where are the coats?
F: Right here on the ground floor. The coat department is in the back of the store, right in front of the elevators.
M: Back of the store? Thanks. Oh. And the restrooms?
F: In the basement, near the elevators.
M: Thanks.
F: No problem.

CONVERSATION 2 [M = Indian]
F: Yes, sir. How can I help you?
M: I'm looking for the shoe department.
F: Men's or women's?
M: Children's, actually.
F: The children's department is upstairs. Take the escalator to the second floor and walk to the back of the store. It's right there. You'll see it.

CONVERSATION 3 [M = U.S. regional]
M: Excuse me. Where's the restaurant?
F: There are two restaurants, sir. There's a coffee shop and a self-service buffet.
M: The coffee shop.
F: That's downstairs in the basement.
M: How do I get there?
F: Just take the escalator and turn right when you get off.

CONVERSATION 4 [M = British English]
M: I want to buy my wife a nightgown.
F: Certainly, sir.
M: Where is the lingerie?
F: The lingerie department is on the top floor, in the front of the store. Go up the stairs and turn right.

CONVERSATION 5 [F1 = Australian]
F1: I'm looking for purses.
F2: Purses? They're in accessories.
F1: Where's that, please?
F2: Go straight down the center of the floor. It's just after you pass the escalators.
F1: Thanks.

C PRONUNCIATION

Suggested teaching time:	5–10 minutes
Your actual teaching time:	_____

- After students read, listen, and repeat, ask *Which words are said louder?* (*first* and *third* in the last two lines) *Why are they said louder?* (because B doesn't understand where the shoe department is; B is checking that she heard right, and A is correcting her)

💿 **Pronunciation Activities**

TOP NOTCH **INTERACTION**

Suggested teaching time: 15–20 minutes
Your actual teaching time: _____

STEP 1

• Refer students back to the Vocabulary on pages 79 and 80 if they need help coming up with items for a list.

STEP 2

• Have students locate the information desk.

• Model the activity by asking a more advanced student where to find a type of clothing. For example, *Excuse me. Where are the coffee makers?* When the student answers, ask for clarification. Use contrastive stress.

Your students can say ...

Shopper: Excuse me. I'm looking for jackets.
Clerk: Men's or Women's? **Shopper:** Men's.
Clerk: Men's Outerwear is on the second floor, in the back of the store. Take the escalator up and then turn right. **Shopper:** Take the escalator up and turn left? **Clerk:** No. Turn right.

Option: Without saying the name of the department, students give directions to a partner from the Information desk to a place in the store. Partners follow the directions and see if they end up in the correct place. **[+5 minutes]**

EXTRAS (optional)

Workbook: Exercises 12
Copy & Go: Activity 27

Pronunciation Supplements

STEP 1. **On the notepad, write things you can find in each department.** (Answers may vary.)

Men's: pants; boxers	Lingerie: panties; nightgowns
Women's: skirts; jeans	Electronics: TVs; printers
Shoes: running shoes	Appliances: microwave ovens

STEP 2. **PAIR WORK.** Look at the department store floor plan and store directory. Role-play conversations between a shopper and an information clerk. Use the items on the notepad.

> Excuse me. Where are the …?

STORE DIRECTORY

Bags and Accessories	Ground Floor
Electronics	Basement
Hosiery	Ground Floor
Lingerie	Ground Floor
Men's Athleticwear	2
Men's Casual	2
Men's Outerwear	2
Men's Shoes	2
Men's Sleepwear	2
Men's Underwear	2
Photo Studio	Basement
Restaurant	Basement
Small Appliances	Basement
Women's Casual	Ground Floor
Women's Shoes	Ground Floor

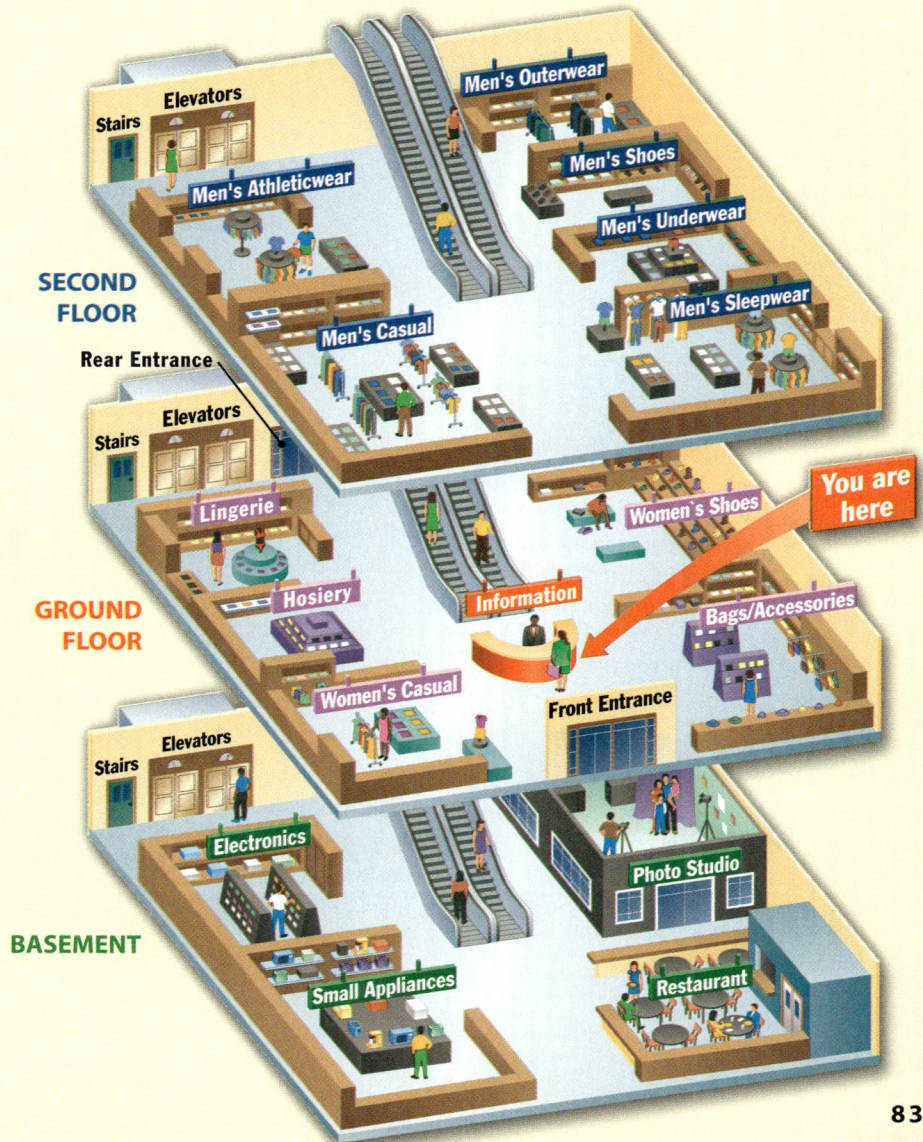

SECOND FLOOR — Stairs, Elevators, Men's Outerwear, Men's Athleticwear, Men's Shoes, Men's Underwear, Men's Casual, Men's Sleepwear, Rear Entrance

GROUND FLOOR — Stairs, Elevators, Lingerie, Women's Shoes, Hosiery, Information, Bags/Accessories, Women's Casual, Front Entrance, You are here

BASEMENT — Stairs, Elevators, Electronics, Photo Studio, Small Appliances, Restaurant

83

FREE PRACTICE

Discuss Culturally Appropriate Dress

A **READING WARM-UP.** What do you wear when the weather is warm?
—when you want to look informal? —when you need to look more formal?

B 🎧 **READING.** Read about clothing do's and don'ts for travelers. Then explain why this information is helpful.

Know before you go . . .

Every culture has unwritten "rules" about appropriate and inappropriate dress. Some cultures have a liberal attitude about clothing, while other cultures are more conservative. Read about some clothing do's and don'ts for three popular travel destinations around the world.

Holland

Holland has a northern climate, so depending on the time of year you're visiting, pack lighter or heavier clothes. One thing people notice about Holland is the way young people dress. Their dress code is "anything goes," so it's not unusual to see some pretty wild clothes there!

Thailand

If you're visiting beautiful Thailand from May to September, pack for the heat. Thailand is generally conservative when it comes to clothing, but at Thailand's magnificent temples, the rules about clothing, and especially shoes, are very strict. If your shoes are too open, they are considered disrespectful, and you will have to change to more modest ones. So be prepared with light but modest clothing and shoes for your Thailand trip.

a Thai temple

Egypt

Summertime is hot in Egypt, so pack light clothing. But be sure to bring warm-weather clothing that is also modest. If you visit a mosque, shorts are definitely out of the question, for both men and women. In mosques, women should wear longer skirts and a head covering, usually a scarf. And the upper part of their arms should be covered with sleeves. For touring other wonderful sights and historical places, casual, comfortable clothing is fine for both men and women.

an Egyptian mosque

SOURCE: *Rough Guide* and *Berlitz* travel guides

LESSON

4 Discuss Culturally Appropriate Dress

A READING WARM-UP

Suggested teaching time:	5 minutes
Your actual teaching time:	_____

• If helpful, explain that *informal* is similar to *casual*. *Formal* is the opposite of *casual*.

• Students answer the questions with a partner or in small groups.

Option: On the board, write the following headings:
Warm weather   Cool weather   Informal   Formal
Ask the class for examples of each type of clothing. Write students' answers under the appropriate heading. **[+5 minutes]**

Option: Ask:
Where do you wear more formal clothes?
What formal clothes do you wear?
Where do you wear more informal clothes?
What informal clothes do you wear?
Are the clothes you're wearing today more formal or more informal?
[+5 minutes]

B 🎧 READING

Suggested teaching time:	10 minutes
Your actual teaching time:	_____

• Explain the terms *liberal* and *conservative*. Have students look at the photo of young people in Holland. Say *Holland has a liberal attitude about clothing. In Holland, young people can wear anything they want. In this culture, is it OK to wear anything, or are people more conservative?*

Option: Have students look through magazines for examples of extremely informal and more conservative dress. **[+10 minutes]**

• After students read and listen, have them read again and underline the adjectives that describe clothing in each place. (Holland: *lighter, heavier, wild*; Thailand: *conservative, light, modest*; Egypt: *light, warm-weather, casual, comfortable*)

Challenge: (If your students are unfamiliar with Thailand) ask:
What do you think the weather is like in Thailand from October through April?
Do you think you'd be allowed to wear shorts in a Thai temple? **[+10 minutes]**

• Have students list clothing do's and don'ts for each country. For example:
Holland
Do: *pack lighter clothes for summer; pack heavier clothes for winter*
Don't: *pack too many very formal clothes*
Thailand
Do: *pack for the heat (in summer); pack conservative clothes; pack light but modest clothes and shoes*
Don't: *wear open shoes at a temple*
Egypt
Do: *pack light clothing (in summer); pack modest clothing; wear a long skirt, long sleeves, and a head covering at a mosque (for women); pack casual, comfortable clothing*
Don't: *wear shorts at a mosque*

Option: Make sure students have understood *wild* and *modest* from the context of the article. (Wild clothing is different, unusual, strange; modest clothing covers your body.) Have pairs write a description of a wild outfit and of a modest outfit. (An outfit is all the clothes worn together at the same time.) For example:

wild	modest
a T-shirt	*a turtleneck*
boxers	*a blazer*
tights	*pants*
boots	*socks*
lots of accessories	*oxfords*

Pairs read one of their descriptions and the class says whether it's wild or modest.
[+10 minutes]

💿 **Extra Reading Comprehension Activities**

💿 **Learning Strategies**

◆ C DISCUSSION

Suggested teaching time:	5–10 minutes
Your actual teaching time:	_____

- To explain, have students refer to their lists of clothing do's and don'ts for each country.
- If you are in Holland, Thailand, or Egypt, students don't need to fill in *This country*.

◆ D PAIR WORK

Suggested teaching time:	10 minutes
Your actual teaching time:	_____

- With a partner, students can write or talk about what to bring for a summer visit to each place.
- Students should refer to their lists of do's and don'ts for each place.
- Review. For each place, ask a few different students what they would pack. Ask the class to listen and check that the clothes are appropriate. For example, for the mosque, no shorts, but a long skirt, long sleeves, and head covering for women; for the pyramids, nothing too warm; for the temple, no sandals.

TOP NOTCH **INTERACTION**

Suggested teaching time:	15–20 minutes
Your actual teaching time:	_____

STEP 1

- Read the first statement out loud. Say *If you have the same opinion, circle* **agree**. *If you have a different opinion, circle* **disagree**.
- If necessary, explain that *essential* means important and necessary.

Option: Take a poll. Read each question out loud to the class. Have students raise their hands (first students who agree, then students who disagree). On the board, write the total number of students who agree and the total number of students who disagree for each statement. Discuss the results. **[+10 minutes]**

STEP 2

- Point out that students don't need to use the word *do* when they write their do's. For example, we say:
  Wear nice pants and a blazer.
  Not ~~Do wear nice pants and a blazer.~~
- If appropriate, students can write a separate set of do's and don'ts for men and women.

STEP 3

- Students compare their notepads. Each student in a group reads his or her do's and don'ts for each place. Students may want to add to their own do's and don'ts as they discuss.

EXTRAS (optional)

Workbook: Exercises 13
Copy & Go: Activity 28

C **DISCUSSION.** Rate the dress code for each country. Then explain each rating you made.

	conservative		liberal		"anything goes!"
Egypt	✓	○	○	○	○
Holland	○	○	○	○	✓
Thailand	✓	○	○	○	○
This country	○	○	○	○	○

(Answers will vary.)

D **PAIR WORK.** Plan your clothes for a July visit to one of the following places.

- an Egyptian mosque
- the pyramids in Egypt
- a casual restaurant in Holland
- a Thai temple

TOP NOTCH
INTERACTION • *Do's and Don'ts*

STEP 1. Take the opinion survey.

What's your personal dress code?

Circle "agree" or "disagree"
for each statement about clothing.

It's OK to wear shorts on the street.	agree	disagree
It's OK for men to wear shorts on the street, but not for women.	agree	disagree
It's essential for men to wear a tie in the office.	agree	disagree
It's OK for women to wear pants in the office.	agree	disagree
It's OK for young people to be less conservative in clothing than adults.	agree	disagree
It's essential for women to cover their heads in public.	agree	disagree

How would you rate yourself?

☐ conservative ☐ liberal ☐ "anything goes!"

STEP 2. On the notepad, write some clothing do's and don'ts for visitors to this country.

in offices and formal restaurants:

in casual social settings:

in religious institutions:

STEP 3. GROUP WORK. Discuss the do's and don'ts for appropriate dress in this country. Does everyone agree?

FREE PRACTICE

UNIT 7
CHECKPOINT

A 🎧 **LISTENING COMPREHENSION.** Listen critically to the conversations about clothes. Infer the name of the **department** where the people are talking.

Outerwear	Lingerie	Hosiery	Bags and accessories	Shoes

1. _Shoes_
2. _Outerwear_
3. _Bags and accessories_

4. _Hosiery_
5. _Lingerie_

B Complete each sentence about clothes with an appropriate word.

1. Two kinds of men's underwear are boxers and ___briefs___.
2. Two kinds of leg coverings for women are pantyhose and ___tights___.
3. Sandals are a kind of ___shoe___.
4. A windbreaker is a kind of ___jacket___.
5. You can't buy just one glove. You have to buy a ___pair___.

C Complete the travel article with the comparative form of each adjective.

When you travel, think carefully about the clothes you pack. As far as color is concerned, ___darker___ colors are
1. dark

usually ___more practical___. For ___cooler___ destinations, a blazer can
2. practical   3. cool

be ___more convenient___ than a windbreaker or cardigan because you can
4. convenient

wear it in ___more conservative___ settings such as offices and ___more formal___
5. conservative   6. formal

restaurants. For travel to ___hotter___ areas of the world,
7. hot

___lighter___ clothes are ___more comfortable___ than ___heavier___ ones.
8. light   9. comfortable   10. heavy

TOP NOTCH **PROJECT**
As a group, write a short entry about this country to the travel guide on page 84. Use your survey, your notepad, and the article as a model.

TOP NOTCH **WEBSITE**
For Unit 7 online activities, visit the *Top Notch* Companion Website at www.longman.com/topnotch.

D Unscramble each sentence.

1. Please / to me / them / show _Please show them to me_ .
2. They / to us / are sending / it _They are sending it to us_ .
3. When / you / are / to her / it / giving _When are you giving it to her_ ?
4. with you / Take / it _Take it with you_ .

E **WRITING.** Imagine you are taking a trip to another country. On a separate sheet of paper, write about where you are going and what you are going to pack. Explain why. Talk about the climate and the culture.

UNIT 7
CHECKPOINT

A 🎧 LISTENING COMPREHENSION

Suggested teaching time:	5–10 minutes
Your actual teaching time:	_____

- Say *Listen to the shoppers and clerks in a department store. Write the name of the department where they are talking.* To review, have volunteers read their answers out loud.

AUDIOSCRIPT

CONVERSATION 1 [F = Japanese]
F: Can you help me?
M: Certainly, ma'am.
F: Do you have these loafers in a larger size? They're a little tight.

CONVERSATION 2 [F = Australian]
F: Excuse me. I'm looking for a nice windbreaker.
M: Certainly. Heavyweight or lightweight?
F: Lightweight. We're going to Thailand. They say it's very hot there this time of year.

CONVERSATION 3 [F1 = Russian]
F1: Excuse me. Where are the less expensive purses?
F2: Just over there, across from the belts.

CONVERSATION 4
M: Do you think you could gift wrap these tights for me? They're a present for my daughter.
F: I'm sorry, but I can't. We don't gift wrap in this department. But if you go to the service desk, they can help you with that.

CONVERSATION 5 [F = Spanish]
F: I just love this nightgown, but pink isn't a good color for me. Do you have it in white?
M: I think we do. What size, madam?
F: Small, please.

B Complete each sentence . . .

Suggested teaching time:	5 minutes
Your actual teaching time:	_____

- Have students check their answers with a partner.

Option: Have students close their books. Ask:
What other kinds of shoes can you name? (oxfords, loafers, running shoes, pumps, flats)
What other kinds of jackets? (windbreaker, blazer)
What other clothing is described as a pair? (pajamas, socks, panties, boxers, briefs, pantyhose, tights, pants, shorts) [+5 minutes]

C Complete the travel article . . .

Suggested teaching time:	5 minutes
Your actual teaching time:	_____

- Be sure students have spelled *hotter* and *heavier* correctly.

Option: To check their work, have students read the paragraph out loud to a partner. [+5 minutes]

Challenge: Ask why darker colors are more practical than lighter colors. (because you don't have to wash them as often) [+5 minutes]

D Unscramble each sentence.

Suggested teaching time:	5 minutes
Your actual teaching time:	_____

- If helpful, remind students that the prepositional phrases come last. Have volunteers write the sentences on the board.

E WRITING

Suggested teaching time:	10–15 minutes
Your actual teaching time:	_____

- Write the following questions on the board:
  Where are you going? When are you going?
  Are people there liberal or conservative about clothing?
  Do you need warm-weather or cold-weather clothes?

- After students answer the questions, have them make a list of what to pack. Remind them to use the adjectives to describe the items of clothing they're packing.

- Have students use their answers to the questions and their lists to write a paragraph.

💿 **Writing Process Worksheets**

TOP NOTCH PROJECT

Idea: Brainstorm on the board adjectives to describe clothing. For example:

tight	liberal	informal
loose	wild	comfortable
light	modest	practical
heavy	casual	long
conservative	formal	short

- Have groups copy from the board the adjectives that describe appropriate clothing in this country.

- Students can use their lists of adjectives together with the survey, notepad, and the article on page 84.

- Lead the class in composing an entry together on the board. Once groups have finished, call on individual students to either contribute a new sentence or make a correction or improvement in organization or wording to what's already on the board. Continue until you have a short entry that's free of errors and well organized. Be sure to include whether this country is more liberal or more conservative about clothing, followed by some specific do's and don'ts.

UNIT WRAP-UP

Suggested teaching time:	15–20 minutes
Your actual teaching time:	_____

Vocabulary

Your students can say . . .

panties, nightgowns, coats, pants, jeans, a parka,
a windbreaker, sweaters, socks, boxers, briefs,
pajamas, gloves, blazers, dresses, purses/bags,
loafers, oxfords, pumps, flats

Option: Competition. Divide the class into groups of
four. One group begins by saying a word or sentence
about the picture and each other group follows by
saying something more. Groups that can no longer say
anything are eliminated until only one group remains.
[+10 minutes]

Social language

• Students can create conversations for one of
the information clerks and the man or woman
at the Information desk, for the clerk and
shopper at the back of the store, or for the clerk
and shopper at the front of the store.

Your students can say . . .

(the shopper and clerk at the back of the store)
A: I'll take the pink coat. **B:** Would you like to try
it on first? **A:** No, thanks. It's for my daughter.
B: How would you like to pay for it? **A:** Charge,
please. And could you gift wrap it for me? **B:** I'm
sorry. We don't gift wrap in this department, but
you can take it to the gift wrap department.
A: Where is it? **B:** Go up the stairs and turn right.

(the clerk and shopper at the front of the store)
A: Excuse me. Do you have this blazer in a smaller
size. **B:** Here you go. This one is a small. See if it's
better. **A:** Yes, it's fine. How much is it? **B:** It's
$75. **A:** That's not too bad.

(the information clerk and shopper with two
children)
A: Excuse me. I'm looking for the children's
department. **B:** The women's department? **A:** No.
The children's department. **B:** It's on the third
floor. You can take the elevator. **A:** Thanks.

Option: Writing activity. In pairs, students write their
conversations in dialogue form. Each pair then writes
each line of their conversation on a slip of paper, mixes
up the order of the slips, and gives them to another
pair. The other pair must then put the conversation
back in the correct order. **[+15 minutes]**

Option: Create characters. As a class, students agree
on a first name for each person in the picture. Next,
working in pairs, students write one line of dialogue
for each person but do not write the name. The next
pair then reads each line of dialogue and writes the
correct name of the speaker after each line.
[+10 minutes]

Grammar

• To help students get started, you can ask a couple
of questions such as *Which is heavier, the parka or the
windbreaker?* (the parka) *Which is bigger, the [color]
blazer or the [color] one?* (the [color] one)

Option: Word prompts. As a class, write a list of
adjectives on the board that students could use to
compare the clothing in the picture, such as *expensive,
cheap, good, warm, pretty, uncomfortable, long, short,* etc.
[+5 minutes]

Your students can say . . .

The parka is heavier than the windbreaker.
The coats are longer than the jackets.
The jeans are more casual than the pants.
The turtleneck sweater is warmer than the V-neck.
The boxers are wilder than the briefs.
The loafers are more comfortable than the pumps.
The [color] blazer is bigger than the [color] blazer.
The black purse is more practical than the
    [color] purse.
The [color] dress is prettier than the [color] dress.
The nightgowns in the front are more modest than
    the nightgowns in the back.
The dresses on the left are more conservative than
    the dresses on the right.

Individual oral progress check (optional)

Use the illustration on page 87 for an oral test.
Have students point to and make three comparisons
about items in the picture. For example, students
could say *The jackets are shorter than the coats.*
Evaluate students on correctness, intelligibility,
and completeness.

Cumulative Vocabulary Activities

You may wish to use the video for Unit 7
at this point. For video activity worksheets,
go to www.longman.com/topnotch.

**Complete Assessment Package
Unit 7 Achievement Test**

- **Vocabulary.** Look at the picture. Then close your book and write the names of the clothing you remember.
- **Social language.** Create conversations for the people. Use the directory.
- **Grammar.** Write comparisons.
  The blazer is more formal than the windbreaker.

BAGS AND ACCESSORIES	1
CHILDREN'S DEPARTMENT	3
ELECTRONICS	3
HAIRDRESSER	4
LINGERIE	1
MEN'S DEPARTMENT	1
PHOTO STUDIO	2
RESTAURANTS	4
SHOES	1
TRAVEL AGENCY	2
WOMEN'S DEPARTMENT	1

INFORMATION DESK

✔ **Now I can ...**

☐ shop for clothes.
☐ pay for clothes.
☐ give and get directions in a store.
☐ discuss culturally appropriate dress.

Getting Away

UNIT GOALS

1 Greet someone arriving from a trip
2 Talk about how you spent your free time
3 Discuss vacation preferences
4 Tell about your experiences on a trip

A **TOPIC PREVIEW.** Look at the travel ads. Which vacations look good to you? Why?

TRAVEL SPECIALS

10 NIGHT Caribbean Cruise

Departs from / Returns to Miami

Miami
Nassau
Cozumel
Belize City
Grand Cayman

Enjoy snorkeling in **Grand Cayman Island**

Go scuba diving in **Belize**

Play with dolphins in **Nassau**

WHAT'S INCLUDED?

✔ Accommodations
✔ Meals
✔ Beverages
✔ Entertainment

ITALY in Six Days!

You'll savor every minute you spend in romantic Italy!

ROME
Discover the Eternal City! Rome is filled with history and romance.

VENICE
Visit historic St. Mark's Square. And don't miss a gondola voyage on the Grand Canal!

Fly-in African Safari
THE SERENGETI NATIONAL PARK

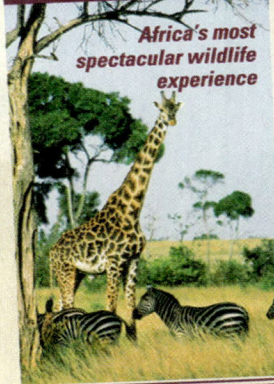

Africa's most spectacular wildlife experience

YOU'LL NEVER FORGET IT!

Duration: 3 days/2 nights
Type: Safari fly-in
Country: Tanzania
Rates (US$): Available on request
Activities include: Birdwatching, wildlife viewing

Walt Disney World Resorts®

Disney MGM STUDIOS

Magic Kingdom®

Something for everyone in your family!
FOUR different theme parks, THREE water parks, shopping, dining, and entertainment.
Choose from over 40 great hotels.

SOURCE: Adapted from www.celebritycruises.com; www.ilove-italy.com; www.ineedavacation.com; www.go2africa.com

B **DISCUSSION.** In your opinion, which of the vacations are good for people who like:

- nature and wildlife?
- history and culture?
- family activities?
- physical activities?

UNIT 8

Getting Away

A TOPIC PREVIEW

Suggested teaching time:	10 minutes
Your actual teaching time:	_____

- Point out the gondolas in the photo of Venice. Explain that a *gondola* is a long narrow boat with a flat bottom and high points on each end. It is used on the canals in Venice, Italy. Gondola rides are very popular with visitors to Venice, but are very expensive.

- Point out that Walt Disney World Resorts are located in Florida in the Southeastern U.S. Point to the photo from the Magic Kingdom®. Explain that a *ride* is a large machine that people ride on for fun at an amusement park like the Magic Kingdom. Explain that a *water park* is an amusement park where all the rides are in water. A *theme park* is an amusement park with themes, such as movies or travel.

- Have students look at the ads. Before students answer the first question in Exercise A, ask *What activities can you do on each vacation?* Have students list the activities for each destination.

Caribbean Cruise	Italy
go snorkeling	go on a gondola
go scuba diving	
play with dolphins	

Walt Disney World	African Safari
go on rides	go birdwatching
go shopping	view wildlife
eat in restaurants	
see shows	

- When students answer the first question in Exercise A, they can use their lists of activities to tell why. For example:
  I want to go to the Caribbean. I can go snorkeling and scuba diving.
  I'd love to go to Italy. I can go on a gondola in Venice.
  Walt Disney World sounds great to me. I can go on rides and see shows.
  The African safari looks good to me. I can go birdwatching and view wildlife.

Option: Ask *Is there a vacation that doesn't look good to you? Why?* Your students can answer, for example, *The Walt Disney World vacation doesn't look good to me. I don't like rides.* [+5 minutes]

Option: Ask questions about the ads:
Which trip is longer, the Caribbean cruise or the Italy trip? (the Caribbean cruise)
Which trip is shorter, the Italy trip or the African safari? (the African safari)
Where can you see dolphins? (in Nassau / the Caribbean)
Do you have to pay for meals and beverages on the cruise? (No, they're included.)
Where's the Serengeti National Park? (in Tanzania)
[+5 minutes]

Option: Have students locate the four different vacation destinations on a world map. [+5 minutes]

B DISCUSSION

Suggested teaching time:	10 minutes
Your actual teaching time:	_____

- To make sure students understand *nature* and *wildlife*, ask for examples of each. For *nature*, your students might say *trees, plants, rivers,* etc. For *wildlife*, your students might say *birds, elephants, zebras, giraffes,* etc.

- Students match their interests to the vacations.

- To review, ask *What do you like? Which vacation is good for you?*

Challenge: To compare their answers, students can suggest vacations to each other. For example:
  A: *I need a vacation. I like history and culture. Any suggestions?*
  B: *What about Italy? You can see the Coliseum and visit St. Mark's Square.* [+5 minutes]

Language note: In British English, a *vacation* is called a *holiday*. In American English, a holiday is a day of celebration and/or commemoration of an event.

◆C◆ 🎧 SOUND BITES

Suggested teaching time:	10 minutes
Your actual teaching time:	_____

- After students read and listen, ask:
  When did Barbara come home from her trip?
    (yesterday)
  How was her trip? (incredible/great)
  How was the weather? (not perfect, but OK)
  How was the food? (amazing)
  Which was better, the weather or the food? (the food)

◆D◆ UNDERSTANDING MEANING FROM CONTEXT

Suggested teaching time:	5–10 minutes
Your actual teaching time:	_____

- To review, have students read their answers out loud.

Option: Ask students to find the source of their answers in the text. **[+5 minutes]**

Language note: In this context, *incredible* means *very good.* However, it can also mean *too strange to be believed* or *very difficult to believe* and have a negative connotation. For example, *We went to a very expensive restaurant, and the food was awful. It was incredible!*

WHAT ABOUT **YOU?**

Suggested teaching time:	10–15 minutes
Your actual teaching time:	_____

- Tell students that they can check more than one box for each question.

Option: Refer back to the travel ads on page 88. Ask:
  What can you see in Venice, Italy? (St. Mark's Square, the Grand Canal)
  What can you see in Cairo, Egypt? (the Pyramids, the Sphinx)
  What can you see in Paris, France? (the Eiffel Tower, the Arc de Triomphe) **[+5 minutes]**

Language note: To *take it easy* means *to relax and not do very much.* The activity of visiting famous or interesting places, especially as a tourist, is known as *sightseeing.*

EXTRAS (optional)

Workbook: Exercises 1–3

Answer the questions about <u>your</u> vacations. Check all that apply.

🌐 TRAVEL SURVEY

Where do you usually go on vacation?
- [ ] I visit family.
- [ ] I go to another city.
- [ ] I go to another country.
- [ ] I go to a beach.
- [ ] Other _____

What do you usually do on vacation?
- [ ] I take it easy.
- [ ] I visit museums and go sightseeing.
- [ ] I do a lot of physical activities.
- [ ] I eat at nice restaurants.
- [ ] Other _____

C 🎧 **SOUND BITES. Read along silently as you listen to a natural conversation.**

GREG: Hi, Barbara. When did you get back? **CN**

BARBARA: Greg! Just yesterday.

GREG: So tell me about your trip.

BARBARA: It was incredible. I had a really great time.

GREG: Good weather?

BARBARA: Not perfect, but generally OK.

GREG: I'll bet the food was great.

BARBARA: Amazing! **CN Corpus Notes:** "Get back" is less formal than "return" and is used more frequently in spoken American English.

D **UNDERSTANDING MEANING FROM CONTEXT. Use the conversation to help you choose the correct answer.**

1. When Greg asks, "When did you get back?" he means _____.
   - **a.** When did you come home?
   - **b.** When did you go on your trip?

2. When Barbara says, "It was incredible," she means _____.
   - **a.** It was a good trip.
   - **b.** It wasn't a good trip.

3. When Greg says, "Good weather?" he means _____.
   - **a.** The weather was good.
   - **b.** Was the weather good?

PARIS

FRANCE

CAIRO EGYPT

1

Greet Someone Arriving from a Trip

🎧 CONVERSATION
MODEL **Read and listen.**

A: So, how was the flight?
B: Pretty nice, actually.
A: That's good. Let me help you with your things.
B: That's OK. I'm fine. **CN**

🎧 **Rhythm and intonation practice**

> **CN** **Corpus Notes:** This use of "fine" to decline help from someone is very common in spoken American English and is often used by customers when talking to sales clerks.

A **GRAMMAR.** **The past tense of be**

Statements

The weather **was** great.
The fruits and vegetables **were** delicious.
There **was** a terrific restaurant in the hotel.
There **weren't** any problems on the flight.

| I He She It | was | We You They | were | **Contractions** wasn't = was not weren't = were not |

Yes / no questions

Was your flight on time?
Were there any good restaurants?

Short answers

Yes, it was. / No, it wasn't.
Yes, there were. / No, there weren't.

Information questions

How was the cruise?
How long was your trip?
How many hours was the flight?

GRAMMAR BOOSTER

PAGES G15–G16
For more . . .

B **Complete the conversations with the past tense of be.**

1. **A:** Did you just get in?
   B: Yes. My flight _____was_____ a little late.
   A: Well, how _____was_____ your vacation?
   B: It was really incredible.

2. **A:** Welcome back! How _____was_____ the drive?
   B: OK. But there _____was_____ a lot of traffic.
   A: Too bad. _____Were_____ you alone?
   B: No. My brother _____was_____ with me.

LESSON

1 ▶ Greet Someone Arriving from a Trip

🎧 CONVERSATION **MODEL**

Suggested teaching time:	10 minutes
Your actual teaching time:	_____

- Have students look at the photo. Ask *Where are the people?* (in an airport)
- Ask students to describe the picture and to guess the situation. Ask:
  Who are the people?
  What are they doing?
  Where are they going?

Students will have differing opinions. Encourage discussion.

Language note: *Pretty* is a common spoken intensifier, but it is not used in formal writing.

Language note: *That's OK, I'm fine* is a more polite way to turn down an offer of help than *No, thanks*.

🎧 Rhythm and intonation practice

Suggested teaching time:	5 minutes
Your actual teaching time:	_____

- Have students repeat each line chorally. Make sure they:
  ○ use rising intonation with *So how was the flight?*
  ○ accurately imitate the intonation of *That's good!*
  ○ use the following stress pattern:

┌─**STRESS PATTERN**─────────────────────┐
```
        •   —   •   •   —
A:  So, how was the flight?

    —   •   —   •   —
B:  Pretty nice, actually.

        —   •   —   •   •   •   •   —
A:  That's good.  Let me help you with your things.

        —   ••   —
B:  That's OK.  I'm fine.
```
└───────────────────────────────────────┘

A GRAMMAR

Suggested teaching time:	10–15 minutes
Your actual teaching time:	_____

- After students read the information in the Grammar box, ask *How is the weather today?* Write a sentence with *is* and an adjective on the board:

  Today the weather is _____.

Then ask *How was the weather yesterday?* Write a sentence with *was* and an adjective on the board:

  Yesterday the weather was _____.

- Ask:
  What is the past tense of is? (was)
  What is the past tense of are? (were)

- Write on the board:

amazing	terrific	pretty bad
incredible	great	terrible
awesome	pretty good	awful

- Have students use the adjectives on the board and the past tense of *be* to describe a trip they took. Ask students to describe the following about the trip to a partner:

the weather	*the shopping*
the food	*the activities*
the entertainment	*the people*

Model the activity. Say *The weather was pretty good. The activities were awesome.*

- Make sure students understand when to use *There was* and *There were*. Ask the class to turn to page 87 and look at the Unit Wrap-Up picture for Unit 7 again. Have them study the picture for 30 seconds and then close their books. Ask *What was there in the picture?* Students answer in complete sentences. Write a few of their sentences on the board. Write singular examples in one column and plural examples in another. For example:

Singular	Plural
There was a windbreaker.	There were shoes.
There was a pink coat.	There were sweaters.

Option: Have students use *There was / There were* to write a few more sentences about the trip they described previously. For example:

  There was a great museum.
  There was a beautiful beach.
  There were incredible restaurants.
  There were lots of activities.

[+5 minutes]

💿 Grammar Self-Checks

B Complete the conversations . . .

Suggested teaching time:	5–10 minutes
Your actual teaching time:	_____

- Write on the board *My flight _____ a little late.* Then ask *What's the subject?* (flight) *Is flight singular or plural?* (singular) *Do you use was or were?* (was)

- If helpful, have students underline the subjects for each item. (1. flight, vacation, it; 2. drive, traffic, you, brother; 3. you, I, you; 4. your parents', It, They, their, it, it)

- To check their work, have students read the conversations with a partner.

◆C▶ ⌒ VOCABULARY

Suggested teaching time:	5 minutes
Your actual teaching time:	_____

• After students listen and repeat, ask a student:
    Was your last trip a flight, a drive, a cruise, a train trip,
    or a bus trip?
    Was it comfortable?
    Was is scenic?
    Was it boring?
    Was it bumpy?
    Was it scary?
    Was it short or long?

  The student should answer *Yes, it was. / No, it wasn't.*
  or *It was short / long.*

• Students ask each other about their last trip in the
  same way.

Option: Read the definitions that follow. Have
students identify the adjective that's defined.
    with beautiful views all around (scenic)
    making you feel afraid or nervous that something bad
      might happen (scary)
    not interesting or fun (boring)
[+5 minutes]

🔶 **Vocabulary Cards**

CONVERSATION **PAIR WORK**

Suggested teaching time:	10–15 minutes
Your actual teaching time:	_____

• Model the activity with a more advanced student.

• Point out how to respond to the positive adjectives
  with *That's good!* and to the negative adjectives with
  That's too bad! Practice first by asking students to
  respond to your statements with the appropriate
  response.
    T: *It was pretty scenic.*   **S:** *That's good!*
    T: *It was pretty long.*   **S:** *That's too bad!*

🔶 **Pair Work Cards**

EXTRAS (optional)

Grammar Booster
Workbook: Exercises 4–8
Copy & Go: Activity 29

3. A: Where ____were____ you last week?

B: Me? I ____was____ at my parents' beach house.

A: Oh. How long ____were____ you there?

B: About three days.

4. A: So, how ____was____ your parents' trip?

B: It ____was____ terrible. They ____were____ so angry.

A: ____Was____ their train on time?

B: No, it ____wasn't____. It ____was____ very late.

C 🎧 **VOCABULARY.** Adjectives for travel conditions. Listen and practice.

It was pretty **comfortable**.

It was pretty **scenic**.

It was pretty **boring**.

It was pretty **bumpy**.

It was pretty **scary**.

It was pretty **short / long**.

CONVERSATION
PAIR WORK

Practice greeting someone arriving from a flight, drive, cruise, train or bus trip. Use the guide, or create a new conversation.

A: So, how was the _____?

B: Pretty _____, actually.

A: That's _____! Let me help you with your things.

B: _____.

comfortable
scenic   } That's good!
short

boring
bumpy } That's too bad!
scary
long

Talk about How You Spent Your Free Time

CONVERSATION MODEL Read and listen.

A: What did you do last weekend?
B: Nothing special. What about you?
A: Well, I went to the beach.
B: How was that?
A: I had a really nice time.

Rhythm and intonation practice

A GRAMMAR. The simple past tense

| I
You
He
She
We
They | studied. | I
You
He
She
We
They | didn't play tennis. |

Did you **have** a good time?   Yes, I did. / No, I didn't.
Where **did** you **go**?   I went to the beach.
When **did** they **arrive**?   On Tuesday.
What **did** he **do** every day?   He slept until noon.

Regular verbs

| visit | visited | play | played |
| watch | watched | study | studied |

Irregular verbs*

buy	bought	have	had
drink	drank	leave	left
eat	ate	meet	met
fly	flew	sleep	slept
get	got	spend	spent
go	went	take	took

*See a complete list on page 128.

In the Split Editions, complete list is on page A5.

GRAMMAR BOOSTER

PAGES G16–G17
For more . . .

B Complete the sentences with the simple past tense.

Dear Vicky,

We're here! The flight was fine. I ___**slept**___ the
 _{1. sleep}
whole time. Yesterday, we ___**went**___ swimming. We
 _{2. go}
___**ate**___ fresh seafood and ___**drank**___ coconut
 _{3. eat} _{4. drink}
milk from coconuts right off the trees. In the evening
we ___**had**___ a wonderful dinner. After the meal,
 _{5. have}
a jazz ensemble ___**played**___ for several hours and
 _{6. play}
we ___**met**___ some very nice people. We ___**didn't leave**___
 _{7. meet} _{8. leave (not)}
until after midnight. We ___**had**___ such a good
 _{9. have}
time! This morning we ___**walked**___ into town and
 _{10. walk}
___**bought**___ postcards. More later! Carol
 _{11. buy}

Vicky Bower

22 High Street

Belleville, NY 10514

USA

LUFTPOST
PAR AVION   VIA AEREA

2 *Talk about How You Spent Your Free Time*

◠ CONVERSATION **MODEL**

Suggested teaching time:	10 minutes
Your actual teaching time:	_____

- Have students look at the photo. Ask:
  How many people are in the photo? (four)
  How many women? (two) *How many men?* (two)
  Where are the people? (at the beach)

- Hold up a calendar. Point to today's date. Then ask *When was last weekend?* Have students tell you the dates.

- After students read and listen, ask:
  Where was A last weekend? (at the beach)
  How was the trip? (nice)
  Was B some place interesting last weekend?
  (No, she wasn't.)

◠ **Rhythm and intonation practice**

Suggested teaching time:	5 minutes
Your actual teaching time:	_____

- Have students find and circle *really* in the conversation. Make sure students stress *really* in the last line.

- Have students repeat each line chorally. Make sure they use the following stress pattern:

```
┌─STRESS PATTERN──────────────────────────┐
│        •  •   •  —  •  —  •              │
│   A:  What did you do last weekend?      │
│       —  •  —  •   —  •  •  —            │
│   B:  Nothing special.  What about you?  │
│       —  •  —  •  •  —                   │
│   A:  Well, I went to the beach.         │
│       —   •  —                           │
│   B:  How was that?                      │
│       •  •  •  —  •  —  •                │
│   A:  I had a really nice time.          │
└──────────────────────────────────────────┘
```

Ⓐ **GRAMMAR**

Suggested teaching time:	5–10 minutes
Your actual teaching time:	_____

- After students read the information in the Grammar box, have them underline the simple past tense in the Conversation Model (did . . . do, went, had).

- Have students look back at the list of everyday activities on page 64. Have them make an ✗ next to the activities they did yesterday. Then students write a sentence with each activity. For example:
  I slept until 9:00 A.M. yesterday.
  I didn't watch TV yesterday.
  I read yesterday afternoon.
  I talked on the phone yesterday.

- Students can use the same list of everyday activities to ask and answer simple past tense yes / no questions with a partner. For example:
  Did you sleep late yesterday?
  Did you watch TV yesterday?
  Did you read yesterday?

  Students answer *Yes, I did* or *No, I didn't.*

- To review, ask a few yes / no questions like the ones above. When a student answers *Yes, I did*, follow up with an information question. For example:
  How long did you sleep?
  What did you watch?
  Who did you talk to?
  Where did you go shopping?
  When did you take a shower?

Language note: *Read* (/rid/) is an irregular verb in the simple past tense. The past tense of *read* is *read* (/rɛd/). The spelling is the same, but the pronunciation is different. Pronounce each and have students repeat.

💿 **Grammar Self-Checks**

Ⓑ **Complete the sentences . . .**

Suggested teaching time:	5–10 minutes
Your actual teaching time:	_____

- To check their work, have students read the postcard out loud to a partner. Ask a few questions about Carol's vacation.
  What did she eat?
  What did she drink?
  What did she do?
  What did she buy?

Challenge: Students think about their own last vacation. With a partner, they ask and answer questions. You may want to have the class first brainstorm questions to ask on the board. Your students can ask:
  Where did you go?
  What sights did you visit?
  What did you do?
  Who did you meet?
  What did you eat?
  What did you drink?
  Did you have a good time?

[+10 minutes]

C Complete each question . . .

Suggested teaching time:	5 minutes
Your actual teaching time:	_____

- Point out that the questions can be <u>yes</u> / <u>no</u> questions (*Did you . . . ?*) or information questions (*What / Where / When did you . . . ?*).
- Remind students to use the base form of the verb with *did*.
- To check their work, have students read the questions and answers with a partner.

D 🎧 PRONUNCIATION

Suggested teaching time:	5 minutes
Your actual teaching time:	_____

- If helpful, explain that *–ed* is pronounced as:
  - /d/ after voiced sounds. The voiced sounds are /b/, /g/, /z/, /v/, /zh/, /j/, /m/, /n/, /ng/, /l/, /r/, and /ð/. With voiced sounds, you feel a vibration when you put your hand on your throat and say them.
  - /t/ after the voiceless sounds /p/, /k/, /s/, /f/, /sh/, /ch/, and /θ/. With voiceless sounds, there's no vibration when you put your hand on your throat and say them.
  - /ɪd/ after /t/ and /d/. Point out that when you pronounce these endings, you split the word before /d/ or /t/ so that the ending begins with a consonant: visi/ted, nee/ded, wai/ted.

Option: On a sheet of paper, students make three columns with the headings /d/, /t/, and /ɪd/. Read the list of words that follows. Students listen for which ending is being used and write the word in the correct column.
   1. *wanted* (/ɪd/)
   2. *packed* (/t/)
   3. *avoided* (/ɪd/)
   4. *cleaned* (/d/)
   5. *walked* (/d/)
   6. *liked* (/t/)
After reviewing as a class, have students practice reading the verbs and pronouncing the endings correctly. **[+10 minutes]**

💿 **Pronunciation Activities**

CONVERSATION **PAIR WORK**

Suggested teaching time:	10–15 minutes
Your actual teaching time:	_____

- If helpful, use a calendar to point out the first four past time expressions. For each, ask the class for dates.
- Model the conversation with a more advanced student. Play the role of Student A. When B responds, ask a question about what he/she did; for example, *What animals did you see?* or *Who won the game?* Then ask about how it was. Student B can answer with the past of *be* and an adjective or by saying *I had a [positive or negative adjective] time.*

Option: Before students practice the conversation, have them think of something they did last weekend, last week, last night, etc. For each past time expression, students write a sentence in the simple past tense. For example, *I went to an art exhibit last weekend.* Then students write a second sentence about whether each activity was a positive or negative experience. For example, *I had a [pretty good] time.* **[+10 minutes]**

💿 **Pair Work Cards**

EXTRAS (optional)

Grammar Booster
Workbook: Exercises 9–13
Copy & Go: Activity 30

💿 **Pronunciation Supplements**

C Complete each question with the simple past tense.

1. **A:** <u>Where did</u> you <u>go</u> last weekend? **B:** We went to the beach.
2. **A:** <u>Did</u> you <u>have</u> a good flight? **B:** Not really. It was pretty scary.
3. **A:** <u>What did</u> you <u>do</u> in the evening? **B:** We listened to music.
4. **A:** <u>When did</u> you <u>arrive</u> at the hotel? **B:** We arrived last Monday.
5. **A:** <u>Did</u> you <u>buy</u> lots of souvenirs? **B:** Yes. We bought some beautiful maps.

D 🎧 **PRONUNCIATION. The simple past tense.** There are three different pronunciations of the simple past tense ending **-ed**. Read and listen. Then repeat.

/d/	/t/	/ɪd/
play**ed**	watch**ed**	visit**ed**
rain**ed**	cook**ed**	need**ed**
call**ed**	stopp**ed**	wait**ed**

CONVERSATION
PAIR WORK

Talk about how you spent your free time. Use the past time expressions.

A: What did you do _____?
B: _____ …

Continue the conversation, using real information or the pictures.

Past time expressions
last weekend
last week
last night
yesterday
over the summer
on your vacation

the zoo

a baseball game

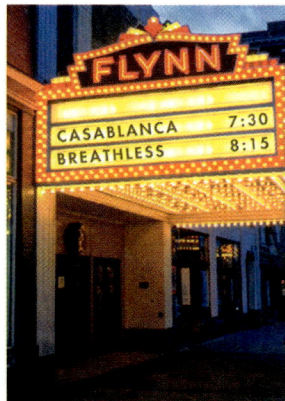

a movie

a museum

3 Discuss Vacation Preferences

A 🎧 **VOCABULARY.** **Adjectives to describe a vacation.** **Listen and practice.**

It was so **relaxing**.   It was so **exciting**. CN   It was so **interesting**. CN It was so **unusual**.

CN Corpus Notes: "Exciting" is one of the 2000 most frequent spoken words. "Interesting" is one of the 1000 most frequent words in spoken American English.

B **READING WARM-UP.** **Describe your dream vacation.**

C 🎧 **READING.**   Read the vacation ads. Then use one or more adjectives from the vocabulary for each vacation.

TOP NOTCH TRAVEL *has your dream vacation!*

Bhutan
Secret of the Himalayas

"Everyone was happy to practice their English and walk with us."

There are many beautiful places on this earth, but Bhutan is unique. Few tourists go there, but you can be one of them. View scenic mountains and meet friendly people dressed in traditional clothing.

www.countrywalkers.com

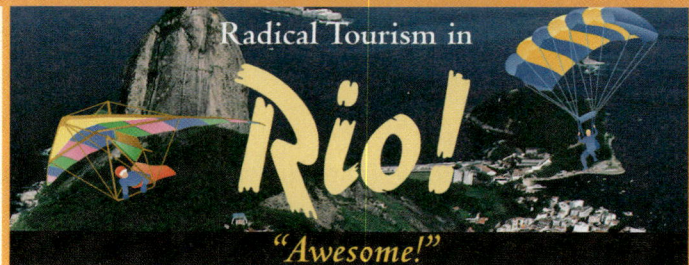

Radical Tourism in
Rio!
"Awesome!"

Are you looking for EXTREME ADVENTURE? How about skydiving or hang gliding over Rio? Jump with us from a plane flying at over 4,000 meters. Or fly slowly like a bird over the famous white sand beaches and mountains of Rio. As close as it gets to heaven—you won't want to come down! No experience required!

www.rioadventuretours.com

EUROPEAN LANGUAGE TOUR

Enjoy Europe, Learn a Language!

"I had a great time and I learned so much!"

Attend classes three to four hours a day and have the afternoon free for sightseeing. Stay with a local family—and practice your new language. Study French, Italian, Greek, and more! Classes available for all levels.

www.europeforvisitors.com

sea mountain
inn and spa

"What an experience!"

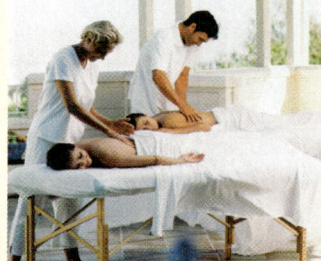

The best of Southern California! Enjoy our scenic Pacific Ocean views. Walk through our Asian gardens and swim in our beautiful pool. Work out in our gym with weights, running machines, or stationary bikes. Eat our delicious and healthful meals and relax with a soothing massage.

www.seamountain.com

LESSON

3 ▶ Discuss Vacation Preferences

Ⓐ 🎧 VOCABULARY

Suggested teaching time:	5 minutes
Your actual teaching time:	_____

Option: Have students look back at the travel ads on page 88. Ask which vacations look relaxing, exciting, interesting, or unusual. **[+5 minutes]**

Option: For each adjective, students think of a vacation they took, an activity they did, a place they visited, etc. Have students say the place or activity. Then ask *Why was it (relaxing / exciting / interesting / unusual)? What did you do?* Students say what they did. Next, say *Tell me about (a relaxing / an exciting / an interesting / an unusual) vacation or activity.* Your students can say, for example:
> *I went to the beach. It was relaxing. I slept late, sat in the sun, and drank tropical drinks.*

[+10 minutes]

Option: Ask for an adjective that means the opposite of both *exciting* and *interesting.* (boring) **[+5 minutes]**

💿 **Vocabulary Cards**

Ⓑ READING WARM-UP

Suggested teaching time:	5 minutes
Your actual teaching time:	_____

• Ask students where they'd like to go. Ask them to use the best one of the adjectives for that place.

• Ask the class *Which vacation looks relaxing? Which vacation looks exciting? Which vacation looks interesting? Which vacation looks unusual?*

Option: Tell students to look only at the photos. Have them label each photo either *relaxing, exciting, interesting,* or *unusual.* **[+5 minutes]**

Ⓒ 🎧 READING

Suggested teaching time:	10–15 minutes
Your actual teaching time:	_____

• If possible, have students locate the four different vacation destinations on a map before they listen and read.

• After students read and listen to all the ads, play the audio program again. Pause after each ad and ask the following questions:
> Bhutan
> *Why is Bhutan a "secret"?* (because few tourists go there)

Rio
> *What do you do when you go skydiving?* (jump from a plane)
> *What do you do when you go hang gliding?* (fly slowly like a bird)

Have students label *skydiving* and *hang gliding* in the photo. (*Skydiving* is on the right, and *hang gliding* is on the left.)

• Ask the following about Sea Mountain:
> *What do you do when you "work out"?* (lift weights, use running machines or stationary bikes)
> *What's happening in the picture?* (The people are getting massages.)

• Relate the reading to students' own lives. Ask questions such as:
> *Have you ever gone skydiving or hang gliding? Do you want to go? Why or why not?*
> *Do you want to learn a new language? What language?*
> *Have you ever had a massage?*

💿 **Learning Strategies**

Option: For each vacation, have students find and list the adjectives that describe it.

Bhutan	Rio	European Language Tour	Sea Mountain
beautiful	radical	none	scenic
unique	awesome		beautiful
scenic	extreme		delicious
friendly			healthful
traditional			soothing

[+10 minutes]

Option: For each vacation, have students find and list the activities you can do.

Bhutan	Rio	European Language Tour	Sea Mountain
go walking	go skydiving	attend classes	go walking
	go hang gliding	go sightseeing	go swimming
		stay with a family	work out
		practice your new language	eat
			have a massage

[+10 minutes]

💿 **Graphic Organizers**

💿 **Extra Reading Comprehension Activities**

▷D PAIR WORK

Suggested teaching time:	10 minutes
Your actual teaching time:	_____

- Talking with their partners, students decide which vacation is best for each person pictured. Have students write the vacation they choose under the person's photo.
- Your students will probably assign the vacations in this order: Sea Mountain Inn and Spa, European Language Tour, Rio, Bhutan. If students have other ideas, encourage them to explain their answers.

▷E WHAT ABOUT YOU?

Suggested teaching time:	5–10 minutes
Your actual teaching time:	_____

- Have students write about their own travel interests. Then tell students to choose the vacation that is best for them. To model this, tell the class about your travel interests and which vacation you would like best. For example, you might say *I like interesting vacations. I like history and culture, and I love to learn new languages. The European Language Tour is a good vacation for me.*
- Ask several students to read their travel interests out loud, leaving out their vacation choice. Have the class guess which vacation they chose.

TOP NOTCH **INTERACTION**

Suggested teaching time:	10–15 minutes
Your actual teaching time:	_____

STEP 1

- Point out that students can check more than one box for each part of the survey.
- Pairs compare their answers. Students can say, for example, *I like interesting and inexpensive vacations. What about you?*

STEP 2

- Have pairs split up and students form small groups with different classmates.
- One student in each group can read each question and make sure that all in the group have a chance to respond.
- To review, have a couple of students respond to each question in open class.

EXTRAS (optional)

Copy & Go: Activity 31

D ▶ **PAIR WORK.** Choose a vacation for each person. Use the ads on page 94. Discuss your answers.

" I work hard all year. I need a vacation where someone will take care of me. "

" I love to meet people and learn about new cultures. I'm over fifty, but I like to learn new things. "

" I'm an athlete and I love sports. I always like to do something new and different. "

" I like to go to places where other people don't go—'off the beaten path.' "

E ▶ **WHAT ABOUT YOU?** Choose a vacation for yourself.

TOP NOTCH
INTERACTION

Do You Need a Vacation?

STEP 1. Take the vacation survey. Then compare your answers with a partner.

What's important to you in a vacation? Check ☑ all that apply.

I like
- ❑ exciting vacations
- ❑ relaxing vacations
- ❑ interesting vacations
- ❑ unusual vacations
- ❑ inexpensive vacations
- ❑ _____ vacations

I like vacations with
- ❑ lots of history and culture
- ❑ lots of nature and wildlife
- ❑ lots of sports or physical activities
- ❑ lots of family activities
- ❑ lots of entertainment
- ❑ people who speak my language
- ❑ beautiful hotels
- ❑ great food
- ❑ warm weather
- ❑ nice beaches
- ❑ friendly people
- ❑ _____

STEP 2. GROUP WORK. Discuss vacation preferences with your classmates. Use your survey for support.

- What's important to you in a vacation?
- How often do you go on vacation?
- Do you need a vacation right now? Why?

95 FREE PRACTICE

4 ▷ *Tell about Your Experiences on a Trip*

A 🎧 **VOCABULARY.** **Problems during a trip.** **Listen and practice.**

The weather **was terrible**.

The people **were unfriendly**.

They canceled my flight.

Someone stole my wallet.

B 🎧 **LISTENING COMPREHENSION.** **Listen to the conversations about vacations and check ☑ all the statements that are true.** **Then listen again and check your work.**

1. ☑ Someone stole her car.   ☐ Someone stole her wallet.   ☑ They canceled her flight.
2. ☑ They canceled her flight.   ☐ They canceled her reservation.   ☐ The people were unfriendly.
3. ☐ They canceled her flight.   ☐ The people were unfriendly.   ☑ Her vacation was too short.

C ▷ **Look at the pictures.** **Write about the problems.**

1. The food __was terrible__.

2. The waiters __were unfriendly__.

3. __They canceled__ my hotel reservation.

4. __He stole__ my purse.

5. The entertainment __was terrible__.

6. __Someone stole__ my luggage.

LESSON 4
Tell about Your Experiences on a Trip

Ⓐ 🎧 VOCABULARY

Suggested teaching time:	5–10 minutes
Your actual teaching time:	_____

- Point out to students that the first two vocabulary items use the past of *be* and the second two use the simple past tense.
- After students listen and repeat the problems, point out that *stole* is an irregular verb form. *Stole* is the simple past tense of *steal*.

💿 **Vocabulary Cards**

Ⓑ 🎧 LISTENING COMPREHENSION

Suggested teaching time:	10 minutes
Your actual teaching time:	_____

- Say *Listen to the conversations. All the people had good vacations, but they also had problems. Check all the problems they had.*
- Make sure students understand that they can check more than one box for each item.

Challenge: Say *In the second conversation, the woman says that Italy is her "dream vacation." Describe your dream vacation. Say as much as you can.* You can discuss in open class, have students discuss in groups or pairs, or have students write a few sentences about their dream vacations. Students should have more to say about their dream vacations now than they had for the Reading Warm-Up on page 94. **[+10 minutes]**

💿 **Learning Strategies**

AUDIOSCRIPT

CONVERSATION 1 [F = Portuguese]
M: Did you do anything special over vacation?
F: Yeah, we went to Disney World.
M: No kidding! How was that?
F: We had a great time ... Except for one thing.
M: What?
F: Well, after we got there, we rented a car.
M: Yeah?
F: Well, on our second day there, someone stole the car.
M: No!
F: Yeah. Oh and that's not all. They canceled our flight coming home. We didn't get back till the next day, so the kids missed school.

CONVERSATION 2 [M = U.S. regional]
M: Martha's back from Italy.
F: Great! Did you speak with her?
M: Yeah. She had a great time.
F: That's nice. How was the food?
M: Great, of course.
F: The people?
M: Wonderful. Warm. Friendly.
F: That's my dream vacation.
M: Well, there was one little problem, though.
F: What?
M: On the last day, they canceled her flight. She didn't get home until three o'clock in the morning.

CONVERSATION 3
F: Hi, I'm back.
M: Hey, how was your vacation?
F: OK.
M: OK? Did you have a good time?
F: Yeah.
M: Was the food good?
F: It was all right.
M: How were the people? Friendly?
F: Pretty much.
M: So, no problems?
F: Not really.
M: Then why do you look so unhappy?
F: It was too short!

Ⓒ Look at the pictures ...

Suggested teaching time:	5–10 minutes
Your actual teaching time:	_____

Challenge: After students complete the sentences, have them look at each row individually. Ask which problem is worse. For example, students look at the first row and you ask *Which problem is worse: The food was terrible or The waiters were unfriendly?* Students give their opinion and tell why. **[+10 minutes]**

TOP NOTCH **INTERACTION**

Suggested teaching time:	25–30 minutes
Your actual teaching time:	_____

STEP 1

• Use one of the Options that follow to help students understand the reading.

Option: For the first article, have students create a chart showing what was good about the trip and what the problems were. Put the chart that follows on the board. Students use the articles to fill in the information.

Hawaii Vacation

good	problems
It was relaxing. The weather was perfect.	The hotel wasn't very good. The food was terrible. The servers were unfriendly.

[+10 minutes]

Option: Put the chart that follows on the board. The chart asks for the same information from the article that students will provide about their own vacation in Step 2. After students read the first article, they fill in the chart with information about the vacation. **[+10 minutes]**

Article 1	
place	Hawaii
weather	perfect
activities	no information
transportation	no information
food	terrible
service	unfriendly
hotel	not very good
people	no information

Graphic Organizers

STEP 2

• To model the activity, talk about a vacation you took. Copy the items from the notepad on the board. Fill in the notepad as you talk. For example:

place: Alaska
weather: cold
activities: kayaking,
  whale watching

transportation: cruise
food / service / hotel / people:
  delicious food, lots of food,
  terrific service, friendly
  people

STEP 3

• Students use their notepads to tell a partner about their vacation. Students should ask questions about each other's vacations.

• Be sure students are aware that NEED HELP? can provide support by reminding them of language they know.

STEP 4

• Using information from their notepads, students write about their vacations. The following is an example of what your students can write:

Your students can say . . .
In the summer of 2002, I went on a cruise to Alaska. The trip was very scenic, but the weather was cold. We went kayaking and whale watching. There was a lot of food on the cruise, and it was delicious! The service was terrific. Our waiters were very friendly, and the Alaskan people were friendly, too. We had a great time.

Writing Process Worksheets

EXTRAS (optional)

Workbook: Exercises 14, 15
Copy & Go: Activity 32

INTERACTION • *How Was Your Vacation?*

STEP 1. **Read two articles students wrote about their vacations.**

> In 2002, I went on vacation to Hawaii. It was very relaxing and the weather was perfect. On the other hand there were some problems. Our hotel wasn't very good. Also, the food was terrible and the waiters and waitresses were unfriendly.

> Last summer, I visited my brother for a week. I took a train and the trip was very scenic. That week, we did a lot of exciting things together. We went horseback riding in the mountains, and we went swimming in the ocean. I also learned how to play golf.

STEP 2. **On the notepad, write notes about a vacation you took.**

place:	transportation:
weather:	food / service / hotel / people:
activities:	

STEP 3. **PAIR WORK.** **Ask about your partner's vacation. Then tell the class about your partner's vacation.**

NEED HELP? **Here's language you already know:**

Ask

How was [the weather]?
What did you do in [the evening]?
Tell me something about ____.
What was wrong with [the food]?
That's [great].
I'm sorry to hear that.
What do you mean?
I'd love to go to ____.

Describe

What do you want to know?
We had a ____ time.
We usually ____.
Sometimes we ____.
The [flight] was [long].
The [beach] was [relaxing].
The [people] were [friendly].

Complain

[The bus driver] drove me crazy!
The ____ didn't work.
The ____ was clogged.
I was in the mood for ____, but …
They didn't accept ____.
The dress code was ____.

STEP 4. **WRITING.** **Write about your vacation. Use your notepad for support.**

FREE PRACTICE

UNIT 8
CHECKPOINT

A 🎧 **LISTENING COMPREHENSION.** Listen critically to people talking about their travel experiences. Then listen again to complete the sentences. Circle the letter of the best answer.

1. It was very _____. **a.** short **(b.)** scary **c.** scenic
2. It was very _____. **a.** scary **b.** unusual **(c.)** relaxing
3. It was very _____. **(a.)** short **b.** scary **c.** scenic
4. It was very _____. **a.** short **(b.)** scenic **c.** boring

B Complete each sentence or question. Use the past tense form.

1. I ___bought___ a lot of souvenirs on my vacation.
    buy
2. Where ___did___ you ___eat___ dinner every night?
                          eat
3. We ___slept___ right on the beach. It ___was___ so relaxing.
         sleep   be
4. My sister ___got___ back last weekend. She ___had___ a great time.
              get   have
5. My friend ___ate___ a lot of good food on her trip to Hong Kong.
              eat
6. When ___did___ she ___arrive___ at the hotel?
                         arrive
7. I had a terrible time. The people ___were___ very unfriendly.
                                       be
8. We ___saw___ an excellent play in London. And it ___was___ very inexpensive.
        see   be
9. My wife and I ___went___ running every morning on the beach.
                   go
10. My brother says he ___met___ a lot of friendly people on his trip.
                        meet

C Complete each conversation with a question in the simple past tense.

1. **A:** ___Where did you go___ on vacation?
   B: We went to Spain.

2. **A:** ___What did you do___ every evening?
   B: We watched TV and read books.

3. **A:** ___When did you___ get back home?
   B: Last night.

🎧 **TOP NOTCH SONG**
"My Dream Vacation"
Lyrics on last book page.

TOP NOTCH PROJECT
Bring in travel ads. In a small group, choose a vacation. Tell the class about it.

TOP NOTCH WEBSITE
For Unit 8 online activities, visit the
Top Notch Companion Website at
www.longman.com/topnotch.

UNIT 8 CHECKPOINT

A 🎧 LISTENING COMPREHENSION

Suggested teaching time:	10–15 minutes
Your actual teaching time:	_____

Challenge: Ask students to describe a scary, relaxing, short, or scenic trip they took. Students can write about the trip or tell a partner or small group.
[+10 minutes]

AUDIOSCRIPT

1. [F = Russian]
F: You want to hear about my flight? Oh, it was terrible. First of all, there was a terrible storm. Everyone was afraid, including me. The children were crying. I was frightened we weren't going to arrive at all! I never want to go on a flight like that again!
N: How was her flight?

2. [M = French]
M: The weather was just wonderful. It was warm and sunny every day. In the morning we went swimming and sat in the sun. We had very nice lunches which we ate right at the beach. After lunch we slept for about an hour, and then we went shopping or walked around the town. In the evening, we just walked along the beach and watched the sun go down.
N: How was his vacation?

3. [F = Australian]
F: Let's see. I left my house about four. There really was no traffic, so it went pretty fast. I got there about, oh, I guess by 5:15. I really thought the trip was going to take at least two hours. Not bad at all.
N: How was her drive?

4. [M = Korean]
M: Well, we took the train there this time instead of flying. The trip was long, but very nice. We had big windows so we could see everything. The mountains were just beautiful, especially in the early morning and late afternoon. And for part of the trip we could actually see the ocean. I loved it. Just beautiful.
N: How was his trip?

B Complete each sentence . . .

Suggested teaching time:	10 minutes
Your actual teaching time:	_____

• If helpful, refer students to page 92 and to the list of irregular verb forms on Appendix page 132.

Language note: A *souvenir* is an object you purchase and keep to remind you of a special occasion or place you have visited.

C Complete each conversation . . .

Suggested teaching time:	5–10 minutes
Your actual teaching time:	_____

Note: In items 1 and 2, students must supply the verb. In item 3, the verb is provided.

• To check their work, have students read the conversations with a partner.

🔵 *Top Notch Pop* Song Activities

TOP NOTCH PROJECT

Idea: Write the questions that follow on the board. Once groups choose an ad, have them read and discuss answers to the questions.

> Why does this vacation look good to you?
> Is it good for people who like nature and wildlife, history and culture, family activities, or physical activities?
> What are the activities you can do?
> How do you get there? Is it a flight, a drive, a cruise, or a train or bus trip?
> Is the vacation more relaxing, exciting, interesting, or unusual?
> Is the vacation expensive or inexpensive?
> What's included in the price of the trip? Hotel? Food? Flight? Entertainment?

Groups plan what to tell the class about their ads. Students decide if one or several people in the group will speak.

Idea: Have groups present their ads as if they're trying to sell their vacation to the class. After all the presentations, the class votes on the best vacation.

UNIT WRAP-UP

Suggested teaching time:	20–25 minutes
Your actual teaching time:	_____

Social language

- Students should create a conversation for the two women. To get them started, ask a few questions:
  Who went on a vacation?
  When did she go?
  How was the flight?

Your students can say ...
A: Hello, [Name]. How was your vacation? **B:** Hi, [Name]. Well, we had a really nice time, but there were some big problems the first day. **A:** What do you mean? **B:** The flight was bumpy and someone stole our luggage. **A:** Really? **B:** Yes. And the hotel was terrible too. **A:** That's too bad. What about the food? **B:** We ate at an awful restaurant. The food was bad and the waiter was unfriendly. **A:** I'll bet the weather was nice. **B:** Incredible! We went swimming, played golf, and went walking on the beach. **A:** That sounds great.

Option: Competition. Divide the class into groups of three. One group begins by saying a word or sentence about the picture. Each group follows by saying something more. Groups that no longer say anything are eliminated until only one group remains. **[+10 minutes]**

Option: Role-play. Have students write the conversation in dialogue form and then role-play their conversation in front of the class. **[+10 minutes]**

Grammar

- Students look at each picture and talk about the woman's vacation. Partners can take turns saying sentences in the past tense.
- Circulate and listen to make sure students are using the past tense correctly.

Your students can say ...
Her flight was bumpy.
Someone stole her luggage.
The hotel was terrible.
The waiter was unfriendly.
The food was terrible.
She went swimming.
She went shopping.
She played golf.
She went to a nice concert.
She went walking on the beach.

Option: Ask students to ask questions about the picture. **[+5 minutes]**

Option: True / False statements. Working in pairs, students write three true statements and three false statements about the picture. For example, *The flight was terrific.* (false) Regroup students into groups of four. Each pair reads their statements out loud to the other pair, who must decide which sentences are true and which are false. **[+10 minutes]**

Writing

- Students write about each picture to tell the story of the woman's vacation. Remind students to use the past tense.
- Encourage students to make up some of the details of her trip. Ask:
  What's her name?
  Where did she go?
  Who did she travel with?

Your students can say ...
In January, [Name] went to Hawaii on vacation. She had a really nice time, but there were also some problems. The flight was very bumpy and long. Someone stole her luggage. The hotel was terrible. She and her husband ate at a bad restaurant. The food was awful, and the waiter was unfriendly.

Later, the vacation was better. The weather was incredible. [Name] went swimming and shopping. She and her husband played golf. In the evening, they sat outside and listened to a band. They went walking on the beach every day. It was very relaxing.

Individual oral progress check (optional)
Use the illustration on page 99 for an oral test. Have students point to and say something about three things that happened on the woman's vacation. For example (pointing to the third picture on the top line) *Someone stole her luggage.* Evaluate students on correctness, intelligibility, and completess.

Cumulative Vocabulary Activities

You may wish to use the video for Unit 8 at this point. For video activity worksheets, go to www.longman.com/topnotch.

Complete Assessment Package
Unit 8 Achievement Test

UNIT WRAP-UP

- **Social language.** Create conversations for the people.
  How was your vacation?

- **Grammar.** Talk about the woman's vacation. Use the past tense.

- **Writing.** Write a story about her vacation.
  The flight was very bumpy ...

Now I can ...

☐ greet someone arriving from a trip.
☐ talk about how I spent my free time.
☐ discuss vacation preferences.
☐ tell about my experiences on a trip.

Taking Transportation

UNIT GOALS

1 Discuss schedules and buy tickets
2 Book travel services
3 Understand airport announcements
4 Describe transportation problems

A **TOPIC PREVIEW.** Look carefully at the departure schedule and the clock. What time is the next flight to São Paulo?

RAPID AIR BRASILIA DEPARTURES

Destination	FLT/No.	Departs	Gate	Status
São Paulo	56	15:50	G4	departed
Belo Horizonte	267	16:10	G3	boarding
Rio de Janeiro	89	16:10	G9	boarding
São Paulo	58	16:50	G4	now 17:25
São Luis	902	17:00	G3	on time
São Paulo	60	17:50	G4	delayed
Porto Alegre	763	17:50	G3	on time
Caracas	04	18:05	G1	canceled
Rio de Janeiro	91	18:10	G9	on time
São Paulo	62	18:50	G4	on time

15:50

"My mom went to Cheju in 2002. She took Asiana."

B **DISCUSSION.** How often do you fly? Complete the chart with flights you took or that someone you know took. Tell your class about them.

Destination	Year	Airline
Cheju, Korea	2002	Asiana

Taking Transportation

A TOPIC PREVIEW

Suggested teaching time:	10–15 minutes
Your actual teaching time:	_____

Culture note: *A.M.* and *P.M.* are only relevant in places where a 12-hour clock is used, such as in the U.S. and Canada. Use of the 24-hour clock, often referred to as *military time*, is more prevalent, especially in more "official" settings (for example, an airport).

- Ask some questions about the departure board:
  What's the name of the airline? (Rapid Air)
  Where does Rapid Air fly? (São Paulo, Belo Horizonte, Rio de Janeiro, São Luis, Porto Alegre, and Caracas)
  What time is it now? (15:50 / 3:50 P.M.)
  Which flight already left? (Flight 56 to São Paulo)
  Which flights are leaving soon? (Flight 267 to Belo Horizonte, Flight 89 to Rio de Janeiro)
  Which flights are late? (Flight 58 to São Paulo, Flight 60 to São Paulo)
  Which flight was canceled? (Flight 04 to Caracas)

- Give students a little time to look at the departure board and figure out when the next flight to São Paulo is. (17:25) Ask *How long do you have to wait for the flight to São Paulo?* (at least an hour and thirty-five minutes) *Where does the flight leave from?* (Gate G4)

Option: Ask *When's the next flight to Rio?* (at 18:10)

- To help students understand the meaning of a *delay*, ask:
  Which flight is delayed? (Flight 60 to São Paulo)
  Is this flight going to leave at 17:50? (no)
  When is it going to leave? (later)
  [+5 minutes]

Language note: A *delay* is a situation in which someone is made to wait. Flights are often delayed because of weather or mechanical problems.

B DISCUSSION

Suggested teaching time:	10 minutes
Your actual teaching time:	_____

- Model the activity by telling the class how often you fly. Then talk about a flight you took. For example, say:
  I fly once in a while, maybe twice a year.
  I went to Dublin, Ireland, in 2003. I took Aer Lingus.

Option: Encourage students to say more about their trip. Model by expanding on your previous answer:
  The flight was a little late because the weather was bad. It was pretty bumpy. The food was awful, but the movie was good.

If helpful, write some previously learned vocabulary on the board. Students can use these words to describe their flights. Remind students to use the past tense.

bumpy	boring	late
scary	short	expensive
comfortable	long	cheap

[+10 minutes]

- To talk about their flights, your students can also say:
  They canceled my flight.
  They lost my luggage.
  The food was _____.
  The movie was _____.

- To encourage students to say more, ask *What did you do on the flight? Did you sleep? What did you eat? Read? Watch? Listen to?*

Option: Students pair up and tell each other about a flight they've taken. Then students find a new partner to tell about the same or another flight. [+10 minutes]

C ⌂ SOUND BITES

Suggested teaching time:	10 minutes
Your actual teaching time:	_____

Note: In this conversation, Marmo is Indonesian and Robert is French.

• Have students look at the photos. Ask *Where are the men?* (at a train station)

Language note: A *bullet train* is a high-speed passenger train, particularly in Japan.

• After students read and listen, ask comprehension questions such as:
Where are they both going? (to Kyoto)
What train are they taking? (the Nozomi)
When is it leaving? (10:20 / in seven minutes)
Where is Robert from? (France)
Is Marmo Chinese? (No, he isn't.)
Where is Marmo from? (Indonesia)
Where is Robert going next week? (Indonesia)

Option: Ask some analytical questions:
What country are the men traveling in? (Japan)
Why are they speaking English? (probably because it's the language they both know / because they don't speak Japanese)

[+5 minutes]

Challenge: Read the explanations below. Ask students to supply the line from the conversation that means the same thing as the explanation.
Marmo is looking for the bullet train to Kyoto. Robert is taking the same train. He knows where the train is. (You can follow me.)
The train is leaving in seven minutes. They have to walk to track 15. There isn't a lot of time. (We should hurry.)
Marmo is Indonesian. Robert is going to Indonesia next week. This is unusual. They are both surprised. (What a small world!)

[+5 minutes]

Language note: The expression *What a small world!* is used to express surprise when people meet by coincidence.

D ◆ Read the statements . . .

Suggested teaching time:	5–10 minutes
Your actual teaching time:	_____

• Review answers as a class. Ask students to demonstrate the source of each fact in the conversation.

• Ask:
Are the trains in our/your country fast or slow?
Are they usually on time or late?

WHAT ABOUT **YOU?**

Suggested teaching time:	10–15 minutes
Your actual teaching time:	_____

• Ask a few students the three questions from the travel survey.

• Ask the students the reasons for their trips. (*study, tourism, work,* etc.)

• If students say they are going to speak English, discuss why. (*It's the language of the country I'm visiting. It's the only possible language in which to communicate,* etc.)

Option: Come up with other questions and possible answers for the survey. Write the new information on the bottom of the chart or on the board. Have students answer and share their answers with the class.

[+10 minutes]

EXTRAS (optional)

Workbook: Exercises 1, 2

C 🎧 **SOUND BITES.** Read along silently as you listen to a natural conversation.

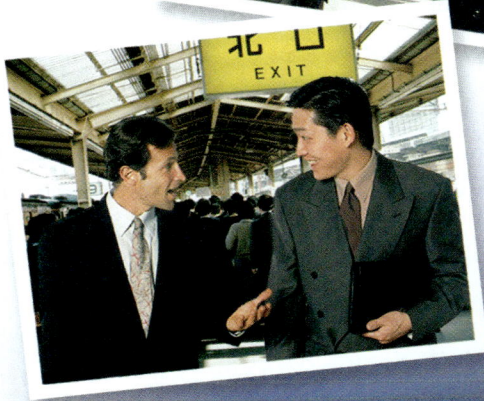

MARMO: Excuse me. Do you speak English?

ROBERT: Yes. But actually I'm French.

MARMO: I'm looking for the bullet train.

ROBERT: Which one?

MARMO: The Nozomi. To Kyoto. Leaving at 10:20.

ROBERT: I'm taking that, too. You can follow me. It leaves from track 15.

MARMO: Thanks. But we should hurry. It's going to leave in seven minutes.

ROBERT: By the way, where are you from? **CN**

MARMO: Jakarta. I'm Indonesian.

ROBERT: No kidding! I'm going to Indonesia next week.

MARMO: Really? What a small world!

D Read the statements critically. Check ☑ the statements that you are sure are true.

☑ **1.** The Nozomi is a bullet train.
☑ **2.** Both travelers are taking the bullet train.
☑ **3.** The train is going to leave soon.
☐ **4.** Robert goes to Indonesia often.

WHAT ABOUT **YOU?**

What are your travel plans?

🌐 TRAVEL SURVEY

Where are you going to travel in the next few years?
☐ Asia   ☐ Africa   ☐ Europe
☐ North America ☐ South America ☐ Other _____

What means of transportation are you going to take?
☐ Airplane   ☐ Ship   ☐ Car
☐ Train   ☐ Bus   ☐ Other _____

What language(s) are you going to speak on your trip?
☐ My native language   ☐ English   ☐ Other _____

Discuss Schedules and Buy Tickets

🎧 CONVERSATION MODEL Read and listen.

A: Can we make the 2:00 bus to Puebla?

B: No, I'm sorry. It left five minutes ago.

A: Oh, no! What should we do?

B: Well, you could take the 2:30.

A: OK. Two tickets, please.

B: One way or round trip?

A: Round trip.

🎧 **Rhythm and intonation practice**

A 🎧 **VOCABULARY. Tickets and trips. Listen and practice.**

PASSENGER TICKET
KOREA BUS LINE
SEOUL > SOKCHO

a one-way ticket

PASSENGER TICKET
KOREA BUS LINE
SEOUL > SOKCHO
SOKCHO > SEOUL

a round-trip ticket

JAPAN RAIL	Kodama (local)	Nozomi (express)
Tokyo	10:13	10:20
Odawara	10:30	–
Atami	11:00	–
Maibara	13:39	–
Kyoto	14:04	12:38

a local   an express

Air China
Flight 009
New York → Los Angeles → Taipei

a direct flight

Air China
Flight 808
New York → Taipei

a non-stop flight

an aisle seat   a window seat

B **Complete the conversations with appropriate words and phrases from the vocabulary.**

1. A: Would you like a window or an aisle?

   B: <u>An aisle seat</u>. I need to stretch my legs.

2. A: Is Flight 009 a <u>non-stop</u> flight?

   B: No. It's a <u>direct</u> flight. It makes two stops, but you don't have to change planes.

3. A: Do you want a <u>round-trip</u> ticket?

   B: Actually, I need a one-way ticket.

4. A: I'm sorry. You missed the express.

   B: Oh, no! Well, can I still make the <u>local</u>?

5. A: Do you want the window or the aisle?

   B: I'd like the <u>window seat</u>, please. I hear the mountains are beautiful.

LESSON 1
Discuss Schedules and Buy Tickets

CONVERSATION MODEL

Suggested teaching time:	10 minutes
Your actual teaching time:	_____

- Have students look at the photo. Ask *What time is it?* (2:05 / 14:05) Point to the woman behind the desk and ask *What is her occupation?*

- After students read and listen, ask:
  Where do they want to go? (to Puebla)
  Can they take the 2:00 bus? (no)
  Why not? (It left at 2:00. It's 2:05 now.)
  When's the next bus? (at 2:30)
  How long do they have to wait? (25 minutes)

- Tell students that *ago* is used to show how far back in the past something happened. To make sure students understand its use, say *It's 2:05 now. The bus left at 2:00. The bus left five minutes ago.*

- Ask *When did we come to class?* Have students use *ago* in their response. Ask individual students *When did you start studying English?*

Rhythm and intonation practice

Suggested teaching time:	5 minutes
Your actual teaching time:	_____

- Have students repeat each line chorally. Have them pay special attention to stress and intonation in the following:
  Oh, no! (emphasis on **no**)
  Well, you could take the 2:30. (emphasis on **could**)
  One way or round trip? (rising intonation in **one way** and falling intonation in **round trip**)

- Make sure students use the following stress pattern:

STRESS PATTERN

A: Can we make the two o'clock bus to Puebla?

B: No, I'm sorry. It left five minutes ago.

A: Oh, no! What should we do?

B: Well, you could take the two thirty.

A: OK. Two tickets, please.

B: One way or round trip?

A: Round trip.

VOCABULARY

Suggested teaching time:	5 minutes
Your actual teaching time:	_____

- After students listen and repeat, point to the Japan Rail schedule and ask *Which train makes stops, a local or an express?* (a local) *Which one is faster?* (an express)

- Point to the Air China flight signs and ask *Which flight makes stops, a direct flight or a non-stop flight?* (a direct flight) *Which one is faster?* (a non-stop flight)

- Ask students to think about the last flight they took:
  Did you have a one-way or a round-trip ticket?
  Was it a direct or a non-stop flight?
  Did you have to change planes?
  Did you have an aisle or a window seat?

  Then ask:
  What about your last train trip?
  Did you have a one-way or a round-trip ticket?
  Did you take a local or an express?
  Did you have an aisle or a window seat?

Students use the Vocabulary to talk about their last airplane and train trips.

Option: Introduce the word *connection*. A connection is a plane, train, or bus that can be used by passengers from an earlier plane, train, or bus who are continuing their trip. When someone has to make a connection, it means they have to change from one plane / train / bus to another. **[+5 minutes]**

Language note: Airlines distinguish between non-stop and direct flights, though the general public tends to use them interchangeably. A direct flight makes an intermediary stop where some passengers get off the plane while others remain. New passengers may get on the plane at this stop.

Vocabulary Cards

Learning Strategies

Complete the conversations ...

Suggested teaching time:	5 minutes
Your actual teaching time:	_____

- To check their work, have students read the completed conversations with a partner.

Language note: When *one way* and *round trip* are used as modifiers, they are hyphenated (*a one-way ticket*). When alone, as in the Conversation Model, they are not hyphenated (*One way or round trip?*).

Language note: In British English, a one-way ticket is called a *single* and a round-trip is a *return*.

C ▸ GRAMMAR

Suggested teaching time:	5–10 minutes
Your actual teaching time:	_____

could

- Say to the class *I don't have any plans this weekend. Give me some ideas about what I could do.* Elicit appropriate suggestions from the class and write them on the board. Students' answers should begin with *You could . . .*

> **Your students can say . . .**
> You could go to the _____ Museum. There's a new exhibit.
> You could eat at _____. The food is really good.
> You could go walking at _____ Park.
> You could see a movie. I saw _____ last night. It was pretty good.

should

- To demonstrate that *should* is used for asking for and giving advice, have students look again at the Rapid Air departure schedule on page 100. Point to the clock on the bottom of the schedule board and say *It's 3:50 now. Which flight to* [name of city] *should I take?*

- For further practice with *should*, elicit advice from the class. Say *I want to get in shape. What should I do? Use* **should** *and* **shouldn't**. Elicit appropriate advice from the class and write it on the board. Make sure students' answer begin with *You should* or *You shouldn't.*

> **Your students can say . . .**
> You should exercise regularly.
> You shouldn't eat junk food.
> You should avoid sweets.
> You should eat healthy foods.
> You should eat small meals.
> You shouldn't drink a lot of soda.

Option: Have students give each other advice about vacation destinations. **[+5 minutes]**

Challenge: Draw two simple faces with speech balloons on the board. In one speech balloon, write *They canceled my flight.* In the other, write *Someone stole my luggage.* Have students use *should* to give advice to each person. For example:
> *They canceled my flight.*
> *You should take the next flight.*
> *Someone stole my luggage.*
> *You should call the police.*

[+5 minutes]

🔲 **Grammar Self-Checks**

D ▸ Complete each sentence . . .

Suggested teaching time:	5–10 minutes
Your actual teaching time:	_____

- Before students complete the exercise, write on the board:

  _____ *a round-trip ticket.*
  She / buy

  Then write incorrect answers on the board. Have students circle the problem with each answer.
  She should ⓢ buy
  She should ⓣⓞ buy

  Elicit the correct answer from the class.
  (She should buy . . .)

- Have students change the same statement into a question. *(Should she buy [that computer]?)* Then have them make it negative. *(She shouldn't buy [that dress].)*

CONVERSATION **PAIR WORK**

Suggested teaching time:	10–15 minutes
Your actual teaching time:	_____

Note: For the first part of the conversation, Student A should choose one of the first three departures listed. Then Student B can suggest the same destination at a later time.

- Point out that Student B is playing the role of a ticket clerk. Student A is a customer.

🔲 **Pair Work Cards**

EXTRAS (optional)

Grammar Booster
Workbook: Exercises 3–7
Copy & Go: Activity 33

C ▶ GRAMMAR. could and should

could CN

Use **could** and the base form of a verb to suggest an alternative or a possibility.

The express bus is full. You **could take** the local instead.

should CN

Use **should** and the base form of a verb to give advice.

You **shouldn't take** that flight. You **should take** the non-stop.

CN Corpus Notes:
"Could" and "should" are two of the 1000 most frequent words in both written and spoken American English.

Questions

Could I **take** the 2:20?   Yes, you **could**. / No, you **couldn't**.

Who **should get** the aisle seat?   I **should**. I like to walk around.

GRAMMAR BOOSTER

PAGES G17–G18
For more . . .

D ▶ Complete each sentence or question with **should** or **could** and the base form of the verb.

1. When ____should we leave____ for the airport? There's going to be a lot of traffic.
   we / leave

2. ____They shouldn't take____ the local bus. It makes too many stops.
   They / not take

3. You have two options. ____You could take____ the express bus or ____you could fly____.
   You / take   *you / fly*

4. That train's always crowded. ____He should get____ his ticket in advance.
   He / get

5. ____He could buy____ it at a travel agency, but it's cheaper on the Internet.
   He / buy

6. Tell her ____she should choose____ the direct flight. It's better than changing planes.
   she / choose

CONVERSATION PAIR WORK

Discuss schedules and tickets. Use the train departure board and the clock. Use the guide, or create a new conversation.

A: Can I make the _____ to _____?
B: No, I'm sorry. It left _____ ago.
A: _____! What should I do?
B: Well, you could take the _____.
A: _____ . . .

Continue the conversation any way you like.

DEPARTURES   7:26 A.M.

To	Departs	Track
WASHINGTON	7:10	6
BOSTON	7:22	9
PHILADELPHIA	7:25	19
WASHINGTON	8:25	8
BOSTON	8:26	24
PHILADELPHIA	8:31	18

CONTROLLED PRACTICE

103

Book Travel Services

🎧 CONVERSATION MODEL Read and listen.

A: I'm going to need a rental car in Dubai.
B: Certainly. What date are you arriving?
A: April 6th.
B: What time do you get in? **CN**
A: Let me check,. . . 5:45.

🎧 **Rhythm and intonation practice**

CN **Corpus Notes:** "Get in" is less formal and more common than "arrive."

A 🎧 VOCABULARY. Travel services. Listen and practice.

a rental car

a taxi

a limousine

a hotel reservation **CN**

CN **Corpus Notes:** Some words are frequently used together with "reservation." Phrases include "have a reservation," "make a reservation," and "get a reservation."

B 🎧 LISTENING COMPREHENSION. Listen to the conversations about travel services. Then listen again and write the service each client needs. Listen again if necessary to check your work.

1. a limousine
2. a hotel reservation
3. a rental car
4. a taxi

C GRAMMAR. Be going to for the future

Use **be going to** + the base form of a verb to talk about the future.

be	going to	base form
I'm	going to	rent a car in New York.
She's	going to	be at the airport.
We're	going to	take a taxi into town.

Are they going to get a round-trip ticket? Yes, they are. / No, they aren't.
Who's going to make the reservation? We are.
When are you going to call? At 8:00.

Remember: The present continuous and the simple present tense can also express future actions.
We're **flying** to Madrid. The plane **leaves** at 6:00.

GRAMMAR BOOSTER
PAGES G18–G19
For more . . .

LESSON 2 ▶ *Book Travel Services*

🎧 CONVERSATION **MODEL**

Suggested teaching time:	5–10 minutes
Your actual teaching time:	————

• After students read and listen, ask *Where is A going?* (Dubai) *When is A arriving in Dubai?* (on April 6th) *What does A need?* (a rental car)

🎧 Rhythm and intonation practice

Suggested teaching time:	5 minutes
Your actual teaching time:	————

• Have students repeat chorally. Make sure they:
  ○ say *sixth*, not *six*.
  ○ use falling intonation with *What date are you arriving?* and *What time do you get in?*
  ○ use the following stress pattern:

```
┌─ STRESS PATTERN ──────────────────────────
│        —  •  •  —  •  —  •  •  —  •  •
│  A:  I'm going to need a rental car in Dubai.
│        —  •  •  —  —  •  •  •  —  •
│  B:  Certainly.  What date are you arriving?
│        —  •  —
│  A:  April sixth.
│          •  —  •  •  —
│  B:  What time do you get in?
│        —  •  •  —  —  •  •  —
│  A:  Let me check....five forty-five.
└──────────────────────────────────────────
```

Ⓐ 🎧 VOCABULARY

Suggested teaching time:	5 minutes
Your actual teaching time:	————

• Explain that a *rental car* is a car you pay to use for a short time.
• After students repeat, ask: *Which services did you use on your last vacation? Where did you go? Did you use a rental car? Did you use a taxi? Did you use a limousine? Did you have a hotel reservation?*

Language note: In informal speech, *limousines* are often called *limos*. An airport limousine is a pre-hired car.

🔘 **Vocabulary Cards**

Ⓑ 🎧 LISTENING COMPREHENSION

Suggested teaching time:	10 minutes
Your actual teaching time:	————

• Ask where Bangkok, Seoul, New York, and Montevideo are. (Thailand, South Korea, the United States, and Uruguay) If possible, show students where each country is on a world map.

Challenge: Have students copy the chart that follows from the board. Students listen again and fill in the information from each conversation. **[+10 minutes]**

	Where is the client going?	What date is the client arriving?	What time is the client arriving?
1.	Bangkok	October 6	No information
2.	Seoul	October 4	No information
3.	New York	October 3	11:30 PM
4.	Montevideo	October 4	8:00 AM

Note: Audioscript is on page T105.

🔘 **Graphic Organizers**

Ⓒ GRAMMAR

Suggested teaching time:	5–10 minutes
Your actual teaching time:	————

• Be sure students understand the concept of future, draw the following timeline on the board:

```
yesterday          today          tomorrow
   ●─────────────────●───────────────●
  past             present          future
```

After students read the information in the Grammar box, ask *What are your future plans?* On the board, write:

| Today . . . | Tomorrow . . . | Next week . . . |
| Tonight . . . | This weekend . . . | Next month . . . |

Have students use *be going to* to write statements about their future activities. (*Today I'm going to play soccer.*)

• Ask *What are you going to do [tonight]?* Have several students read their sentences out loud. Check that students use the correct form of *be going to* with the base form of a verb. (*Tonight I'm going to lift weights at the gym.*)

• Have students find and underline the three ways future actions are expressed in the Conversation Model. (**I'm going to need** . . . ; What date **are** you **arriving**?; What time **do** you **get in**?)

Option: Point out that it's sometimes possible to use *be going to* + the base form of a verb, the present continuous, or the simple present tense to talk about the same future action. Elicit three different ways to express Speaker A's arrival date and time (1. He**'s going to arrive** in Dubai on April 6 at 5:45. 2. He**'s arriving** in Dubai on April 6 at 5:45. 3. He **arrives** in Dubai on April 6 at 5:45.) **[+5 minutes]**

Language notes: In casual conversation, the words *going to* are often pronounced "gonna." However, in written English, the words are always spelled *going to*. The simple present tense is often used for the future when discussing travel dates, schedules, and times.

🔘 **Grammar Self-Checks**

AUDIOSCRIPT (from page T104)

CONVERSATION 1 [F = Spanish]
M: Good morning. How can we assist you today?
F: I'm flying to Bogota on October 6th, and I need a limousine.
M: Certainly. For you alone?
F: No. I'll be traveling with my three children. We'll have lots of luggage.
M: That's no problem. I can book you a limo with a large trunk for the luggage. Are you going to need a hotel reservation in Bogota?
F: No, thank you. Bogota is my home.

CONVERSATION 2 [M2 = U.S. regional]
M1: Yes, sir. Can I help you with something?
M2: I hope so. I'm arriving in Seoul on October 4th, and I need a hotel reservation. I'm very concerned because I don't speak any Korean.
M1: Don't be concerned, sir. The hotel staff all speak English.

CONVERSATION 3 [F = Chinese]
F: Excuse me. I need some help with a rental car reservation overseas.
M: Yes, of course. Please have a seat. I'll be right with you. Now, ma'am. Where do you need that car?
F: In New York, at John F. Kennedy airport. I arrive on the third.
M: Of October?
F: Yes. At 11:30 P.M. Is that too late to get a car?
M: Certainly not. Nothing's too late in New York!

CONVERSATION 4 [M2 = Eastern European]
M1: Excuse me. Do you work here?
M2: Yes, sir. How can I assist you this afternoon?
M1: I'm arriving in Montevideo from Porto Alegre on October 4th at eight o'clock in the morning. I have a reservation at the Hotel del Centro. I'll need either a taxi or a limousine. Are there limousines from the airport to the hotel?
M2: Let me check . . . Actually, no. You'll need to take a taxi.
M1: Is it possible to make a reservation? I have a lunch meeting and I want to be sure I don't have to wait for the taxi. Is that possible?
M2: Anything is possible. If you'll just give me a moment, I'll go online to see what the options are.

D Complete each sentence . . .

Suggested teaching time:	5 minutes
Your actual teaching time:	_____

Option: On a sheet of paper, have students rewrite the sentences using the present continuous. (1. They're buying . . . 2. When's she calling . . . ? 3. Are we reserving . . . ? 4. Who's meeting . . . ?) **[+5 minutes]**

E Complete the e-mail . . .

Suggested teaching time:	5 minutes
Your actual teaching time:	_____

• To check their work, have students read the e-mail out loud to a partner.

Option: Write the following on the board:
  airline:
  flight number:
  place of departure:
  departure time:
  destination:
  arrival time:

Have students find the travel information in the e-mail. Ask volunteers to come up and write in the correct answers. (*Atlas Airlines, 6702, Mexico City, 4:45 P.M., Chicago, 9:50 P.M.*) **[+5 minutes]**

Challenge: Ask the class:
  What time is Mara's flight going to arrive? (10:00 P.M.)
  What's the name of the airport in Chicago? (O'Hare)
[+5 minutes]

CONVERSATION **PAIR WORK**

Suggested teaching time:	5–10 minutes
Your actual teaching time:	_____

• Ask questions about the tickets. For each ticket, ask:
  What's the form of transportation? (flight, train, bus)
  What's the destination? (Cuzco, Washington, Sokcho)
  What's the arrival date? (April 11, June 26, August 13)
  What's the arrival time? (19:15 / 7:15 P.M., 9:10 P.M., 11:55)

Option: Have students bring in their own plane, train, or bus tickets. Students use their own tickets to practice the conversation. **[+10 minutes]**

Pair Work Cards

EXTRAS (optional)

Grammar Booster
Workbook: Exercises 8–12
Copy & Go: Activity 34

D ▸ **Complete each sentence or question with be going to and the base form of the verb.**

1. _They are going to buy_ tickets for the express.
   _{they / buy}

2. When _is she going to call_ the travel agent?
   _{she / call}

3. _Are we going to reserve_ seats for everyone or just for us?
   _{we / reserve}

4. Who _is going to meet_ him at the airport?
   _{meet}

E ▸ **Complete the e-mail. Circle the correct forms.**

● ● ●

Here's my travel information: I (**1.** leaving / **('m leaving**)) Mexico City at 4:45 P.M.
on Atlas Airlines flight 6702. The flight (**2.** arriving / **arrives**) in Chicago at
9:50 P.M. Mara's flight (**3.** be going to get in / **is getting in**) ten minutes later, so
we (**4.** **'re meeting** / meeting) at the baggage claim. That's too late for you to
pick me up, so I (**5.** **'m going to take** / taking) a limo from O'Hare. Mara
(**6.** goes to / **is going to**) come along and (**7.** **spend** / spending) the night with us.
Her flight to Tokyo (**8.** not leaving / **doesn't leave**) until the next day.

CONVERSATION
PAIR WORK

Book a rental car, taxi, limousine, or hotel. Use the tickets for arrival information. Use the guide, or create a new conversation.

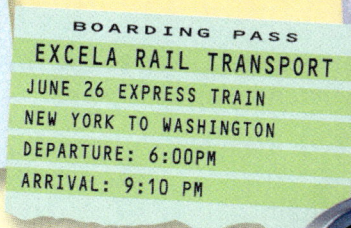

PASSENGER TICKET AND BAGGAGE CHECK
AIR CUZCO   APRIL 11   FLIGHT 22
DEPARTURE: 18:00   ARRIVAL: 19:15
LIMA TO CUZCO
88985376124   0 988 7631986534 7

BOARDING PASS
EXCELA RAIL TRANSPORT
JUNE 26 EXPRESS TRAIN
NEW YORK TO WASHINGTON
DEPARTURE: 6:00PM
ARRIVAL: 9:10 PM

Seoul Touristbus
FROM Seoul
TO Sokcho
DATE 13 August
DEPARTS 07:45
ARRIVES 11:55

A: I'm going to need _____ in _____.
B: _____. What date are you arriving?
A: _____.
B: What time does the _____ arrive?
A: Let me check.... _____.
B: _____...

Continue the conversation in your own way ...

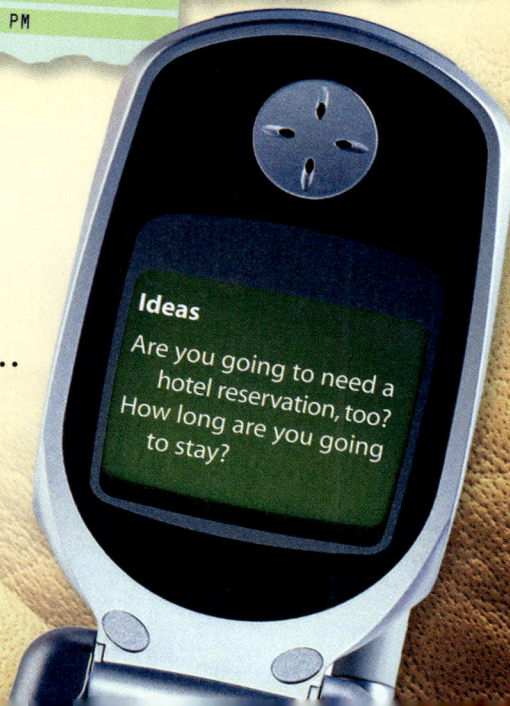

Ideas
Are you going to need a hotel reservation, too?
How long are you going to stay?

105

3 Understand Airport Announcements

A 🎧 **VOCABULARY.** Airline passenger information. **Listen and practice.**

a passenger   an agent
a boarding pass

security

an overbooking

a cancellation

B 🎧 **LISTENING COMPREHENSION.** Listen to the airport announcements and check ☑ the problems that are announced.

- ☑ a delay
- ☐ a cancellation
- ☐ an overbooking

- ☑ a gate change
- ☐ a security problem
- ☑ a mechanical problem

C 🎧 Now listen again and write the flight information.

1. flight number: __692__
2. original departure gate: __26B__
3. final departure gate: __16C__
4. final departure time: __7:00__

D 🎧 **PRONUNCIATION.** Stating alternatives. **Listen to the rhythm and intonation of alternatives. Then listen again and repeat.**

- Well, you could take the train, or take the bus.
- They could wait or reserve a later flight.
- Would you like a one-way ticket or a round-trip ticket?

Antofagasta, Chile

LESSON 3
Understand Airport Announcements

A 🎧 VOCABULARY

Suggested teaching time:	5–10 minutes
Your actual teaching time:	_____

Option: Read the definitions that follow. Students identify the correct vocabulary word or phrase.
1. *There are not enough seats on the plane for all the people who have tickets.* (an overbooking)
2. *The person who takes your boarding pass when you get on an airplane.* (an agent)
3. *The flight is not going to go today.* (a cancellation)
4. *The place where you leave the airport building to get on an airplane.* (a gate)
5. *The place where they use a machine to check travelers and their luggage before they go to their gates.* (security)
6. *A kind of ticket that you show the agent to get on the plane.* (a boarding pass) [**+5 minutes**]

💿 **Vocabulary Cards**

B 🎧 LISTENING COMPREHENSION

Suggested teaching time:	10 minutes
Your actual teaching time:	_____

• When you review, ask *Was there a delay? Was there a cancellation?* etc. Students answer *Yes, there was* or *No, there wasn't.*

Note: The accented speakers in this listening comprehension are Spanish.

AUDIOSCRIPT

[F and M = Spanish]
F: Lanca Airlines, flight 692, with service to Antofagasta, Chile, and continuing service to Santiago is now ready for boarding through gate 26B. Passengers with boarding passes should pass through security and proceed immediately to the gate.

F: This is a gate change for Lanca Airlines, flight 692, with service to Antofagasta, Chile, and Santiago. The new gate is gate 16 C. This is a gate change for Lanca Airlines, flight 692, with service to Antofagasta, Chile, and Santiago. The new gate is gate 16 C.

M: This is an announcement for passengers on Lanca Airlines flight 692 with service to Santiago with an intermediate stop in Antofagasta. Ladies and gentlemen, please take your seats. The captain informs me that there is a mechanical problem, and the new departure time will be at seven o'clock. If you are traveling on flight 692, please take your seat. The flight has been delayed. The new departure time is seven o'clock. We're sorry for the delay.

M: Ladies and gentlemen, Lanca Airlines, flight 692 to Antofagasta, with continuing service to Santiago is now available for boarding through gate 16C. Passengers requiring assistance or with small children will be boarded first. We're now ready to board passengers in the Wide World Alliance or those passengers with first-class or business-class boarding passes. Have a good flight.

C 🎧 Now listen again . . .

Suggested teaching time:	10 minutes
Your actual teaching time:	_____

• After students complete the exercise, ask *Is flight 692 direct or non-stop?* (direct)

D 🎧 PRONUNCIATION

Suggested teaching time:	5–10 minutes
Your actual teaching time:	_____

• Point out how intonation rises on the first of two alternatives and falls on the second.

Option: Partners plan a trip together. They suggest alternatives to each other, practicing the correct rhythm and intonation. To make the activity more interesting, students can choose from the alternatives their partner suggests. (*I'd like to go to Europe.*) [**+10 minutes**]

Your students can say . . .
We could go to Europe or to South America.
We could fly or take a cruise.
Do you want to get a rental car or use public transportation?

Europe	or	to South America
fly	or	take a cruise
a rental car	or	use public transportation

💿 **Pronunciation Activities**

TOP NOTCH **INTERACTION**

Suggested teaching time:	15–20 minutes
Your actual teaching time:	_____

STEP 1

- Have pairs look at the picture and say all they can about it. Students should use complete sentences to talk about the picture.

┌─ **Your students can say . . .** ─────────────
The man is an agent.
The airline is Rapid Air.
The flight number is 58.
The flight is going / is going to go to São Paulo.
The flight leaves / is leaving / is going to leave at 17:25 (5:25).
The flight leaves / is leaving / is going to leave from gate G9.
It's 16:35 (4:35) now.
└──

- Read the announcement out loud or have students read it independently.

- Remind students that when something is overbooked, it means there are more passengers than seats. The airline sold too many tickets.

- Ask:
    What's the problem with the flight? (it's overbooked)
    What does the airline want someone to do? (take a later flight)
    What does the person who volunteers to take a later flight get? (a free ticket for another flight)

Option: Have students find and circle the word *volunteer* in each speech balloon. Ask what part of speech *volunteer* is in each context. (It's a noun in the first balloon, a verb in the second.) Ask *How many volunteers does the airline need?* (one volunteer) *Would you like to volunteer? Why or why not?* **[+5 minutes]**

STEP 2

- Write the following questions on the board:
    What time is flight 58 going to arrive?
    When's the next flight to São Paulo?
    What time does it arrive?
    What time is your very important dinner?

- Read each question out loud and elicit answers from the class. Write the answers on the board.

- Remind students to practice the correct rhythm and intonation when they state alternatives.

- Be sure students are aware that NEED HELP? can provide support by reminding them of language they know.

STEP 3

- Ask individual students *What are you going to do?* and *What's your partner going to do?* To encourage students to say more, ask *Why?*

┌─ **Your students can say . . .** ─────────────
I'm going to take flight 58. I have to be on time for the dinner.
My partner's going to volunteer. He wants a free ticket. He's going to go to Rio in February.
└──

Option: Ask students if they have ever had tickets for an overbooked flight. If they have, ask those students:
    Where were you going?
    Were you traveling alone or with someone?
    Was there a later flight you could take?
    Did they offer you a free round-trip ticket?
    Have you used your free ticket?
    If so, where did you go?
[+5 minutes]

EXTRAS (optional)

Workbook: Exercises 13
Copy & Go: Activity 35

 Pronunciation Supplements

INTERACTION • *Overbooked!*

STEP 1. Read the announcement by the gate agent for Rapid Air flight 58 from Brasilia to São Paulo.

> Good afternoon, ladies and gentlemen. Flight 58 is overbooked. We apologize. We need one volunteer to give up a seat on this flight.

> There are seats available on all later flights to São Paulo. If you volunteer to take a later flight, Rapid Air will give you a free round-trip ticket anywhere. The free ticket is good for one year.

16:35

RAPIDAIR
GATE G9

DESTINATION	FLIGHT	DEPARTS	STATUS
São Paulo	58	Now 17:25	See Agent

STEP 2. **PAIR WORK.** You and your partner have tickets on Flight 58. Read the facts.

- The time is now 16:35.
- You have a very important dinner in São Paulo at 20:30.
- The flight takes two hours.

Now look at the departure schedule and discuss your alternatives.

DEPARTURES			
São Paulo	56	16:20	departed
Rio de Janeiro	89	16:40	boarding
São Paulo	58	16:50	now 17:25
São Paulo	60	17:50	on time

> What are you going to do?

> I'm going to volunteer.

NEED HELP? Here's language you already know:

Discuss plans

What are you going to do?
What should we do?
You could ____.
We should ____.
What about ____?
Can we make the ____?

It departed ____ ago.
What time does ____ arrive?
Is it direct / non-stop?
I'm going to ____.

STEP 3. **DISCUSSION.** Tell the class what you decided and why. How many students decided to take a later flight?

4 ▷ Describe Transportation Problems

A 🎧 **VOCABULARY.** **Transportation problems.** **Listen and practice.**

We **had an accident**. | We **had mechanical problems**. | We **missed our train**. | We **got bumped** from the flight. | We **got seasick**.

B 🎧 **LISTENING COMPREHENSION.** **Listen to the conversations.** **Then listen again and complete each statement with a phrase from the vocabulary.**

1. They got ___seasick___.
2. They had ___an accident___.
3. They got ___bumped___.
4. They had ___mechanical problems___.
5. They missed ___their flight___.

C **READING WARM-UP.** **Do your trips always go well?**

D 🎧 **READING.** **Read the news clippings.** **Which clipping is the most interesting?** **Explain your opinion.**

Runaway train travels 70 miles

A train from the CSX Company left Stanley Yard today when the engineer accidentally hit the power lever instead of the brake. The train was caught 70 miles later, near Toledo, Ohio. There were no injuries.

MYSTERY CRUISE SHIP ILLNESSES END

Incidents of sickness are now over, according to a cruise industry spokesperson. He was referring to numerous outbreaks of illness on cruises in recent weeks.

Dave Forney of the Centers for Disease Control and Prevention agrees. Poor sanitation in handling food was probably responsible for the recent outbreaks. "It's always important to wash hands and prepare food safely," adds Forney.

TURKEYS ENTER COCKPIT

On March 9, a small plane operated by Atlantic Coast Airlines was en route from Dulles International Airport near Washington to LaGuardia Airport in New York, when the aircraft was struck by two wild turkeys. There were four crew members and fifty passengers on board. The pilot reported that the turkeys entered the cockpit through the pilot's window. No one was injured.

SOURCES: cnn.com and ntsb.gov

E **Complete each statement to predict what each person probably said.**

1. The train engineer probably said, "_____."
   a. I almost had an accident.
   b. I almost missed the train.

2. The cruise industry spokesperson probably said, "_____."
   a. The passengers ate bad food.
   b. The passengers got seasick.

3. The pilot of the plane probably said, "_____."
   a. We had mechanical problems.
   b. We almost had an accident.

LESSON

4 Describe Transportation Problems

A ⌒ VOCABULARY

Suggested teaching time:	5 minutes
Your actual teaching time:	_____

Language note: If someone *gets bumped* from a flight, it means they lost their seat on this flight (usually due to overbooking). To be *seasick* means to feel very nauseated because of movement of a boat or ship. Someone who gets sick because of the motion on a plane is said to be *airsick*. Also, *carsick* means to get sick because of the motion of a car.

🌀 **Vocabulary Cards**

B ⌒ LISTENING COMPREHENSION

Suggested teaching time:	5–10 minutes
Your actual teaching time:	_____

• When you review, have students check that they used the correct possessive adjective, *their*, in item 5.

Option: Students listen again for the means of transportation in each conversation. (1. ship 2. limo 3. airplane 4. airplane 5. airplane) **[+5 minutes]**

AUDIOSCRIPT

CONVERSATION 1 [M1 = British English]
M1: You'll never believe what happened on our holiday.
M2: What?
M1: Well we took this great cruise, and we were seasick the whole time.
M2: You're kidding! What bad luck.

CONVERSATION 2
F: How was the trip with your family?
M: It ended well. But it started badly.
F: What do you mean?
M: Well, the airport limo had an accident.
F: Did anyone get hurt?
M: No. But it was really scary.

CONVERSATION 3 [F = Chinese]
M: How did it go?
F: Pretty good, except for one thing.
M: What was that?
F: We got bumped from our flight.
M: Oh, no!
F: Well, it turned out OK. They put us on a later flight, but we got in too late for the party.

CONVERSATION 4 [F2 = Spanish]
F1: What time does your parents' flight arrive?
F2: Well, it was supposed to arrive at five, but they called to say it was late.
F1: How come?
F2: Some kind of mechanical problem. It's leaving at eight so they won't be in until ten.

CONVERSATION 5
F: What are you doing home?
M: We missed our flight.
F: Oh, no. What are you going to do?
M: It's OK. We're going to take the first flight out in the morning.

C READING WARM-UP

Suggested teaching time:	5 minutes
Your actual teaching time:	_____

• Review the frequency adverbs (from Unit 6) that students can use in their responses: *always, almost always, usually, often, sometimes, hardly ever,* and *never.*

• To model the activity, answer the question yourself. Give one or two specific examples. For example: *My trips usually go well, but not always. I went on a cruise to Mexico. I was seasick the first day. Also, I had an accident in a rental car in Germany.*

D ⌒ READING

Suggested teaching time:	5–10 minutes
Your actual teaching time:	_____

• Pause the audio program after each article. Ask a few comprehension questions:
  Runaway train . . .
  What did the engineer want to do? (hit the brake)
  What did he do? (hit the power lever)
  Could he stop the train? (no, not at first)
  Was there an accident? (No.) *Was anyone hurt?* (No.)
  Mystery cruise . . .
  Why did people get sick on cruises? (The food was bad.)
  Why was the food bad? (Food preparers didn't wash their hands.)
  Are people getting sick now? (No.)
  Turkeys enter . . .
  What was the airplane's destination? (LaGuardia Airport in New York)
  What happened? (Turkeys / Birds struck the pilot's window.)
  Did the flight arrive? (Yes.) *Was anyone hurt?* (No.)

Language note: In the runaway train clipping, the word *hit* means to press a part in a machine or vehicle to make it work (*hit the brake*).

🌀 **Learning Strategies**

E Complete each statement . . .

Suggested teaching time:	5 minutes
Your actual teaching time:	_____

• Ask students to explain their answers.

🌀 **Extra Reading Comprehension Activities**

T108

TOP NOTCH **INTERACTION**

Suggested teaching time:	20–25 minutes
Your actual teaching time:	_____

STEP 1

• If helpful, explain that a *ferry* is a boat that takes people across a river or a narrow area of water. Give an example. You can say *Many tourists in Europe take a ferry from England to France;* or better still, give an example of a local ferry.

Vocabulary Cards

STEP 2

• Point out that to ask about airplane trips, it is more natural to say *Where did you fly?* than *Where did you take the airplane?* Ask *What is the past tense of* fly? (flew)

• To model the activity, look at a student's book. Say *[Name] took a ferry. Where did you take the ferry, [Name]?* Make sure students note that the past tense form of *take* is *took*.

Option: Have students walk around and find one classmate who took each means of transportation. For each form of transportation, students write a sentence about a classmate. Students write eight sentences, like this: *[Name] took [a bus] to [Place].* **[+10 minutes]**

STEP 3

• Write the items from the notepad on the board. To model the activity, make notes about a trip when you had transportation problems.

STEP 4

• Use your notepad to tell the class about your trip. Relate the information that is on the notepad but also give more information and details.

• Have the class ask you a few questions about your trip.

• Give students a few minutes to think about how to tell their stories.

• After each student tells a story, classmates should ask at least two questions.

STEP 5

• Students use their notepads to write their stories. Encourage them to include more information and details.

Option: Have volunteers read their stories to the class. **[+5 minutes]**

Writing Process Worksheets

EXTRAS (optional)

Workbook: Exercises 14–16
Copy & Go: Activity 36

TOP NOTCH
INTERACTION • *Travel Woes*

STEP 1. Circle all the transportation you have taken. Then add other transportation you have taken.

bus

train

ferry

airplane

helicopter

taxi

limousine

other _____

STEP 2. Ask your partner questions about the transportation he or she circled.

> 66 When was the last time you took a train? 99

STEP 3. Choose a trip when you had transportation problems. On the notepad, make notes about the trip.

means of transportation:

when:

destination:

good memories:

problems:

STEP 4. GROUP WORK. Tell your story to the class. Ask your classmates questions about their trips.

STEP 5. WRITING. Write the true story of what happened. Use your notepad for support.

> Last summer I went to Tanzania. I traveled from Dar es Salaam to Songea. The bus was very comfortable and not expensive. It had air-conditioning and a bathroom.
> But I always get bus sick, so . . .

UNIT 9
CHECKPOINT

A 🎧 **LISTENING COMPREHENSION.** Listen to the conversations. Then listen again and write the number of the conversation below each picture.

_5_ _3_ _1_ _4_ _2_

B **Complete each sentence with an appropriate word or phrase.**

1. If you don't want to drive to the airport, a ___taxi___ is very convenient and practical.
2. A ___limousine___ is a large car with a driver.
3. If you are not returning, you should buy a ___one-way___ ticket.
4. A ___non-stop___ flight is faster than a direct flight.
5. In order to board a plane, you have to give a ___ticket___ to the agent at the gate.

C **Write an answer to each statement.**

1. "Can we still make the 6:00 ferry?" **YOU** _____.
2. "Why are you buying a one-way ticket?" **YOU** _____.
3. "Oh, no! When did it leave?" **YOU** _____.

D **Complete the conversation with be going to and the indicated verbs.**

A: On Saturday, ___we are going to leave___ for Cancun.
 1. we / leave

B: Really? ___Are you going to rent___ a car there? There are some great
 2. you / rent

  places to explore.

A: No. I think ___we are going to stay___ on the beach and rest.
 3. we / stay

  By the way, where ___are you and Margo going to go___ for your vacation?
 4. you and Margo / go

B: I'm not sure. But ___I am going to travel___ to Bangkok on business
 5. I / travel

  next month. And ___I am going to take___ a few days off to go
 6. I / take

  sightseeing. I hear it's great.

E **WRITING.** On a separate sheet of paper, write a paragraph about your next trip. Use the questions for support.

- Where are you going to go?
- What kind of transportation are you going to take?
- When do you leave?
- Who are you traveling with?
- What are you going to do when you are there?
- When do you get back?

> **TOP NOTCH PROJECT**
> Use the Internet to plan travel arrangements. Use real schedules and travel services.

> **TOP NOTCH WEBSITE**
> For Unit 9 online activities, visit the *Top Notch* Companion Website at www.longman.com/topnotch.

UNIT 9
CHECKPOINT

A 🎧 LISTENING COMPREHENSION

Suggested teaching time:	5–10 minutes
Your actual teaching time:	_____

• Before students listen, have them look at each picture and identify the vocabulary word or phrase that's shown. *(security, an aisle seat / a window seat, a rental car, an overbooking, a limousine)* Students can write the word or phrase above the corresponding picture.

Option: Introduce another air travel vocabulary word. Explain that to get *an upgrade* is to get a better seat on an airplane than the one that you paid for. **[+5 minutes]**

Challenge: Ask *Do airport security rules drive you crazy?* Lead a class discussion. **[+10 minutes]**

AUDIOSCRIPT

CONVERSATION 1
M: Is she going to rent a car in New York?
F: I'm pretty sure she is.

CONVERSATION 2
F: How are you going to get to the airport?
M: We're going to take a limousine.

CONVERSATION 3
M1: What kind of seat would you like, sir?
M2: I like a view. A window seat, please.

CONVERSATION 4
M: Hey! They're offering a free ticket on a later flight to people who didn't get a seat.
F: That's great. But I don't think that airlines should sell more seats than they have!

CONVERSATION 5 [M = Spanish]
F: Look at all those people waiting to get through security!
M: These new rules are driving me crazy!

B Complete each sentence . . .

Suggested teaching time:	5 minutes
Your actual teaching time:	_____

Option: Ask some questions:
Why is a taxi more practical than a limo? (because it's cheaper)
What's more expensive, a round-trip ticket or a one-way ticket?
Do you prefer non-stop or direct flights? Why?
[+5 minutes]

C Write an answer . . .

Suggested teaching time:	5 minutes
Your actual teaching time:	_____

• To check their work, have students take turns reading the questions and their answers with a partner.

D Complete the conversation . . .

Suggested teaching time:	5 minutes
Your actual teaching time:	_____

• To check their work, have students read the conversation with a partner.

E WRITING

Suggested teaching time:	10–15 minutes
Your actual teaching time:	_____

• Have students make notes in response to the questions before they begin writing.

• Encourage students to include more details and information.

Your students can say . . .
I'm going to go to San Diego, California. The weather is great there! I'm going to fly, and then I'm going to need a rental car. I'm traveling with my husband. We leave on November 5th and get back on November 19th. We're going to relax on the beach every day. We're going to go bike riding and walking. We're also going to go to the zoo and visit Mexico.

🌐 **Writing Process Worksheets**

TOP NOTCH PROJECT

Idea: Students can work independently or in pairs. Have them choose a destination.

Idea: Students use the Internet to find the following:
a means of transportation
a departure time
an arrival time
the cost of the transportation
a hotel or other accommodations
transportation at their destination (rental car, taxi, limo, public transportation, etc.)

If students need help finding travel websites, you can suggest www.travelocity.com, www.orbitz.com, and www.expedia.com.

Note: Websites in students' native language are OK too, as long as the information they report is in English.

Idea: Students can tell the class about their travel plans and what websites they used to find them.

Idea: If students don't have easy access to the Internet, use travel agency information.

UNIT WRAP-UP

Suggested teaching time:	15–20 minutes
Your actual teaching time:	_____

Social language

- Before students do the activity, ask them some questions about the picture:

  What is the couple doing on June 6th? (planning a vacation)
  Where do they decide to go? (Hawaii.)
  What happened to Flight 3450? (It was canceled.)
  What happened when the couple got to Hawaii? (They missed the 14:45 bus.)
  What could they do? (They could take the bus at 15:15 or 15:45.)

- Point out that students can also use language from Unit 8, *Getting Away*, especially if they choose the first picture.

Option: Have students write sentences to describe the problems in the picture. For example, *The flight was canceled. They missed the bus.* **[+5 minutes]**

┌─ **Your students can say . . .** ─────────┐

Picture 1
Travel agent: How can I help you? **Wife:** We need a vacation. [To husband] Where should we go? **Husband:** I don't know. **Travel agent:** Well, what do you like? Do you like history and culture, or nature and wildlife? **Husband:** We like nature. We like warm weather and nice beaches, too. **Travel agent:** You could go to Hawaii. It's scenic and relaxing. **Wife:** Sounds perfect. [To husband] What do you think? Should we go to Hawaii? **Husband:** Sure. Let's go. **Travel agent:** Great. When are you going to leave? **Wife:** On August 22nd. **Travel agent:** And how long are you going to stay? **Husband:** Two weeks. **Travel agent:** OK, I can book your flight and hotel reservations. Are you going to need a rental car? **Wife:** Yes, please. **Travel agent:** You're going to have a really nice time.

Picture 2
Wife: Oh, no! They canceled our flight. **Husband:** What should we do? **Wife:** Well, we **could** take a later flight. **Husband:** What time's the next flight? **Wife:** At 8:30. Flight 3460. It leaves from the same gate. **Husband:** OK. We have to wait one hour. We could have dinner. **Wife:** Good idea.

Picture 3
Wife: Can we make the 14:45 bus? **Tour bus agent:** No, I'm sorry. It left. **Husband:** Oh, no! We missed our bus. What should we do? **Tour bus agent:** Well, you could take the 15:15 bus. It leaves in 30 minutes. **Wife:** OK. That's fine.

└──┘

Option: Role play. Have students write the conversation in dialogue form. Have volunteers act out their conversations in front of the class. **[+10 minutes]**

Option: Scrambled sentences. In pairs, have students write their conversations in dialogue form. Each group then writes each line of their conversation on a slip of paper, mixes up the order of the slips, and gives them to another group. The other group must then put the conversation back in the correct order. **[+10 minutes]**

Writing

- Before students begin writing, ask:

  What's the date in the first picture? (June 6th)
  What's the date in the second picture? (August 22nd)
  What's the date in the third picture? (August 23rd)

- Have students use the past tense to tell the story. Suggest that they give the couple names.

┌─ **Your students can say . . .** ─────────┐

On June 6th, [Mary and George Benson] went to a travel agent. She showed them different vacations. They liked the trip to Hawaii. They could relax and see interesting sites. They booked a volcano tour in Hawaii.

On August 22nd, [Mary and George] went to the airport. There was a problem. The airline canceled their flight. They had to take the next flight. It left an hour later. On August 23rd, [Mary and George] arrived at 14:45 for their tour. The bus left at 14:45. They just missed their bus. They had to wait for the next bus at 15:15.

[Mary and George] had a really nice time on their vacation, but they also had to wait a lot!

└──┘

Option: Have students use the simple present to write the story in the pictures. **[+10 minutes]**

┌─ **Individual oral progress check (optional)** ─┐

Use the illustration on page 111 for an oral test. Have students ask you questions about the pictures. For example, the student could point to the bus schedule in the last frame and ask *What bus should they take?* You could answer *They should take the 15:15 bus.* Evaluate students on correctness, intelligibility, and completeness.

└──┘

Cumulative Vocabulary Activities

You may wish to use the video for Unit 9 at this point. For video activity worksheets, go to www.longman.com/topnotch.

Complete Assessment Package
Unit 9 Achievement Test

- **Social language.** Choose one picture. Create a conversation for the people. Use <u>could</u> and <u>should</u>.

- **Writing.** Tell the story in the pictures. Use the times and dates.

GATE 12B

AUGUST 22			
HAWAIIAN AIRLINES TO HONOLULU			
FLIGHT	GATE	DEPARTURE	STATUS
3450	12B	07:30	CANCELED
3460	12B	08:30	ON TIME

June 6

CONSTELLATION HOTEL

Hawaii Volcano Tour

RA COSTAS

Hawaii
Volcano Tour

14:45

AUGUST 23

Volcano Tour
Bus Schedule
Departures
14:45
15:15
15:45

Now I can...

- ☐ discuss schedules and buy tickets.
- ☐ book travel services.
- ☐ understand airport announcements.
- ☐ describe transportation problems.

Hawaii
Volcano Tour

111

Shopping Smart

UNIT GOALS

1 Ask for a recommendation
2 Bargain for a lower price
3 Discuss tipping customs
4 Talk about a shopping experience

A > **TOPIC PREVIEW.** Look at the information in the travel guide for Toronto. Do you ever use traveler's checks, credit cards, or ATMs?

When you're in TORONTO …

TRAVELER'S CHECKS ▶
The easiest and safest way to carry money in Canada is in traveler's checks.

CREDIT CARDS
You can use credit cards at most stores and restaurants. However, some smaller businesses don't accept them. Make sure you always carry some cash.

◀ **CHANGING MONEY**
Banks usually offer the best exchange rates. Remember to bring your passport.

ATMs ▶
Get cash 24 hours a day from ATMs (called *bank machines* in Canada) at banks, bus and train stations, and large supermarkets.

▲ **TIPPING**
Leave a tip of about 10–15% of a restaurant bill or taxi fare. Restaurant bills for larger groups may include a service charge. Also tip hairdressers and hotel staff.

BARGAINING ▶
While shopping in Toronto, it's generally not the custom to bargain for a lower price.

75!
50!
65!

SOURCE: based on information from www.roughguides.com

B > **DISCUSSION.** How do you pay for things when you travel? Do you usually bargain for a lower price when you go shopping? Where is it OK to bargain? Are you a good bargainer?

Toronto
Ontario

Weston
Willowdale
Woodbridge

Shopping Smart

A TOPIC PREVIEW

Suggested teaching time:	10–15 minutes
Your actual teaching time:	_____

- If helpful, point out Toronto's location on a map of Canada. Let students know that the information on the travel guide page is based on customs in Toronto.

- After students read the page from the travel guide, make sure they understand the language in red. Read the descriptions that follow.

    Machine where you put your card in and take money out. (ATM)

    Leaving money for your waiter or waitress after you eat in a restaurant. (tipping)

    Similar to cash, but only you can use them. You sign them when you buy them and then again when you use them. (traveler's checks)

    Asking for a lower price. (bargaining)

    Trading money from one country for money for another country. (changing money)

    Small plastic cards that you can use to buy something now and pay for it later. (credit cards)

- Ask a few questions about the information in the travel guide. For example:

    How much should you tip at restaurants in Toronto? (10–15 percent)

    Where can you find ATM machines in Toronto? (at banks, bus and train stations, and large supermarkets)

    What should you bring with you when you want to change money? (your passport)

    Is it OK to bargain in Toronto? (No, not really.)

B DISCUSSION

Suggested teaching time:	10 minutes
Your actual teaching time:	_____

- After students discuss answers to the questions with a partner or in a small group, lead a class discussion. Ask:

    How do you usually pay for things when you travel?
    Where is it OK to bargain?
    Where is it not OK to bargain?

Option: Ask for two volunteers to stand and role-play bargaining for the class. Have them decide who is the clerk and who is the customer. Offer them an object to bargain over. **[+10 minutes]**

Option: Have students close their books. Say *You're going on a trip to Toronto. What should you do? What shouldn't you do?* Possible answers are:

    I should bring traveler's checks and credit cards.
    I should change money at banks.
    I should bring my passport.
    I should look for ATMs at banks, bus and train stations, and supermarkets.
    I should tip 10–15 percent in restaurants.
    I shouldn't bargain.

[+5 minutes]

C 🎧 SOUND BITES

Suggested teaching time: 10 minutes
Your actual teaching time: _____

- Have students look at the photos. Ask:
    What are the women doing? (shopping)
    What are the women looking at in the second picture? (a plate)
- After students read and listen, ask:
    What is Kay doing? (She's looking for a gift for her mother.)
    What's the problem? (She doesn't have much cash.)
    How does Amy say she can pay? (She can use a credit card.)
    Does Kay like the ceramic plate? (yes)
    What's the problem with it? (It's expensive.)
    What does Amy say she should do? (bargain / ask for a better price)

D UNDERSTANDING MEANING FROM CONTEXT

Suggested teaching time: 5–10 minutes
Your actual teaching time: _____

- After students complete the exercise, ask a few questions using the new language:
    *Imagine you're looking into your fridge right now. What do you have? What are you **out of**?*
    *Do you think the plate is really beautiful? What do you own that's **gorgeous**?*

WHAT ABOUT **YOU?**

Suggested teaching time: 10–15 minutes
Your actual teaching time: _____

- To review, ask several different students the question. Ask questions such as: *Are you often out of cash? How often do you [get money from an ATM] / [use a credit card]?*

EXTRAS (optional)

Workbook: Exercises 1, 2

C 🎧 **SOUND BITES.** Read along silently as you listen to a natural conversation.

KAY: Oh, no. I'm almost out of cash. And I'm looking for a gift for my mother.

AMY: That's OK. I'm sure these shops accept credit cards. Let's go in **CN** here. They have really nice stuff.

KAY: Good idea.

AMY: What about this?

KAY: It's gorgeous, but it's a bit more than I want to spend. **CN**

AMY: Maybe you could get a better price.

KAY: You think so?

AMY: Well, it can't hurt to ask.

D **UNDERSTANDING MEANING FROM CONTEXT.** Choose the best answer.

1. When Kay says, "I'm almost out of cash," she means _____.
   a. I don't have much money.   **b.** I have a lot of money.

2. When Amy says, "It can't hurt to ask," she means _____.
   a. It's a good idea to ask.   **b.** It's not a good idea to ask.

3. When Kay says, "It's gorgeous," she means _____.
   a. It's very pretty.   **b.** I don't really like it.

4. When Amy says, "Maybe you could get a better price," she means _____.
   a. This is a good price.   **b.** Bargain with the salesperson.

WHAT ABOUT **YOU?**

What do _you_ usually do when you're out of cash?

☐ I go to the bank.
☐ I use a credit card.
☐ I get money from an ATM.
☐ other _____.

CN **Corpus Notes:** "Accept credit cards" is more frequently used than "take credit cards," even though the verb "take" is much more common than the verb "accept."

CN **Corpus Notes:** In spoken American English, the word "gorgeous" is used to describe things much more often than it is used to describe people.

1 ▶ Ask for a Recommendation

🎧 CONVERSATION MODEL Read and listen.

A: I'm looking for a digital camera. Which is the least expensive?

B: The X80. But it's not the best. How much can you spend?

A: No more than 350.

B: Well, we've got some good ones in your price range.

A: Great. Could I have a look? **CN**

🎧 **Rhythm and intonation practice**

CN Corpus Notes:
"Take a look" is more common than "have a look" in American English, but both are acceptable.

A ▶ **GRAMMAR.** Superlative adjectives

Use superlative adjectives to compare more than two people, places, or things.

> Which camera is **the cheapest** of these three?
> Which brands are **the most popular** in your store?

adjective	comparative	superlative	adjective	comparative	superlative
cheap	cheaper	**the cheapest**	comfortable	more comfortable	**the most comfortable**
nice	nicer	**the nicest**	portable	more portable	**the most portable**
easy	easier	**the easiest**	difficult	less difficult	**the least difficult**
big	bigger	**the biggest**	expensive	less expensive	**the least expensive**

> **Irregular forms**
> good → better → **the best**
> bad → worse → **the worst**

GRAMMAR BOOSTER

PAGES G19–G20
For more . . .

B ▶ **Write the superlative form of the adjective. Use <u>the</u>.**

1. A: All of these cameras are easy to use.

   B: But which is ____the smallest____?
   <small>small</small>

2. A: All of our sweaters are pretty warm.

   B: But which brand makes ____the heaviest____ ones?
   <small>heavy</small>

3. A: She wrote at least six books about Italy. They're pretty interesting.

   B: Which of her books is ____the most interesting____?
   <small>interesting</small>

4. A: Do you want to take a taxi, bus, or train to the airport?

   B: Which is ____the most convenient____?
   <small>convenient</small>

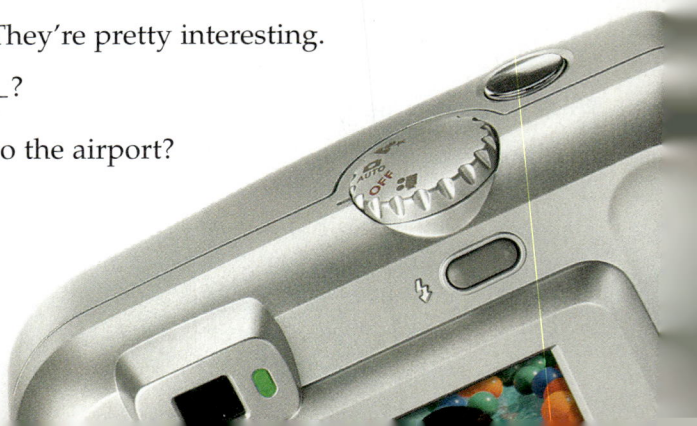

LESSON

1 ▶ Ask for a Recommendation

🎧 CONVERSATION **MODEL**

Suggested teaching time:	5–10 minutes
Your actual teaching time:	_____

• Have students look at the photo. Ask:
  Where are the women? (in a store / an electronics store)
  What are the women looking at? (a camera)
  Which one is the clerk? (the woman on the right)
  Which one is the shopper? (the woman on the left)

• After students read and listen, ask:
  What is the woman shopping for? (a digital camera)
  Is the X80 expensive or inexpensive? (inexpensive)
  Is it very good? (no)
  Are there good digital cameras for less than 350? (yes)

• Make sure students understand *in your price range.* Ask *How much can the shopper spend?* (no more than 350) Say *So any camera that costs less than 350 is in her price range. Is a camera that costs 400 in her price range?* (no)

Language note: When the currency is understood, it is common to just say a number, such as *three hundred fifty* or *three-fifty.* Feel free to substitute a price in a currency familiar to your students.

🎧 Rhythm and intonation practice

Suggested teaching time:	5 minutes
Your actual teaching time:	_____

• Have students find and circle *least* and *best.* Make sure students stress *least* and *best.*

• Ask students to underline the questions in the conversation and identify if they have falling or rising intonation.

• Have students repeat each line chorally. Make sure they use the following stress pattern:

┌─ **STRESS PATTERN** ──────────────────────┐

  • __ • • __ • • __   •
A: I'm looking for a digital camera.

  __   • • • __ •
Which is the least expensive?

  • __ • • • __   •
B: The X eighty. But it's not the best.

  __   • • • __
How much can you spend?

  __ __ • __ • __   •
A: No more than three fifty.

  __   • • __ • • • • __   •
B: Well, we've got some good ones in your price range.

  • • • __ •
A: Great. Could I have a look?

└──┘

🔶 A ❯ GRAMMAR

Suggested teaching time:	5–10 minutes
Your actual teaching time:	_____

• After students read the information in the Grammar box, ask:
  *Which is **warmer**, a cardigan or a blazer?* (a blazer)
  *Which is **the warmest**, a cardigan, a blazer, or a parka?* (a parka)
  *Which is **more expensive**, a bus trip or a flight?* (a flight)
  *Which is the **most expensive**, a bus trip, a flight, or a cruise?* (a cruise)
  *Which is **better**, Mexican food or Thai food?* (Answers will vary.)
  *Which is the **best**, Mexican food, Thai food, or Indian food?* (Answers will vary.)

• Explain that comparative adjectives are used to compare two people, places, or things. Superlative adjectives are used to compare three or more people, places, or things. Point out that students should use *the* with superlative adjectives (*the largest*).

• Ask *What's the difference between the adjectives on the left side of the box and the ones on the right side of the box?* (The adjectives on the right are longer / have more syllables.) Point out that with adjectives of two or more syllables, we use *most* or *least* to form the superlative.

• Have students find and underline the superlative adjectives in the travel guide on page 112. *(easiest, safest, most, best)*

Option: Practice superlative sentences with a transformation drill. Write on the board *This one is the nicest.* Say the adjective *cheap* and elicit from the class the sentence *This one is the cheapest.* Then point to a student and say *small.* Elicit the sentence *This one is the smallest.* In this manner, continue to elicit superlative sentences by prompting students with adjectives. **[+10 minutes]**

🌀 Grammar Self-Checks

🔶 B ❯ Write the superlative form . . .

Suggested teaching time:	5 minutes
Your actual teaching time:	_____

• To check their work, have students read the conversations with a partner.

• Have students check their spelling of *the heaviest* in item 2.

C ⌒ VOCABULARY

Suggested teaching time:	5 minutes
Your actual teaching time:	_____

• After students listen and repeat, ask *Which of these electronic products do you use regularly?*

Option: Write on the board:
> *Which of the electronic products do you think*
> *is generally . . .*
>   *. . . the most expensive?*
>   *. . . the cheapest?*
>   *. . . the most convenient?*
>   *. . . the most popular?*
>   *. . . the biggest?*
>   *. . . the smallest?*
>   *. . . the easiest to use?*
>   *. . . the most difficult to use?*

Have students discuss their answers to the questions in groups. **[+10 minutes]**

💿 **Vocabulary Cards**

D ⌒ LISTENING COMPREHENSION

Suggested teaching time:	10 minutes
Your actual teaching time:	_____

Challenge: Ask *What are the customers looking for in each electronic product?* Have students listen again for the superlative that describes the product in each conversation. (1. the best 2. the smallest 3. the fastest 4. the easiest to use) **[+10 minutes]**

AUDIOSCRIPT

CONVERSATION 1 [M = Indian]
F: Hi, I'm looking for a camcorder.
M: Are you looking for any particular brand?
F: Not really. Which one is the best?

CONVERSATION 2 [F2 = Portuguese]
F1: We've got three brands to choose from. They're all pretty small.
F2: Well, which MP3 player is the smallest?
F1: I'd say the X23 is a little smaller than the others.

CONVERSATION 3 [M = Chinese]
M: I need one that's really fast.
F: Well, these scanners over here are all pretty fast.
M: Yes, but which one is the fastest?

CONVERSATION 4 [M2 = Eastern European]
M1: Do you already have a digital camera?
M2: No, I don't. What do you recommend?
M1: I'd go with the Prego. It's the easiest to use.

CONVERSATION **PAIR WORK**

Suggested teaching time:	10–15 minutes
Your actual teaching time:	_____

• Before students practice the conversation, ask:
What electronic products do you see in the ads? (digital cameras, MP3 players, camcorders) For each ad, you can ask questions like:
> *What's the brand name?*
> *What's the model number?*
> *What's good about the _____?*
> *How much does the _____ cost?*
> *Which _____ is the cheapest?*
> *Which _____ is the easiest to use?*
> *Which _____ the most popular?*
> *Which _____ the most expensive?*

Option: Bring in ads for electronic products, or ask students to bring them in. Students use the ads to practice the conversation. **[+10 minutes]**

💿 **Pair Work Cards**

EXTRAS (optional)

Grammar Booster
Workbook: Exercises 3–6
Copy & Go: Activity 37

C ⌂ VOCABULARY. Electronic products. Listen and practice.

 **a digital camera**

 **a camcorder**

 **a DVD player**

 **an MP3 player**

 **a scanner**

D ⌂ LISTENING COMPREHENSION. Listen to the conversations at an electronics store. Then listen again and write the electronic product the people are talking about.

1. _a camcorder_   2. _an MP3 player_   3. _a scanner_   4. _a digital camera_

CONVERSATION
PAIR WORK

Ask for a recommendation. Use the ads, changing the prices to local currency if you wish. You can use this guide, or create a new conversation.

A: I'm looking for _____.
Which is the _____?

B: The _____. But it's not _____.
How much can you spend?

A: No more than _____.

B: _____ …

Continue the conversation in your <u>own</u> way . . .

...deas
...he nicest
...he most popular
...he lightest
...the most practical
...the easiest to use

MP3 Players

RICO SL-S225 **$129** *Practical*

PUSAN X23 **$109** *Easy to Use*

POWER X MUSIC MASTER **NEW! $199**

Digital Cameras

HONSHU X24 **$209** *Very Popular*

HONSHU B100 **$149**

PREGO 5 **NEW! $299**

Camcorders

VISION 720 **$949** *Very Light*

PUSAN 5X **$829** *Easy to Use*

DIEGO P500 **$679** *Popular*

CONTROLLED PRACTICE

115

Bargain for a Lower Price

🎧 **CONVERSATION MODEL** Read and listen.

A: How much do you want for that rug?

B: This one?

A: No, that one's not big enough. The other one.

B: 300.

A: That's a lot more than I want to pay. I can give you 200.

B: How about 225?

A: OK. That sounds fair.

🎧 **Rhythm and intonation practice**

A **GRAMMAR.** too and enough

When something is not satisfactory:

| Those rugs are **too small**. | OR | Those rugs are **not big enough**. |
| That camera is **too heavy**. | OR | That camera is **not light enough**. |

When something is satisfactory:

This PDA is **small enough**. I'll take it.

GRAMMAR BOOSTER

PAGE G21
For more . . .

B Complete the conversations with the adjectives from the box. Use **too** or **enough**.

| noisy | fast | expensive | small | hot | big |

1. A: That microwave oven needs to be <u>fast enough</u> for my family. We're very busy.
B: Oh, yes. The X11 is our fastest model.

2. A: These pumps aren't <u>big enough</u>. They're very uncomfortable.
B: I'm so sorry. Let me get you a larger size.

3. A: My photocopier is <u>too noisy</u>. It's driving me crazy!
B: Then let me show you a quieter model.

LESSON 2 *Bargain for a Lower Price*

🎧 CONVERSATION **MODEL**

Suggested teaching time:	10 minutes
Your actual teaching time:	_____

• Have students look at the photo. Ask:
  Where are the men? (in a store)
  What are the men looking at? (rugs, carpets)
  Which one is the salesperson? (the man on the right)
  Which one is the shopper? (the one on the left)

• After students read and listen, ask
  What is the original / first price for the rug? (300)
  How much does the shopper say he can pay? (200)
  What is the final price for the rug? (225)
  What did the shopper do? (He bargained for a lower price.)

Culture note: The acceptability of bargaining varies around the world. In some cultures, bargaining is expected and a merchant never expects the customer to accept the first price. In others, bargaining is very limited or discouraged altogether.

🎧 Rhythm and intonation practice

Suggested teaching time:	5 minutes
Your actual teaching time:	_____

• Have students repeat each line chorally. Make sure they:
  ◦ use falling intonation with *How much do you want for that rug?* and *How about 225?*
  ◦ use rising intonation with *This one?* (a shortened form of *Do you mean this one?*) Make sure students put stress on *this*.
  ◦ emphasize *that* in *No, that one's not big enough* and *other* in *The other one.*
  ◦ use the following stress pattern:

STRESS PATTERN

A: How much do you want for that rug?

B: This one?

A: No, that one's not big enough. The other one.

B: Three hundred.

A: That's a lot more than I want to pay.

I can give you two hundred.

B: How about two twenty-five?

A: OK. That sounds fair.

Ⓐ GRAMMAR

Suggested teaching time:	5–10 minutes
Your actual teaching time:	_____

• After students read the information in the Grammar box, have them look at the Conversation Model again. Ask *What was the problem with the first rug?* (It wasn't big enough.) Have students underline *not big enough* in the model. Then have students change *not big enough* to a phrase with *too* that has the same meaning. (too small) Have students read the first three lines of the new conversation with a partner.

• Draw a sad face on the board. Next to it write:
  <u>too</u> + *an adjective*
  <u>not</u> + *an adjective* + *enough*

• Draw a happy face on the board. Next to it write:
  an adjective + <u>enough</u>

• Say *Think of something you own that you don't like. Why don't you like it? Write a sentence with <u>too</u> or <u>enough</u>.* Ask a few students to read their sentences. Your students can say, for example, *My car is too old.*

• Say *Think of something you own that you like. Why do you like it? Write a sentence with enough.* Ask a few students to read their sentences. Your students can say, for example, *My computer is fast enough.*

💿 **Grammar Self-Checks**

Ⓑ Complete the conversations . . .

Suggested teaching time:	5–10 minutes
Your actual teaching time:	_____

• If helpful, explain that *noisy* means *loud*. It's the opposite of *quiet*. To make sure students understand, ask *What are some places that are noisy?* (concerts, cafeterias, basketball games)

• To check their work, have students read the conversations with a partner.

T116

C 🎧 PRONUNCIATION

Suggested teaching time:	5 minutes
Your actual teaching time:	_____

Option: Bring in clothing catalogs, or ask students to bring them in. Students practice using rising intonation to confirm the subject by asking about items in the catalog. For example: **A:** Do you like that jacket? **B:** The black one? **A:** Yes. **B:** I like it a lot. [+10 minutes]

💿 **Pronunciation Activities**

D 🎧 VOCABULARY

Suggested teaching time:	5 minutes
Your actual teaching time:	_____

• After students listen and repeat, ask questions about the handicrafts. Say *Look at this plate, this vase, this necklace, this bowl, this painting, and this rug.* Ask:
> *Which one do you think is . . .*
>> *. . . the most beautiful?*
>> *. . . the nicest gift?*
>> *. . . the most expensive?*
>> *. . . the least expensive?*
>> *. . . the most practical?*

💿 **Vocabulary Cards**

💿 **Learning Strategies**

CONVERSATION **PAIR WORK**

Suggested teaching time:	10–15 minutes
Your actual teaching time:	_____

• Tell students to point and use rising intonation when they say *This one?*
• Students can use a currency of their own choice to give prices.
• Student A can also say *That's too expensive* to begin bargaining.

💿 **Pair Work Cards**

EXTRAS (optional)

Grammar Booster
Workbook: Exercises 7–10
Copy & Go: Activity 38

💿 **Pronunciation Supplements**

4. A: We ordered the <u>hot</u> appetizers. These aren't <u>hot enough</u>.

   B: Of course, sir. I'll take care of that right away.

5. A: How about this pocket TV? It's pretty small.

   B: That's definitely <u>too small</u>. Thanks.

6. A: This jacket is a bargain. It's only $495.

   B: I'm sorry. That's just <u>too expensive</u> for me.

C ∩ **PRONUNCIATION.** **Confirming and clarifying information.** **Listen to the rising intonation to confirm. Then repeat.**

   A: How much is that rug?

   B: This one? ➚

   A: That's right.

   A: Could I have a look at that sweater?

   B: The red one? ➚

   A: No, the black one.

D ∩ **VOCABULARY.** **Handicrafts.** **Listen and practice.**

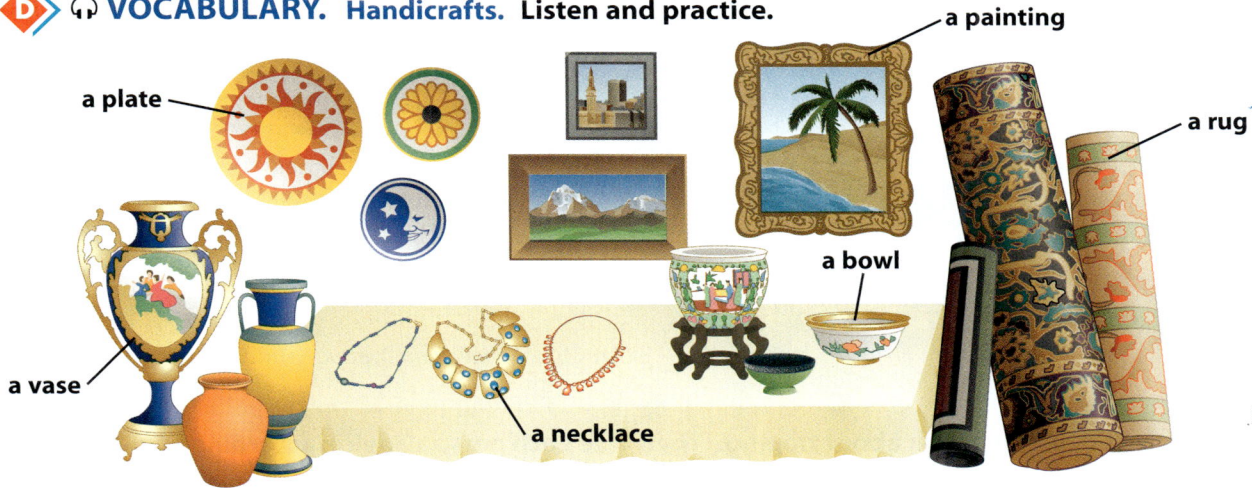

a plate · a painting · a rug · a bowl · a vase · a necklace

CONVERSATION
PAIR WORK

With a partner, bargain for a lower price. Use the pictures above, giving a price to each item. Start like this:

A: How much do you want for that _____?

B: This one?

A: _____ …

Continue the conversation in your <u>own</u> way . . .

3 ▶ Discuss Tipping Customs

Ⓐ READING WARM-UP. Do you think tipping is a good idea or a bad idea?

Ⓑ 🎧 READING. Read the article about tipping customs. Is any of the information surprising to you? Explain.

Did you remember to leave a tip?

In some countries tipping is very common. In others, tipping is not expected. Here are some tipping customs from around the world.

🇦🇺 Australia

Australians are pretty relaxed about tips—people do not usually expect them. Many people will be quite surprised if you give them a tip. Customers do leave a 10–15% tip in nicer restaurants, but don't tip taxi drivers. Instead, you can just say "Keep the change," and round off the fare.

🇫🇷 France

A service charge is almost always included on the bill in restaurants and cafés. If you are satisfied with the service, leave an additional small tip for the server. Tip porters about 1 euro for each piece of luggage, and leave the maid who cleans your hotel room about 1 euro per day. Taxi drivers expect 10–15% of the fare. And don't forget to tip your tour guide.

🇺🇸 🇨🇦 US and Canada

Tip waiters and taxi drivers anywhere from 15–20% of the total bill—depending on how satisfied you are with the service. A service charge is sometimes added to a restaurant bill if there are six or more people at the table, so you don't have to leave an additional tip. At airports and hotels, porters expect about $1 per bag. In some fast-food restaurants and coffee bars, there is a cup for small tips near the cashier.

Note: In some countries, it's not customary to give tip Before you travel, check local tipping customs to be su

SOURCES: *Lonely Planet, Rough Guide, Fodor's* travel guides

Ⓒ Read each person's question about tipping. Then give each person advice, according to the reading.

❝ I'm going to Paris, France. I'm staying in a small hotel for about six days. How much should I tip the maid? ❞

❝ I'm studying English in Sydney, Australia, and I just took a taxi home. The fare is AUS$3.60. How much should I give the taxi driver? ❞

❝ I'm visiting friends in Los Angeles, in the United States. I took ten people out for dinner. The bill is US$360. How much more should I leave for the tip? ❞

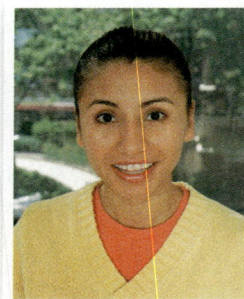

❝ I just arrived in Montreal, Canada, and took a taxi from the airport. The fare is CAN$6.90. How much should I tip the driver? ❞

3 ▶ *Discuss Tipping Customs*

A 🎧 READING WARM-UP

Suggested teaching time:	5 minutes
Your actual teaching time:	_____

Culture note: In some countries, tipping is unknown. If your students come from a country where tipping is not customary, they may have strong opinions about why it is a bad idea.

B 🎧 READING

Suggested teaching time:	10–15 minutes
Your actual teaching time:	_____

• After students read and listen, ask:
  Where is tipping not expected? (Australia)
  Where is it common? (France, the U.S. / Canada)

• Make sure students understand the phrase *round off the fare.* Write the following taxi fares/prices on the board. Round off the first fare. Ask students to round off the other fares. Substitute local currency for these dollar amounts:
  $4.75 ($5)
  $6.50 ($7)
  $3.40 ($4)

Option: Students read again and fill in the chart that follows with information from the reading.
[+10 minutes]

How much to tip each person?

	Australia	France	U.S. & Canada
a server in a restaurant	*no tip (10-15% in nicer restaurants)*	*included on the bill (can leave a small tip)*	*15-20% (included on the bill for 6+ people)*
a taxi driver	*round off the fare*	*10-15%*	*15-20%*
porters		*1 euro per bag*	*$1 per bag*
a hotel maid		*1 euro per day*	
others		*tour guide*	*tip cups*

💿 **Graphic Organizers**

Language note: Another word for *maid* is *housekeeper*; *chambermaid* is also used. Where the person who cleans the room is male, that person is referred to as a *housekeeper*.

💿 **Learning Strategies**

C Read each person's question . . .

Suggested teaching time:	10–15 minutes
Your actual teaching time:	_____

• Have students read the people's questions independently and then identify the country and the service for each one. (France, maid; Australia, taxi; U.S., restaurant server; Canada, taxi)

• Students note their advice below each photo. For help deciding what advice to give, students can refer to the charts they completed.

• With a partner, students take turns reading the people's questions and giving advice.

Your students can say . . .

You should tip the maid $6.
You should pay the taxi driver $4.
You should look at the bill. If there's a service charge, don't leave a tip. If there's not a service charge, leave $54–$72.
You should tip the driver $1–$1.50.

💿 **Extra Reading Comprehension Activities**

TOP NOTCH **INTERACTION**

Suggested teaching time:	20–25 minutes
Your actual teaching time:	_____

STEP 1

- Check students' understanding of *appreciation* from the context. Say *If you have good service, what do you want to say to the person who served you?* (thank you) *So to show appreciation is to express thanks.*

- After students complete the poll, see what the most popular opinions about tipping are. Read each item. Have students raise their hands for *agree, disagree,* or *not sure.* Note the most popular response for each item on the board. Discuss any items with *disagree* or *not sure* as the most popular opinion.

- Have students match the expression in the cartoon (*When in Rome, do as the Romans do!*) with one of the items on the opinion poll (item 2). Give other specific examples of following this advice. For example:

  When you're in Thailand, you should wear closed shoes to a temple.
  When in Egypt, women should cover their heads in a mosque.
  When you're in the U.S., you should tip 15–20 percent in restaurants.

  Elicit the meaning of the expression *When in Rome, do as the Romans do!* (When you're visiting another city, you should act like the local people do.)

Option: Have students write examples of *When in Rome, do as the Romans do!* for your city. Students can write their own sentences or they can complete the following statements:

  When you're in [your city], you should eat . . .
  When you're in [your city], you should drink . . .
  When you're in [your city], you should wear . . .
  When you're in [your city], you should play . . .
  When you're in [your city], you should listen to . . .
  When you're in [your city], you should watch . . .
  When you're in [your city], you should read . . .
  When you're in [your city], you should go to . . .
  When you're in [your city], you should . . .

[+10 minutes]

STEP 2

- Students can use *should* to write their tipping rules or to explain how to show appreciation for good service.

STEP 3

- Students can make changes to their rules based on their discussion with classmates. If their rules are different, they can also discuss the reason why their rules are different.

EXTRAS (optional)

  Copy & Go: Activity 39

STEP 1. What are your opinions about tipping when traveling in a country where tipping is customary? Take the opinion poll. Then compare your answers with your class.

When in Rome, do as the Romans do!

OPINION POLL

	I agree	I disagree	I'm not sure
1. Tipping is the best way to show appreciation for good service.	☐	☐	☐
2. When you're visiting another country, you should always follow its tipping customs.	☐	☐	☐
3. If the service is not good, you shouldn't tip.	☐	☐	☐
4. Restaurant bills should always include a service charge.	☐	☐	☐

STEP 2. PAIR WORK. On the notepad, write some suggestions for showing appreciation for good service in this country. If tipping is customary, explain how much to tip.

waiters / waitresses:

taxi drivers:

hotel maids:

baggage porters:

other:

STEP 3. GROUP WORK. In small groups, compare your notes. Does everyone agree?

4 ▶ Talk about a Shopping Experience

A 🎧 **VOCABULARY.** Talking about prices. **Listen and practice.**

She got a good price.

NOTE: Prices can be converted to local currency if you wish.

She saved a lot of money.

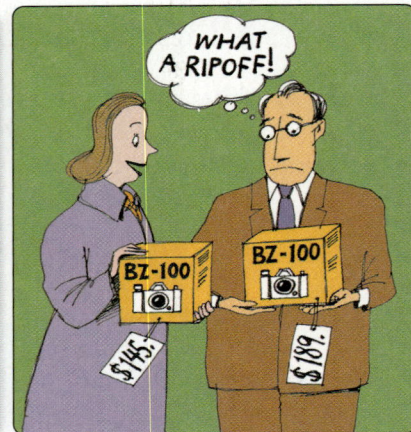

He paid too much. **CN**

CN **Corpus Notes:** The noun "ripoff" is used much more frequently in spoken rather than written American English. It is usually used in an informal way.

B 🎧 **LISTENING COMPREHENSION.** **Listen to the conversations about shopping. Then listen again and complete the chart.**

What did the shopper buy?	got a good price	saved a lot of money	paid too much
1. a bowl	✔		
2. a necklace	✓		
3. a camcorder			✓
4. a DVD player		✓	

C ▶ **DISCUSSION.** **Read this true story about a shopping experience. Then discuss the questions.**

Several years ago, I was in Saudi Arabia on business, and I wanted to buy a small rug. I wanted to spend no more than $350 USD. I found a beautiful and unusual rug, but the asking price was too high for me: $900. The salesman and I talked about the price for a long time. Finally, he shook my hand, and I thought that was the end of the conversation.

I left the store, and he looked very surprised. Then I was surprised! He actually had agreed to my offer of $350. That's why he shook my hand. Of course, I bought the rug. What a great deal!

1. How much money did the salesman want? How much did the shopper pay?

2. Why was the shopper surprised?

3. Do you think the shopper got a good price?

LESSON

4 Talk about a Shopping Experience

A 🎧 VOCABULARY

Suggested teaching time:	5–10 minutes
Your actual teaching time:	_____

- Before students listen and repeat, have them look at the pictures. Ask:
  What is the BZ-100? (a [digital] camera)
  How much did the woman in the first picture pay for the BZ-100? ($145)
  How much did the woman in the second picture pay for the BZ-100? ($99)
  How much did the man in the third picture pay for the BZ-100? ($189)
  Who got the best price? (the woman in the second picture)
  Who got the worst price? (the man in the third picture)

- Make sure students understand *saved, a deal,* and *a rip-off.*

  ◦ Have students look at the second picture. Ask:
  What is the regular price for the BZ-100? ($150)
  How much did the woman pay? ($99)
  So how much did she save? ($51)

  ◦ Point to the woman in the second picture. Say *She paid the lowest price. She got a great deal.* Then point to the man in the third picture. Say *He paid the highest price. He paid too much.*

Option: Give high, low, and fair prices for electronic or other items. Have the class say whether the price is *a rip-off, a great deal,* or *a good price.* **[+5 minutes]**

Language note: Students should be careful with *What a rip-off!* It can be rude in certain situations. For example, it's not OK to say *What a rip-off!* directly to a salesperson. It is more appropriate for complaining to a friend about a bad purchase at a later time.

🔹 **Vocabulary Cards**

B 🎧 LISTENING COMPREHENSION

Suggested teaching time:	10 minutes
Your actual teaching time:	_____

Option: Have students listen again and note how much each person paid. For item 4, students can listen for how much the man saved. **[+5 minutes]**

AUDIOSCRIPT

CONVERSATION 1 [F = Sri Lankan]
M: I just got some gifts for my family. Look.
F: How much did you pay for that bowl?
M: It's really nice, isn't it? I paid 250 pesos.
F: It's beautiful. I think you got a pretty good price.

CONVERSATION 2
F: Look at this great souvenir I bought.
M: What a beautiful necklace! Very nice! Was it expensive?
F: No. Only 30 pounds.
M: No kidding! It looks much more expensive than that.

CONVERSATION 3 [M2 = Arabic]
M1: I got a really great price on this camcorder.
M2: Do you think? How much was it?
M1: Only twelve hundred euros.
M2: Twelve hundred euros? You paid way too much. A camera like that should cost less.

CONVERSATION 4
M: Guess what? I just saved a ton of money on this DVD player.
F: How did you do that?
M: They were having a sale. $100 off.
F: Wow. What a deal!

C DISCUSSION

Suggested teaching time:	10–15 minutes
Your actual teaching time:	_____

- After students read independently, ask:
  What did the shopper buy? (a rug)
  Where did he buy it? (in Saudi Arabia)
  Did he bargain? (Yes, he did.)
  In Saudi Arabia, when a salesperson shakes your hand, what does it mean? (that he agrees to your price)
  Did the shopper understand this? (no)
  What did he do? (He left the store.)

- Make sure students know that *USD* stands for *U.S. dollars.*

TOP NOTCH **INTERACTION**

Suggested teaching time:	20–25 minutes
Your actual teaching time:	_____

STEP 1

• Ask the first question (*In your own city or town, what is the best restaurant?*) to the whole class. Elicit opinions. When students give their opinions, ask *Why?*

• Pairs discuss the questions and note a local place for each one. Students should also talk about why they think each place is the best, nicest, etc.

STEP 2

• Each pair of students can join another pair to form a group.

• Point out that students can say *I / We agree* or *I / We disagree* and then give their own opinion.

Option: Take a class poll. Write the ten categories (best restaurant, nicest hotel, etc.) as headings on the board. Students write their choices under the headings. Remind students to look at the places already listed and not write the same place twice. Then read the places listed. Have students vote for one place in each category by raising their hands. **[+10 minutes]**

STEP 3

• Say *Have you ever bargained for a lower price? Was it a good experience or a bad experience? What happened?* If students have never bargained, they can write notes about some other good or bad shopping experience.

• In addition to the questions on the notepad, have students note whether they got a good price, saved a lot of money, or paid too much.

STEP 4

• Before students begin writing, tell your own story about a good or bad shopping experience.

• Students use their notepads to write the story. They can also use the story on page 120 as a model.

┌─ **Your students can say . . .** ─────────────┐

Two summers ago, I went to Morocco with a friend. We went shopping, ate good food, and practiced our Arabic. I saw a beautiful vase. The saleswoman wanted $60 Canadian. That wasn't in my price range. I only had $40 cash. I offered her $30. She said $35. Then I said $33. She agreed. I got the vase for $33. I saved $27. What a great deal!

└──┘

Challenge: Students read a classmate's story. Based on the story, they create a conversation between their classmate / the shopper and a salesperson. To model the activity, create a conversation as a class between the shopper and the salesman in the story on page 120. **[+10 minutes]**

Challenge: Students act out the conversations they created. **[+10 minutes]**

🔄 **Writing Process Worksheets**

EXTRAS (optional)

Workbook: Exercises 11, 12
Copy & Go: Activity 40

INTERACTION • *It's the Best!*

STEP 1. PAIR WORK. Discuss the questions with a partner.

1. In your own city or town, what is . . .
   - the best restaurant?
   - the nicest hotel?
   - the most expensive department store?
   - the most unusual market?
   - the most interesting museum?

2. Where can you buy . . .
   - the least expensive fruits and vegetables?
   - the nicest flowers?
   - the best electronics products?
   - the most unusual souvenirs?
   - the wildest clothes?

STEP 2. DISCUSSION. Discuss your choices.

> " The Savoy Hotel has the biggest rooms and the best food. "

> " The Central Market is too expensive. The fruits and vegetables at the Old Town Market are much better and cheaper. "

STEP 3. On your notepad, write notes about a good or bad shopping experience you had. Then tell the class about your experience.

What did you buy?	
Where did you buy it?	
How much money did the salesperson want?	
Did you bargain?	
How much did you pay?	

STEP 4. WRITING. Write the story of your shopping experience.

UNIT 10
CHECKPOINT

A 🎧 **LISTENING COMPREHENSION.** Listen to the conversations and write the name of the item. Then listen again critically. Check ☑ if the item is satisfactory or not satisfactory to the customer.

		satisfactory	not satisfactory
1.	_a camcorder_	☐	☑
2.	a necklace	☑	☐
3.	paintings	☐	☑
4.	a digital camera	☑	☐

B **Complete the sentences.**

1. If you're out of cash, you can get money from _____an ATM_____.

2. If there's a service charge on the restaurant bill, you don't have to leave a _____tip_____.

3. In many countries, it's OK to _____bargain_____ for a lower price.

4. You can get the best _____exchange rates_____ at banks.

5. _____Traveler's checks_____ are a safe and easy way to carry money when traveling.

6. What a ripoff. I paid _____too much_____.

7. Wow! What a great deal. I _____saved_____ a lot of money.

C **Write each sentence in another way. Use <u>too</u> or <u>enough</u>.**

1. That vase is too heavy. _That vase isn't light enough_.

2. Those cameras aren't cheap enough. _Those cameras are too expensive_.

3. This PDA is too big. _This PDA isn't small enough_.

4. These drinks aren't cold enough. _These drinks are too warm_.

5. That restaurant is too noisy. _That restaurant isn't quiet enough_.

D **Write sentences about stores in your city. Use the superlative.**

Winston's Department Store has the cheapest clothing.

1. _____.

2. _____.

3. _____.

4. _____.

🎧 **TOP NOTCH SONG**
"Shopping for Souvenirs"
Lyrics on last book page.

TOP NOTCH PROJECT
With a partner, write advice about tipping customs for a traveler to this country.

E **WRITING.** On a separate sheet of paper, use your sentences to write a paragraph for a visitor to this city.

TOP NOTCH WEBSITE
For Unit 10 online activities, visit the Top Notch Companion Website at www.longman.com/topnotch.

UNIT 10 CHECKPOINT

A. LISTENING COMPREHENSION

Suggested teaching time:	5–10 minutes
Your actual teaching time:	_____

Challenge: Students listen again and write the problem with the two items that are not satisfactory. Have students use *too + [adjective]* or *not + [adjective] + enough* to express the problem. (Answers: 1. too expensive; 3. too big, not pretty enough) **[+10 minutes]**

AUDIOSCRIPT

CONVERSATION 1 [M = Korean; F = Japanese]
M: Can I help you, ma'am?
F: I'm looking for a small camcorder.
M: Well, we have several brands. This one is the smallest.
F: It's nice, but it's more than I want to spend.

CONVERSATION 2
F: Can I help you, sir?
M: Yes. How much do you want for that necklace?
F: Which one? This one?
M: That's right.
F: Oh, that's a nice one. Is it for your wife?
M: Yes.

CONVERSATION 3 [M = Arabic]
M: What about this one, ma'am?
F: No, that one's too big.
M: How about this one?
F: No, that one's not pretty enough. Are these the only paintings you have?
M: No. We have more in the back.

CONVERSATION 4
F: How much can you spend?
M: No more than three hundred.
F: Well, this is a very nice digital camera in your price range.
M: Great. Let me have a look.

B. Complete the sentences.

Suggested teaching time:	5 minutes
Your actual teaching time:	_____

• If students need help, refer them to pages 112 and 120.

C. Write each sentence . . .

Suggested teaching time:	5 minutes
Your actual teaching time:	_____

• If necessary, ask students the opposites of *heavy, cheap, big, cold,* and *noisy* before they begin work on the exercise. (light, expensive, small, warm/hot, quiet)

D. Write sentences . . .

Suggested teaching time:	5 minutes
Your actual teaching time:	_____

• Students can look back at Step 1, item 2 on page 121 for ideas.

Option: Students can read their sentences to a partner. Partners say whether they agree or disagree with each sentence. **[+5 minutes]**

E. WRITING

Suggested teaching time:	10–15 minutes
Your actual teaching time:	_____

Option: Create an opening sentence for students' paragraphs as a class; for example, *When you're in [your city], shop where the local people shop.* **[+5 minutes]**

Top Notch Pop Song Activities

TOP NOTCH PROJECT
Idea: Students should use their notepads to write about their country's tipping customs. After students write about tipping customs in their country, they can look at a travel guide for their country and compare their rules/advice with the book's.

Idea: Have students research tipping customs in a country they plan to visit or would like to visit.

T122

UNIT WRAP-UP

Suggested teaching time: 15–20 minutes
Your actual teaching time: _____

Vocabulary

> **Your students can say . . .**
>
> necklaces, purses, belts, vases, gloves, rugs, bowls, digital cameras, camcorders, laptops, an ATM, a taxi, luggage, computers, shoes, T-shirts, sweaters, shorts, a hotel

Option: Memory game. Students look at the picture for 20 seconds and then close their books. In teams, students state one sentence about the picture. If the sentence is true, the team gets a point. If the team says something that is not true (for example, *There's a movie theater in the picture*) they do not get a point. Each team can make only one sentence at a time. Each sentence can be used only once. Students may not make notes or use notes made for prior activities. **[+10 minutes]**

Social language

> **Your students can say . . .**
>
> (the shoppers at the top left)
> **Man:** Do you like this T-shirt? **Woman:** Not really. It's too wild, and it's not warm enough. What about that sweater? **Man:** The [color] one? **Woman:** No, the [color + "one" or style, e.g. blue turtleneck]. **Man:** It's too boring.
>
> (the salesman and the shopper at the top right)
> **Salesman:** Can I help you? **Shopper:** I'm looking for a gift for my sister. **Salesman:** What about this rug? **Shopper:** It's gorgeous. How much do you want for it? **Salesman:** $200. **Shopper:** That's a lot more than I want to spend. I can give you $100. **Salesman:** How about $150? **Shopper:** OK. That sounds fair.
>
> (the shopper and the electronics salesman)
> **Shopper:** I'm looking for a [what the salesman is pointing at]. Which one is the best? **Salesman:** The GX1000. It's [adjective appropriate for item] and [adjective appropriate for item]. **Shopper:** Sounds great. **Salesman:** But it's not the cheapest. **Shopper:** How much is it? **Salesman:** [Price appropriate for item, a little high because it's the best] **Shopper:** That's in my price range. Could I have a look?
>
> (the man and woman standing in front of the ATM)
> **Man:** Oh, no. I'm almost out of cash. What should I do? **Woman:** You could use the ATM. **Man:** Good idea. Thanks. **Woman:** No problem.
>
> (the woman and man holding sweaters)
> **Woman:** Come take a look. I got a great deal on this sweater. **Man:** Really? How much did you pay? **Woman:** $15. **Man:** I bought the same sweater. It was $55. **Woman:** You paid too much. Where did you buy it? **Man:** At Lane's Department Store. What a rip-off!

Option: Role play. Have two volunteers act out their conversation in front of the class. Have the class listen and guess which people in the picture they are portraying. **[+10 minutes]**

Writing

- Remind students to use the present continuous to describe what people are doing. Remind them not to use the present continuous with *have, want, need,* or *like*.

- To talk about the couple with the sweaters, students need to tell what happened before the moment pictured. They should use the past tense.

- Students may also include some sentences about what people are going to do next.

Option: Have students tell the story in the past tense. **[+10 minutes]**

> **Your students can say . . .**
>
> A man and woman are shopping for clothes. They're looking at a wild T-shirt. / A woman is buying a rug for her sister. She's bargaining for a lower price. / A woman is at an electronics store. She's looking for a digital camera. / There's a great deal on DataWhiz at the electronics store. DataWhiz is the most popular brand. Lots of people are buying them. / A woman is changing money at the bank. Banks have the best exchange rates. / A man is almost out of cash. He's going to use the ATM. / A woman and a man bought the same sweater. The woman got a great deal. She saved a lot of money. The man paid too much. / A woman is tipping a porter at the Top Notch Hotel. She's giving him $1. / A man is tipping a taxi driver. He's going to stay at the hotel.

> **Individual oral progress check (optional)**
>
> Use the illustration on page 123 for an oral test. Divide the class into pairs. Have each pair select two people in the picture and then role-play, asking and answering questions. For example, students could point to the man and woman holding sweaters in the front of the currency exchange and say **A:** *How much did you pay for that sweater?* **B:** *$55.* **A:** *I paid $15 for my sweater. You paid too much.* Evaluate students on correctness, intelligibility, and completeness.

Cumulative Vocabulary Activities

You may wish to use the video for Unit 10 at this point. For video activity worksheets, go to www.longman.com/topnotch.

Complete Assessment Package
Unit 10 Achievement Test
Review Test 2
Speaking Test 2

UNIT WRAP-UP

- **Vocabulary.** Name all the things you can in the picture.
- **Social language.** Create conversations for the people.
- **Writing.** Describe what the people are doing.

CURRENCY EXCHANGE

TODAY'S RATES
US
UK
JP
EU

ATM

SALE
25% OFF
EVERYTHING
GUARANTEED

TOP NOTCH
HOTEL

DataWhiz
OUR # 1 BRAND

$15 USD

$55 USD

TAXI

✓ *Now I can...*

- ☐ ask for a recommendation.
- ☐ bargain for a lower price.
- ☐ discuss tipping customs.
- ☐ talk about a shopping experience.

Alphabetical word list

This is an alphabetical list of all productive vocabulary in the **Top Notch 1** units. The numbers refer to the page on which the word first appears or is defined. When a word has two meanings, both are in the list.

A

a/an   56
absolutely   80
accept   58
accessory   76
accident   108
across the street   20
activity   88
actress   5
address   20
aerobics   64
agent   106
air-conditioning   48
airline   105
airplane   109
airport   66
aisle seat   102
alike   34
almost always   68
always   68
amazing   89
an   56
another   79
appetizer   52
apple   55
appliance   45
appropriate   84
around the corner   20
arrival   102
arrive   100
art exhibit   19
artist   6
at   18
athlete   6
athletic field   69
ATM   112
aunt   28
avoid   70
awesome   42
awful   44

B

back   82
bad   78
bag   76
baggage porter   118
banana   55
bank   113
bargain   116
baseball game   93
basement   82
basketball   64

basketball player   5
bathrobe   76
bathroom   45
be   90
beach   89
beautiful   78
bedroom   45
bedtime   17
beef   55
belt   76
better   78
between   20
beverage   52
big   78
bike riding   64
black   79
blazer   80
blond   38
blue   81
boarding pass   105
book   104
boring   91
both   34
bottled water   53
boxers   76
brand   42
bread   55
briefs   79
broccoli   55
brother   28
brother-in-law   28
brown   78
bullet train   101
bumpy   90
bus   109
business   4
busy   18
but   34
butter   55
buy   77

C

cake   55
call   93
camcorder   115
can   66
cancel   96
cancellation   106
candy   55
cardigan   80
carrot   55
cash   80
casual   83
CD burner   43
CD player   44

cell phone   43
certainly   80
change money   112
charge   80
cheap   78
check   58
cheese   55
chef   10
chicken   55
child   28
choice   53
clam   55
class   6
classical music   16
classmates   8
clean   64
clerk   77
clogged   48
close   48
clothes   76
clothing   79
coat   82
coconut oil   55
coffee   54
coffee maker   44
coffee shop   82
color   79
come   8
comfortable   91
complain   48
complaint   48
computer programmer   10
concert   19
conservative   85
convenient   46
cook   64
cookie   55
corn oil   55
corner   20
couch potato   65
could   103
cousin   28
crab   55
crazy   41
credit card   58
crew neck   80
cruise   90
culture   84
cute   29

D

dairy product   55
dancing   64
dark   86

daughter   5
decline   18
delay   106
delayed   100
delicious   57
depart   100
department   76
department store   76
departure   102
dessert   53
destination   109
different   34
difficult   114
digital camera   115
dinner   64
direct flight   102
directions   20
dish   57
divorced   31
do aerobics   64
down the street   20
dress   78
dress code   85
drink   92
DVD player   115

E

early   17
easy   114
eat   54
egg   54
either   34
electronic product   115
electronics   43
elevator   82
e-mail address   11
English   64
enough   116
entertainment   19
entrée   52
escalator   82
evening   68
event   19
every day   65
every weekend   65
exciting   94
expensive   78
express   102

F

fair   116
family   28

family member   31
family name   4
fan   17
fast   116
father   28
father-in-law   28
fatty   60
favorite   24
fax machine   44
ferry   109
fine   78
first   82
first name   4
fish   55
flats   80
flight   90
flight attendant   10
flight number   105
flush   48
fly   92
food   55
free   18
fridge   48
fried   56
from   6
front   82
fruit   55
funny sound   48

G

gadget   40
gate   105
get   92
get bumped   108
get seasick   108
get to know   4
get up   72
gift   77
gift wrap   77
given name   4
glasses   38
gloves   79
go   18
go down   82
go out (to eat)   54
go up   82
golf   64
golf course   69
good   78
good time   92
gorgeous   113
grains   55
grandfather   28
grandmother   28

grandparent   28
grape   55
graphic designer   10
great   42
green   81
grilled   53
ground floor   82
guaranteed   46
guitar   64
guy   29
gym   68

H

hair dryer   44
hardly ever   68
have   30
have to   66
he   8
health   60
healthful   60
healthy   60
heavy   78
helicopter   109
hello   44
her (possessive adjective)   8
hers (possessive pronoun)   80
Hi   44
him   80
hip-hop music   25
his   8
history   88
hometown   12
hosiery   76
hot   78
hot sauce   57
hotel maid   118
hotel reservation   104
house   64
housework   36
how many   32
how much   116
how often   68
how old   8
hurry   101
husband   28

I

I   8
ice   53
important   77
in   18
in moderation   60
in shape   70

in the evening 68
inappropriate 84
incredible 89
inexpensive 42
in-law 28
interesting 94
interpreter 10
introduce 5
invitation 18
iron 48
it 8
its 8

J
jacket 78
jazz 16
jeans 80
juice 54
junk food 70

K
kids 29
kitchen 45

L
lamb 55
language 4
laptop 43
large 78
last name 4
Latin music 16
leather 76
leave 92
left 20
length 78
less 78
lettuce 54
liberal 84
lift weights 64
light 78
like 30
limousine 104
lingerie 76
live 30
living room 45
loafers 80
local 102
location 20
long 78
look 30
loose 78

M
machine 41
main course 53
make (a bus or
   train) 102
manager 10
married 4
me 80
meal 60
means 109
meat 55
mechanical
   problems 108
medium 77
meet 8

memory 109
men 4
menu 52
microwave oven
   44
milk 55
miss 108
Miss 4
model 42
modest 84
more 78
morning 68
mother 28
mother-in-law 28
movie 19
MP3 player 115
Mr. 4
Mrs. 4
Ms. 4
much 54
museum 21
musician 10
my 8

N
nationality 4
nature 88
need 68
nephew 28
never 65
nice 114
nickname 8
niece 28
nightgown 76
noisy 116
non-stop flight
   102
noodles 55

O
occupation 4
office 64
often 68
oils 55
OK 89
old 81
olive oil 55
on 18
on sale 76
on time 100
on the corner 20
on the left side
   20
on the right side
   20
once a week 65
once in a while
   65
one way 102
onion 55
only child 31
open 48
orange 55
order 53
our 8

out of cash 113
out of shape 70
outerwear 76
overbooking 106
oxfords 80

P
pack 84
pair 78
pajamas 76
panties 79
pants 79
pantyhose 79
parent 28
park 69
passenger 106
pasta 55
pay 80
PDA 43
pepper 55
phone 64
photo 29
photo album 28
photocopier 44
photographer 10
physical 88
pie 55
piece of junk 44
pilot 10
play *n* 19
play *v* 64
polo shirt 80
pool 69
pop music 24
popular 46
portable 46
portion 60
pretty *adj* 78
pretty *adv* 42
price 77
price range 114
printer 41
problem 48
pumps 80
purse 83

R
R&B music 25
rain 93
rap music 25
read 64
recommendation
   115
red 77
regularly 70
relationship 28
relaxing 94
religious
   institution 85
rent a car 104
rental car 104
reserve 105
restaurant 83
rice 55
right 20

rock 16
room 49
round-trip 102
rug 116
running 64
running shoes 76

S
salad 52
sale 76
salesperson 10
salt 54
salty 61
sandals 80
sandwich 54
sausage 55
save 120
scanner 115
scary 91
scenic 91
schedule 102
seafood 55
second 82
security 106
selection 77
service 77
she 8
shopper 77
shopping 64
short 38
shorts 76
should 103
shower 64
shrimp 55
side 20
sightseeing 89
similar 34
singer 5
single 4
sink 48
sister 28
sister-in-law 28
size 77
skirt 84
skydiving 69
sleep 64
sleepwear 76
sleeves 84
small 78
snack 60
soccer 64
socks 76
sometime 66
sound 116
soup 52
souvenir 121
speak 4
special 76
spell 3
spend 92
spicy 57
squid 55
stairs 82
stapler 3

steal 96
stop 93
store directory 83
straight 82
strict 84
student 5
study 4
stuff 113
style 17
suggestion 42
superlative 114
sweater 77
sweatpants 80
sweatshirt 80
sweet 61
sweet tooth 70
sweets 55
swimming 64

T
take 82
take a shower 64
take a taxi 104
talk 19
tall 38
taxi 104
taxi driver 118
teacher 5
tennis 64
tennis court 69
terrible 44
terrific 42
than 78
the 56
theater 20
their 8
them 80
there are 54
there is 54
they 8
third 82
ticket 102
tights 76
time 18
tip *n* 58
tip *v* 112
title 4
today 68
toilet 48
tomato 52
tonight 68
too 34
top floor 82
track (athletic)
   69
track (train) 101
traffic 90
train 109
transportation
   109
travel 4
travel agency 83
traveler's check
   112

trip 89
try on 77
T-shirt 80
turn 82
turn off 48
turn on 48
turtleneck 80
TV 43
twins 31

U
uncle 28
underwear 76
unfriendly 96
unisex 76
unusual 94
us 8
usually 68

V
vacation 94
vegetable 55
visit 92
V-neck 80

W
wait 93
waiter 118
waitress 118
walking 64
want 68
warm 78
was 90
watch 64
water 56
waterproof 78
we 8
weather 89
weekend 65
weights 64
were 90
what 8
what time 32
when 68
where 8
who 8
widowed 31
wife 5
wild 121
wildlife 88
windbreaker 76
window 48
window seat 102
women 4
work *n* 65
work *v* 30
worse 78
wrong 41

Y
yogurt 55
you 8
your 8

Z
zoo 93

Social language list

This is a unit-by-unit list of all the productive social language from *Top Notch 1*.

Welcome to *Top Notch!*

Hi, my name's [Peter].
I'm [Alexandra].
Everyone calls me [Alex].
Good morning. / Good afternoon.
Good evening. / Good night.
What do you do?
I'm a [student]. And you?

[Alex], this is [Emily]. [Emily], this is [Alex].
Nice to meet you, [Emily].
Well, it was nice meeting you.
See you later.
Bye. / Good-bye.
Take it easy. / Take care.
What's this called in English?

That's right.
How do you say [your last name]?
What's your [last name], please?
I'm sorry. Could you repeat that?
Sure.
How do you spell [your first name]?
Thanks. / Thank you.

Unit 1

This is [my teacher].
Please call me [Tom].
Let me introduce you to [my wife, Carol].
Good to meet you.
Pleasure to meet you.
Are you [Bill]?

No, I'm [David].
That's [Bill] over there.
Are you [a student]?
As a matter of fact, [I am].
Is she from [São Paulo]?
Those are the [new students].
Who's that?

Come. I'll introduce you.
I'd like you to meet [Kate].
What's your name?
Where's he from?
How old are they?
Could you say that louder?

Unit 2

Do you want to see [a concert] on [Saturday]?
That's not for me.
I'm not really a [rock] fan.
What about [Sergio Mendes]?
Now that's more my style!
There's a [show] at [eleven thirty].
That's past my bedtime!
No problem.

Perfect.
See you then.
Are you free on [Friday]?
Really? (to show enthusiasm)
I'd love to go.
I'd love to go, but I'm busy on [Friday].
What time?
Too bad.
Maybe some other time.

When's the [concert]?
What time's the [movie]?
Where's the [play]?
Excuse me. (to get someone's attention)
I'm looking for [The Bell Theater].
That's right [around the corner], on the [left] side of the street.
I'm sorry, I'm not from around here.
Thanks, anyway.

Unit 3

What are you up to?
Come take a look.
Let me see.
Who's that [guy]? / Who are [those two]?
Really! (to show surprise)
Tell me something about [your family].
Sure.
What do you want to know?

Do you have any [brothers or sisters]?
I have [one younger sister].
Do they look like you?
Not really.
So what does [your sister] do?
That's great!
How about [your brother]?
How many [children] do you have?
How are you alike?

How are you different?
Do you look alike?
We wear similar clothes.
Do you both [like basketball]?
She [likes basketball], and I do too.
She doesn't [like fish], and I don't either.
He [likes coffee], but I don't.

Unit 4

This [printer] is driving me crazy!
It's not working.
It's just a lemon!
What do you mean?
What's wrong with it?
Hey, [Bob]! (as a greeting)
What are *you* doing here? (to express surprise)

I'm looking for [a laptop].
Any suggestions?
What about [a Pell]?
Really? (to ask for clarification)
How's it going?
Fine, thanks.
I'm sorry to hear that.
That's too bad. / That's a shame.

The [window] won't open / close.
The [iron] won't turn on / off.
The [fridge] is making a funny sound.
The [toilet] won't flush.
The [toilet] won't stop flushing.
The [sink] is clogged.
Hello? (to answer the telephone)
This is room [211]. Can I help you?

Unit 5

Are you ready to order?
Do you need some more time?
I think I'll start with [the soup].
Then I'll have [the chicken].
That comes with [salad], doesn't it?

There's a choice of vegetables.
Tonight we have [carrots].
Certainly.
Anything [to drink]? / And [to drink]?
What is there to [eat]?

Is that all?
I'm in the mood for [seafood].
Sorry. You're out of luck.
Let's go out!
Good idea!

I'll have the [pasta] for my [main course].
What does that come with?
What kind of [soup] is there?
I think I'll have the [salad].
What do you feel like eating [tonight]?
The [special] sounds delicious.

What about the [chicken]?
Sounds good.
Excuse me! (to get attention in a restaurant)
We're ready to order.
Would you like to start with [an appetizer]?

And for your [main course]?
We have [a nice seafood special] on the menu.
We'll take the check, please.
Is the tip included?
Do you accept credit cards?

Unit 6

Where are you off to?
I'm on my way to [the park].
Do you want to play together sometime?
That would be great.
No way.
He's a couch potato.
Too bad.

I'm crazy about [tennis].
Why don't we [play basketball] sometime?
Great idea.
When's good for you?
Sorry, I can't. (to express regret)
I have to [meet my sister at the airport].
That sounds great.

You too?
Actually, I usually go [in the evening].
How come?
Well, have a great time.
He's in shape / out of shape.
We don't eat junk food.
[They] avoid sweets.
[I have] a sweet tooth.

Unit 7

Excuse me. (to ask for assistance in a shop)
How much is that [V-neck] / are those [pants]?
That's not too bad.
Do you have it / them in [a larger size]?
It is / These are too [short].
Here you go.
Would you like to try it / them on?
No, thanks.

Would you be nice enough to [gift wrap it / them for me]?
Of course.
We have a pair in [brown].
See if they are better.
Let me see if I can find you something better.
Yes, they're fine.
I'll take the [loafers].
How would you like to pay for them?

Excuse me? (to ask for clarification)
Cash or charge?
Go straight.
Turn left / right.
Go down / up the stairs.
Take the escalator / elevator / stairs.
It's on the top / first / ground floor.
It's in the basement.
It's in the front / back.

Unit 8

When did you get back?
Just [yesterday].
Tell me about your trip.
I had a [really great] time.
I'll bet the [food] was [great].
Amazing! (to express delight)
How was the [flight]?
I was [pretty bumpy], actually.

Let me help you with your [things].
Thanks a lot.
Did you just get in?
My [flight] was [a little late].
Welcome back!
OK.
What did you do [last weekend]?
Nothing special.

What about you?
It was so [relaxing].
[The weather] was terrible.
[The people] were unfriendly.
They canceled [my flight].
Someone stole [my wallet].

Unit 9

Do you speak [English]?
I'm looking for [the bullet train].
Which one?
I'm taking that, too.
You can follow me.
It leaves from [track 15].
We should hurry.
By the way, where are you from?
No kidding!

What a small world!
Can we make the [2:00 bus]?
It left / departed [five minutes] ago.
Oh, no!
What should we do?
One way or round-trip?
I'm going to need [a rental car] in [Dubai].
What date are you arriving?

What time do you get in?
Let me check.
We had an accident / mechanical problems.
We missed our [train].
We got bumped from the flight.
We got seasick.

Unit 10

I'm almost out of cash.
Let's go in here.
What about this?
It's a bit more than I want to spend.
Maybe you could get a better price.
You think so?
It can't hurt to ask.
How much can you spend?

No more than [amount].
Could I have a look?
How much do you want for [that rug]?
This one?
The other one.
I can give you [amount].
That sounds fair.
This jacket is a bargain.

I'm sorry. That's just too much for me.
Pretty good!
What a great deal!
What a rip-off!
She got a good price.
She saved a lot of money.
He paid too much.

Pronunciation table

These are the pronunciation symbols used in *Top Notch 1*.

Vowels

Symbol	Key Words
i	beat, feed
ɪ	bit, did
eɪ	date, paid
ɛ	bet, bed
æ	bat, bad
ɑ	box, odd, father
ɔ	bought, dog
oʊ	boat, road
ʊ	book, good
u	boot, food, flu
ʌ	but, mud, mother
ə	banana, among
ɚ	shirt, murder
aɪ	bite, cry, buy, eye
aʊ	about, how
ɔɪ	voice, boy
ɪr	deer
ɛr	bare
ɑr	bar
ɔr	door
ʊr	tour

Consonants

Symbol	Key Words	Symbol	Key Words
p	pack, happy	z	zip, please, goes
b	back, rubber	ʃ	ship, machine, station, special, discussion
t	tie	ʒ	measure, vision
d	die	h	hot, who
k	came, key, quick	m	men
g	game, guest	n	sun, know, pneumonia
tʃ	church, nature, watch	ŋ	sung, ringing
dʒ	judge, general, major	w	wet, white
f	fan, photograph	l	light, long
v	van	r	right, wrong
θ	thing, breath	y	yes
ð	then, breathe		
s	sip, city, psychology		
t̬	butter, bottle		
t˺	button		

Non-count nouns

This list is an at-a-glance reference to the non-count nouns used in *Top Notch 1*.

aerobics	candy	dancing	fruit	ice	music	running	sightseeing	traffic
air-conditioning	cash	dessert	golf	juice	nature	salad	skydiving	transportation
basketball	cheese	dinner	grain	junk food	oil	salt	sleepwear	TV
beef	chicken	electronics	health	lamb	outerwear	sausage	soccer	walking
bike riding	clothing	English	history	lettuce	pasta	seafood	soup	water
bread	coffee	entertainment	hosiery	lingerie	pepper	service	squid	weather
broccoli	crab	fish	hot sauce	meat	pie	shopping	swimming	wildlife
butter	culture	food	housework	milk	rice	shrimp	tennis	yogurt
cake								

Irregular verbs

base form	simple past	past participle	base form	simple past	past participle	base form	simple past	past participle
be	was / were	been	get	got	gotten	see	saw	seen
begin	began	begun	give	gave	given	sell	sold	sold
break	broke	broken	go	went	gone	send	sent	sent
bring	brought	brought	grow	grew	grown	sing	sang	sung
build	built	built	have	had	had	sit	sat	sat
buy	bought	bought	hear	heard	heard	sleep	slept	slept
catch	caught	caught	hit	hit	hit	speak	spoke	spoken
choose	chose	chosen	hurt	hurt	hurt	spend	spent	spent
come	came	come	keep	kept	kept	stand	stood	stood
cost	cost	cost	know	knew	knew	steal	stole	stolen
cut	cut	cut	leave	left	left	swim	swam	swum
do	did	done	lose	lost	lost	take	took	taken
drink	drank	drunk	make	made	made	teach	taught	taught
drive	drove	driven	mean	meant	meant	tell	told	told
eat	ate	eaten	meet	met	met	think	thought	thought
fall	fell	fallen	pay	paid	paid	throw	threw	thrown
find	found	found	put	put	put	understand	understood	understood
fit	fit	fit	quit	quit	quit	wake up	woke up	woken up
fly	flew	flown	read	read	read	wear	wore	worn
fall	fell	fallen	ride	rode	ridden	win	won	won
feel	felt	felt	run	run	run	write	wrote	written
forget	forgot	forgotten	say	said	said			

GRAMMAR BOOSTER

Grammar Booster

Note about the Grammar Booster

Many will elect to do the Grammar Booster as self-study. If you choose to use the Grammar Booster as a classroom activity instead, included in these pages are some suggestions similar to those found in the corresponding units. There is also space for you to make notes of your own teaching ideas. These may be helpful in the future.

UNIT 1 **LESSON 1**

Verb be: usage

- Ask a volunteer to read the rule in the Grammar box. Call on other students to read the example sentences.
- Write the following sentence on the board:
  Yao Ming is a basketball player.
- Ask *What's the subject of the sentence?* (Yao Ming)

Challenge: Ask *Is Yao Ming a proper noun, a pronoun, or a noun?* (a proper noun)

- Point to the sentence on the board. Ask the class to change Yao Ming to a subject pronoun:
  He
  Yao Ming is a basketball player.

Verb be: forms

Affirmative statements

- Have a volunteer read the information about affirmative statements. Ask another to read the example sentences.
- Read the subject pronouns and forms of be out loud and have students repeat:
  I am, you are, he is, she is, it is, we are, they are
- Call out different subjects — proper nouns, pronouns, and nouns — and have students respond with the correct form of be. For example:
  we (are)
  Meryl Streep (is)
  the students (are)
  I (am)

Contracted forms

- Have students read the information about contracted forms of be independently.
- Call on a student to read the contracted forms of be out loud and have the rest of the class repeat.
- Explain that contractions of proper nouns + be and pronouns + be are used in both speaking and informal writing.

- Write the following sentence on the board:
  He is Chinese.
- Cross out He is in the sentence on the board. Elicit the contracted form:
  He's
  He is Chinese.

Negative contractions

- Have students read the information about negative contractions independently.
- On the board, write:
  Yao Ming is Chinese. He _____ American.
- Ask for two different ways to fill in the sentence correctly ('s not, isn't).

Verb be: yes / no questions; affirmative and negative short answers

- Have students read the information in the box independently.
- Ask:
  Is Yao Ming Chinese? (Yes, he is. NOT Yes, he's.)
  Is Yao Ming American? (No, he's not. / No, he isn't.)

Ⓐ Choose an answer . . .

- Before students do the exercise, have them circle the subject in each question (1. they; 2. you; 3. he; 4. she; 5. I; 6. it).
- Ask *Are the subjects nouns or pronouns?* (pronouns) Point out that the short answers also contain subject pronouns.
- Have students complete the exercise. To check their work, have students take turns asking and answering the questions with a partner.

Option: For additional practice, have students change the affirmative answers to negative and the negative to affirmative.

Challenge: Have students look only at the short answers and write new questions.

┌─ **Additional Teaching Ideas** ─────────┐
│   │
│   │
│   │
│   │
│   │
│   │
│   │
└──┘

GRAMMAR BOOSTER

The *Grammar Booster* is optional. It provides more explanation and practice, as well as additional grammar concepts.

UNIT 1 Lesson 1

Verb be : usage

Use the verb <u>be</u> to give information about the subject of a sentence. The subject of a sentence can be a noun or a pronoun.

noun   subject
The **teacher** is Chinese.

pronoun subject
We're Peruvian.

Verb be: forms

Affirmative statements

There are three forms of the verb <u>be</u> in the present tense: <u>am</u>, <u>are</u>, and <u>is</u>.

I **am** a student.
You **are** late.
He
She   }   **is** in the room.
It

We **are** married.
They **are** Canadian.

Contracted forms

In speaking and informal writing, contract <u>be</u> with subject nouns and pronouns.

I am a student. = **I'm** a student.
You are late. = **You're** late.

He is in the room. = **He's** in the room.
Peter is a singer. = **Peter's** a singer.

Negative contractions

There are two ways to contract in negative sentences.

He's not Brazilian. OR **He isn't** Brazilian.   **They're not** teachers. OR **They aren't** teachers.

Note: There's only one kind of negative contraction for <u>I am not</u>: **I'm not**.

Verb be: yes / no questions; affirmative and negative short answers

It's common to answer <u>yes</u> / <u>no</u> questions with short answers (or just <u>Yes</u> or <u>No</u>). Don't use contractions with affirmative short answers.

<u>yes</u> / <u>no</u> question	affirmative	negative
Are you a salesperson?	Yes, I am. NOT ~~Yes I'm~~.	No, I'm not.
Is he Italian?	Yes, he is. NOT ~~Yes he's~~.	No, he's not / he isn't.
Are they students?	Yes, they are. NOT ~~Yes they're~~.	No, they're not / they aren't.

A   **Choose an answer for each question.**

  d   **1.** Are they Chinese?
  b   **2.** Are you hungry?
  e   **3.** Is he a teacher?
  c   **4.** Is she Russian?
  f   **5.** Am I in your class?
  a   **6.** Is it 3:00?

a. Yes, it is.
b. No, I'm not.
c. No, she isn't.
d. Yes, they are.
e. Yes, he is.
f. Yes, you are.

1. Is Tokyo in China? ___*No, it isn't*___ .   **4.** Is Paris a country? ___No, it isn't___ .

2. Is Spanish easy? ___No, it isn't/Yes, it is___   **5.** Are you a musician? ___No, I'm not/Yes, I am___ .

3. Are cats animals? ___Yes, they are___ .   **6.** Are Korea and Japan in Asia? ___Yes, they are___ .

UNIT 1 Lesson 2

Information questions with be

Use <u>Who</u> to ask about people, <u>What</u> to ask about things, <u>Where</u> to ask about places, and <u>How old</u> to ask about age.

singular nouns	plural nouns
Who's your teacher?	**Who are** the new students?
What's your name?	**What are** their names?
Where is your father from?	**Where are** your classmates from?
How old is your sister?	**How old are** your children?

Possessive nouns and possessive adjectives

Possessive nouns

Add 's to a name or a noun.

Where is **Mary's** father from?   What's your **mother's** name?

Add an apostrophe (') to plural nouns that end in -s.

What are the **students'** names?

Possessive adjectives

Where's Mary's father from? → Where's **her** father from?
What's Emilio's last name? → What's **his** last name?
What's Lee and Gan's address? → What's **their** address?

A ▷ **Choose an answer for each question.**

___e___ **1.** What's your name?   **a.** Wales, actually. He's British.

___a___ **2.** Where is he from?   **b.** Kwon-su and Toshinaga.

___c___ **3.** Where's her mother from?   **c.** Sasha's mother? San Francisco, I think.

___b___ **4.** Who are they?   **d.** Twelve and ten.

___d___ **5.** How old are your cousins?   **e.** I'm Milos. But everyone calls me Mishka.

B ▷ **Write questions with <u>What</u> and a possessive adjective.**

1. A: ___*What's their address*___ ?   **4. A:** ___What's her nickname___ ?

   B: Lin and Ben's? It's 2 Bay St.   **B:** Sandra's nickname is Sandy.

2. A: ___What's his phone number___ ?   **5. A:** ___What's your number___ ?

   B: His phone number? It's 21-66-55.   **B:** Our number? Oh, it's 555 298-0093.

3. A: ___What's his last name___ ?   **6. A:** ___What's his address___ ?

   B: Dave's last name? It's Bourne.   **B:** Ray's? His address is 456 Rue Noire.

B Answer the questions . . .

- Before students do the exercise, have them circle the subject in each question. (1. Tokyo; 2. Spanish; 3. cats; 4. Paris; 5. you; 6. Korea, Japan)
- For the noun subjects, have students note the corresponding pronoun. For example, Tokyo: *it*
- Have students complete the exercise. To check their work, have students take turns asking and answering the questions with a partner.

Option: Have students write a true statement to clarify each negative response. For example, for item 1, *Is Tokyo in China? No, it isn't. It's in Japan.*

Challenge: Have each student write a similar type of question on a slip of paper. Students stand up and circulate. They pair up, ask and answer each other's questions, and then exchange slips. Students continue to circulate, repeating these steps for about 5 minutes.

UNIT 1 **LESSON 2**

Information questions with <u>be</u>

- Have students read the information in the box independently.
- Point out that in questions with <u>be</u> as the main and only verb, the subject of the sentence follows <u>be</u>.
- Write the following on the board:
    Yao Ming
    basketball player
    Chinese
    Shanghai, China
    The Little Giant
- In pairs, have students create an information question with <u>be</u> for each answer.
    Yao Ming (What's his name? / Who is he?)
    basketball player (What's his occupation?)
    Chinese (What is his nationality?)
    Shanghai, China (Where's he from?)
    The Little Giant (What's his nickname?)

Option: Pairs create a similar set of answers for a different famous person. Each pair joins another pair to make a group of four. One pair asks the other information questions with <u>be</u> to try to guess the identity of the other pair's famous person. They cannot ask what the person's name is. The first and last questions each pair asks can be <u>yes</u> / <u>no</u> questions: *Is it a man or a woman?* (so they know what pronoun / possessive adjective to use) and *Is it _____ ?* (to guess the person's identity).

Option: To practice information questions with <u>be</u> with plural nouns, cut out photos of famous couples from a magazine, or have students bring in photos. Give one photo to each small group of students. Students write information questions with <u>be</u> about the couple. For example:
    Who are they?
    What are their occupations?
    Where are they from?
    How old are they?

Each group takes a turn coming to the front of the room to show their photo and ask the class their questions.

Possessive nouns and possessive adjectives

- After students read the information in the box, focus their attention on the second rule and example.
- Write the following sentences on the board:
    My friend's name is Maria.
    My friends' names are Maria and Steven.
- Ask the class what the difference in meaning is between the two sentences. Elicit or point out that the first sentence refers to one friend and gives <u>her</u> name; the second sentence refers to two friends, and gives <u>their</u> names.
- Explain that when two names are given, the apostrophe s ('s) is only on the second name.
    (What's Lee and Gan's address?)

A Choose an answer . . .

- After students complete the exercise, have them take turns asking and answering the questions with a partner.

Option: Have students find and underline the possessive adjectives in the questions. (1. your; 3. her; 5. your)

B Write questions . . .

- Before students do the exercise, have them circle the possessive nouns and adjectives in the responses.
- For the responses with possessive nouns, have students note the corresponding possessive adjective. For example, Lin and Ben's: *their.*
- Have students complete the exercise. To check their work, have students take turns asking and answering the questions with a partner.

┌─ **Additional Teaching Ideas** ─────────────┐
│   │
│   │
│   │
│   │
│   │
│   │
│   │
│   │
└───┘

UNIT 2 LESSON 1
Prepositions of time and place

Time

- Have students read the information about prepositions of time independently.
- To practice, call out specific moments in time, periods of time, and days and dates in random order. The class responds with the correct preposition and the time that you called out. For example:

  Teacher: *August*
  Class: *in August*

  If helpful, use the following list:

  Saturday (on)   midnight (at)
  4 o'clock (at)   New Year's Eve (on)
  2005 (in)   January (in)
  March 28 (on)   Monday morning (on)
  spring (in)   the morning (in)
  sunset (at)

Place

- Have students read the information about prepositions of place independently.
- To practice, call out specific physical locations and names of streets, larger locations, cities, countries, continents, and interior locations in random order. As with the prepositions of time above, the class responds with the correct preposition and the place that you called out.

  If helpful, use the following list:

  Book World (at)   Moscow (in)
  Canada (in)   the art exhibit (at)
  New Street (on)   Lyons Avenue (on)
  Asia (in)   the library (at)
  the left side of the street (on)   the classroom (in)

A ▷ Complete each sentence . . .

- After students complete the exercise, have them take turns reading the sentences out loud with a partner.

Option: On the board, draw the charts that follow without the answers. Have students copy and complete the charts with the times and places from the exercise.

Prepositions of time	in:	the 19th century, the afternoon, November
	on:	Friday, the weekend, January 1, Thursday morning
	at:	8:30

Prepositions of place	in:	the center of town, Africa
	on:	Grove Street, the right side of the street
	at:	the public library, work

Challenge: Have students use the prepositions, times, and places in the charts to create their own sentences. For example, *Our English class is in the afternoon.*

Additional Teaching Ideas

Prepositions of time and place

Time

Use on with the names of days or dates.

on Thursday	on Monday morning	on New Year's Day
on the weekend	on Sundays	on a weekday

Use in with periods of time (but not with names of days).

in 1998	in July	in [the] spring
in the morning	in the 20th century	in the 1950s

Use at with specific moments in time.

at 9:00	at ten thirty-five	at 6 o'clock
at sunrise	at noon	at midnight

Place

Use on with the names of streets and specific physical locations.

on Main Street	on Smith Avenue	on the corner
on the street	on the right	on the left

Use in with the names of cities, countries, continents, and other large locations.

in the neighborhood	in the center of town	in Caracas
in Thailand	in Africa	in the ocean

Use at for buildings and addresses.

at the theater	at the supermarket	at the bank
at the train station	at 10 Main Street	at 365 Smith Avenue

A **Complete each sentence or question with on, in, or at.**

1. When's the movie? The movie is ____on____ Friday ____at____ 8:30.

2. ____On____ the weekend, I'm going to the concert ____at____ the public library.

3. Where is he? He's not here right now. He's ____at____ work.

4. Where's his office? It's ____in____ the center of town.

5. When was her mother born? She was born ____on____ January 1.

6. When does the movie take place? It takes place ____in____ the 19th century ____in____ Africa.

7. There is a ticket booth ____in____ the center of town.

8. Is the concert hall ____on____ Grove Street?

9. I think the theater is ____on____ the right side of the street.

10. Let's go to the early show. The concert is outside, and the weather gets really hot ____in____ the afternoon.

11. This concert occurs every second year ____in____ November.

12. I'll see you ____on____ Thursday morning in front of the theater, OK?

Look at the tickets. Ask questions with <u>When</u> or <u>What time</u>. Ask a question with <u>Where</u>. Then write an answer to each question.

1.

METRO
★ HILL STREET MALL ★
8:55PM   Friday, Oct. 17
Phantom of the Opera

questions: <u>What time does the show start?</u>

answers: <u>It starts at 8:55 P.M.</u>

2.

ELECTRIC MAYHEM
M I D N I G H T   C O N C E R T
THE CAT CLUB
SAT.   OCTOBER 23 $18

SAT · OCTOBER 23 · THE CAT CLUB · MIDNIGHT CONCERT · ELECTRIC MAYHEM · $18

questions: <u>Where's the show?</u>

answers: <u>It's at the Cat Club.</u>

UNIT 3 Lesson 1

The simple present tense: usage

Use the simple present tense to talk about facts and habitual actions in the present.

facts	**habitual actions**
Hank **speaks** French very well.	I **go** to bed at 10:00 p.m. every night.
I **work** at 43 Fork Road.	She **eats** lunch at Safi's Cafe on Fridays.

The simple present tense: form

Add –s to the base form of the verb for third-person singular (<u>he</u>, <u>she</u>, <u>it</u>).

I **like** Japanese food.	He **likes** Mexican food.
You **study** Korean.	She **studies** English.
They **open** at 7:00.	It **opens** at 8:00.
We **work** at a restaurant.	

Use <u>don't</u> (do not) and <u>doesn't</u> (does not) and the base form of the verb to make negative statements.

I **don't go** to bed before 10:00 p.m.   Hank **doesn't speak** Spanish very well.

The simple present tense: yes / no questions

Use <u>do</u> or <u>does</u> and the base form to make <u>yes</u> / <u>no</u> questions in the simple present tense.

Do you **speak** Portuguese?   **Does** she **live** near you?   (NOT ~~Does she lives near you?~~)

A Write negative sentences.

1. Hank likes jazz. (His brother) <u>His brother doesn't like jazz</u>.
2. Vic lives in Lima. (His sisters) <u>His sisters don't live in Lima.</u>
3. Kate works in a hospital. (Her sister) <u>Her sister doesn't work in a hospital</u>.
4. My sister has a big family. (My brother) <u>My brother doesn't have a big family</u>.
5. My older brother speaks Japanese. (My younger brother) <u>My younger brother doesn't speak Japanese</u>.
6. Han's niece takes a bus to school. (His nephew) <u>His nephew doesn't take a bus to school</u>.

B) Look at the tickets. Ask questions . . .

- On the board, write the headings: *When* and *Where*.
- Before students do the exercise, have them list the information about when and where that is available for each show.

  1. *When*　　*Where*　　2. *When*　　*Where*
     8:55 p.m.　Metro　　　midnight　The Cat Club
     Friday,　　Hill Street　Saturday
     Oct. 17　　Mall　　　October 23

- Have students write *in, on,* or *at* before each time or place listed. (at 8:55, on Friday, at the Metro, at the Hill Street Mall, at midnight, on Saturday, at The Cat Club)
- Students use their lists to ask and answer questions with a partner. Then have them use their lists to write questions and answers.

UNIT 3 **LESSON 1**

The simple present tense: usage

- Have students read the information in the first box independently.
- Use the simple present to tell the class about your typical weekday. For example:

  I wake up at 7:00 A.M.　　*I go home at 5:00 P.M.*
  I go to work at 8:00 A.M.　*I eat dinner at 7:00 P.M.*
  I eat lunch at 12:30 P.M.　*I go to bed at 11:00 P.M.*

- Have pairs take turns describing their typical weekday to a partner.

Option: With a new partner, have students discuss facts about themselves like where they live, what languages they speak, how many brothers and sisters they have, and so on.

The simple present tense: form

- Have students read the information in the second box independently.
- To make the first rule clear, write on the board:

  I, you, we, they <u>live</u>
  he, she, it <u>lives</u>

- To make the second rule clear, write on the board:

  I, you, we, they <u>don't live</u>
  he, she, it <u>doesn't live</u>

- Point out that in third-person singular, there is no *-s* on the main verb.

  She doesn't like Mexican food. (NOT ~~She doesn't likes Mexican food.~~)

- Point out that when <u>or</u> connects two verbs in a negative statement, <u>don't</u> or <u>doesn't</u> is not repeated before the second verb.

  I don't eat or drink at work. (NOT ~~I don't eat or don't drink at work.~~)

The simple present tense: yes / no questions

- Have students read the information in the third box independently.
- To make the rule clear, write on the board:

  <u>Do</u> *I, you, we, they* <u>live</u> . . . ?
  <u>Does</u> *he, she, it* <u>live</u> . . . ? (NOT ~~Does he, she, it lives . . . ?~~)

- Explain that for <u>yes</u> / <u>no</u> questions in the simple present tense, <u>do</u> or <u>does</u> is used before the subject.
- Students should not use <u>do</u> or <u>does</u> for <u>yes</u> / <u>no</u> questions with <u>be</u>.

  Does she speak German?
  Is she from Germany? (NOT ~~Does she from Germany?~~)

Option: Draw the chart below on the board. Then choose a student and write his or her name in the first box. Ask the student *Do you like basketball? Do you like Italian food?* etc. The student answers *Yes, I do* or *No, I don't.* When the student answers *Yes, I do* put an X in the appropriate box. To review, tell the class about the student's likes and dislikes. For example, *Martin likes Italian food, art exhibits, and coffee. He doesn't like basketball, rap music, or horror movies.* Students copy the chart on a sheet of paper and walk around the room asking their classmates *Do you like . . . ?* and filling in their charts. To review, each student tells the class about another student's likes and dislikes.

	basketball	Italian food	rap music	art exhibits	coffee	horror movies
Martin		✗		✗	✗	

A) Write negative sentences.

- Have students look at the exercise. Read each new subject out loud. Have the class call out the corresponding subject pronouns. (1. His brother: he; 2. His sisters: they; 3. Her sister: she; 4. My brother: he; 5. My younger brother: he; 6. His nephew: he)
- Point to the information about negative statements on the board. Have students do the exercise.
- Call on volunteers to read their answers to the class.

Option: Make <u>yes</u> / <u>no</u> questions from the sentences in items 1, 2, 3, and 6. Have the class respond with short answers. For example, *Does Vic live in Lima?* (Yes, he does.) *Does Han's nephew take a bus to school?* (No, he doesn't.)

┌─ **Additional Teaching Ideas** ─────────────────┐
│   │
│   │
│   │
│   │
│   │
│   │
└──┘

B Practice. Write <u>yes</u> / <u>no</u> questions.

- Before students do the exercise, have them look at the answers to the questions. Ask them to circle the subjects. (1. he / My brother; 2. I; 3. we; 4. my in-laws; 5. she / my niece)
- Tell students to:
  1. look at each subject
  2. decide whether to use <u>Do</u> or <u>Does</u>
  3. change the subject pronoun or possessive adjective, if necessary
  4. write the question
- To check their work, have students take turns asking and answering the questions with a partner.

UNIT 3 LESSON 2

The simple present tense: form of information questions

- Have students read the information in the box independently.
- Choose a few of your family members. Write their names and your relationship on the board. Include individual family members and couples. For example:

  My aunt [Lynne]
  My parents [Robert] and [Karen]
  My brother [Gary]
  My brother- and sister-in-law [Tim] and [Michelle]

- Write What, Where, When, and How many on the board. Have the class use the question words to ask you about your family members. For example:

  What does your aunt do?
  Where do your parents live?
  When do you see your brother?
  How many children do your brother- and
    sister-in-law have?

- Have students choose a few of their own family members, both individuals and couples, and write their names and relationships on a slip of paper. Students exchange slips and take turns asking information questions about each other's family members. Circulate and check that students are forming their questions correctly.

A Complete the questions.

- Before students do the exercise, have them look at the answers to the questions. Ask students to note whether each answer tells <u>what</u>, <u>where</u>, <u>when</u> / <u>what time</u>, <u>how many</u>, or <u>who</u>. Review as a class.
- Remind students to look at the subjects to decide whether to use *do* or *does*. Remind them also to not to use <u>do</u> or <u>does</u> with <u>Who</u>.
- To check their work, have students take turns asking and answering the questions with a partner.

UNIT 4 LESSON 1

The present continuous: spelling rules

- Have students read the spelling rules on pages G5 and G6 independently.
- Write these words on the board:

  talk, take, hit, mow

- Call on students to write the present participle form (talking, taking, hitting, mowing). Point out the dropped -<u>e</u> in <u>taking</u> and the double consonant in <u>hitting</u>.
- Write the following words on the board:

  begin, open

- Contrast the two words according to the last point in the Grammar box. Ask: *For the present participle, which verb doubles the last consonant?* (begin—beginning) *Why?* (because the stress is on the second syllable)

──Additional Teaching Ideas──

Practice. Write <u>yes</u> / <u>no</u> questions.

1. <u>*Does your brother*</u> drink coffee?   No, he doesn't. My brother drinks tea.
2. <u>Do you look like your</u> sister?   Yes, I do. I really look like my sister.
3. <u>Do you have any</u> children?   No, we don't have any yet.
4. <u>Do your in-laws live</u> in Chile?   No, my in-laws live in Argentina.
5. <u>Does your niece speak</u> English?   Yes, she does. My niece speaks it very well.

▶ ## UNIT 3 Lesson 2

┌─ **The simple present tense: form of information questions** ─

Use <u>do</u> or <u>does</u> and the base form of the verb to ask information questions.

>   **Where do** your in-laws **live**?   **What does** your sister **do**?
>   **When do** you **visit** your parents?   **What time does** she **go**?

Don't use <u>do</u> or <u>does</u> with <u>Who</u>. Always use the third-person singular to ask information questions with <u>Who</u> in the simple present tense.

>   **Who** lives here? My parents **do**.

Use <u>How many</u> with plural nouns.

>   **How many** children **do** you **have**?   **How many** books **does** she **have**?
>   **How many** aunts and uncles **do** you **have**?   **How many** languages **does** he **speak**?

A **Complete the questions.**

1. <u>What does</u> your father ___<u>do</u>___? He's a doctor.
2. <u>Where do</u> your grandparents ___<u>live</u>___?   They live in Seoul.
3. <u>How many</u> children <u>do you have</u>? I have two boys and three girls.
4. <u>How often</u> <u>do you visit</u> your in-laws?   We visit them on Sundays.
5. <u>Where does</u> your brother ___<u>live</u>___? He lives across the street from me.
6. <u>Who</u> speaks French?   My uncle does.
7. <u>When do</u> you ___<u>study</u>___? I study early in the morning at around 7:00.
8. <u>Who</u> has four children?   My cousins do.
9. <u>When does</u> your son ___<u>eat</u>___ breakfast?   He eats breakfast at 8:00.

▶ ## UNIT 4 Lesson 1

┌─ **The present continuous: spelling rules** ─

To form a present participle, add <u>–ing</u> to the base form of the verb.

>   talk → talk**ing**

If the base form ends in a silent (unvoiced) <u>–e</u>, drop the <u>–e</u> and add <u>–ing</u>.

>   leave → leav**ing**

In verbs of one syllable, if the last three letters are a consonant-vowel-consonant*
sequence, double the last consonant and then add **–ing** to the base form.

C V C

s i t → si**tt**ing

BUT: If the verb ends in **–w**, **–x**, or **–y**, don't double the final consonant.

blow → **blowing**

fix → **fixing**

say → **saying**

In verbs of more than one syllable that end in a consonant-vowel-consonant sequence,
double the last consonant only if the spoken stress is on the last syllable.

permit → permi**tt**ing   BUT order → ordering

*Vowels = a, e, i, o, u
Consonants = b, c, d, f, g, h, j, k, l, m, n, p, q, r, s, t, v, w, x, y, z

A ▷ **Write the present participle for the following base forms.**

1. turn	_turning_	7. stop	stopping	13. sew	sewing	19. change	changing
2. rain	raining	8. exit	exiting	14. listen	listening	20. be	being
3. run	running	9. sit	sitting	15. do	doing	21. have	having
4. help	helping	10. eat	eating	16. write	writing	22. put	putting
5. open	opening	11. buy	buying	17. begin	beginning	23. go	going
6. close	closing	12. mix	mixing	18. use	using		

The present continuous: statements

Form the present continuous with a form of **be** and the present participle.

affirmative statements	negative statements
I**'m studying** English.	I**'m** not **studying** French.
You**'re studying** French.	You**'re** not **studying** English.
He**'s reading** a book.	He**'s** not **reading** a newspaper.
She**'s reading** a newspaper.	She**'s** not **reading** a book.
We**'re watching** TV.	We**'re** not **watching** a video.
They**'re watching** a video.	They**'re** not **watching** TV.

B ▷ **Change each affirmative statement to a negative statement. Use contractions.**

1. She's going to the supermarket. __She's not going to the supermarket__.

2. He's calling his wife this afternoon. __He's not calling his wife this afternoon__.

3. I'm buying tickets for a rock concert tonight. __I'm not buying tickets for a rock concert tonight__.

4. The Roberts are feeding their kids early. __The Roberts are not feeding their kids early__.

5. Jack is taking the bus to the movies. __Jack is not taking the bus to the movies__.

C ▷ **Write answers to the questions.**

1. Are you studying English this year? __Yes, I'm studying English this year__.

2. When are you taking a vacation? __I'm taking a vacation next month__.

A Write the present participle for the following base forms.

- Read the list of verbs in Exercise A (page G6) out loud. Have students circle the verbs that are more than one syllable (5. open 8. exit 14. listen 17. begin).

- On a separate sheet of paper, have students make a six-column chart like the one below. Ask them to fill in the headings for the first four columns: <u>talking</u>, <u>leaving</u>, <u>sitting</u>, and <u>blowing</u> / <u>fixing</u> / <u>saying</u>.

- As students complete the exercise, have them write each present participle under the example that follows the same spelling rule.

- Review as a class. Explain that the present participle of <u>be</u> is <u>being</u>.

- Now have students look at the two-syllable verbs. Say each verb out loud and have students underline the syllable that is stressed in each (5. <u>o</u>pen 8. <u>e</u>xit 14. <u>lis</u>ten 17. be<u>gin</u>).

- Ask students to fill in the headings for the last two columns on their chart: <u>permitting</u> and <u>ordering</u>. Students write the present participle for each two-syllable verb under the example that follows the same spelling rule.

- Review as a class.

talking	leaving	sitting	blowing / fixing / saying	permitting	ordering
turning	closing	running	buying	beginning	opening
raining	writing	stopping	mixing		exiting
helping	using	putting	sewing		listening
eating	changing				
being	having				
doing					
going					

The present continuous: statements

- Have students read the information in the box independently.

- Read the first affirmative sentence out loud. Say *When I say this sentence, it means that the action (studying) is happening right now, at the same time I am saying this sentence.*

- Remind students not to repeat the subject and the verb <u>be</u> when the subject is doing two things. (*Sylvia is walking and talking.* NOT ~~Sylvia is walking and Sylvia is talking.~~)

- Read down the list of affirmative statements. Ask a volunteer to tell you what the main verb is in each statement.

Option: On the board, draw three large squares. In each square, draw a stick person (or people) doing something specific (reading a book, painting a house, playing soccer). Point to the first picture and ask *What is this person doing?* (or *she* or *they*, depending on the drawing). Elicit responses from students. If you hear an inappropriate response, say *No, he's not (riding a bike)* to provide input of the negative form.

Option: Have students draw a picture of a person or people doing an activity. Encourage students to include as much detail as possible (for example, the title of the book the person is reading, the name of the restaurant or store, etc.). Then divide the class into small groups. Students take turns showing their drawing to their group members and asking *What is (he / she) doing?* or *What are they doing?*

B Change each affirmative statement . . .

- Before students do the exercise, have them look at the negative statements in the box. Ask *Where is <u>not</u> in the negative statements?* (between <u>be</u> and the main verb)

- After students complete the exercise, call on volunteers to read their answers to the class.

Option: Have students note whether each statement describes an action that is in progress *now* or a *future* action. (1. now; 2. future; 3. future; 4. now; 5. now / future)

C Write answers to the questions.

- After students complete the exercise, review as a class. Read the first question and call on a student to answer. The student answers, then reads the next question and calls on another student to answer. Continue until all the questions are answered.

Additional Teaching Ideas

The present continuous: questions

• Read the first affirmative statement from the statements box on page G6 out loud. Have the class change the statement into a yes / no question. For example:

Teacher: *I'm studying English.*
Class: *Are you studying English?*

Continue in this way until you have gone through the whole list. You may also come up with statements of your own.

• Have students ask information questions about a statement. For example:

Teacher: *I'm studying English.*
Class: *Where are you studying?*

Continue this way until you have gone through the list. You may also come up with statements of your own.

◆D▷ Complete each conversation . . .

• Before students do the exercise, tell them to circle the subjects in the responses to help them identify which pronoun they should use.

• Ask *Which are responses to yes / no questions?* (items 1 and 2) *Which are responses to information questions?* (items 3 and 4)

• To check their work, have students take turns asking and answering the questions with a partner.

UNIT 5 **LESSON 1**

Non-count nouns: categories and verb agreement

• Have students read the information in the box independently.

• Have students form small groups. Assign each group one of the categories. Groups write a sentence with a non-count noun in their category. Student can use one of the non-count nouns listed or their own non-count noun. The non-count noun should be the subject of the sentence.

• One student from each group writes the group's sentence on the board. Read the sentences out loud and make any necessary corrections as a class. For each sentence, ask what the category is and what the verb is. Check that the verb is singular.

• Your students might say:

Music makes the world go 'round. (abstract ideas)
Golf is difficult. (sports and activities)
Cancer kills many people. (illnesses)
Snow is beautiful. (natural events)
English is useful for business and travel. (academic subjects)
Coffee has caffeine. (foods)

◆A▷ Complete each sentence . . .

Note: In Exercise A, it is acceptable for students to write negatives unless incorrect (i.e., item 4).

• Remind students to use the third-person singular forms of the verbs in parentheses.

• After students complete the exercise, call on volunteers to read their answers to the class.

Option: Have students complete the following sentences with their own non-count nouns. Call on volunteers to share their answers with the class.

_____ is my favorite beverage.

_____ is very good for you.

_____ isn't good for you.

_____ is my favorite subject.

_____ creates problems for many students.

_____ is my favorite sport.

┌─ **Additional Teaching Ideas** ──────────────┐
│   │
│   │
│   │
│   │
│   │
│   │
│   │
│   │
└──┘

3. Is it raining now? _No, it's not raining now_ .

4. Where are you eating dinner tonight? _I'm eating dinner at home tonight_ .

5. Are you listening to music now? _No, I'm not listening to music now_ .

The present continuous: questions

Yes / no questions: Place <u>be</u> before the subject of the sentence.

> **Is she** watching TV?   **Are we** meeting this afternoon?
> **Are you** driving there?   **Are they** talking on the phone?

Information questions: Use question words to ask information questions.

> **When** are you going?   **Who**'s talking on the phone?
> **What** are you doing right now?   **Why** are you buying that pocket translator?

D **Complete each conversation with a question in the present continuous.**

1. A: _Is he watching TV_ ?
     B: No. Evan's not watching TV right now.

2. A: _Is she working this morning_ ?
     B: Yes, she's working this morning.

3. A: _Who are you calling_ ?
     B: I'm calling Janet Hammond.

4. A: _When is she coming home_ ?
     B: She's coming home later tonight.

▶ UNIT 5 Lesson 1

Non-count nouns: categories and verb agreement

Non-count nouns are common in the following categories:

> **abstract ideas:** health, advice, help, luck, fun
> **sports and activities:** tennis, swimming, golf, basketball
> **illnesses:** cancer, AIDS, diabetes, dengue
> **natural events:** rain, snow, wind, light, darkness
> **academic subjects:** English, chemistry, art, mathematics
> **foods:** rice, milk, sugar, coffee, fat

All non-count nouns require a singular verb.

> Fat **isn't** good for you.
> Mathematics **is** my favorite subject.

A **Complete each sentence with the correct form of the verb.**

1. Coffee ___is___ my favorite beverage.
               be

2. Rice ___is___ very good for you, even when you are sick.
          be

3. Influenza ___causes___ pain and fever.
             cause

4. Mathematics ___creates___ problems for many students, but not for me!
                create

5. Darkness ___frightens___ some people, but I don't know why.
            frighten

6. Medical advice ___helps___ people answer questions about their health.
              help

B Complete each statement with a countable quantity. (Note: More than one phrase of quantity may be possible.)

liquids

1. This soup is too salty. It has _a cup of_ salt in it!

2. She must be very thirsty. This is her third _glass of_ water.

3. My car has a big gas tank. It holds _20 gallons of_ gas.

solids

4. I ate _5 slices of_ cheese and now I feel sick.

5. A club sandwich doesn't have two _slices of_ bread. It has three _slices of_ bread.

6. I like my tea sweet. Please put in _2 spoonfuls of_ sugar.

C Complete each question with **How much** or **How many.**

1. _How much_ bread do we need? I put two loaves in the shopping cart.

2. _How much_ salt did you put in the beef stew? I can't eat it.

3. _How much_ hot pepper do you like? This food is already very spicy!

4. _How many_ spoonfuls of sugar do you want in your tea? Two, please.

5. _How much_ oil should I put in this salad? A half cup?

6. _How much_ cheese is there in the kitchen? I think we need to get some more.

7. _How many_ slices of bread do you want? Only one, thanks.

8. _How many_ cups of coffee did you drink? Your hands are shaking!

Non-count nouns: expressing quantities

- Have students read the information in the box independently.

- If possible, bring in objects or pictures to make the meaning of the countable phrases clear. For example, bring in a loaf of bread. Hold it up and say *bread*. Then say *one loaf of bread*. Next, count the slices of bread. Say *one slice of bread, two slices of bread*, etc. Do the same with <u>piece</u>. Show pictures of white bread, wheat bread, and rye bread. Say *three kinds of bread*.

Note: One gallon = 3.8 liters

B ▷ Complete each statement ...

- Before students do the exercise, tell them to circle the non-count noun that comes after the answer space in each item.

- Review as a class. Call on volunteers to read their statements. Elicit a couple of possible responses for each item.

Option: Have students write a description of "The Perfect Sandwich." For example, *The perfect sandwich has two slices of bread. It has two pieces of chicken and three slices of cheese. It has lettuce, but it doesn't have tomatoes.*

Questions with <u>How much</u> and <u>How many</u>

- Have students read the information in the box independently.

- Write the following on the board:
  1. _____ students are in this class?
  2. _____ glasses of water do you drink every day?
  3. _____ sugar do you put in your coffee?
  4. _____ bread do you buy every week?
  5. _____ cousins do you have?
  6. _____ cheese do you put on your sandwiches?
  7. _____ TV do you watch?

  Have students complete the questions with <u>How much</u> or <u>How many</u>. (Answers: 1. How many 2. How many 3. How much 4. How much 5. How many 6. How much 7. How much) Then have them answer the questions in pairs.

C ▷ Complete each question ...

- Before students do the exercise, have them look at the nouns that follow each answer space. Ask *Which are count nouns?* (4. spoonfuls; 7. slices; 8. cups) *How do you know they are count nouns?* (They end in -<u>s</u>.)

- To check their work, have students take turns reading the questions and responses with a partner.

Words that can be count nouns or non-count nouns

- Have students read the information in the box independently.

- Read each example out loud. First read the non-count use, then the count use. When you read the count use, draw a simple picture on the board. Draw two chickens, three TVs, and a lamp. After you read each count use example, point to the picture(s) and count. Explain that in each example the non-count use is general and the count use refers to specific objects.

Language note: In informal speaking, some non-count nouns may be used as count nouns. For example: *I'd like two teas and two waters* means *I'd like two cups of tea and two glasses of water.*

┌─Additional Teaching Ideas─────────┐
│   │
│   │
└────────────────────────────────────┘

Plural count nouns: spelling rules

- Have students read the information in the box independently.
- Pronounce the plural forms under each rule and have students repeat.

Note: The plural form of cup is pronounced as /s/. The plural forms of the nouns that add *-es* are pronounced as /əz/, with the exception of tomatoes. The plural forms of tomatoes and all other nouns listed are pronounced as /z/.

D Write the plural form ...

- Before students do the exercise, tell them to underline the last letter of each count noun. Remind students that if the noun ends in *-ch* or *-sh*, they should underline the last two letters.
- After students complete the exercise, ask *For which nouns did you need to do more than add -s?* (french fries, sandwiches, potatoes) Have volunteers write these plural forms on the board.

Option: Pronounce the plural forms in Exercise D and have students repeat. Then have students write the headings /əz/, /s/, and /z/ on a sheet of paper. Pronounce each plural form again. Have students listen for how the plural form is pronounced and write the word under the appropriate heading.

/əz/	/s/	/z/
slices	cups	clams
sandwiches		olives
		spoonfuls
		pears
		french fries
		vegetables
		potatoes

Review as a class. Then have students use their lists to practice pronouncing the plural nouns with a partner.

Option: Ask students to name other plural nouns. Have them tell you which heading the new word should go under.

UNIT 5 **LESSON 2**

A Write <u>a</u> or <u>an</u> ...

- Remind students to use *an* before count nouns that begin with a vowel and *a* before count nouns that begin with a consonant.
- After students complete the exercise, call on volunteers to read their answers to the class.

<u>Some</u> and <u>any</u>

- Call on a student to read the first point in the Grammar box. Call on other students to read the example sentences.
- Ask volunteers to read the second point in the Grammar box and the example. Continue in this way until all points and examples are read.
- Ask *Is <u>milk</u> count or non-count?* (non-count) *Are <u>bananas</u> count or non-count?* (plural count) Then, to clarify the information in the box, write on the board:

affirmative statements	negative statements	questions
some milk	any milk	any milk, some milk
some bananas	any bananas	any bananas, some bananas

Language note: *An apple a day keeps the doctor away* is a familiar aphorism.

┌─ **Additional Teaching Ideas** ─────────┐
│   │
│   │
│   │
│   │
└──┘

Plural count nouns: spelling rules

Add –s to most nouns.

cup	**cups**	appetizer	**appetizers**
apple	**apples**		

If a noun ends in a consonant and –y, change the y to i and add –es.

cherry	**cherries**	berry	**berries**

Add –es to nouns that end in –ch, –o, –s, –sh, –x, or –z.

lunch	**lunches**	radish	**radishes**
tomato	**tomatoes**	box	**boxes**
glass	**glasses**		

But do not change the y when the letter before the y is a vowel.

boy	**boys**

D **Write the plural form of the following count nouns.**

1. clam ___clams___
2. slice ___slices___
3. cup ___cups___
4. olive ___olives___

5. spoonful ___spoonfuls___
6. pear ___pears___
7. french fry ___french fries___
8. sandwich ___sandwiches___

9. vegetable ___vegetables___
10. potato ___potatoes___

UNIT 5 Lesson 2

A **Write a or an. If the noun is a non-count noun, write X.**

1. He has __X__ diabetes.
2. She would like to eat __a__ pear.
3. "__An__ apple a day keeps the doctor away."
4. Would you like __an__ appetizer?
5. There's __an__ egg on the shelf.

6. Does the restaurant serve __X__ rice with the chicken?
7. We'd like __X__ water, please.
8. He always gives __X__ good advice.
9. Let's go to __a__ concert tonight.
10. My family loves __X__ music.

Some and any

Use some and any to describe an indefinite number or amount.

There are **some** apples in the fridge. (Indefinite number: we don't know how many.)
Are there **any** oranges? (Indefinite number: no specific number being asked about.)
They are bringing us **some** coffee. (Indefinite amount: we don't know how much.)
Now we have **some**. (Indefinite amount: we don't know how much.)

Use some with non-count nouns and with plural count nouns in affirmative statements.

      non-count noun   plural count noun
We need **some** milk and **some** bananas. (affirmative statement)

Use any with non-count nouns and plural count nouns in negative statements.

      non-count noun   plural count noun
We don't want **any** cheese, and we don't need **any** apples.
They don't have **any**.

Use any or some in questions with count and non-count nouns.

Do you need **any** cookies or butter?
Do you need **some** cookies or butter?

Change the following sentences from affirmative to negative.

1. There is some coffee in the kitchen.
   <u>*There isn't any coffee in the kitchen*</u> .

2. There are some beans on the table.
   <u>There aren't any beans on the table</u> .

3. We have some leftovers.
   <u>We don't have any leftovers</u> .

4. They need some onions for the soup.
   <u>They don't need any onions for the soup</u> .

5. She's buying some fruit at the market.
   <u>She's not buying any fruit at the market</u> .

6. The Reeds want some eggs for breakfast.
   <u>The Reeds don't want any eggs for breakfast</u>

7. I want some butter on my sandwich.
   <u>I don't want any butter on my sandwich</u> .

8. There is some chicken in the fridge.
   <u>There isn't any chicken in the fridge</u> .

9. They need some cheese for the pasta.
   <u>They don't need any cheese for the pasta</u> .

Complete each statement with <u>some</u> or <u>any</u>.

1. I don't want _____any_____ more coffee, thank you.

2. There isn't _____any_____ salt in this soup.

3. We don't see _____any_____ sandwiches on the menu.

4. They need _____some_____ sugar for their tea.

5. The restaurant is making _____some_____ cakes for the party.

6. It's too bad that there isn't _____any_____ soup.

7. I don't see _____any_____ menus on those tables.

8. There are _____some_____ eggs for the omelet.

UNIT 6 Lesson 1

┌─ **Can: form** ─────────────────────────────────────

Use <u>can</u> with the base form of a verb.

> She **can play** golf very well.
> NOT She ~~cans play~~ golf very well.
> NOT She ~~can plays~~ golf very well.
> NOT She ~~can to play~~ golf very well.

There are three negative forms of <u>can</u>.

> He **can't** swim. = He **cannot** swim. = He **can not** swim.

└──

Correct the following sentences.

1. Can you ~~coming~~ *come* to the party next week?

2. My brother-in-law can't ~~plays~~ *play* basketball tomorrow.

3. I'm going to the pool with Diane, but I ~~no can~~ *can't* swim.

4. Alice can ~~to~~ go running after work.

5. Can Lisa ~~visits~~ *visit* her cousins next weekend?

B ▶ **Change the following sentences . . .**

• Before students complete the exercise, review the negative forms of present tenses:

    There is / are → There isn't / aren't
    We have → We don't have (simple present tense)
    She's buying → She's not buying (present continuous)

• After students complete the exercise, call on volunteers to read the negative sentences out loud.

C ▶ **Complete each statement with <u>some</u> or <u>any</u>.**

• To check their work, have students read the completed statements to a partner.

Option: Have students change the statements to questions. For example, *1. Do you want any / some more coffee?*

UNIT 6 **LESSON 1**

<u>Can</u>: form

• Have students read the information in the box independently.

• Have 5–10 students write a sentence on the board about something they can or can't do. Remind students that they can use any of the negative forms of <u>can</u>. Students should write their names next to their sentences.

• As a class, make any necessary corrections to the sentences on the board. Check that students do not use <u>to</u> after <u>can</u> or <u>can't</u>. For example: *I can speak English,* NOT *I can to speak English.*

• To reinforce not adding *-s* in the third-person singular, rewrite one of the sentences on the board in the third person. For example:

    I can sing. → *[Julia] can sing.*

A ▶ **Correct the following sentences.**

• Review as a class. Ask for volunteers to read the corrected sentences. For item 3, elicit all three negative forms of *can.*

┌─ **Additional Teaching Ideas** ─────────┐
│   │
│   │
│   │
│   │
│   │
│   │
│   │
│   │
│   │
└──┘

Can: information questions

- Have students read the information in the box independently.

- Have students look at the sentences their classmates wrote on the board again. Read the affirmative statements out loud. Ask the class to create <u>yes</u> / <u>no</u> questions from the statements. Write the <u>yes</u> / <u>no</u> questions on the board. For example:

    I can play golf. ➞ *Can you play golf?*

- Then ask students to change the <u>yes</u> / <u>no</u> questions to information questions by adding a question word at the beginning. For example:

    Can you play golf? ➞ *When can you play golf?*

B Complete the questions, using <u>can</u>.

- Have students look at the examples in the box again. Ask *Where is <u>can</u> in the information questions?* (after the question word, before the subject) Point out that in questions with *Who,* there is no subject.

- To check their work, have students take turns reading the questions and responses with a partner.

Have to: form

- Ask a volunteer to read the rule in the Grammar box. Call on other students to read the example sentences.

- Write the following list of obligations on the board. Students tell a partner which ones they have to do and which ones they don't have to do this week. Then each student tells the class one thing her partner has to do and one thing her partner doesn't have to do.

    go to class
    go shopping
    study English
    work
    make dinner
    go running
    clean the house

C Correct these sentences.

- Review as a class. Ask for volunteers to read the corrected sentences.

Have to: information questions

- Have students read the information in the box independently.

- Tell students that in a question, a form of <u>do</u> (<u>do</u>/<u>does</u>, <u>don't</u>/<u>doesn't</u>) is used with <u>have to</u>, For example:

    <u>Do</u> *you* <u>have to</u> *go there?*
    Where <u>does</u> *she* <u>have to</u> *go?*

┌─ **Additional Teaching Ideas** ─────────┐
│   │
│   │
│   │
│   │
│   │
│   │
│   │
│   │
└──┘

Can: information questions

Where **can** I go running around here?	Try the park.
When **can** you **come** for dinner?	How about tomorrow night?
How often **can** you **go** running?	No more than twice a week. I'm pretty busy.
What languages **can** you **speak**?	I can speak Italian.
Who **can drive**?	I can.

B **Complete the questions, using can.**

1. **A:** _____Where can I do_____ aerobics around here? (Where / I / do)

   B: Why don't you try Total Fitness? They have great instructors.

2. **A:** _____When can we study_____ English together? (When / we / study)

   B: Let's get together tomorrow night. OK?

3. **A:** We need some fresh air. _____Where can we go_____ walking? (Where / we / go)

   B: Well, we can go over to Grant Park. It's very nice.

4. **A:** _____How often can Larry play_____ golf? (How often / Larry / play)

   B: Not very often. He's starting a new job.

5. **A:** _____Who can make_____ dinner tonight? (Who / make)

   B: What about Katherine? She's not doing anything.

Have to: form

Use __have to__ or __has to__ with the base form of a verb. Use __has to__ for the third-person singular.

I **have to go** to class at 9:00.
She **has to go** to class at 8:00.
NOT She ~~has to goes~~ to class at 8:00.
NOT She ~~has to going~~ to class at 8:00.

C **Correct these sentences.**

1. My brother-in-law ~~have~~ *has* to work on the weekend.

2. Do you ~~has~~ *have* to meet Mr. Green at the airport?

3. We don't have to ~~making~~ *make* dinner tonight. We're going out.

4. Ms. Davis has to ~~fills~~ *fill* out an application for her English class.

5. Does she have to ~~watches~~ *watch* TV now? I'm trying to study.

Have to: information questions

What does he **have to do** Saturday morning?	He has to clean the house.
How often does she **have to work** on the weekend?	Not often.
When do they **have to go** shopping?	Tonight. The party's tomorrow.
Who **has to write** the report?	Marian.
Where do you **have to go** this morning?	To the airport.

Complete the questions.

1. **A:** <u>What does</u> she <u>have to</u> do tomorrow?
   B: She has to go to English class.

   How often
2. **A:** <u>does</u> he <u>have to</u> take the medicine?
   B: Every three hours.

   What time
3. **A:** <u>does</u> she <u>have to</u> go to the park?
   B: At around eight.

4. **A:** <u>What do</u> they <u>have to</u> do after class?
   B: Nothing special.

5. **A:** <u>When do</u> we <u>have to</u> turn off the machine?
   B: Never! Don't ever turn it off.

6. **A:** <u>When do</u> you <u>have to</u> pick up your sister?
   B: At about two thirty.

UNIT 6 Lesson 2

The simple present tense: non-action verbs

Some verbs are non-action verbs. Most non-action verbs are not usually used in the present continuous, even when they are describing a situation that is happening right now.

I **want** a sandwich. NOT I'm wanting a sandwich.

Some common non-action verbs:

be   have   know   like   love   miss   need   see   understand   want

Some non-action verbs have action and non-action meanings.

non-action meaning	action meaning
I **have** two sandwiches. (possession)	I'm **having** a sandwich. (eating)
I **think** English is difficult. (opinion)	I'm **thinking** about her. (the act of thinking)

A **Write the verbs in the simple present tense or the present continuous.**

Dear Kevin,

It's 2:00 and I <u>'m thinking</u> of you. The kids <u>are playing</u> outside. I <u>see</u>
   1. think   2. play   3. see
them through the window right now. They <u>have</u> a small table and chairs and
                                   4. have
they <u>are having</u> a late lunch.
   5. have
I <u>want</u> to mail this letter before the post office closes. I <u>know</u> you're
  6. want   7. know
working hard and we all <u>miss</u> you.
                   8. miss

Maggie

The simple present tense: frequency adverbs

Frequency adverbs generally follow forms of the verb <u>be</u> and precede all other verbs.

be	frequency adverb
I **'m**	**usually** at the pool on Saturdays.

frequency adverb	verb
I **usually**	**go** to the pool on Saturdays.

<u>Sometimes</u>, <u>usually</u>, <u>often</u>, <u>generally</u>, and <u>occasionally</u> can also go at the beginning or the end of a sentence. Don't use the other frequency adverbs there.

Sometimes I go to the pool on Sundays.
I go to the pool **often**.
NOT <u>Never I go to the pool.</u> OR <u>I go to the pool never.</u>

◆D Complete the questions.

- Remind students to use <u>does</u> with *he / she / it* and <u>do</u> with *I / you / we / they*.
- To check their work, have students take turns reading the questions and responses with a partner.

Option: With a partner, students take turns asking and answering the questions in Exercise D, using their own words.

UNIT 6 **LESSON 2**

The simple present tense: non-action verbs

- Have students read the information in the box independently.
- Write the common non-action verbs on the board. Pronounce each one and have students repeat.
- Ask for volunteers to use one of the verbs from the list to say something about themselves. For example, *I love rap music.* Write the sentence and the student's name on the board next to the verb (*I love classical music. [Name]*). Try to elicit one sentence for each of the verbs. Review the meaning of any verbs the class can't create a sentence for.
- Give students about 30 seconds to review the sentences on the board. Then erase the sentences. Students tell a partner as much as they can remember about their classmates. Circulate and make sure students add the third-person singular *-s* to the verbs. (*[Name] loves classical music.*)
- To make sure students understand how some non-action verbs have action and non-action meanings, have them complete the following sentences:
   I have . . .
   I'm having . . .
   I think . . .
   I'm thinking about . . .
- To review, ask a few students to read their sentences for each prompt. Your students might respond:
   I have a car.
   I'm having chicken for dinner tonight.
   I think English is easy.
   I'm thinking about the concert on Friday.

◆A Write the verbs . . .

- Before students do the exercise, have them look at the verbs below the answer spaces. Have them circle the non-action verbs.
- To review, ask for a volunteer to read each paragraph out loud.

Language note: While most non-action verbs are not usually used in the present continuous, exceptions to this rule may be heard in spoken language in some places. (*I'm wanting a sandwich.*)

The simple present tense: frequency adverbs

- Have students read the information in the boxes on pages G12 and G13 independently.
- Write the following lists of verbs and frequency expressions on the board. Ask students to create sentences about their own habits and activities by using one word from each list. Have students write five sentences.

be	*always*
play	*almost always*
go	*usually / often / generally*
eat	*sometimes / occasionally*
exercise	*hardly ever / not ever*
drink	*never / not ever*
talk	*(once) a week*
study	*(twice) a year*
cook	*a lot*

- Students read their sentences out loud in small groups. The group checks for correct word order in all sentences.
- Have students look at their own sentences and rewrite any sentences that can be written correctly in a different order.

┌─────────────────────────────┐
Additional Teaching Ideas

└─────────────────────────────┘

The simple present tense: time expressions

- Call on a student to read the first point in the Grammar box. Ask another student to read the example sentences.

- Do the same for the second point and the example sentences in the Grammar box.

- Read the time expressions out loud and have students repeat. Use a calendar to demonstrate the meanings of the expressions.

- Tell students that the simple present tense is used to tell or ask about habits, customs, regular occurrences, routines or facts.

B> These sentences . . .

- Have students number the seven rules in the boxes at the bottom of page G12 and top of page G13.

- As students rewrite each sentence in Exercise B, have them note the number of the rule they used to correct the sentence. Do item 1 together as a class. Elicit the correct sentence and then the number of the appropriate rule (number 1).

- To review, ask for volunteers to read the corrected sentences and tell what rule they used for each. For items 2 through 10, students should have noted the following rule numbers: 2. 1; 3. 1; 4. 6; 5. 5; 6. 1 / 2; 7. 3 / 4; 8. 6; 9. 1 / 2; 10. 6.

UNIT 7 LESSON 1

Comparative forms of adjectives

- Have students read the information in the box independently.

- Read the two sentences at the bottom of the box out loud. Point out that in comparative sentences, the comparative is followed by *than*.

- Elicit some examples of comparative sentences with *than* from the class. Write them on the board.

Additional Teaching Ideas

In negative sentences, most frequency adverbs can precede OR follow <u>don't</u> or <u>doesn't</u>.

> Hank **usually** doesn't go running on the weekend.
> Hank doesn't **usually** go running on the weekend.

But note that <u>always</u> CANNOT precede <u>don't</u> or <u>doesn't</u>.

> I don't **always** have breakfast in the morning.
> NOT I ~~always don't have~~ breakfast in the morning.

Don't use <u>never</u> with a negative verb. Use the frequency adverb <u>ever</u> with negative verbs.

> I **never** eat sweets. = I **don't ever** eat sweets.
> NOT I ~~don't never~~ eat sweets.

The simple present tense: time expressions

Time expressions generally go at the beginning or the end of a sentence.

> I go to the pool **three times a week**.   **Three times a week**, I go to the pool.

The time expression <u>a lot</u> can appear only at the end of a sentence.

> I go to the pool **a lot**.   NOT ~~A lot I go to the pool.~~

> **some time expressions**
> every week
> every other day
> once a month
> twice a year
> three times a week
>
> **other expressions**
> once in a while
> a lot

B ▷ **These sentences are not written correctly. Rewrite them correctly.**

1. She plays usually golf on Sunday.
   <u>She usually plays golf on Sunday</u>.

2. They go to the park hardly ever.
   <u>They hardly ever go to the park</u>.

3. I always am hungry in the afternoon.
   <u>I am always hungry in the afternoon</u>.

4. We once in a while have eggs for breakfast.
   <u>Once in a while, we have eggs for breakfast</u>.

5. Pat doesn't never exercise.
   <u>Pat doesn't ever exercise/Pat never exercises</u>.

6. Never I go swimming at night.
   <u>I never go swimming at night</u>.

7. Victor doesn't drink always coffee.
   <u>Victor doesn't always drink coffee</u>.

8. Connie and I play twice a week tennis together.
   <u>Connie and I play tennis twice a week together</u>.

9. We go often bike riding in the afternoon.
   <u>We often go bike riding in the afternoon</u>.

10. She is every day late for class.
    <u>She is late for class every day</u>.

UNIT 7 Lesson 1

Comparative forms of adjectives

Add <u>–er</u> to one-syllable adjectives. If the adjective ends in <u>–e</u>, add <u>–r</u>.

> cheap → cheap**er**   loose → loose**r**

If an adjective ends consonant-vowel-consonant, double the final consonant before adding <u>–er</u>.

> hot → ho**tt**er

For most adjectives that end in <u>–y</u>, change the <u>y</u> to <u>i</u> and add <u>–er</u>.

> pretty → prett**ier**   busy → bus**ier**

To make the comparative form of most adjectives of two or more syllables, use <u>more</u> or <u>less</u>.

> She's **less practical** than her sister.   DVDs are **more popular** than videos.

A Write the comparative form of the following adjectives.

	comparative			comparative
1. tall	_taller_	6. casual	more casual
2. pretty	prettier	7. wild	wilder
3. comfortable	more comfortable	8. informal	more informal
4. heavy	heavier	9. late	later
5. light	lighter	10. sad	sadder

B Complete each sentence with a comparative form.

1. This purse is _____nicer_____ than that one.
   nice

2. He's a _____better_____ student than she.
   good

3. Holland is _____smaller_____ than Thailand.
   small

4. Thailand is _____larger_____ than Holland.
   large

5. Women's shoes are usually _more expensive_ than men's shoes.
   expensive

UNIT 7 Lesson 2

Direct objects

The subject of a sentence performs the action of the verb, and a direct object receives the action of the verb.

subject		direct object
I	like	**this house**.
My husband	likes	**that suit**.

A Underline the subjects in the following sentences. Circle the direct objects.

1. We're visiting (Africa) this summer.
2. Many people rent (cars) when they travel.
3. I love Egyptian (food).
4. Sanford and Mary never eat (meat).
5. You can't enter (school) before eight o'clock.
6. Do you have the (tickets)?
7. Marie wants (coffee) with cream.

Indirect objects

When a sentence contains a direct object and prepositional phrase, you can use an indirect object to say the same thing.

prepositional phrase	indirect object
I'm buying the gloves **for her**.	I'm buying **her** the gloves.
Give the sweater **to Ben**.	Give **Ben** the sweater.

B Rewrite each sentence, changing the prepositional phrase into an indirect object.

1. She buys groceries for us. _She buys us groceries_.

2. Laura sends a check to them every month. _Laura sends them a check every month_.

3. At night we read stories to them. _At night we read them stories_.

4. They serve meals to us in the dining room. _They serve us meals in the dining room_.

5. They never give gifts to me on my birthday. _They never give me gifts on my birthday_.

A ▸ Write the comparative form of the following adjectives.

- On a separate sheet of paper, have students make a five-column chart like the one below.
- As students complete Exercise A, have them write each present participle under the example that follows the same spelling rule.
- Review as a class. Pronounce each of the comparative forms on the chart and have students repeat.

cheap**er**	loos**er**	hott**er**	pretty → prett**ier**	less practical/ more popular
taller	later	sadder		more comfortable
lighter			heavier	more casual
wilder				more informal

Option: Have students write sentences with the comparatives from Exercise A. For example, *Flats are more comfortable than pumps.*

B ▸ Complete each sentence with a comparative form.

- After students complete the exercise, call on volunteers to read the sentences.

Option: Have students add the comparatives from Exercise B to the chart they made in Exercise A. Ask *Which comparative is irregular and doesn't have a place on the chart?* (better)

UNIT 7 **LESSON 2**
Direct objects

- Have students read the information in the box independently.
- Read the two examples out loud. Ask:
  What do I like? (this house)
  What does my husband like? (that suit)
- Explain that direct objects answer the question <u>What?</u>

Challenge: Have students write their own sentences following the *subject + verb + direct object* pattern. Suggest that students use the verbs *like, love, have, want, need.* Ask several volunteers to write a sentence on the board. Have different volunteers come to the board to underline the subjects and circle the direct objects in the sentences.

A ▸ Underline the subjects ...

- Review the answers to Exercise A as a class. Then have students look at the underlined subjects. Ask *Are there any subject pronouns?* (yes) *What are they?* (We, I, You, you) Have students look at the circled direct objects. Ask *Are there any object pronouns?* (No. The direct objects are all nouns.)

- Ask *What are the object pronouns?* On the board, write the headings *Subject pronouns* and *Object pronouns.* Have students list both on a sheet of paper. Tell students they will use the object pronouns in the indirect object exercises that follow.

Option: Ask whether each subject and direct object in Exercise A is a noun or a pronoun (1. pronoun, noun; 2. noun, noun; 3. pronoun, noun; 4. noun, noun; 5. pronoun, noun; 6. pronoun, noun; 7. noun, noun)

Indirect objects

- Have students read the information in the box independently.
- Read each pair of examples out loud. Ask *Who am I buying the gloves for?* (for her) *Who do I give the sweater to?* (to Ben) Say *Indirect objects answer the question <u>Who?</u>*
- Write the two sentence patterns with indirect objects on the board:
  subject + verb + direct object + preposition and *indirect object*
  subject + verb + indirect object + direct object
- Tell students they have won a contest at a local department store. They can buy four gifts and spend any amount of money. Students write sentences about what and for whom they are buying. Have students use prepositional phrases in their sentences. For example:
  I'm buying a DVD player for my parents.
- Now have students rewrite their sentences using the other pattern, with the indirect object first. For example:
  I'm buying my parents a DVD player.
- Finally, have students rewrite their sentences using an object pronoun in place of the indirect object noun. For example:
  I'm buying them a DVD player.
- Point out that it's also possible to say *I'm buying a DVD player for them.*

B ▸ Rewrite each sentence ...

- Before students do the exercise, have them underline the prepositional phrase in each sentence.
- Point to the sentence patterns on the board and ask which one item 1 follows (*subject + verb + direct object + preposition and indirect object*). Ask students which pattern to follow when they rewrite the sentences (*subject + verb + indirect object + direct object*).
- Review as a class. Have volunteers read the rewritten sentences.

┌─ **Additional Teaching Ideas** ─┐

└─────────────────┘

C ▷ Rewrite each sentence . . .

- Before students do the exercise, have them underline the indirect object in each sentence.

- Ask which sentence patterns item 1 follows (*subject + verb + indirect object + direct object*). Ask students which pattern to follow when they rewrite the sentences (*subject + verb + direct object + preposition and indirect object*).

- Review as a class. Have volunteers read the rewritten sentences.

D ▷ Add the indirect object to each sentence.

- Before students do the exercise, have them circle the direct object in each sentence.

- Remind students that *preposition + indirect object* goes after the direct object; *indirect object* alone goes before the direct object.

- To review, have volunteers read their answers.

UNIT 8 LESSON 1
The past tense of <u>be</u>: form

- Ask a volunteer to read the rule in the Grammar box. Call on other students to read the example sentences.

- Write on the board:

  I, she, he, it was / wasn't
  you, we, they were / weren't

- Tell students that in informal writing and in speaking, use the contractions <u>wasn't</u> and <u>weren't</u> in negative statements and short answers.

- Write *yesterday* and *last winter* on the board. Ask the class what other past time expressions they know. Write these on the board. For example:

last night	last summer
last weekend	last year
last week	in 2000
last month	

- Read the list out loud and have students repeat.

- To make sure students understand the expressions, have pairs write a date / time for each one. For example, if today is Thursday, March 4, <u>last night</u> was Wednesday, March 3.

- Review as a class. To make sure students know that past time markers can go at the beginning or the end of a sentence write an example for each on the board:

  Last week he was in Thailand; He was in Thailand last week.

The past tense of <u>be</u>: questions

- Call on a student to read the first rule in the Grammar box. Ask other volunteers to read the example questions.

- Do the same for the second rule and example questions.

- Write the following two sentences on the board:

  My dinner was terrific.
  Their passports were on the table.

- Ask the class to change the sentences to <u>yes</u>/<u>no</u> questions. (*Was your dinner terrific? Were their passports on the table?*)

- Now ask the class to create an information question for each sentence. (*How was your dinner? Where were their passports?*)

Option: Show students how to form negative questions. (*Wasn't your flight on time?*)

A ▷ Complete the conversations . . .

- If helpful, have students underline the subjects before they do the exercise. Note that for item 2, speaker B, students should underline *fresh seafood* as the subject for the first answer space.

- To check their work, have students read the conversations with a partner.

┌─ **Additional Teaching Ideas** ─────────────┐
│   │
│   │
│   │
│   │
│   │
│   │
│   │
│   │
└───┘

C Rewrite each sentence, changing the indirect object into a prepositional phrase.

1. He always gives me a check when I ask. <u>*He always gives a check to me when I ask*</u>.

2. I send them the tickets and they give me a receipt. <u>I send the tickets to them and they give me a receipt</u>

3. Michael's assistant shows him the phone messages every day after lunch.
<u>Michael's assistant shows the phone messages to him every day after lunch</u>.

D Add the indirect object to each sentence. Don't add words.

to me **1.** They send it on Monday. <u>*They send it to me on Monday*</u>.

you **2.** Do they give breakfast on the tour? <u>Do they give you breakfast on the tour</u>?

her **3.** We always tell the truth. <u>We always tell her the truth</u>.

for him **4.** They make extra time. <u>They make extra time for him</u>.

UNIT 8 Lesson 1

The past tense of be: form

Use was or were for affirmative statements. Use wasn't or weren't for negative statements.

I **was** there yesterday.   They **were** there, too.
She **wasn't** my teacher.   They **weren't** my classmates.

The past tense of be: questions

Begin yes / no questions with Was or Were.

Was your flight on time?   **Were** you late?

Begin information questions with a question word followed by was or were.

How long was the flight?   **Where were** your passports?

A Complete the conversations with **was, were, wasn't,** or **weren't.**

1. **A:** _____Were_____ you out of town last week?

   B: No, I __wasn't__. Why?

   A: Well, you __weren't__ at work, so I wasn't sure.

2. **A:** How __was__ the food?

   B: Incredible! There __was__ lots of fresh seafood and the fruit __was__ delicious.

3. **A:** So __was__ your vacation OK?

   B: Well, actually it __wasn't__. The food __was__ terrible and the people __were__ unfriendly. What more can I say?

4. **A:** Where __were__ you last weekend?

   B: I __was__ on vacation.

   A: Really? How __was__ it?

5. **A:** How long __was__ your vacation?

   B: Only a week. But you know something? After a week, the kids and I __were__ pretty tired.

B ▷ Write questions with the scrambled words.

1. A: _____Was your vacation very long_____?
　　　　your / vacation / was / very long

B: No, it wasn't. It was pretty short, actually.

2. A: _____Where was your luggage_____?
　　　　your luggage / was / where

B: My wife had it. I thought someone
had stolen it!

3. A: _____Was the drive comfortable_____?
　　　　the drive / was / comfortable

B: Perfect.

4. A: _____Were you on the morning flight_____?
　　　　you / were / on the morning flight

B: Yes, I was.

UNIT 8 Lesson 2

The simple past tense: usage

Use the simple past tense to talk about a completed action in the past.

　　My grandparents went to Paris.　　　　We played tennis and went running every day.

The simple past tense: form

Regular verbs: spelling rules

Form the past tense of most verbs by adding –ed to the base form.

　　play → play**ed**

For verbs ending in –e or –ie, add –d.

　　smile → smile**d**　　　tie → tie**d**

For one-syllable verbs ending in one vowel + one consonant, double the consonant and add –ed.

　　stop → stop**ped**　　　plan → plan**ned**

Two-syllable verbs ending in one vowel + one consonant: If the first syllable is stressed, add –ed.

　　vi - sit → visit**ed**

If the second syllable is stressed, double the consonant and add –ed.

　　pre - fer → prefer**red**

For verbs ending in a consonant and –y, change the –y to –i and add –ed.

　　study → stud**ied**

Irregular verbs

Do not use –ed. See Appendix page 128 for a list of irregular verbs in the simple past tense form.
　　　　　　　　　Note: Page A5 in the Split Editions.

Negative statements

Use didn't + the base form of a verb.

　　He **didn't go** to his grandmother's last weekend.　　They **didn't have** a good trip.
　　NOT He didn't goes to his grandmother's last weekend.　　NOT They didn't had a good trip.

The simple past tense: questions

Begin yes / no questions with Did. Use the base form of the verb.

　　Did you **go** swimming every day?　　　NOT Did you went swimming every day?

Begin information questions with a question word followed by did.

　　Where did you go shopping?　　**When did** you leave?　　**What did** you eat everyday?

Ⓑ▷ Write questions . . .

- Before students do the exercise, have them look at the scrambled words below each answer space. Ask *Which are* yes / no *questions?* (items 1, 3, and 4) *Which are information questions?* (item 2)

- Ask *What do* yes / no *questions begin with?* (was or were) *What do information questions begin with?* (a question word followed by was or were)

- To check their work, have students read the conversations with a partner.

UNIT 8 **LESSON 2**
The simple past tense: usage

- Have students read the information in the box independently.

- Ask *What did you do last summer?* Elicit a few simple past tense sentences from the class.

The simple past tense: form

Regular verbs

- Ask a volunteer to read the first rule in the Grammar box and the example that follows. Call on other students to read the other five spelling rules and the corresponding examples.

Irregular verbs

- Read the list of irregular simple past verb forms on Appendix page 128 (in the Split Editions, the list is on page A5). Have students repeat.

- Review the meanings of any verbs that are unfamiliar to students.

Negative statements

- Write the following sentences on the board:
    My grandmother went to Paris.
    We played soccer and went swimming every day.
    They smiled at the baby.

- Have students rewrite the sentences as negative statements. (My grandmother didn't go to Paris. We didn't play soccer and we didn't go swimming. They didn't smile at the baby.)

The simple past tense: questions

- Call on a student to read the first rule in the Grammar box. Ask another student to read the example question and the incorrect question.

- Ask another volunteer to read the second rule in the Grammar box. Call on other students to read the example questions.

- Write the two sentences from *The simple past tense: usage* box on the board. Ask the class to change the sentences to yes/no questions. (*Did your grandparents go to Paris? Did you play tennis and go running every day?*) Write the questions on the board. Cross out went in the two sentences and underline Did and go in the two questions.

- Now ask the class to create an information question for each sentence. (*Where did your grandparents go? What did you do every day?*)

┌─ **Additional Teaching Ideas** ─────────┐
│   │
│   │
│   │
│   │
│   │
│   │
│   │
│   │
│   │
└──┘

A Write the simple past tense form . . .

- Read the list of words in Exercise A. Have students put a check mark (✓) next to the verbs that are two syllables (return, travel, arrive, offer, hurry).

- Have students look at the verbs that are checked and circle the ones that end in a vowel followed by a consonant (travel, offer). Pronounce these two verbs again. Have students underline the syllable that is stressed (travel, offer).

- On a separate sheet of paper, have students make a six-column chart like the one below.

- Have students complete Exercise A. As they do so, have them write each simple past tense verb under the example that follows the same spelling rule.

- Review as a class.

played	smiled/tied	stopped	visited	preferred	study → studied
returned	liked		traveled		cried
stayed	changed		offered		tried
rained	arrived				hurried
waited					

Option: Have students write the headings /ɪd/, /t/, and /d/ on a sheet of paper. Read the past tense forms from Exercise A out loud. Have students listen for how the ending is pronounced and write the verb under the appropriate heading.

/ɪd/	/t/	/d/
waited	liked	returned
		changed
		cried
		tried
		stayed
		traveled
		arrived
		rained
		offered
		hurried

B Write the simple past tense form . . .

- Have students look at the irregular verbs and write as many of the simple past tense forms as they can without referring to the list on page 128. Then have them look at the list to check their work and fill in any forms they didn't know.

Option: Have students write simple past tense sentences with the irregular verbs.

C Complete the conversations . . .

- Before students do the exercise, have them look at the words below each answer space. Ask *Which are information questions?* (items 1, 2, and 4) *Which are yes / no questions?* (items 3 and 5)

- Ask *What do yes / no questions begin with?* (did) *What do information questions begin with?* (a question word followed by did)

- Point out that while the simple present has two forms — do and does — for negative statements and questions, the simple past has only one — did. To illustrate, read the answer to item 1 several times, changing the subject each time. For example, *Where did she go . . .? Where did we go . . .? Where did Tim go? Where did Rita and Paul go?*

- To check their work, have students read the conversations with a partner.

UNIT 9 LESSON 1

Modals can, should, could: meaning

- Have students read the information in the box independently.

- On the board, write:

can	could	should
ability	suggest an alternative	give advice
possibility	make a weak suggestion	express criticism

- Explain that modals are words that come before verbs. They change the meaning of the verbs in some way.

Modals: form

- Have students read the information in the boxes on pages G17 and G18 independently.

- As a class, create an affirmative sentence for each of the three modals on the board. Add the sentences to the lists on the board. Write each sentence exactly as the student says it, even if there are mistakes. For example:

  can
  ability
  possibility
  Marina can play the guitar.

- Now have the class create a negative sentence for each modal. Add these sentences to the lists on the board. Write each sentence exactly as the student says it, even if there are mistakes. For example:

  can
  ability
  possibility
  Marina can play the guitar.
  Eric can't come to class on Friday.

┌─ **Additional Teaching Ideas** ─────────────┐
│   │
│   │
│   │
│   │
└──┘

A Write the simple past tense form of the following verbs.

1. return   *returned*
2. like   *liked*
3. change   *changed*
4. cry   *cried*

5. try   tried
6. stay   stayed
7. travel   traveled
8. arrive   arrived

9. rain   rained
10. wait   waited
11. offer   offered
12. hurry   hurried

B Write the simple past tense form of these irregular verbs.

1. eat   *ate*
2. drink   *drank*
3. swim   *swam*
4. go   *went*

5. write   wrote
6. meet   met
7. run   ran
8. begin   began

9. buy   bought
10. read   read
11. pay   paid
12. understand   understood

C Complete the conversations with questions in the simple past tense. Use a capital letter to begin sentences.

1. **A:** _Where did you go on vacation last summer_ ?
      you / go / where / on vacation last summer
   B: We went to the mountains. It was very nice.

2. **A:** _When did you get back from vacation_ ?
      you / get back / when / from vacation
   B: We got back last week. I'm sorry we didn't call you.

3. **A:** _Did they have a good flight_ ?
      they / have / a good flight
   B: Well, they said it was really scenic. So I guess so.

4. **A:** _What did you do in London_ ?
      you / do / what / in London
   B: We went to see some plays and we visited a few museums.

5. **A:** _Did your parents enjoy their trip_ ?
      your parents / enjoy / their trip
   B: Well, almost. There were some problems, but I think they had a good time.

UNIT 9 Lesson 1

Modals can, should, could: meaning

Use can to express ability or possibility.

Jerome **can** speak Korean.   **Can** you be there before 8:00?

Use could to suggest an alternative or to make a weak suggestion.

They **could** see an old movie like *Titanic*, or they **could** go to something new.

Use should to give advice or to express criticism.

You **should** think before you speak.

Modals: form

Modals are followed by the base form of the main verb of the sentence, except in short answers to questions.

Who **should read** this?   They **should**.   **Can** you **see** the moon tonight?   Yes, I **can**.

Never add –s to the third-person singular form of modals.

He **should** buy a ticket in advance.   NOT He shoulds buy a ticket in advance.

Never use <u>to</u> between modals and the base form.

You **could take** the train or the bus.   NOT ~~You could to take the train or the bus.~~

Use <u>not</u> between the modal and the base form.

You **shouldn't stay** at the Galaxy Hotel.   They **can't take** the express.

Modals: questions

In <u>yes</u> / <u>no</u> questions, the modal comes before the subject. In information questions, the question word precedes the modal.

<u>yes</u> / <u>no</u> questions

Should I buy a round-trip ticket?
Can we make the 1:05 flight?
Could she take an express train?

information questions

Which trains **could** I take?
Who can give me the information?
When should they leave?

A ▶ **Complete each sentence or question.**

1. Who ___**should buy**___ the tickets?
   _{should buy / should to buy}

2. Where ___**can I find**___ a hotel?
   _{I can find / can I find}

3. You ___**could walk**___ or ___**take**___ the bus.
   _{could to walk / could walk}   _{take / taking}

4. ___**Should I call**___ you when I arrive?
   _{I should call / Should I call}

5. We ___**can't take**___ the bus; it left five minutes ago.
   _{can to not take / can't take}

6. When ___**should you give**___ the agent your boarding pass?
   _{should you giving / should you give}

7. Which trains ___**can get**___ me there before dinnertime?
   _{can get / can getting}

UNIT 9 Lesson 2

Expression of future actions

There are four ways to express future actions using the present tenses. These are similar in meaning.

<u>be going to</u>

<u>be going to</u> + base form usually expresses a future plan or certain knowledge about the future.

I'm going to spend my summer in Africa.   She**'s going to get** a rental car when she arrives.
It**'s going to rain** tomorrow.

The present continuous

The present continuous can also express a future plan.

We**'re traveling** tonight.   They **aren't wearing** formal clothes to the wedding.
We **aren't eating** home tomorrow.

The simple present tense

The simple present tense can express a future action, almost always with verbs of motion: <u>arrive</u>, <u>come</u>, <u>depart</u>, <u>fly</u>, <u>go</u>, <u>head</u>, <u>leave</u>, <u>sail</u>, and <u>start</u>, especially when on a schedule or timetable. When the simple present tense expresses the future, there is almost always a word, phrase, or clause indicating the future time.

This Monday the express **leaves** at noon.

The present tense of <u>be</u>

The present tense of <u>be</u> can describe a future event if it includes a word or phrase that indicates the future.

The wedding **is on Sunday**.

Modals: questions

- Have students read the information in the box independently.
- Have the class add a <u>yes</u>/<u>no</u> and information question for each modal to the lists on the board from the previous modals exercise. Write each question exactly as the student says it, even if there are mistakes. For example:

  can
  ability
  possibility
  Marina can play the guitar.
  Eric can't come to class on Friday.
  Can we have a party for our last class?
  Who can speak three languages?

- Read each of the rules under *Modals: form* and *Modals: questions* out loud. After you read each rule, pause and ask the class to check the correctness of the sentences or questions on the board.

(A) Complete each sentence or question.

- Before students do the exercise, write the patterns for sentences with modals on the board:

  affirmative: subject + modal + base form of verb
  negative: subject + modal + <u>not</u> + base form of verb
  question: [question word +] modal + subject + base form of verb

- To review, call on volunteers to read their answers out loud.

UNIT 9 **LESSON 2**
Expressions of future actions

- Call on a student to read the first point in the Grammar box. Ask another student to read the example sentences.
- Continue in this manner until all four ways to express future actions and their corresponding examples have been read.
- Read the list of verbs of motion out loud and have students repeat. Review the meanings of any that are unfamiliar to students.
- Ask *To use the simple present tense to express a future action, what do you need?* Write on the board and fill in as you elicit the answers from students:

  Simple present tense for future action:
  1. a verb of motion
  2. a word, phrase, or clause indicating future time

- Use one example from each set of examples in the box to create a chart on the board:

be going to	*present continuous*	*simple present tense*
I'm going to spend my summer in Africa.	*We're traveling tonight.*	*This Monday the express leaves at noon.*

- Have students rewrite each of the three sentences in the other two forms, if possible. Students' completed chart should look like this:

be going to	*present continuous*	*simple present tense*
I'm going to spend my summer in Africa.	*I'm spending my summer in Africa.*	*X*
We're going to travel tonight.	*We're traveling tonight.*	*We travel tonight.*
This Monday the express is going to leave at noon.	*This Monday the express is leaving at noon.*	*This Monday the express leaves at noon.*

- Point out that <u>travel</u> is also a verb of motion. Since <u>We're traveling tonight</u> contains a verb of motion and a word indicating future time, <u>tonight</u>, the sentence can be rewritten in the simple present: <u>We travel tonight</u>.

Additional Teaching Ideas

TG18

A. Answer the following questions.

• Remind students that they can express their future plans in more than one way. Write your own response to question 1 on the board. Ask a volunteer to change it to another form. For example, *I'm visiting my sister in London this summer.* → *I'm going to visit my sister in London this summer.*

• After students complete the exercise, elicit a response to each question. Ask another student to express each response in a different form.

Option: In pairs, students take turns asking and answering the questions in Exercise A using their own words.

B. Read the arrival . . .

• Have students look at the schedules. Ask about the form of transportation for each (bus, flight / airplane, train). Point out that the schedules show future departure and arrival times.

• If students are not sure what verbs to use, refer them back to the list of motion verbs on page G18.

• To review, have volunteers read their answers to the class. Check that students include the third-person singular *-s* in the statements and use the base form of the verb in the questions.

UNIT 10 **LESSON 1**
Comparison with adjectives

• Ask a volunteer to read the first point in the Grammar box. Have another volunteer read the example sentence.

• Call on another pair of students to do the same for the second point in the Grammar box.

• Read the adjective, comparative adjective, and superlative adjective out loud and have students repeat.

• Write the names of these three products on the board:
  Computer (Price: 500)
  Sweater (Price: 40)
  Hair dryer (Price: 10)

• Ask students to write two sentences comparing the items. Tell them to use a comparative adjective in one sentence and a superlative adjective in the other.

• Ask several students to read one of their sentences. After each sentence, ask whether a comparative or a superlative adjective was used. Your students can write:
  [The computer] is more expensive than [the sweater].
  [The hair dryer] is the cheapest.
  [The computer] is larger than [the hair dryer].

Superlative adjectives: form

• Call on a student to read the first rule in the Grammar box. Ask another student to read the examples.

• Continue in this manner until all the rules and examples have been read.

• Write the following on the board:
  A cat is ___, a tiger is _____ but a cheetah is _____. (fast)
  A car is ___, a truck is _____ but a train is _____. (heavy)
  A bench is _____, a chair is _____ but a sofa is _____. (comfortable)

• Have students copy the sentences and complete them using the adjective in parentheses in the adjective, comparative adjective, and superlative adjective forms. Ask three volunteers to come write their answers on the board. Review as a class.

┌─ **Additional Teaching Ideas** ─────────┐
│   │
│   │
│   │
└──┘

A　**Answer the following questions.**

1.　What are your plans for the summer?
_____ (Answers will vary.) _____

2.　What are you going to do this weekend?
_____

3.　What are you doing this evening?
_____

B　**Read the arrival and departure schedules. Then complete each question or statement with the simple present tense.**

TOMORROW'S BUS TO **NEW YORK CITY**		THURSDAY'S FLIGHT TO **GUATEMALA CITY**	THIS WEEKEND'S TRAIN TO **BEIJING**

1.　The bus __arrives__ at 11:00. It __departs__ at 8:00.

2.　When __does__ the flight __arrive__? At 1:30.

3.　The flight __departs__ at 23:30.

4.　What time __does__ the train __arrive__ in Beijing? At ten-twenty at night.

5.　__Does__ the train __depart/ leave__ at seven? Yes, it does.

UNIT 10 Lesson 1

┌─ **Comparison with adjectives** ─────────────────────────

Comparative adjectives compare two people, places, or things.

　　Mexico City is **bigger than** Los Angeles.

Superlative adjectives compare more than two people, places, or things.

　　Mexico City is **the biggest** city in the Americas. (compared to all the other cities in the Americas)

adjective	comparative adjective	superlative adjective
cheap	**cheaper (than)**	**the cheapest**
expensive	**more expensive (than)**	**the most expensive**

└──

┌─ **Superlative adjectives: form** ─────────────────────────

Add –est to one-syllable adjectives. If the adjective ends in –e, add –st. Remember to use the with superlatives.

　　cheap → **the** cheap**est**　　　　　　loose → **the** loose**st**

If an adjective ends with consonant-vowel-consonant, double the final consonant before adding –est.

　　hot → the ho**tt**est

For most adjectives that end in –y, change the y to i and add –est.

　　pretty → the prett**iest**　　　　　　busy → the bus**iest**

To make the superlative form of most adjectives of two or more syllables, use the most or the least.

　　Car trips are **the least relaxing** vacations.　　Safaris are **the most exciting** vacations.

└──

A ► Write the comparative and superlative form of the following adjectives.

	comparative	superlative		comparative	superlative
1. tall	taller	tallest	9. informal	more informal	most informal
2. easy	easier	easiest	10. interesting	more interesting	most interesting
3. liberal	more liberal	most liberal	11. conservative	more conservative	most conservative
4. heavy	heavier	heaviest	12. light	lighter	lightest
5. unusual	more unusual	most unusual	13. casual	more casual	most casual
6. pretty	prettier	prettiest	14. comfortable	more comfortable	most comfortable
7. exciting	more exciting	most exciting	15. relaxing	more relaxing	most relaxing
8. wild	wilder	wildest			

B ► Complete each sentence with a comparative or superlative adjective.

1. That dinner was __the most delicious__ meal on our vacation.
   delicious

2. This scanner is definitely __better__ than that one.
   good

3. The Caribbean cruise is __the most relaxing__ of our vacation packages.
   relaxing

4. The Honshu X24 is a good camera, but the Cashio Speedo 5 is __easier__ to use.
   easy

5. We have several brands, but I'd say the R300 is __the most popular__.
   popular

6. Sunday is going to be __the worst__ day of the week. It's the end of my vacation!
   bad

7. I like that vase, but I think this one is __more beautiful__.
   beautiful

8. The Italian bowl was a good deal, but the Portuguese one was __nicer__.
   nice

C ► Complete the conversations with a superlative adjective.

1. **A:** Well, we've got several brands to choose from.

   B: Which one's __the best__?
   good

2. **A:** Would you like to see these scanners?

   B: Sure. But which one's __easier__ to use?
   easy

3. **A:** I'm looking for a PDA. Which brand is __lighter__?
   light

   B: Oh, that would be the Delio P500.

4. **A:** How much can you spend?

   B: Not too much. Which is __the least expensive__?
   expensive

5. **A:** I love these plates. They're so unusual. Should we buy one?

   B: Sure. Which one do you think is __the most attractive__?
   attractive

A) Write ...

- On a separate sheet of paper, have students make a five-column chart like the one below.

- As students complete Exercise A, have them write each superlative form under the example that follows the same spelling rule. Students may use <u>most</u> or <u>least</u> for adjectives of two or more syllables.

- Review as a class. Pronounce each of the superlative forms on the chart and have students repeat.

cheap**est**	loose**st**	hot**test**	pret**ty**→pretti**est** busy→busi**est**	least relaxing/ most exciting
tallest			easiest	most liberal
wildest			heavier	most unusual
lightest				most exciting
				most interesting
				least informal
				least conservative
				least casual
				least comfortable
				least relaxing

B) Complete each sentence ...

- Remind students that sentences that compare two things use a comparative adjective and that superlatives are used to compare more than two things.

- Point out that after students decide whether the sentence needs a comparative or a superlative, they have to determine the correct form.

- To review, ask volunteers to read the sentences out loud.

C) Complete the conversations ...

- Point out that <u>Which?</u> is the question word used with comparatives and superlatives. Have students circle <u>which</u> in each conversation.

- To check their work, have students read the conversations with a partner.

Additional Teaching Ideas

UNIT 10 **LESSON 2**

Intensifiers <u>too</u>, <u>really</u>, and <u>very</u>

- Have students read the information in the box independently.
- Be sure students know that intensifiers come before the adjective.

A ▸ **Complete each sentence . . .**

- Before students do the exercise, point out that more than one answer is possible for each item.
- Review as a class. Elicit more than one answer for each item.
- Point out that the only sentences that can accept *too* are items 2, 3, 7, and 8. Read these answers out loud: *too unhealthy, too expensive, too slow, too tight.* Emphasize that these all have negative meaning.

B ▸ **Complete the conversations . . .**

- On the board, write:

+ / satisfactory	− / not satisfactory
adjective + <u>enough</u>	<u>too</u> + adjective
	<u>not</u> + adjective + <u>enough</u>

- If helpful, point out that students should use <u>enough</u> in the negative sentences. (A negative sentence with <u>too</u> expresses that something is satisfactory. *It's not too sweet* means that it's just right.)
- To check their work, have students read the conversations with a partner.

┌─ **Additional Teaching Ideas** ─────────────┐
│   │
│   │
│   │
│   │
│   │
│   │
└───┘

UNIT 10 Lesson 2

Intensifiers too, really, and very

Intensifiers make the meaning of adjectives stronger.

Too expresses the idea of "more than enough." **Too** has a negative meaning.

These shoes are **too** expensive. I'm not going to buy them.   That movie is **too** scary. I don't want to see it.

Very and **really** don't have negative meaning.

These shoes are **very** expensive. I like them.   That movie is **really** scary. I'm going to love it.

A ▶ **Complete each sentence with a phrase using <u>too</u>, <u>really</u>, or <u>very</u>.**   *(Answers will vary, but may include the following.)*

1. Beach vacations are _really relaxing_. I love them.
2. French fries are _really unhealthy_. You shouldn't eat them every day.
3. A safari vacation is _too expensive_. I don't have enough money to go.
4. This movie is _really good_. I want to see it.
5. Our house is _really wonderful_. I don't want to sell it.
6. English is _very popular_. Many people study it.
7. This printer is _too slow_. I need a new one.
8. Those pants are _too tight_! You should wear something more conservative.

B ▶ **Complete the conversations. Write the adjectives with <u>too</u> or <u>enough</u>.**

1. **A:** How about this necklace? Should we buy it for your mother?

   B: No. It isn't _pretty enough_. I want something nicer.
   <u>pretty</u>

2. **A:** Look. I bought this rug today. Do you think it's too small?

   B: No. I think it's _big enough_.
   <u>big</u>

3. **A:** I'm sending this steak back to the chef.

   B: Why? What's wrong?

   A: It's just not _good enough_.
   <u>good</u>

4. **A:** How was your vacation?

   B: Well, to tell the truth, it just wasn't _relaxing enough_.
   <u>relaxing</u>

5. **A:** Did you buy a microwave oven?

   B: I looked at some yesterday. But they were _too expensive_.
   <u>expensive</u>

6. **A:** You don't eat candy?

   B: No. It's _too sweet_ for me.
   <u>sweet</u>

7. **A:** How's that soup? Is it _hot enough_?
   <u>hot</u>

   B: No, it's fine. Thanks.

8. **A:** Do you want any ice in your water?

   B: No, thanks. It's _cold enough_.
   <u>cold</u>

🎧 TOP NOTCH POP LYRICS

Going Out [Unit 2]

Do you want to see a play?
What time does the play begin?
It starts at eight. Is that OK?
I'd love to go. I'll see you then.
I heard it got some good reviews.
Where's it playing? What's the show?
It's called "One Single Life to Lose."
I'll think about it. I don't know.

(CHORUS)
Everything will be all right
when you and I go out tonight.

When Thomas Soben gives his talk—
The famous chef? That's not for me!
The doors open at nine o'clock.
There's a movie we could see
at Smith and Second Avenue.
That's my favorite neighborhood!
I can't wait to be with you.
I can't wait to have some food.

(CHORUS)

We're going to have a good time.
Don't keep me up past my bedtime.
We'll make a date.
Tonight's the night.
It starts at eight.
The price is right!
I'm a fan of rock and roll.
Classical is more my style.
I like blues and I like soul.
Bach and Mozart make me smile!
Around the corner and down the street.
That's the entrance to the park.
There's a place where we could meet.
I wouldn't go there after dark!

(CHORUS: 2 times)

The World Café [Unit 5]

Is there something that you want?
Is there anything you need?
Have you made up your mind
what you want to eat?
Place your order now,
or do you need more time?
Why not start with some juice—
lemon, orange, or lime?
Some like it hot, some like it sweet,
some like it really spicy.
You may not like everything you eat,
but I think we're doing nicely.

(CHORUS)
I can understand every word you say.
Tonight we're speaking English at The
World Café.

I'll take the main course now.
I think I'll have the fish.
Does it come with the choice of another
    dish?
Excuse me waiter, please—
I think I'm in the mood
for a little dessert, and the cake looks good.

Do you know? Are there any low-fat
desserts that we could try now?
I feel like having a bowl of fruit.
Do you have to say good-bye now?

(CHORUS)

Apples, oranges, cheese and ham,
coffee, juice, milk, bread, and jam,
rice and beans, meat and potatoes,
eggs and ice cream,
grilled tomatoes—
That's the menu.
That's the list.
Is there anything I missed?

(CHORUS)

A Typical Day [Unit 6]

The Couch Potato sits around.
He eats junk food by the pound.
It's just a typical day.
Watching as the world goes by,
he's out of shape and wonders why.
It's just a typical day.

(CHORUS)
Every night he dreams that he's
skydiving through the air.
And sometimes you appear.
He says, "What are you doing here?"

He cleans the house and plays guitar,
takes a shower, drives the car.
It's just a typical day.
He watches TV all alone,
reads and sleeps, talks on the phone.
It's just a typical day.

(CHORUS)

I'm sorry.
Mr. Couch Potato's resting right now.
Can he call you back?
He usually lies down every day of the week,
and he always has to have a snack.
Now all his dreams are coming true.
He's making plans to be with you.
It's just a typical day.
He goes dancing once a week.
He's at the theater as we speak!
It's just a typical day.

(CHORUS)

My Dream Vacation [Unit 8]

The ride was bumpy
and much too long.
It was pretty boring.
It felt so wrong.
I slept all night,
and it rained all day.
We left the road,
and we lost the way.
Then you came along
and you took my hand.
You whispered words
I could understand.

(CHORUS)
On my dream vacation,
I dream of you.

I don't ever want to wake up.
On my dream vacation,
this much is true:
I don't ever want it to stop.

The food was awful.
They stole my purse.
The whole two weeks went
from bad to worse.
They canceled my ticket.
I missed my flight.
They were so unfriendly
it just wasn't right.
So I called a taxi,
and I got inside,
and there you were,
sitting by my side.

(CHORUS)

You were so unusual.
The day was so exciting.
I opened up my eyes,
and you were gone.
I waited for hours.
You never called.
I watched TV
and looked at the walls.
Where did you go to?
Why weren't you near?
Did you have a reason
to disappear?
So I flew a plane
to the south of France,
and I heard you say,
"Would you like to dance?"

(CHORUS)

Shopping for Souvenirs [Unit 10]

I go to the bank at a quarter to ten.
I pick up my cash from the ATM.
Here at the store, it won't be too hard
to take out a check or a credit card.
The bank has a good rate of exchange,
and everything here is in my price range.
The easiest part of this bargain hunt
is that I can afford anything I want.

(CHORUS)
Whenever I travel around the world,
I spend my money for two.
Shopping for souvenirs
helps me to be near you.

I try to decide how much I should pay
for the beautiful art I see on display.
To get a great deal, I can't be too nice.
It can't hurt to ask for a better price.

(CHORUS)

Yes, it's gorgeous, and I love it.
It's the biggest and the best,
though it might not be the cheapest.
How much is it—more than all the rest?
I'll pass on some good advice to you:
When you're in Rome, do as the Romans do.
A ten percent tip for the taxi fare
should be good enough when you're staying
    there.

(CHORUS)

Workbook Answer Key

Note: In communicative exercises where several answers are possible, this answer key contains some examples of correct answers, not all possible answers. Any valid answer in this type of exercise should be considered acceptable.

UNIT 1

Exercise 1
1. true   **2.** false   **3.** false   **4.** no information   **5.** false

Exercise 2
2. b   **3.** d   **4.** a

Exercise 3
Answers will vary.

Exercise 4
1. c   **2.** a   **3.** b   **4.** c

Exercise 5
1. am, meet, too
2. that, over, Is, think

Exercise 6
2. Are they   **3.** Is she   **4.** Is he   **5.** Are you   **6.** Are you

Exercise 7
2. Yes, he is.   **3.** No, she isn't. / No, she's not.   **4.** Yes, they are.

Exercise 8
3. A: Is he married?
    B: No, he's not. / No, he isn't.
4. A: Are you from Kyoto?
    B: Yes, we are.
5. A: Are Bill and Cliff here today?
    B: No, they aren't. / No, they're not.
6. A: Is she from Ireland?
    B: Yes, she is.
7. A: Are you in my class?
    B: No, I'm not.

Exercise 9
Answers will vary.

Exercise 10
1. His, he
2. you, your
3. their, they
4. we, our, Her, She

Exercise 11
2. What's   **3.** How old is   **4.** What's   **5.** Where are
6. Who are

Exercise 12
1. c   **2.** d   **3.** f   **4.** b   **5.** a   **6.** g   **7.** e

Exercise 13
1. Who are they?   **2.** What are their names?   **3.** Where are they from?   **4.** How old is she?

Exercise 14
Answers will vary.

Exercise 15
1. false   **2.** false   **3.** true   **4.** true   **5.** no information

Exercise 16
Answers will vary.

Exercise 17
Answers will vary.

Exercise 18
Answers will vary. Following is one example of what students may write:

> Meet Eldrick Woods. His nickname is Tiger. He is an athlete. He lives in Orlando, Florida, USA. He is from Cypress, California.

GRAMMAR BOOSTER
Exercise A
1. a   **2.** c   **3.** b   **4.** b   **5.** b

Exercise B
1. b   **2.** d   **3.** e   **4.** f   **5.** c   **6.** a

Exercise C
2. He's   **3.** It's   **4.** He's   **5.** It's   **6.** They're   **7.** you're not
8. I'm

Exercise D
1. Their   **2.** His   **3.** Her   **4.** Your   **5.** My, my   **6.** Our

Exercise E
2. What's your teacher's name?   **3.** Where are you from?
4. Who are they?   **5.** What's your name?   **6.** What's your address?

JUST FOR FUN
Exercise 1

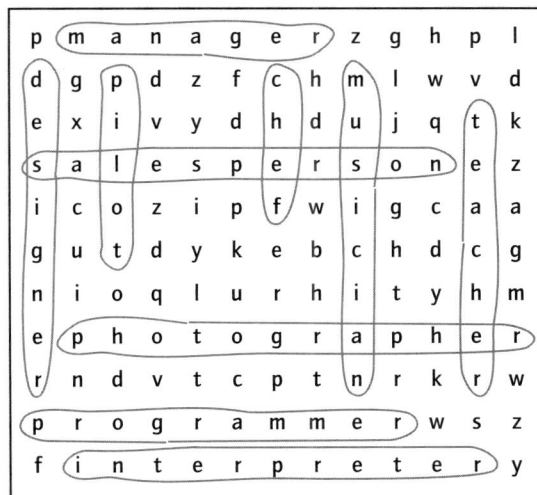

Exercise 2
1. Mexican   **2.** Canadian   **3.** Turkish   **4.** Argentinean
5. Brazilian   **6.** Lebanese

UNIT 2

Exercise 1

Who is playing?	What kind of music?	Where is it?	What time is the show?	How much are tickets?
Marc Anthony	Latin	Havana Club	10:30 p.m.	$25
James Carter	jazz	Riverfront Park	12:45 p.m.	$10
The White Stripes	rock	Continental Club	11:30 p.m.	$15
Alfred Brendel	classical	City Music Hall	8:00 p.m.	$45

Exercise 2

Answers will vary.

Exercise 3

Answers will vary. Following is one example of what students may write:

> I like jazz music, but rock music isn't really my style. A concert at 11:00 p.m. is too late, but a concert at 8:00 p.m. is perfect for me.

Exercise 4

1. c   2. b   3. b   4. a

Exercise 5

1 Are you busy on Saturday night?
6 10:00 p.m.? Well, I'd like to go, but that's past my bedtime.
4 Really? Sounds great! What time's the play?
3 A Comedy of Errors is at the Community Theater.
5 At 10:00 p.m. It's a late show.
2 No, I'm not. Why?
7 Too bad. Maybe some other time.

Exercise 6

1. on   2. in   3. at, on   4. at, in   5. at, in   6. on   7. at

Exercise 7

2. What time's the concert?   3. Where's the school?
4. Where's Tim?   5. When's his class?   6. Where's the concert?   7. When's your class?

Exercise 8

Answers will vary.

Exercise 9

1. d   2. b   3. a   4. c

Exercise 10

2. It's down the street.   3. It's across the street.
4. It's around the corner.   5. It's on the corner of Hill Street and Valley Road.   6. It's on the left.

Exercise 11

Conversations will vary. Following is one example of what students may write:
A: Excuse me. I'm looking for the Coffee Stop Café.
B: The Coffee Stop Café? It's on Second Street. It's around the corner.
A: Thanks. And one more question. Where's the Salsa Club?
B: Do you know the address?
A: Yes, it's 131 Aspen Street.
B: Oh, that's down the street, on the left side of the street.
A: Thanks.

Exercise 12

Answers will vary.

Exercise 13

1. On Saturday, May 10
2. At the Park Arts Theater
3. At 7:00 p.m.
4. At the Park Arts Theater
5. The Korean Dance: "Bu–che Chum" Fan Dance Troupe

Exercise 14

1. Saturday   2. Park Arts Center   3. Rand Park   4. play
5. dance   6. concert   7. 5:00 PM

Exercise 15

1. true   2. false   3. no information   4. false

Exercise 16

Answers will vary.

GRAMMAR BOOSTER

Exercise A

1. on   2. at   3. in   4. at   5. in   6. in   7. on   8. in

Exercise B

1. a   2. c   3. a   4. b   5. c   6. a   7. c

Exercise C

2. on   3. at   4. on   5. in   6. at   7. on   8. at   9. on
10. at   11. on

Exercise D

2. A: Where's the play?
   B: The play is at The Landry Theater.
3. A: Where's the supermarket?
   B: The supermarket is on Park Road.
4. A: When's the exhibit?
   B: The exhibit is in January and February.

JUST FOR FUN

Exercise 1

Across
4. movie   6. exhibit   8. play
Down
1. free   2. concert   3. right   5. thirty   7. bad

Exercise 2

1. actor   2. musician   3. artist   4. writer

UNIT 3

Exercise 1

Answers will vary. Following are some examples of what students may write:

Family Relationships		
Words for males	Words for females	Words for males and females
son	daughter	children
father	mother	parents
grandfather	grandmother	grandparents
husband	wife	in-laws
uncle	aunt	cousins
father-in-law	mother-in-law	
brother-in-law	sister-in-law	
nephew	niece	

Exercise 2

1. parents   2. grandparents   3. cousin   4. husband
5. niece   6. children

Exercise 3

Note: Order of some of the answers may vary.
2. Jane is a _daughter_, a _sister_, a _sister-in-law_, and an _aunt_.
3. Evan is a _grandson_, a _son_, a _brother_, and a _nephew_.
4. Mark is a _grandfather_, a _father_, a _husband_, and a _father-in-law_.

Exercise 4

1. c **2.** b **3.** c **4.** a **5.** a

Exercise 5

1. lives **2.** works **3.** likes **4.** doesn't like
5. doesn't have **6.** has **7.** live **8.** work

Exercise 6

1. e **2.** c **3.** d **4.** a **5.** b

Exercise 7

1. true **2.** no information **3.** false

Exercise 8

2. They're divorced. **3.** She's a widow. **4.** They're twins.

Exercise 9

men (are older)

Exercise 10

Answers will vary. Following is one example of what students may write:
2. Does your brother look like you? **3.** Do you have any photos of your family? **4.** Does your daughter like this music? **5.** Does the manager work on Saturdays?

Exercise 11

Answers will vary.

Exercise 12

1. does **2.** does **3.** do **4.** does **5.** do **6.** do

Exercise 13

1. c **2.** e **3.** a **4.** b **5.** d **6.** f

Exercise 14

2. _Where do_ your cousins _live_? **3.** _When does_ your mother _visit_ you? **4.** _How many_ concert tickets _do you have_?
5. _What time do you go_ to school? **6.** _Who does_ your younger brother _look like_?

Exercise 15

Answers will vary.

Exercise 16

1. In the United States. **2.** They are triplets. **3.** No, they don't.

Exercise 17

1. a, c **2.** a **3.** c **4.** a

Exercise 18

2. Chris and Lola both like coffee. / Chris likes coffee and Lola does, too. **3.** Joon is a new student but Kris isn't.
4. Mia doesn't have a large family and Greg doesn't either.
5. Jay looks like his father but his brother doesn't.

Exercise 19

Answers will vary. Following is one example of what students may write:
They have the same occupation. Shaquille is an athlete and Ming is, too. They are from different countries. Shaquille has a big family but Ming doesn't. Shaquille is married but Ming isn't. They like similar music. They both like rap music.

GRAMMAR BOOSTER
Exercise A

1. a **2.** b **3.** d **4.** e **5.** c **6.** f

Exercise B

2. Yes, they do. **3.** Yes, I do. **4.** No, he doesn't.
5. No, we don't.

Exercise C

2. _Does she eat_ / _Does your sister eat_ meat?
3. _Does he drink_ / _Does your grandfather drink_ coffee?
4. _Do you like_ jazz?
5. _Do you have any_ nieces and nephews?

Exercise D

1. a **2.** b **3.** b **4.** a **5.** b **6.** b **7.** a

Exercise E

2. Where does Jon work?
3. When do they start class?
4. What kind of music do you like?

JUST FOR FUN
Exercise 1
Across
1. nephew **2.** alike **3.** aunt **4.** single
Down
5. law **6.** cousins **7.** younger **8.** parents
9. twins **10.** different

Exercise 2

1. Harry **2.** Shirley **3.** Mark **4.** Barbara **5.** Cynthia
6. Rick **7.** Beth **8.** Alex **9.** Ted **10.** Kelly

UNIT 4

Exercise 1

1. true **2.** false **3.** false **4.** false

Exercise 2

Answers will vary.

Exercise 3

Answers will vary.

Exercise 4

1. c **2.** a **3.** a **4.** c

Exercise 5

2. he's / he is looking **3.** isn't / is not working **4.** Are you going **5.** I'm leaving **6.** are you calling **7.** he's / he is using

Exercise 6

2. No, they're not. They're / They are looking at a catalog.
3. No, I'm not. I'm / I am shopping for a PDA. **4.** No, she's not. She's / She is going to the movie at 7:30.

Exercise 7

2. Is he using the computer now? **3.** Are they buying a CD burner? **4.** Is Karla working today?

Exercise 8

2. is going to the computer show **3.** are you buying
4. is your sister going to Vienna

Exercise 9

1. She's / She is having lunch with Elias. **2.** Yes, she's / she is going shopping. She's / She is looking for a DVD player.
3. No, she's / she is not eating dinner. She's / She is seeing / watching a movie with Dan.

Exercise 10
Answers will vary.

Exercise 11
1. How's it going?   2. What's wrong with it?
3. What brand is it?   4. Any suggestions?

Exercise 12
1. e   2. c   3. b   4. a   5. d

Exercise 13
Answers will vary but may include the following:
2. Pell computers are terrific!   3. Too bad.   4. It's a lemon!

Exercise 14
Answers will vary.

Exercise 15
1. true   2. false   3. false   4. no information

Exercise 16
2. is leaving   3. is going   4. is talking   5. is buying
6. is using   7. is making   8. is sending   9. are cleaning
10. making

Exercise 17
Answers will vary. Following is one example of what students
may write:
    The employees at the Techo office are having problems.
The number Frank is trying to reach on the phone is busy. The
photocopier is broken / jammed. The sink in the kitchen is
clogged, and the coffee maker is overflowing.

Exercise 18
convenient, portable, popular

Exercise 19
Answers will vary.

GRAMMAR BOOSTER
Exercise A
2. My mother's buying a newspaper   3. They're walking to
school   4. It's raining all the time   5. The bus is stopping
in front of my house   6. He's running in the park   7. We're
closing the store   8. He's writing the report

Exercise B
2. Sonia and Lee are not / aren't drinking tea.   3. Ted is not /
isn't doing homework.   4. You are / You're not listening.
5. I am / I'm not reading a book.   6. We are / We're not eating
at your house.   7. The fax machine is not / isn't printing.

Exercise C
1. d   2. b   3. c   4. a   5. g   6. e   7. f

Exercise D
2. Where are they playing soccer?   3. What is Sam eating?
4. When is Lidia coming home?   5. Why are you using my
computer?

JUST FOR FUN
Exercise 1
1. coffee maker   2. PDA   3. microwave oven
4. hair dryer   5. photocopier   6. printer   7. cell phone
new word: machine

Exercise 2
2. a photocopier   3. a hair dryer   4. a refrigerator

UNIT 5

Exercise 1
2. Cleo's Café   3. Louis' Restaurant   4. Louis' Restaurant

Exercise 2
Answers will vary.

Exercise 3
Answers will vary but may include the following:
1. fruits: bananas, grapes, oranges, mangoes   2. vegetables:
carrots, broccoli, onions   3. oils: olive oil, coconut oil
4. meat: chicken, sausage   5. dairy products: butter,
cheese, milk   6. sweets: candy, pie   7. seafood: fish,
shrimp, crab   8. grains: rice, noodles, bread

Exercise 4
milk, fruit, chicken, vegetables (carrots, potatoes, and peppers)

Exercise 5
There is fish, sausage, milk, cheese, broccoli, yogurt, and a
banana. There isn't any lettuce or any juice. There are apples,
eggs, and grapes. There aren't any carrots, oranges, or onions.

Exercise 6
Answers will vary.

Exercise 7
2. a   3. e   4. c   5. d   6. b

Exercise 8
1. do the bagels come   2. kind of bread   3. to drink
4. kinds of dessert

Exercise 9
1. a   2. a or the   3. a   4. an   5. a   6. the   7. the
8. a   9. the   10. the   11. a

Exercise 10
Answers will vary.

Exercise 11
2. There is clam chowder and chicken vegetable soup.
3. Yes, there is.   4. Yes, there are.   5. Yes, it is.   6. No,
it doesn't / does not.   7. There is pasta salad and mixed
green salad.

Exercise 12
Answers will vary. Following is one example of what students
may write:
Appetizers: grilled shrimp, mixed green salad
Soups: black bean, chicken vegetable, clam chowder
Entrees: fish, chicken, lamb
Desserts: ice cream, apple pie, cake, cookies
Beverages: water, milk

GRAMMAR BOOSTER
Exercise A
Count: cookie, egg, onion
Non-count: water, fun, fish, fruit, cheese, bread, help

Exercise B
1. How many   2. How much   3. How much
4. How many   5. How much
Answers to questions will vary.

Exercise C
2. a   3. a   4. an   5. a   6. X   7. a

Exercise D
1. some/any, some   2. some/any, any   3. any, some
4. some/any, any, some

JUST FOR FUN
Exercise 1
1. choice 2. sweets 3. snacks 4. meals 5. fatty
6. high **new word:** health

Exercise 2
1. menu 2. appetizers 3. fruit 4. check 5. portion
6. ice cream

UNIT 6

Exercise 1
1. C 2. I 3. D 4. G 5. F 6. A 7. H 8. E 9. B

Exercise 2
Answers will vary.

Exercise 3
1. b 2. b 3. c 4. a

Exercise 4
1. have to 2. have to 3. has to 4. have to 5. has to
6. have to 7. have to

Exercise 5
Answers will vary. Following are examples of what students
may write:
2. I have to work late on Friday. 3. My parents have to
go shopping this weekend. 4. My brother can sleep late
tomorrow morning. 5. My friend has to cook dinner tonight.

Exercise 6
2. Paula / She has to clean the house on Sunday afternoon.
3. Yes, Paula / she has to work on Friday.
4. Paula / She will be seeing a movie with Sara on Sunday
   night at that time.
5. Yes, Paula / she can sleep late on Sunday morning.

Exercise 7
2. Can you play basketball tonight?
3. Do you have to meet your brother at the airport?
4. Can I call you tomorrow?
5. Does Frank have to buy a new printer?
6. Do they have to take the exam on Friday?

Exercise 8
1. athletic field 2. gym 3. court, course 4. pool
5. track

Exercise 9
1. b / f 2. e / b / f 3. f 4. d 5. a 6. c

Exercise 10
1. a 2. a 3. b 4. b 5. a 6. c

Exercise 11
Answers will vary.

Exercise 12
2. do you go walking / for a walk 3. do you usually cook
dinner 4. do they go dancing 5. do you do aerobics
6. does Kyle play soccer

Exercise 13
2. Stan is talking on the phone right now. 3. My daughter
never studies English. 4. We're going dancing tonight.
5. I'm sleeping late tomorrow morning. 6. He's taking a
shower now. 7. They drive to work at least once a week.
8. She's / She is working late next Tuesday. 9. I always go
swimming on Mondays and Wednesdays. *OR* I always swim
on Mondays and Wednesdays.

Exercise 14
Ron Miller: is in shape; has a sweet tooth
Nina Hunter: is out of shape, avoids sweets

Exercise 15
1. false 2. false 3. no information 4. false 5. true
6. false

Exercise 16
Answers will vary.

GRAMMAR BOOSTER
Exercise A
2. When can she come? 3. How many languages can you
speak? 4. What time can you meet me? 5. How often
can you play golf?

Exercise B
2. Where do you have to 3. What time do I have to
4. Why does she have to
5. What do we have to

Exercise C
1. b 2. c 3. c 4. b 5. c

Exercise D
2. Joel walks to school every day. 3. My sisters don't call
me every week. 4. Their class doesn't meet every day.
5. They play tennis three times a week.

JUST FOR FUN
Exercise 1
Across
1. avoid 2. court 3. soccer 4. gym 5. never
Down
1. always 6. couch 7. riding 8. diet 9. course

Exercise 2
1. tennis 2. soccer 3. golf 4. basketball
5. weight lifting 6. bicycling

UNIT 7

Exercise 1
2. C 3. D 4. B 5. E 6. G 7. A

Exercise 2
1. service 2. price 3. selection

Exercise 3
1. b 2. a 3. a 4. a

Exercise 4
1. (+) <u>–r</u>: looser; nicer
2. (+) <u>–er</u>: taller; sweeter; younger
3. (−) –y (+) <u>–ier</u>: spicier; friendlier; healthier
4. double the final consonant (+) <u>–er</u>: hotter; thinner; fatter
5. more: more comfortable; more important; more
   convenient
6. irregular forms: worse

Exercise 5
Answers will vary, but may include the following:
2. A personal computer is less portable than a laptop.
3. A hair dryer is cheaper than a photocopier.
4. Running shoes are more comfortable than pumps.
5. Your grandparents are older than your children.
6. A salad is healthier than french fries.
7. A microwave oven is faster than a conventional oven.

Exercise 6

Answers for 1, 3, and 4 may vary.
1. cheaper **2.** black **3.** more expensive **4.** warmer
5. US women's 5–10

Exercise 7

Answers will vary.

Exercise 8

1. Certainly. **2.** Charge, please. **3.** The V-neck or the crew neck? **4.** That's too bad.

Exercise 9

1. a shirt **2.** a blazer **3.** a skirt **4.** pantyhose
5. pumps **6.** a sweatshirt **7.** a windbreaker
8. sweatpants **9.** socks **10.** running shoes

Exercise 10

Answers will vary.

Exercise 11

1. them **2.** it **3.** her **4.** me **5.** us **6.** them, you
7. them, them, him

Exercise 12

1. Lingerie **2.** Electronics **3.** Men's Underwear

Exercise 13

Answers will vary.

GRAMMAR BOOSTER
Exercise A

2. warmer than **3.** more expensive than **4.** older than
5. larger than **6.** faster than **7.** more comfortable
8. healthier than

Exercise B

Answers will vary.

Exercise C

2. When does she wash it? **3.** How often does he eat it?
4. Why does your teacher / she invite them? **5.** What time does Monica / she meet him?

Exercise D

2. Tina buys him gifts. Tina buys gifts for him.
3. The teacher gives us homework. The teacher gives homework to us.
4. The waiters serve them food. The waiters serve food to them.

JUST FOR FUN

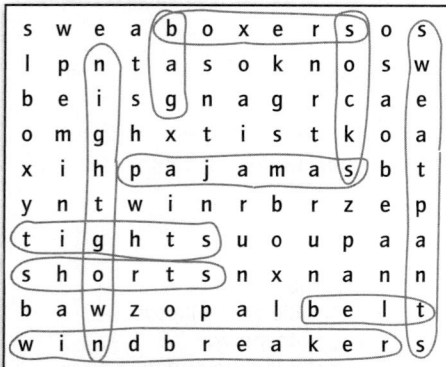

UNIT 8

Exercise 1

1. f **2.** e **3.** b **4.** c **5.** d **6.** a **7.** g

Exercise 2

Answers will vary.

Exercise 3

Answers will vary.

Exercise 4

1. No, thanks. **2.** Pretty boring. **3.** No, not too bad.
4. That's too bad. **5.** Well, that's good.

Exercise 5

2. The accommodations were pretty nice. **3.** Our room was a little small. **4.** There weren't any good family activities.
5. There were a lot of friendly people. **6.** The flight wasn't very long.

Exercise 6

2. Was the movie theater open?; it was **3.** Was the weather good?; it wasn't **4.** Was there a movie on your flight?; there wasn't **5.** Were there any problems at the airport?; there were

Exercise 7

1. Where were you last weekend? **2.** How was it?
3. Where was the resort? **4.** How long was the drive?
5. And how was the weather? **6.** How long were you there?

Exercise 8

Answers will vary.

Exercise 9

1. called **2.** arrive **3.** study **4.** got **5.** stopped
6. go **7.** bought **8.** did **9.** left **10.** eat

Exercise 10

1. c **2.** d **3.** a **4.** b

Exercise 11

1. bought, didn't spend **2.** flew, took **3.** had, ate, drank, watched **4.** left, got

Exercise 12

2. Did you go with Jane? **3.** Did you like the art exhibit?
4. When did you leave? **5.** What did she buy? **6.** Where did you play tennis? **7.** How long did you stay?

Exercise 13

Answers will vary.

Exercise 14

1. D **2.** B **3.** C **4.** A **5.** E **6.** F

Exercise 15

1. scenic **2.** perfect **3.** relaxing **4.** unusual **5.** scary
6. terrible

GRAMMAR BOOSTER
Exercise A

1. b **2.** c **3.** f **4.** a **5.** g **6.** d **7.** e

Exercise B

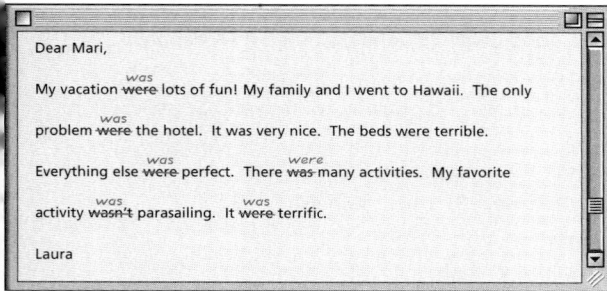

Dear Mari,

My vacation ~~were~~ *was* lots of fun! My family and I went to Hawaii. The only

problem ~~were~~ *was* the hotel. It was very nice. The beds were terrible.

Everything else ~~were~~ *was* perfect. There ~~were~~ *was* many activities. My favorite

activity ~~wasn't~~ parasailing. It ~~were~~ *was* terrific.

Laura

Exercise C

1. When was your last vacation?   **2.** How long was it?
3. How was the hotel?   **4.** Was the weather good?
5. How many people were with you?
The responses to the questions will vary.

Exercise D

Answers will vary but may include the following:
2. The weather wasn't very good yesterday.   **3.** How long did the trip take last time?   **4.** We didn't stay in a hotel last summer.   **5.** I used to cook clams at the beach at night.
6. Everyone had a good time last weekend.   **7.** My flight was canceled an hour ago.

Exercise E

2. Where did you go on vacation?   **3.** When did they go to the gym?   **4.** Who did you visit?   **5.** How much money did he spend?

JUST FOR FUN
Exercise 1

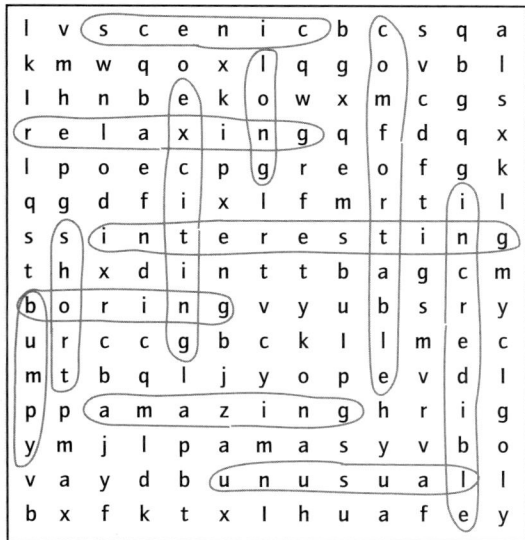

Exercise 2

2. baseball game   **3.** art museum   **4.** aerobics   **5.** golf
6. cruise   **7.** safari

UNIT 9

Exercise 1

1. true   **2.** false   **3.** false   **4.** true   **5.** false   **6.** true

Exercise 2

1. e   **2.** a   **3.** d   **4.** c   **5.** b

Exercise 3

1 Can I help you?
7 Let's see. The local leaves from track 23, lower level.
6 That sounds OK. What's the track number?
4 Oh, no! What should I do?
2 Yes. Can I still make the 10:05 express train to Antwerp?
3 Sorry, you missed it.
5 Well, you could take a local train. There's one at 11:05.
8 Thanks very much.

Exercise 4

1. b   **2.** a   **3.** c   **4.** c

Exercise 5

1. c   **2.** b

Exercise 6

1. You should take; You could take   **2.** You should hurry; You could make   **3.** She should buy   **4.** We could take; should we take   **5.** We could be; Should we call   **6.** they could not get

Exercise 7

2. You should take the 7:25.   **3.** You should be at the Scarsdale train station at 9:22.   **4.** You should take a local (train).

Exercise 8

1. arriving   **2.** late   **3.** reservation   **4.** going
5. limousine   **6.** rental   **7.** should

Exercise 9

1. d   **2.** a   **3.** c   **4.** b

Exercise 10

2. is going to buy the tickets   **3.** are you going to need the car rental   **4.** are they going to arrive   **5.** Are we going to make

Exercise 11

Answers will vary.

Exercise 12

Answers will vary.

Exercise 13

2. a passenger   **3.** a gate agent   **4.** a passenger
5. a passenger   **6.** a gate agent

Exercise 14

1. d   **2.** c   **3.** e   **4.** b   **5.** a

Exercise 15

1. false   **2.** false   **3.** true   **4.** true   **5.** false

Exercise 16

Answers will vary.

GRAMMAR BOOSTER
Exercise A

2. Where could he **get** a train to Hampstead?
3. Bette can't **take** a flight to Tokyo.
4. When **could we** leave?
5. How late can he **board**?
6. He **should** choose an aisle seat.

Exercise B

2. he can   **3.** you could   **4.** you can't   **5.** they should

Exercise C

2. They're going to run two miles   **3.** We're going to have a party   **4.** I'm going to school   **5.** You are going to do a great job

JUST FOR FUN
Exercise 1

1. volunteer   **2.** problems   **3.** boarding   **4.** reservation   **5.** security   **6.** could   **new word:** travel

Exercise 2

one

UNIT 10

Exercise 1

1. d   **2.** e   **3.** f   **4.** b   **5.** c   **6.** a

Exercise 2

Answers will vary.

Exercise 3

1. b   **2.** b   **3.** b   **4.** a

Exercise 4

1. c   **2.** a   **3.** e   **4.** b   **5.** d

Exercise 5

2. Which camera is the cheapest? OR Which camera is the most difficult to use?   **3.** Which camera is the lightest?   **4.** Which camera is the easiest to use?   **5.** Which camera is the heaviest?

Exercise 6

Answers will vary but may include the following:
1. You should try the Diego Mini 3000. It's the lightest.
2. You should try the Prego 5. It's the easiest to use.
3. You should look at the Honshu X24. It's the cheapest.

Exercise 7

1. bowl   **2.** enough   **3.** too   **4.** much   **5.** more   **6.** give   **7.** about   **8.** fair

Exercise 8

1. too boring   **2.** old enough   **3.** too unfriendly   **4.** too big   **5.** long enough   **6.** comfortable enough   **7.** too difficult

Exercise 9

1. What a rip-off!   **2.** The tall one?   **3.** You think so?   **4.** What a good deal!   **5.** Thanks. Keep the change.

Exercise 10

1. seller   **2.** buyer   **3.** buyer   **4.** buyer   **5.** seller   **6.** buyer

Exercise 11

1. false   **2.** true   **3.** true   **4.** false

Exercise 12

Answers will vary.

GRAMMAR BOOSTER
Exercise A

1. more beautiful, the most beautiful   **2.** intelligent, more intelligent   **3.** bigger, the biggest   **4.** convenient, the most convenient   **5.** busier, the busiest   **6.** fast, faster   **7.** safe, the safest   **8.** noisier, the noisiest

Exercise B

2. worse   **3.** the most interesting   **4.** better; faster; more powerful; best   **5.** the most popular; cheapest; more expensive; lighter

Exercise C

2. It's not spicy enough.   **3.** They're too uncomfortable.   **4.** It's too noisy.   **5.** The train isn't fast enough.   **6.** It's too boring.

JUST FOR FUN
Exercise 1
Across

1. worst   **2.** least   **3.** price   **4.** bargain
Down
5. spend   **6.** deal   **7.** tip   **8.** range   **9.** service

Exercise 2

2. large, small   **3.** difficult, easy   **4.** interesting, boring   **5.** expensive, cheap   **6.** different, similar   **7.** light, heavy   **8.** short, long   **9.** good, bad